Dr. Noel Due's work provides us a careful, scholarly, chronological analysis of biblical worship. It provides a thorough account, especially, of the worship of the patriarchs and that of the temple era. It does an excellent job of showing how Jesus fulfills Israel's worship. I have on a number of occasions wanted to have a book like this to assign to my seminary students in classes on worship, and I'm very grateful to Dr. Due for meeting that need in an excellent way. His treatment of Scripture gives real authority to his practical recommendations for worship today, which the church should certainly heed.

John M. Frame
Professor of Systematic Theology and Philosophy
Reformed Theological Seminary, Orlando, Florida

Here, at last is a book about worship which truly honours and uplifts the Lord Jesus Christ, as its central theme and object. Moving systematically through the whole of the Scriptures, Dr Due shows how worship provides both the fulfilment of our humanity and the focus of our sinful rebellion. Here is close scholarly observation, blended with sharp, contemporary relevance. It is a treasure-trove of insightful analysis of major themes, central doctrines and even whole or part books of the Bible, as they relate to 'the chief end of man'. This *tour de force* of Biblical theology is a gale of fresh spiritual air: it is brilliant.

Rev David Jackman
Cornhill Training Course, London

Created For Worship

From Genesis to Revelation to You

Noel Due

MENTOR

Dedication

For Tim, Steven, and Merran,
who by the grace of God,
learned to worship him in their childhood.

Copyright © Noel Due 2005

ISBN 1-84550-026-1

10 9 8 7 6 5 4 3 2 1

Published in 2005
in the
Mentor Imprint
by
Christian Focus Publications, Ltd.,
Geanies House, Fearn,Ross-shire,
IV20 1TW, Scotland

www.christianfocus.com

Cover design by Alister Macinnes

Printed and bound in Scotland by
Bell and Bain, Glasgow

Contents

Acknowledgements

Thanks are due to many people, not least to Prof. Andrew McGowan and the staff and students of the Highland Theological College, Dingwall, Scotland, whose encouragement and stimulating fellowship have been given by God himself. To Martin Cameron, who has served as 'Librarian on Call' and given cheerful assistance at every turn. To Alistair Wilson, whose well ladened shelves I mined regularly. To Hector Morrison and Jamie Grant, who have read the first drafts: their comments have always been insightful and incisive. To Nick Needham, whose informal comments and staff room discussions have often sent me back to think again. To the 'informal readers' Trish Rigby and Liz Priest, whose eyes have spotted a wrong reference or three. And most of all to my wife, Bev, who has patiently endured many absences (both physical and mental!) over the years of our life together. In the face of such help I must lay claim to the remaining deficiencies myself.

Chapter 1

The Battle for Worship

We are going to begin our exploration of the biblical theme of worship in an unusual place. Most books on worship (at least those that are concerned to establish a biblical basis for their discussion) begin by formulating a definition of worship, or by looking at the range of Hebrew and Greek words that are used to describe the actions, attitudes and characteristics of biblical worship. We will cover such things in due course, but we are not going to begin there. Instead we will start with four different sections of Scripture, each of which gives us an indication of the central importance of worship to human life and to the destiny of the creation, and each of which reveals something of the great battle for worship that surrounds us.[1]

The first of these sections involves the events preceding Jesus' public preaching and teaching ministry, and in particular the event of the temptation in the wilderness. The second section comes from the books of the Psalms (themselves great and powerful expressions of the worship life of God's Old Testament people, Israel). We will see that Psalm 115 embodies one of the most important biblical principles regarding worship – one which we will see emerging in a number of different ways throughout this book. The third section we will look at is a part of Paul's opening letter to the Romans where the current conditions of humanity are directly linked with the matter of worship. Finally we will give some attention to a portion of the Book of the Revelation, in which the pivotal nature of worship is accentuated and its importance for heaven and earth made plain. In these passages some of the great issues that inform our understanding of worship are thrown into sharp relief, and in them we see with stark clarity the intensity of the battle for true worship, and the scope of the issues at stake.

Jesus' Baptism and Temptation

The synoptic Gospels all record the temptation of Jesus. While Matthew (Matt. 4:1-11) and Luke (Luke 4:1-12) give fuller accounts than Mark (1:12-13), all three place it in the same location relative to the events that precede the opening phase of Jesus' public ministry. In all three, the experience of the temptation follows on immediately from his baptism and before his public ministry begins. It thus stands at the very gateway of his life's work. For this reason the battle is intense and its outcome crucial. Even in Mark's abbreviated account[2] the emphasis is on the clash itself with Satan. 'Jesus in the wilderness is confronted with Satan and temptation. It is the clash itself which is important; it is going on in Jesus' whole ministry'.[3] Failure here, at this point, would be to lose all. What, then, is the significance of the temptation, both in relationship to the baptism, and in relationship to the unfolding public ministry?

1. The Meaning of Jesus' Baptism

(a) Identification and Proclamation of the Lamb of God
The baptism was a public event, as great in its significance for Jesus as for those who witnessed it. The event itself, and the declaration heard from heaven, 'You are my Son, in You I am well pleased,' were at once personal (with regard to Jesus) and declarative (with regard to John the Baptist and others who witnessed it). Here Jesus is introduced to the public stage, and as he takes up his life's work his Father bears testimony to his eternal love for him in the bestowal of the Holy Spirit upon him. The event is saturated with meaning and thus it cannot be reduced to one single line of significance. Even the fact that it was at once a baptism in water and the occasion for the descent of the Spirit tells us this. It was a baptism and an anointing, and both of these in the context of a proclamation, first from heaven and then to the multitudes.

The synoptic accounts all indicate that John the Baptist was the one who saw the Spirit descend on Jesus and who heard the voice from heaven. But John's account of the Baptist's ministry (John 1:29-34) leaves us in no doubt that he proclaimed to the assembled crowds that which he had seen and heard. According to John 1:31 the importance of John's baptizing ministry lay in its purpose to mark out or declare Jesus to Israel. 'And I did not recognize him, *but in order that he might be manifested to Israel*, I came baptizing in water' (NASB), thus emphasizing the declarative nature of the event and (of particular importance in John's Gospel) the role of John the Baptist as the *witness* to the truth. Both the event itself and John's ongoing ministry as witness, declared to Israel that her king had come. Moreover, it is also important to see that John proclaimed Jesus to be the Lamb of God in this context (John 1:29; 1:36). Jesus was recognized as the Lamb by virtue of what John had seen and heard in the baptism. The baptism/anointing cannot therefore be separated from Jesus' role as atoning sacrifice. He is at one and the same time the great Davidic king and the Sacrificial Lamb, and both of these by virtue of the Spirit's anointing.

(b) Kingship

Through the baptism and abiding presence of the Spirit bestowed on him there, Jesus was deliberately and publicly set apart by his Father for his work as Messianic King. In the Old Testament the kings of Israel were all anointed. This is seen in the accounts of Saul (1 Sam. 9:16; 10:1 cf. 15:1, 17) and David, for example, who was anointed three times: by Samuel, by the men of Judah, and by the elders of Israel respectively (1 Sam. 16:3, 12-13; 2 Sam. 2:4, 7; 2 Sam. 5:3, 17). Solomon was also anointed, by Zadok the priest and Nathan the prophet immediately preceding the death of David (1 Kings 1:34, 39, 45 cf. 1 Chron. 29:22). In Solomon's case (in 1 Kings 1:32-48) and in that of Jehoash (in 2 Kings 11:9-20), we have the accounts of two enthronement ceremonies with approximately 150 years between them. In making this observation De Vaux concludes, 'there can be no doubt that all the kings of Israel were consecrated in the Temple, and anointed by a priest'.[4] Thus, in Israel the reigning king was Messiah (the anointed one)[5], who ruled on Yahweh's authority and under his covenantal grace.[6] In the Old Testament, the king is thus characteristically designated as the 'anointed one' (e.g. Psalms 18:50; 20:6; 84:9 cf. 2 Kings 9:3) who had his place not by right, but by Yahweh's gracious choice.

Moreover, the anointing of the king was intimately tied to the reception of the Spirit. This is seen very clearly in the accounts of Saul (1 Sam. 10:10) and David (1 Sam. 16:13) and less clearly in the account of Solomon.[7] This link between kingship and Spirit also gives the necessary context for David's prayer in Psalm 51:11: 'Do not cast me away from your presence; do not take your Holy Spirit from me.' While there is doubtless deep personal devotion in this prayer, the request involves more than personal piety. The prayer may be understood as a plea that the anointing of the Spirit – so necessary for David to fulfil his duties as the anointed king – be not taken away from him. The removal of the Spirit is given special prominence in narrative describing David's predecessor, Saul. Saul had lost the enduring kingship of Israel through his own disobedience and unrepentant heart. The Spirit of Yahweh and all the blessing that this entailed had been taken away, and a spirit of madness had been sent to him by way of judgment (1 Sam. 16:14). While Saul was still king in name and function, he was no longer the one to carry kingship forward in Israel. There would be no dynasty of Saulite kings, as there would later be a dynasty of Davidic monarchs. In Psalm 51 the repentant David is seen in contrast to the self-justifying Saul, and the link between kingship and Spirit is thus preserved.

Here in the baptism, we see Jesus being anointed with the Spirit of his Father to enable him to fulfill his kingly task of bringing the Lord's righteousness to the ends of the earth. In the bestowal of the Spirit, Jesus is marked out as the King of Israel,[8] but as a king whose reign and rule do not end with Israel. His kingship came *from* Israel, but is *for* the whole world, and thus his baptism/anointing has universal connotations. He is the Lamb of God who takes away the sin of the world, and the Davidic king to whom all of the nations belong. When the reality of this event and all that it meant was sorely tested in the wilderness, it was not the outcome of one ethnic group or nation which lay in the balance, but the destiny of the whole earth.

(c) Sonship

In Israel, the anointed king was understood to be the adopted son of Yahweh, as seen particularly in the great royal Psalms 2 and 110. Israel's chosen king was regarded as none other than the adopted son of God, who was charged with shepherding Israel, God's nation-son (Exod. 4:22-23). The king could do so, however, only under the authority of God, as his vice-regent (hence Psalm 23, where the shepherd-king of Israel indicates his own submission under the Shepherd-King Yahweh). Psalm 2 expresses the point in the language of the Davidic covenant (Ps. 2:6ff. cf. 2 Sam. 7:13f.). In the Old Testament no credence is given to kingship which does not share the character of obedient sonship, whether this be in the kingship Psalms or in the wider kingship theology of the Old Testament. The king was Yahweh's 'beloved', the son of his choosing and the object of his gracious affections. In response, the kings of Israel were to love the Lord and his Law, and lead the nation in covenantal faithfulness to him. They were to shepherd the nation with integrity of heart (so Ps. 78:70-72 cf. I Kings 9:4f.), and to walk in humble worship and adoration before the Creator God who had adopted Israel as his son, and appointed them to rule over this chosen nation. Israel, God's 'national' son (Exod. 4:22-23), had a chosen son on the throne, who was to care for the nation's welfare by walking in obedience to his and the nation's Creator/Father.

By virtue of the above, we can see that the anointing of the king was a pledge of love and assurance of Yahweh's covenantal faithfulness. It also laid upon the king covenant obligations to walk in obedience to the Lord, such obedience being particularly emphasized in the matter of worship.[9] Such worship would be faithful to Yahweh's covenant Law, as expressed externally in the Temple, but as known internally in the attitude of a humble and obedient heart (cf. Ps. 51:17). He was to respect and honour the Temple worship because the Temple was the dwelling place of the Name of God who had chosen him to be his adopted son. Thus, one of the prime aspects of his shepherd/guardian role over Israel was the preservation of true worship (e.g. 1 Kings 15:9-14; 2 Kings 12:1-3), including the removal of the high places and the promotion of true worship in the Temple. The reigns of Hezekiah and Josiah are particularly commended in this regard, under whose sway we see a root and branch reform of worship in the land (2 Kings 18:1-8; 2 Kings 23:1-25).

In short: where the kings of Israel led the nation in true worship of Yahweh, blessing was the result, and their reigns were commended in the writings of the former prophets. Where they refused to lead the nation in their covenantal obligations regarding worship, they and the nation reaped the curse of God's judgment. Their epitaph is entirely negative, often linking them with 'Jeroboam the son of Nebat, who caused Israel to sin' (e.g. 1 Kings 16:26; 21:22; 22:52 etc.), especially by raising up false worship centres and encouraging idolatry (of which we will say more later).

The anointing of Jesus with the Spirit at his baptism thus identifies him as the covenant king of Israel, who is both the vice-regent of God and the covenantally obligated ruler of God's people. His mission as the great Davidic King would hinge entirely on his worship of God. Its successful outcome would be a worshiping people, led by his own faithfulness to the throne of his Father. Jesus' role as the purifier of the Temple (e.g. John 2:13-22) and the transformer of worship (e.g. John 4:19-24) is thus fully fitting for his kingly ministry over Israel and for his construction of a new Temple, far greater than that of Solomon or Herod.

(d) Priesthood

The anointing of Jesus at his baptism also has other connotations, specifically to do with priesthood. Like the ideas of sonship and kingship, the concept of priesthood implicitly speaks of God's sovereign choice and his subsequent commissioning for the task. The writer to the Hebrews gives voice to the principle that is assumed throughout the Old Testament that 'no one takes this honour for himself, but only when called by God, just as Aaron was' (Heb. 5:4 ESV). Indeed in the account of Korah's rebellion in Numbers 16-17 we see the action of God's judgment falling on those who presume to take the honour of priesthood to themselves, without God's divine command. God had chosen Aaron and his line to be priests, just as much as he had prescribed the system of worship in which the priests were to serve. Those who were born into the tribe of Levi had the privilege of operating as priests to God, taking it in turns to serve at the temple, and receiving special benefits in lieu of their possession of land.

The accounts of the consecration of Aaron and his sons in Exodus 29 and Leviticus 8 make it clear that the priests were carefully prepared for their tasks. Aaron and his sons were all washed in water, dressed in their specified priestly robes, and then Aaron specifically was anointed with fragrant oil. The action is taken up in the symbolism of Psalm 133, which describes the beauty of unity as being like 'the precious oil on the head, running down on the beard, on the beard of Aaron, running down on the collar of his robes!' (Ps. 133:2). In other words, the unity of God's people (possibly particularly in worship) is akin to the fragrant blessing and anointing of the Spirit symbolized in the anointing of the earthly leader of their worship. Thus, Jesus' baptism in water (corresponding to the washing of Aaron) and anointing with the Spirit (corresponding to Aaron's anointing with oil) indicates that he is now the new High Priest, come to offer a better sacrifice and lead his people in true worship.[10] However, it also indicates something more in relationship to the theme of priesthood.

In the Old Testament there is another significant priestly figure, who features in the account of Abraham's return from the battle with the five kings in Genesis 14. Melchizedek stands as a more ancient and greater priest, but in contrast to Aaron's priestly line which continued through the Levites from one generation to the next, Melchizedek's 'line' seems to be limited to himself, at least in terms of human descent. The writer to the Hebrews describes him, however, as being the older and more abiding model of priesthood, which transcended the Aaronic and Levitical priesthood in both age and significance (Heb. 7:1-3). He predated both Aaron and the tribe of Levi, and in Abraham all subsequent lines of priesthood bowed down to Melchizedek, implicitly recognizing his superiority (Heb. 7:5-10). Thus, while there seems to be no direct continuation of Melchizedek's priesthood in functional terms (i.e. there was no earthly worship centre in which a line of his descendants operated), the fact that this priesthood antedates the Levitical priesthood by more than four hundred years and that Abraham was content to bow in worship and offer tithes is not to be ignored. It is therefore significant that Psalm 110 mentions *this* priesthood in relation to the matter of kingship in Israel, rather than the priesthood that was already functioning in accordance with the covenant made at Sinai.

Psalm 110 clearly indicates that God's anointed ruler shared in a priestly role. Of the king it is said, 'the LORD has sworn and will not change his mind, "You are a priest forever after the order of Melchizedek"' (Ps. 110:4). Thus Weiser comments:

> The psalm ... very forcefully emphasizes – the solemn way in which the divine oracle is introduced cannot be without significance here – the priesthood will forever remain vested in the king after the order of Melchizedek, that Canaanite priest-prince of Jerusalem in ancient times (cf. Gen. 14:18) who likewise combined both these offices in his one person. When David took over the Jebusite kingship of the city of Jerusalem these two offices were conferred on him and, as the psalm shows, continued to be held by the Davidic dynasty.[11]

Thus it seems that in Israel the legitimate king of David's line was a priest, but of a different order to the priesthood which operated in the Temple. The kings were in the line of Melchizedek's priesthood, not Aaron's. This does not mean that the king in Israel was free to operate independently of the Temple and its sacrifices; but by virtue of his special relationship with Yahweh as his adopted son and his linkage with the figure of Melchizedek in the ancient past, the king in some ways transcended the Temple and its cultus. Whether Israel (or even the king himself) fully understood it or not, he stood as testimony in Israel's midst to a different, universal order of priesthood – an order of priesthood that in itself contained the innermost meaning of the Temple worship (that God's covenant blessings were ultimately for all the nations), and to which it would at length give way.

Psalm 110 and Psalm 2 are the most quoted Psalms in the New Testament. When the New Testament writers interpret the ministry of Jesus, it is as though they use these Psalms as the lens through which they view the whole of Jesus' life and ministry, including his ascension. Whatever the original occasions of these Psalms' composition, both serve to underscore the fact that the real King of Israel is Yahweh, and that the earthly throne of Israel is occupied only by his gift to his anointed/adopted son. It became clear, however, that if ever and however these Psalms were applied to the earthly kings of Israel, their fulfillment transcended their reigns. 'With the eclipse of the Davidic dynasty the psalm [110] lived on as an expression of faith in God's ultimate fulfillment of his king-centered purposes for his people' and thus 'the great assurances of the psalm fell deep into the well of time till they finally plunged in the waters of NT revelation'.[12]

(e) Prophetic Empowerment

That the baptism/anointing of Jesus had kingship at its core is beyond doubt. There are, however, other considerations which are of some significance. We have already alluded to the fact that Jesus' baptism and temptation took place immediately before his public teaching and preaching ministry began. At the very outset of that ministry Jesus himself uses the following description: 'The Spirit of the Lord is now upon me, because he has anointed me to preach the gospel to the poor. He has sent me to proclaim release to the captives and the recovery of sight to the blind, to set free those who are downtrodden, to proclaim the favourable year of the Lord' (Luke 4:18 NASB).

This is, of course, a quote from Isaiah 61:1ff. All of the Gospels are united on the fact that Jesus' ministry was first and foremost a ministry of proclamation. He came teaching and preaching the word of God in the power of the Spirit. He was anointed, therefore, as the

Prophet,[13] foretold by Moses in Deuteronomy 18:15, who would teach the truth of Law to the nation and bring salvation to the Gentiles (cf. Matt. 12:18f.). Just as all the Old Testament prophets were anointed by the Spirit for their task, Jesus was likewise anointed, but in his case 'without measure' so that the very words he spoke were 'spirit and life' (John 6:63).

The baptism/anointing stands, therefore, as the public attestation of Jesus' threefold office of King, Priest and Prophet. These, of course, cannot be isolated from one another, but they do allow us to focus on different aspects of Jesus' life and work. The three offices are of immense importance for the matter of worship. In their Old Testament contexts, each, in its own way, was an office filled by the anointed servants of Yahweh to lead the nation in true worship and thus ensure its reception of the covenant blessings that accompany such covenant faithfulness.[14]

(f) Trinitarian Communion

Thus far we have concentrated on the Spirit's anointing which took place in Jesus' baptism for his threefold office and thus for his work as Saviour. But the anointing also has a deeply personal significance for Jesus himself, particularly as seen in its connection with the proclamation from heaven, 'You are my beloved Son, in you I am well pleased.'[15] That the anointing took place 'while he was praying' (Luke 3:21) is meaningful in this regard. The context is that of communion, of mutuality, of speaking and being heard, of listening and responding in love. It was a declaration of love by the Father, spoken in the words from heaven, and testified to in the bestowal of the Spirit. As such this was a Trinitarian event. The Father, Son and Spirit are revealed in their relationships to one another, open now for human eyes to see and ears to hear. But it is significant to note that this great Trinitarian revelation has the blessing of sinners as its ultimate goal. This event was the greatest revelation of the Trinitarian life that had ever been seen in history, and it takes place in the context of an anointing and empowering to enable the redemption of sinners (and ultimate restoration of the whole Creation under its rightful King). This was not simply the baptism of the great King, but the anointing of the Lamb of God for his sacrificial death. Jesus needed and was given the Spirit and the voice from his Father to prepare him for that terrible event.

(g) Identification with Sinners
This aspect of the baptism is underlined by Jesus' words in Matthew 3:15. In answer to John's objection to his being baptized, Jesus says, 'Let it be so now, for thus it is fitting for *us* to fulfill all righteousness' (ESV). The plural pronoun is important. By it we see that Jesus identified himself with the sinners he came to save. In Matthew 3:5f. we are told of the impact of John's ministry as 'Jerusalem, and all Judea, and all the districts around the Jordan' were going out to him to be baptized in the Jordan River, 'as they confessed their sins'. John refused to baptize the Pharisees and Sadducees, whom he characterized as a 'brood of vipers', and who did not bring forth fruit that was in keeping with repentance. Jesus, therefore, aligns himself with the repentant sinners coming to be baptized by John, whose Gospel of the Kingdom had turned their hearts away from their sins and towards the God who is Jesus' Father. But their baptism could only ever be effective on the basis of another baptism that the Son of God would undergo on the cross (Luke 12:50). This baptism into the judgment of death would be the means by which the sinners with whom he here identifies would be forgiven, and the means by which sinners would come to know God as their Father too.

(h) Personal Assurance
In the light of all these things, we must also affirm that the baptism was of enormous personal importance for Jesus. There can be no doubt that he knew the purpose for his coming into the world. On the one hand this was the redemption of sinners, but on the other it was the destruction of all the works of the devil.[16] These are not two separate purposes, but one, and to be accomplished through the one cross under the empowering of the Spirit. With the reality of that cross before him, the intensity of the conflict with all the forces of evil along the way, and the ultimate descent into death itself, Jesus needed to know, at the very outset, that no matter where these things would take him, he was still the beloved of his Father. The events to come would lead him to the place of utter dereliction, and to get there, and to come through it, he needed the assurance of the Father's love. He was (and is) a man, and in his humanity he needed all the power of the presence of the Father to accomplish this new exodus for his people. In this vein Sinclair Ferguson comments that

the descent of the Spirit, and Jesus' new experience of him, serve to assure Jesus of the Father's love ... the Spirit is a Spirit of Sonship and assurance, who will bear witness with his spirit that he is the Son of God, and who will enable him, even in Gethsemane, to call God *Abba!* Father!... The Spirit thus seals and confirms the bond of love and trust between the Father and the incarnate Son.[17]

2. Jesus as the Second Adam and True Israel of God

Each of the areas we have spoken of above, and all of them together, serve to emphasize the fact that the whole of Jesus' life and ministry was (and is) for the sake of others. All of the offices and layers of meaning indicated above have their goal not in themselves, but for those who are thus represented in him. He is the Lamb, the Prophet, the Priest, the King and the Beloved Son whose whole life is bound up with his service to the Father for the sake of the blessing of the nations. And all of the 'for-other-ness' of Jesus' life hinges upon his worship. He is shown to be both the true man, of Adam's line, and the true (faithful) Israel of God. In terms of biblical theology, these two great figures, Adam and Israel, stand as testimonies both to God's gracious faithfulness and to the tragedy of disobedient sonship.

In Luke's Gospel, Jesus' genealogy is placed immediately between the baptism and the temptation. In this linear genealogy Jesus' line of descent is taken all the way back to Adam, 'the son of God' (Luke 3:38). The first son, Adam, faced the temptation in the Garden. The second Adam now had to face it in the wilderness. Here he took his stand in and under the conditions of the curse that the first Adam's disobedience had occasioned. Where the first had failed in the midst of plenty, would the second succeed in the midst of deprivation? In hunger and want, in the wilderness state of creation that was brought about through the curse of the first Adam's failure, would he himself fail to obey the word of God his Father?

In Matthew's Gospel we see a slightly different, though not contradictory, emphasis. Where Luke's genealogy ends with Adam, Matthew's begins with Abraham, and draws particular attention to David as Abraham's descendant (Matt. 1:1-16). As the seed of Abraham, via David, Jesus stands as the representative of Israel, and its true King. Thus Matthew gives us an account of Jesus' period of refuge in Egypt (Matt. 2:13ff.), the meaning of which is given: 'so that the prophecy might be fulfilled, Out of Egypt did I call my son.' Israel had been chosen by Yahweh to be a royal priesthood in the midst of the nations. This calling, which they abrogated, would now be taken up in this new Son, who is a King Priest forever, after the order of Melchizedek. Would he fail like Israel, who resisted/grieved the Spirit in the wilderness (Isa. 63:10 cf. Acts 7:51-53)? Would he repeat their sin in refusing to hear and obey the voice of God (Deut. 6:1-9 cf. 2 Kings 17:13-15)? Or would he prove himself to be a faithful Son in contrast to Israel's constant rebelliousness? In short, would he live for himself, or for his Father?

3. The Temptation: General Considerations

'The temptation is an inevitable and significant concomitant phenomenon of the wilderness. Of all the side themes of the wilderness tradition, both in the Old and New Testament, it is the most frequent one.'[18] In the wilderness, all that was affirmed personally to Jesus and publicly of Jesus was tested in the depths of his own physical, spiritual and emotional life. We cannot begin to estimate the intensity of the hunger pains he suffered, or the physical extremity to which this severe period of testing brought him, except that we are told in Matthew 4:11 that at the end of the ordeal 'angels came to minister to him'. The only other occasion where such a statement is made is in Luke's account of Gethsemane, where at the end of that terrible trial 'an angel from heaven appeared to him, strengthening him' (Luke 22:43).[19] For Jesus, the temptation in the wilderness was every bit as demanding as the depths of Gethsemane. It took him to the uttermost limits of endurance in every aspect of his humanity: physically, emotionally and spiritually.

It is clear that Jesus had been anointed by the Father with the Spirit for the vocation ahead of him, but the first great work of the Spirit in this phase of his life was to take him to the very brink of human endurance in the wilderness, there to face the evil one head on. The confrontation with the devil was no accident, but rather the express purpose of the Spirit's leading.[20] Here, at the point of human extremity, would he trust and obey the Word of God?[21]

The repeated phrase in Matthew's account 'If you are the Son of God ...' highlights the nature of the temptation.[22] Just as Adam (the son in the Garden) and Israel (the son in the wilderness) were tested in their obedience, so was the Son tested in his obedience to the Father's word. Would his messianic mission be accomplished according to his own understanding, or according to his Father's? Would he serve himself, or serve the One who had sent him, even if at the point of his deepest physical hunger that One seemed not to be near him?

4. The Temptation and Worship
Standing at the centre of the account in Luke and the culmination of the account in Matthew is the express issue of worship. In Matthew the exchange is reported like this:

> Again, the devil took him to a very high mountain and showed him all the kingdoms of the world and their glory. And he said to him, 'All these I will give you, if you will fall down and worship me.' Then Jesus said to him, 'Be gone, Satan! For it is written, "You shall worship the Lord your God and him only shall you serve"' (Matt. 4:8-10, ESV)

The 'very high mountain' is not a literal topographical feature (a mountain from which one can see the whole earth is impossible), but the Satanic parody of the mountain of revelation, seen throughout the Scriptures.[23] Here he offers to Jesus that which has already been promised to him by the Father, as the Messianic King.[24] The implicit question is whether he would obtain the inheritance and its glory by worshipping Satan or by worshipping God. It was precisely here that both Adam and Israel failed. 'As in the very first account of testing, failed by Adam and Eve (Gen. 3:1-7), the question centres on a choice between the will of Satan and the will of God, which involves implicitly the rendering of worship to one or the other'.[25] Would Jesus, by outward obeisance or inward attitude of heart, give way to the worship of Satan, thus breaking the first commandment? Would he thus repeat Israel's sin and become bound to the power of the idols, behind whom Satan stands?[26]

In seeking to be worshipped, Satan's ploy was to bring the Son captive to himself. The issue of worship was not (and is not) a peripheral issue in the life of the Son of God, but lies at its very core. It is the key on which all hinges, not just for his own sake, but for the sake of the whole of the creation. All of Jesus' life was an expression of his worship to God his Father as he served him in thought, word and deed, and ultimately as he set the captives free from Satan's power through his sacrificial death.

In promising Jesus the kingdoms of this world in exchange for his worship, Satan was offering a path 'that side stepped the cross and introduced idolatry'.[27] He sought at the very outset to corrupt the holy principle of Jesus' life, as expressed in the first commandment, that he would have no other gods than his Father in heaven. This being the case, Jesus would have no divided allegiance, no other focus of his obedience and no other object of his affections. He would love that which his Father loved, and hate that which he hated, and worship him in the doing of his will to the uttermost – with all his heart and soul and mind and strength.

It is for this reason that Jesus' response to the temptations is in and through the word of God. He does not quote the Scriptures as some sort of talisman, but uses them to express his *active obedience* to that word. It is this active obedience which gives him the power to resist the evil one and which enables him to prevail. He stands here, anointed by the Spirit as the representative head of a new humanity, as its champion on the field of battle. This humanity will not be free until it is free to worship 'in Spirit and in truth', and such freedom can only come about through Jesus' own worship – such worship and service ultimately being expressed to the point of death on the Cross.

We should not interpret Jesus' dismissal of the temptations by the word of God in any perfunctory manner, as though Jesus was just quoting texts as ammunition. To dismiss these temptations with the word of God was at the same time to choose actively the way of the Cross. It was to take up the full burden of responsibility involved in the fact that the Son did not come down from heaven to live for himself, but to die for others. Where the first Adam failed and brought the tyranny of false worship to the race, the obedient worship of the second Adam would lead a new humanity to the liberating glory of the worship for which it was created.

5. Conclusion

The foregoing brief discussion makes it clear that Jesus Christ is the one who enables true worship, and the one who redeems human beings from the curse of false worship. The battle at the very outset of his public ministry recapitulated that of Adam and Israel, and revolved around his own worship of God for the sake of others. This worship affected and informed every aspect of his life. When we speak of 'worship' then, we are not speaking about *an* activity of one's life, but speaking of *the* activity of one's life, which gives that life its entire focus and direction. It is a core orientation rather than a peripheral action.

Psalm 115

1. The Setting of the Psalm

We now turn to the second main portion of Scripture to be discussed in this opening chapter. Psalm 115 is a psalm which majors on the contrast between Yahweh and the other so called gods of the nations. While commentators often locate the Psalm in the setting of post-exilic Judah,[28] perhaps during the discouraging times faced by Nehemiah's returnees at the time of the stalled rebuilding programme in Jerusalem,[29] it is universally agreed that it is a cultic/liturgical psalm. Its background may well be the earlier worship of the Temple, but it formed a central portion of Israel's post-exilic worship, especially through its use during the Passover festival, about which we say a little more below (and significantly more, later in the book).

Whether this precise setting of the returning (and discouraged) exiles can be finally defended or not, the themes of the Psalm certainly match such times. The Psalm reflects a period of national despair and no little suffering, where the God of Israel is being mocked by the surrounding nations (verse 2), because his people seem to have been abandoned. The nations cry out, 'Where is their God'? Yahweh seems either not able, or not willing, to defend his covenant promises to his people. They seem to be defeated, and languish under the gaze of their enemies. From the point of view of the nations, Yahweh seems to have abandoned his own flock.

2. The Content of the Psalm

Throughout the Scriptures, the nations are often portrayed in hostile opposition to Yahweh and his purposes (just look at Psalm 2, for example), and throughout the Old Testament, the glory and power of the nations is seen to be bound up with their gods. Israel's god, from the nations' point of view, seems to have failed. However, the singers of the Psalm cry out to God in faith (verse 1), looking for him to affirm the glory due to his holy name, on the basis of his covenantal faithfulness (*chesed*). It is Yahweh's own glory and reputation that seems to be at stake in the nations' taunting, and this forms the substance of the cry/affirmation of the psalmist.

The fact that this Psalm is part of the great Egyptian Hallel[30] should not be lost on us. The Egyptian Hallel (Psalms 113–118) was sung during the great pilgrim feast of Passover, which recounted in

Israel's communal liturgical experience, year after year, the events of Yahweh's deliverance in the exodus. Israel knew that he had acted for her in faithfulness to the covenant promises made to their father Abraham, and that by God's own outstretched arm they had been delivered from the gods of Egypt (Exod. 12:12). Psalm 115 thus provided both an historical focus for Israel (in recalling the events of the past, which forged them as a nation) and a contemporary expression of hope (that Yahweh really is the one, true, living God, and all of the so called gods of the nations are mere idols). In contrast to the idols of the nations, Yahweh 'is in the heavens; he does whatever he pleases' (verse 3). He is thus both King over all, and absolutely free in his dealings with both Israel and the surrounding nations.

The contrast between Yahweh and the nations' gods is developed throughout Psalm 115. Verses 4-8 emphasize the inability of the idols to act. The psalmist highlights the fact that they are 'the work of human hands' (verse 4) and that, as such, they share the inanimate nature of the metal and wood from which they are created. They can do nothing, a theme echoed in many other places in the Old Testament (e.g. Isa. 44:9-20; Jer. 10:1-9), and consequently, they 'do not speak, reveal, promise, or utter any spoken word'.[31] Instead of placing false trust in such worthless objects, the Psalm urges God's people to put their trust in him (three times in verses 9-11) and thus live in the blessing of God (verses 12-15), who is 'the maker of heaven and earth'. Not only this, the clear implication here is that God has spoken and acted in the past, and that his words and deeds should be remembered by Israel in the present. The final section of the Psalm reprises some of the earlier themes, and adds to them the abiding reality that men and women are but mere mortals (verse 17), whose joy and delight it is to bless and praise the Lord while they live on the earth (verse 18).

3. The Significance of the Psalm for Our Theme

Psalm 115 is significant on many levels. In terms of the history of Israel, it finds its significance in its liturgical function and, through this, its direct declaration of the nature of Yahweh as the covenant faithful God. He is the one who not only acts in history to deliver his people, but who speaks to them and rules over all things with sovereign care. On the level of its abiding pastoral significance it is 'a stirring lesson to the people of God in every age concerning survival in an alien, hostile environment.... The reality of a relationship with God imparts strong resistance to rival human ideologies and creates a hope so certain to believing hearts that its prospect can already induce praise (cf. Rom. 5:2; 8:38-39; 1 Peter 1:3-9)'.[32] However, there is another level of significance in this psalm that will be emphasized even more in the later sections of this book

Psalm 115:8 simply says, 'Those who make them become like them; so do all who trust in them' (ESV). The 'them' here are the idols, who stand in contrast to Yahweh. Notice what is said. Those who fashion idols to worship (those who are involved in the perpetuation of idolatry) and those who put their trust (*batach*) in the idols themselves (i.e. the worshipers, who have placed their faith in these objects) both come to resemble the very things they make and worship. Their false trust leads them to reflect the character of the object in which they put their trust. Just as the idols are dull to the real world, and especially the world of Yahweh's voice, their worshipers are dull to him and to his word. Their senses are as dead as those of the idols themselves.[33] In simple terms, the idols that have been formed by human hands then form human beings into *their* likeness. In other words, men and women are shaped morally by the objects they worship. Worship is not a static event, but a dynamic one. Engaging in false worship actually has an impact on the worshiper. To engage in idolatry affects the moral and spiritual condition of a person, or a nation. The character of the idol is borne in upon the soul of the society as much as it is borne in upon the soul of the individual.

Thus the moral and spiritual character of the king in Israel was to reflect the character of Yahweh. His rule over the nation was to depict Yahweh's rule over him. Through its obedience to the covenant and the joyful submission to Yahweh's law, the nation itself was to be a moral and spiritual witness to the surrounding nations. In Israel they were to see the nature and purposes of God displayed. Whereas the gods of the nations shaped those nations into dull and lifeless entities (at least as far as hearing and rejoicing in the word of Yahweh was concerned), Israel ought to have been shaped by their allegiance to and love of Yahweh in all his covenant-making glory.

The sorry story of Isael's history, however, is that this allegiance was not given freely and consistently. For the most part, they turned from their God-ordained vocation to be Yahweh's priest-nation and embraced the very idolatry of the nations surrounding them. In Israel's own experience, then, they became dull to the very One whom they should have heard most joyously. Their eyes became blind, their ears became deaf and their voice grew mute through their abandonment of their worship of Yahweh (e.g. Isa. 42:17-20; 43:8). They were often became as dull to the voice of God as the surrounding nations. And at the core of this national tragedy was the matter of their worship.

Romans 1:18-32

1. The Gospel in Romans

The analysis of the matter of worship contained in the brief reflections above finds a resonating voice in the third section of Scripture we are to consider. The apostle Paul clearly had a variety of reasons for writing to the Christians in Rome. In part, he wanted to take care of some travel arrangements. It seems that Paul was planning a trip to Spain (15:22-29) and that he had intended to travel there from Rome. Paul states that he had wanted to visit on other occasions (he had never met the Roman believers face to face), but that he had been prevented from coming (1:13; 15:22). He plainly wanted to be blessed in ministry among them, both in the giving and receiving of that joy which only the fellowship of the gospel can bring, and to have the opportunity to proclaim that gospel wider afield in Rome (1:11, 13, 15). But whatever the personal reasons for its authorship, the letter to the Romans has been rightly seen as one of the great foundational letters of apostolic Christianity. In it, Paul gives a sort of handbook of Christian teaching, laying out not just the nature of the apostolic gospel, but also spelling out its implications. These have to do with big issues, such as the relationship between Jews and Gentiles, and smaller ones, such as the payment of taxes. And one issue that impinges on both the nature of the gospel and its implications is the matter of worship.

We will have cause to examine some of the material in Paul's theology of worship in more detail later. For now, however, we want to examine the central place that the issue of worship has for the nature of the gospel itself. In Romans 1:16-17 Paul has stated his theme: the gospel (the good news) of salvation, for all nationalities, Jew and Greek (here used as a shorthand form for speaking about the Gentiles). He declares that he is not ashamed of this gospel (though this implies that the gospel itself is regarded unfavourably by many) and that this gospel is the means by which God's power is at work in the world. Through it, God's righteousness is revealed to the nations, and through belief in this gospel men and women can be saved.

2. The Gospel and the Wrath of God
In view of the theme of the good news, then, the opening statement of Romans 1:18 seems quite abrupt and out of place. Paul writes: 'For the wrath of God is revealed from heaven against all ungodliness and unrighteousness of men, who by their unrighteousness suppress the truth' (ESV). The little connective 'for' is important. It 'introduces all of the section that follows: It is necessary for God to reveal his righteousness in the gospel *because* God has also found it necessary to reveal his wrath against sin.'[34] The matter of the gospel, understood as good news, only makes sense when we see that there is such a thing as bad news! Men and women of all nationalities need the gospel, because of the state in which they already exist. They exist under the wrath of God. God is holy. Anything that does not match with that holiness is subject to just, holy wrath. God's holy love would not be either loving, or holy, if he did not exercise wrath against sin and evil.

While the wrath of God may be spoken of as something that lies in the future, to be fully revealed and experienced at the end of history (e.g. Rom. 2:5, 8; 5:9; cf. 1 Thess. 1:10), here in this passage it is best to take it as something that is *already* in operation, in the present experience of men and women. Despite attempts to avoid this aspect of the 'bad news' (for example, by redefining the term 'wrath', or arguing that this is a primitive idea in the history of religion and that we can now look beyond it to a more positive and genial view of God), 'to do justice to what the apostle is saying we must include in our understanding of this passage the idea that part of the meaning of salvation is that God's *wrath* is averted.'[35] The experience of God's wrath now, as well as the prospect of a day of reckoning to come, provides the arena in which the 'good news' must be understood. If there is no 'bad news' of wrath, the 'good news' is of little importance.

Why is this wrath revealed? The passage tells us that God is constantly speaking to men and women through the creation, and directly in their own hearts. Men and women are left without excuse 'for what can be known about God is plain to them, because God has shown it to them. For his invisible attributes, namely, his eternal power and divine nature, have been clearly perceived, ever since the creation of the world, in the things that have been made' (Rom. 1:19-20). This statement defines the limits of what some theologians call 'natural revelation'. God speaks in and through the created world, 'nature', but this revelation does not bring a saving knowledge of God to human beings. Indeed, it confirms them as being under the wrath of God, since 'although they knew God, they did not honor him as God or give thanks to him, but they became futile in their thinking, and their foolish hearts were darkened' (Rom. 1:21).

It is of paramount importance to understand that in this passage, men and women are actually engaged in a process of *suppressing* the truth (1:18), and this is matched by the action of *exchanging* it for a lie (1:23, 25). Schreiner is entirely correct, therefore, to head the section of his commentary dealing with Romans 1:18-32 as 'Their Rejection of God'. However, it is particularly important that we note the nature of this suppression and exchange, the means by which this rejection is enacted.

3. Worship and the Wrath of God
Romans 1:21 clearly expresses these matters in terms of worship. 'For although they knew God, they did not honor (*edoxasan*) him as God or give thanks (*eucharistēsan*) to him, but they became futile in their thinking, and their foolish hearts were darkened' (ESV). The verb here translated as 'honour' is from the word *doxa* ('glory'), and its transliterated form is embedded in English words such as 'doxology' and 'doxological'. The basic form of the verb for giving thanks (*eucharistō*) is likewise transliterated and embedded in English words such as 'eucharist' or 'eucharistic'. Even on this simple level, we can see that the vocabulary used here is worship orientated language. However, at a more fundamental level (and here we preempt a later discussion to some degree) we can see that one of the most obvious consequences of the doctrine of creation is that human beings were structured for worship. The Shorter Catechism, in response to the question, 'What is the chief end of man?', answers, 'Man's chief end is to glorify God and to enjoy him for ever.' In placing this question at the very head of all the questions in the Catechism, the Westminster Divines were making a profound theological and pastoral statement.

To put the matter in terms of the thesis of this book, human beings were created for worship. This is both a defining feature of our nature, and the actual reality of our existence. To worship God is to serve him in love and in trustful obedience to his word.

We have seen above, that for Jesus in the wilderness, the temptation to worship Satan was at the same time the temptation to abandon trust in God and his word. True worship and faith belong together. 'As God's creature, man was bound to render glory and thanksgiving to his Creator; this means not merely to acknowledge his existence, and to employ the words and rites of religion, but to recognize his lordship and live in grateful obedience, in fact (in the Pauline sense) to believe, to have faith.'[36] Human beings were created to worship God and to express their devotion to him in obedient faith. Where this worship is abandoned, the result is not a state of 'no worship', but a state of 'false worship'.

For a human being there can be no vacuum of non-worship. One is either submitted to God in the doing of his will and the glorifying of his name, or one is submitted to someone, or something else. The error described in Romans 1:18ff., is not the *neglect* of worship, but the *exchange* of worship. Men and women are inveterate worshipers. Worship belongs to their essential structure. The expression of human sin is that the worship for which they were created is exchanged for idolatrous worship. They sin, not by *not* worshiping, but by worshiping wrongly. 'Human unrighteousness most fundamentally consists in a refusal to worship God and a desire to worship that which is in the created order. Unrighteousness involves the refusal to give God his proper sovereignty in one's life.'[37]

4. How the Wrath of God is Revealed

Whether the exchange of worship spoken of above is expressed in classical representations of idolatry, or whether it is expressed in more subtle ways (where no physical idol is in fact present), the biblical reality is that men and women are shaped by their worship. Inner motivation and affections that make their impact on outward attitudes and actions should not be thought of as free-standing aspects of personality. The psychology of human motivation and volition, from a biblical perspective, is entirely linked with the spiritual dimension of one's worship.

In idolatry, human beings express their in-built desire for worship. This false worship, designed to suppress the truth of God, is the means by which men and women seek to give voice to their innate spirituality. There is no doubt, however, that its motive is self-centred and self-seeking.[38] Idols always promise more than they deliver. However, human beings prefer to worship them than God, since they seem to make fewer moral demands upon them, and promise much more freedom. There is a deep irony in all this, of course, plainly expressed in the way in which God's wrath is revealed from heaven against this rebellious activity.

In verses 24, 26, and 28 Paul speaks of God's action in 'giving up' (*paredōken*) men and women to their choices. This threefold use of the concept of 'giving up' is directly matched to the threefold action of 'exchanging' described in verses 23, 25 and 26. It emphasizes the judicial, deliberative action of God in judgment, as he lets men and women reap the harvest of that which they have sown. However, we should not think of this as merely passive, of merely letting one stew in one's own juice! Moo comments that the meaning of the verb 'demands that we give God a more active role as the initiator of the process. God does not simply let the boat go – he gives it a push downstream. As a judge hands over a prisoner to the punishment his crime has earned, God hands over the sinner to the terrible cycle of increasing sin'.[39]

Such an understanding is entirely in keeping with the concept's Old Testament background, especially as seen in such places as Ezekiel 16. Here we see a dramatic (indeed, terrifying) picture of Israel handed over to her many lovers (the idols, and the nations from which these have come) who leave her defiled, bleeding, naked and ashamed. The language is symbolic, but the action is not. In the juridical action of giving men and women over to their idolatrous exchange, God's wrath is experienced in the midst of all the pain, shame, isolation, degradation and destruction that human sin brings. God's wrath is revealed in the horror of the breakdown of all human relationships, in the haunting and howling of the human conscience in its sin, and in the destruction of human society that is the necessary corollary of the selfish pursuit of the idols.

The freedom from obligation to God that the idols seem to offer, is in fact nothing other than abject slavery. As men and women seek to control their future and attain physical or spiritual security through idolatry, they are in actuality reduced to penury. The idols 'have no future, no inheritance to offer, no goal to reach. Not being sovereign they can promise nothing substantial. Since man lives on hope as well as faith and love, the idols cheat him, turning him into a derelict, depriving him of true faith, hope and love'.[40]

By the worship of idols, human beings compound their enslavement to powers of darkness, who stand behind and energize all idolatrous action. In all of this they meet God's wrath. As Barth has commented, 'when God has been deprived of His glory, men are also deprived of theirs.'[41] Idolatry destroys human dignity and freedom, and it ushers people directly into the experience of the wrath of God, whom they are seeking to reject.

5. Conclusion

Romans 1:18-32 is a foundational passage for understanding all of Paul's theology. The fact and nature of sin; the experience of the wrath of God; the reality of this wrath and the need for propitiation; the fact that this propitiation must be provided as a gift of God's grace; these and many other related themes are explicitly discussed or inescapably implied in this passage. They are seen with greater force when we consider that it is only the opening salvo of a whole section (running from Rom. 1:18-3:20) in which the utterly sinful state of the whole of humanity (both Gentile *and* Jew) is revealed for what it is.

Of most significance for our theme, however, is the fact that this opening salvo centres on the nature of worship. Human beings are clearly portrayed as creatures who must worship, and whose sin lies in the fact that they do not choose to worship as they should. Their hatred of God is expressed in the fact that they exchange his truth for a lie, such an exchange being manifest in their idolatry. Where the Creator should be praised, they turn to serve the creature. Idols dominate their life and relationships, rather than the glorious liberty of the worship of God. By implication, if there is to be redemption, there must be a reverse exchange. The bondage and deceitfulness of idolatry must be removed, to be replaced by the truth of God and the liberty of his worship. By the nature of the case this could only be brought about by God himself. It does alert us, however, to the real goal and scope of redemption: the restoration of true worship and the destruction of the false.

Revelation 4–5

1. Revelation = Unveiling

The last of the passages to which we will turn in this opening chapter comes from the final book of the Bible. The book of Revelation is, as

its name means, an 'unveiling'.⁴² The book shows us what is going
on behind the scenes, opening our eyes to the actions of unseen spiritual
powers and revealing the plan and purpose of God that is being worked
out in human history. It is at one and the same time a letter to the
Church, a prophecy regarding the future, and an unveiling of the
meaning of history in the light of the action of God in the present.
Throughout, the message is conveyed in terms of dream, vision, image
and symbolism, all of which is steeped in Old Testament imagery.
Biblical scholars point to the distinct nature of this type of literature
by designating it 'apocalyptic' in style. While it speaks of things that
are true, they may not be literal (e.g. a literal 'bottomless pit' is
impossible, but we well know what it means!). Apocalyptic literature
conveys to us that which can only be communicated by stretching
language to its limits and by drawing upon clusters of allusions to
biblical themes, expressing in visual forms concepts that are otherwise
impossible to grasp.

2. The Throne Room in Heaven

The two chapters to which we refer are crucially placed within the
structure of the book. In the opening chapter John has been given a
vision of the risen and glorified Jesus, who is seen in the midst of his
churches (Rev. 1:9-20) and who commands that letters be written to
the seven specific congregations there named. These letters all
demonstrate the intimate knowledge that the Head of the Church has
of every situation, and portray the intensity of his loving care for the
various congregations to whom he speaks. The congregations are in
a variety of states, ranging from deep poverty and hostile persecution
(e.g. Smyrna in 2:8-11) to great wealth and spiritual lethargy
(e.g. Laodicea in 3:14-22).

On the other side of Revelation 4 and 5 lies a powerful disclosure
of the battle that rages behind the scenes of history. The great enemies
of God and his people are revealed and the vindicating judgments of
God are opened up for us to see. What is clear is that without such
revelations being given, we would not be able to comprehend the real
meaning of the events of history, nor see the plan and purpose of God
being worked out. Witherington comments,

> But that this sort of information is only conveyed through visions and
> dreams and oracles makes clear that without revelation, without the
> unveiling of divine secrets and mysteries, humans would be in the dark

about such matters. It is the message of apocalyptic literature that the meaning and purpose of human history cannot be discovered simply by empirical study or analysis of that history.[43]

Through John's eyes – opened by the Holy Spirit (Rev. 4:2) – in Revelation 4 and 5 we are given a description of the throne room in heaven. This is the nerve centre which governs everything else in the book. The destiny of the churches (which are the focus of the first three chapters) and the destiny of the world (which is the focus of the rest of book) are alike bound up with the sovereign will of God. No matter how much the forces of darkness might threaten the people of the Lamb, and no matter how deep the suffering they must endure, nothing happens outside of the sovereign purposes of God. This vision of absolute rule is both a message of comfort for the people of God (they *will* be vindicated) and the guarantee of judgment for God's enemies (they *will* be destroyed). There is nothing uncertain about the outcome.

What dominates the scene in these chapters is thus the 'throne' and the one who sits on it. The repetition is emphatic in the extreme (4:2, 3, 4, 5, 6, etc.!). In chapter 5 there is a strong emphasis on the 'scroll' (vv. 1, 2, 3, 4, 5, etc.) which comes from the right hand of the one on the throne and which governs the unfolding drama of the rest of the book.[44]

What is particularly striking for our theme is that the presence and action of the throne elicits continual worship from the heavenly creatures who surround it. There is unceasing declaration of the Lord's holy character (4:8) and perpetual praise, glory and thanksgiving offered to him (4:9-10). In chapter 4 this is primarily because of his role as the creator and sustainer of all things, as the hosts of heaven sing, 'Worthy are you, our Lord and God, to receive glory and honor and power, for you created all things, and by your will they existed and were created' (v. 11).

In Revelation 5, the focus is on God's role as redeemer, and praise ascends to the Lamb in particular (vv. 9, 12, 13), though the actions of the throne and the Lamb are seen as one. The scene in these chapters portrays the worship of the whole of creation. Not only the heavenly creatures around the throne, but the angelic beings and every element of creation itself is seen to express its praise and glory to God, so that John says, 'And I heard every creature in heaven and on earth and under the earth and in the sea, and all that is in them, saying, "To him who sits on the throne and to the Lamb be blessing and honor and glory and might forever and ever!"' (v.13). This reinforces what we have seen earlier: that the whole of creation is in fact structured for worship, and that its destiny is bound up with its worship. Moreover, the Lamb is given unending praise for his action in redeeming people from every nation under heaven and making them 'a kingdom and priests to our God, and they shall reign on the earth' (Rev. 5:10). We will return to some of these themes in due course, but it is plain that the creation cannot come to its full glory unless the king-priesthood of humanity be reinstated.

Revelation is replete with other descriptions of the heavenly beings or the people of God at worship (e.g. John himself in chapter 1; the saints in 7:9-15; the twenty four elders of heaven in 11:15-17; and so on), but these passages all reflect the character of Revelation 4 and 5 and give us reiterations of its themes. In addition, there is a strong thread of temple images and motifs that runs throughout the book, and which forms the culmination of the new heavens and earth's experience of the presence of God. He is with his people in the new Jerusalem, and where one would have expected there to be a physical temple in the midst of the new city of God, God himself is the Temple, i.e. the dwelling place of his people (21:22f.).

While we will have cause to return to some of these things at a later point, here we simply need to highlight the connection between worship, power and victory that is implicit in what has been said. At various points and in various ways Tremper Longman III and Daniel Reid comment on the connection between worship and God's role as the Divine Warrior. For example, they suggest that the pattern of warfare, victory, kinship, house building and celebration evident in other ancient Near Eastern writings is seen also in the biblical accounts. In particular they draw attention to the events of the exodus, the history of the early kings of Israel, and the structure of the sections of the book of Revelation to indicate that the worship of God was both the context for, and outcome of, the holy war of God and his people against their enemies.[45] They argue that the biblical term 'a new song' (as seen, for example, in Psalm 96:1; Isaiah 42:10; Revelation 5:9; 14:3) 'is a technical term for a victory song [which celebrates] the new situation brought about by God's warring activity',[46] and draw attention to the relationship between Jesus as the Warrior King and the Temple, which is his Father's house.[47] In these and other ways, the authors suggest that connections between the concepts of Divine warfare, his victory over his enemies and the establishment of true worship are substantial and deliberate.

In reflecting on such links, and drawing upon much of his own material,[48] Geoffrey Bingham has drawn attention to the inherent connection between worship and power.[49] The people of God are empowered by God in the context of their worship and in the ministry of the Word and Spirit that forms the matrix of their life as the worshiping community of God. Conversely, the discussion of idolatry throughout the Bible is predicated on the assumption that those who worship idols are seeking power from them, either for such blessings as fertility and fruitfulness, or for victory in battle and expansion of their empires. In this way the Temple-Sanctuary of God is the place of his people's protection and empowerment, while the temple-sanctuaries of the idols exist as sinful alternatives to this place of true empowerment. As such they have been deliberately established as a 'network' of ensnaring and destructive centres where the power and presence of Satan may interact more freely with the fleshly sin of the world (used here in its theological sense of that activity of wicked humanity that is opposed to God and his purposes) to maintain his command and control mechanisms over sinful humanity. In this light it is not surprising to see the prominence given to the cosmic battle for worship in the Revelation.

3. Revelation: the Cosmic Battle for Worship

The book of Revelation portrays the battle for worship in very stark terms. For example, the blasphemous beast in Revelation 13 deceives the unredeemed world into worshipping it (vv. 8, 12), and slaughters those who refuse to worship in this way (v. 15). The idolatry of the nations is clearly seen, along with the stubbornness of heart and rebellion which such worship manifests (e.g. 9:20-21; 16:9, 11). We see the powers of evil in hostile action against the witnesses of God, seeking to obliterate their testimony from the earth (e.g. 6:9; 11:7; 20:4), and we see the great powers of the city of man intent on destroying the people of God (e.g. 17:3-6).

Over and against all of this evil action, the book also clearly shows that God is engaged in bringing judgment upon his enemies (and those who are thereby the enemies of his people), and the fact that he works in such ways is itself a cause for worship (e.g. 11:15-18; 15:3-4;

16:4-7; 19:1-8). The righteous, powerful and holy action of God in defeating his enemies must, perforce, overthrow all false systems of worship. This is a theme to which we will return a little later, but it does expose a principle that is seen throughout the Bible: God brings judgment on enslaving and dehumanising forms of worship in order to liberate his people into the freedom of the glory of worshiping him, the thing for which they have been created. All in all, the book of the Revelation gives us a picture of worship that emphasises its power and importance for the whole of creation, and it allows us to see that which we would not normally perceive: that the whole of history may be interpreted through the lens of the battle for worship.

Conclusion

Much recent writing on worship (particularly at the evangelical and Reformed end of the spectrum) has been engaged in contributing to or commenting on the so-called 'Worship Wars' evident in many contemporary churches and denominations. Much of this writing has to do with matters of worship style (robes and choir, or jeans and rock band?), the relationship between worship and evangelism (should we make our services non-threatening and seeker friendly?), or on the meaning and scope of the regulative principle (exclusive unaccompanied psalmody, or other material as well?).

The material that we have considered in this chapter, however, has initiated us into something of the more substantial worship war that lies behind the biblical narrative. The four sections of Scripture we have considered indicate that worship lies at the heart of true human identity and vocation. It is not something that affects the periphery of human existence, or something that can be confined to one particular venue or time (e.g. the sanctuary between 11:00 and 12:00 on Sunday). Rather, the battle for worship lies at the heart of the very meaning of the biblical narrative itself. Cranfield is right to identify four broad uses of the term worship:[50] adoration of God; the public worship of the assembled people of God; the private religious expressions of devotion to God of families or individuals; and worship as a whole of life activity. The aim of this book is to highlight the interconnections between these elements, and in so doing we will see that from creation to new creation, the issue is one of worship. This is why the matter is so important, and why we cannot allow the discussion to be reduced to form and function alone.

Chapter 2

Worship in the Biblical Prologue
(Genesis 1–11)

Introduction

Having seen something of the dimensions of the battle for worship in the previous chapter, we are now about to embark on a brief, but necessary, overview of the matter of worship in the biblical narrative. In this and the next two chapters we are going to focus on the matter of worship in the Old Testament. Throughout the discussion we want to remain alert to the 'big picture' questions relating to the significance of the battle for worship, and the ways in which this battle is expressed.

In this chapter we will be focusing on the first eleven chapters of Genesis. These form the prologue, not just to the book of Genesis itself, but to the entire Bible. The themes that emerge in these eleven chapters govern the unfolding drama of the biblical narrative, not least in the matter of worship. They are taken up throughout the Old Testament, and taken forward into the New Testament in the person and ministry of Jesus Christ. Ultimately they find their fulfilment in the new creation, so powerfully described in Revelation, the closing book of the Bible, where the allusions to Genesis 1–11 are profuse.

1. Worship in Eden, and Before

(1) Worship Predates the Creation of Human Beings
For a number of reasons (e.g. the fact that we, as human beings, are the ones engaged in worship) the tendency is to begin treatments of the matter of worship with comments relating to the creation of human beings. However, this would be to limit the definition of worship to a human activity directed towards God. This is too narrow. God's decision to create the universe is the effective cause of worship. He creates, and that which springs into being through his Word and Spirit as a result of his creative will, worships. The worship of humanity may stand at the pinnacle of the worship of creation, but it is not the sum total of worship.

It is clear, for example, that the angelic beings worship. On a number of occasions in the Scriptures we see the veil which separates time from eternity drawn aside, and on every occasion we see worship being offered in the courts of heaven. In Job 38:7 we read that, at the time of the creation of the world, 'the morning stars sang together, and all the sons of God shouted for joy' (NASB). From the way in which the phrase 'sons of God' is used elsewhere in the Scriptures (e.g. Job 1:6; 2:1; 38:7; Pss. 29:1; 89:6) we know that it refers to the angelic beings.[1] At the creation of the world they were moved to sing praises to God and bring adoration to him, doubtless for the wonder of what they saw unfolding before their eyes. Perhaps, too, there is a hint of wonder at the creation of human beings, made in God's image and for his glory.

Similarly in Isaiah 6, that chapter of great prophetic vision and call, the *seraphim* are involved in worshipping God, declaring his holiness, in what has come to be known as the Trishagion (lit. 'three holies') 'Holy, Holy, Holy is the LORD [Yahweh] of hosts, the whole earth is full of his glory' (Isa. 6:3).[2] At the time of the coming of the Son of God into the world, the angelic host is seen again praising and worshipping God (Luke 2:13ff.). Throughout the book of the Revelation, all the angelic creatures, the living beings and the celestial elders are seen in constant worship (e.g. chapters 4 and 5), a picture which is reflected in Hebrews 12:22 where believers are said to 'have come to Mount Zion and to the city of the living God, the heavenly Jerusalem, and to innumerable angels in festal gathering'.

The fact that there are different categories of heavenly beings mentioned in the Scriptures also alerts us to the diversity and fecundity of God's creative action. For example, we read of *seraphim* (Isa. 6:2, 6);[3] *cherubim* (e.g. Gen. 3:24; Exod. 25: 18-20; Num. 7:89; 1 Sam. 4:4; 2 Sam. 6:2; 1 Kings 6:25; 2 Chron. 3:7; Ps. 99:1; Isa. 37:16; Ezek. 10:1; Heb. 9:5);[4] living creatures (Ezek. 1:5; Rev. 4:6-9; 5:6; 6:1; 14:3; 15:7; 19:4);[5] and elders (Rev. 4:4, 10). Each of these groups or orders has a different role, and each serves God, not simply in the expression of worship through praise and adoration offered up in song, but in the doing of his will. Just as the Son's active obedience in his earthly life revealed his worship of the Father, so their obedience is worshipful service of their Creator. Their expressions of adoration and praise are not ones of outward show, but the vocalizations of the thrust of their whole beings.

However, it is not simply the sentient celestial creation that worships. The whole of the creation is shown to worship God. This is particularly evident within the Psalter of Israel (e.g. Ps. 148; Ps. 96; cf. 1 Chron. 16:23-33), but not exclusively so (see, for example, Rev. 5:13). An analysis of these passages demonstrates that the non-sentient creation worships God by doing his will. It exists for him, and obeys him. This is seen in the very language of Genesis itself. Henri Blocher, commenting on Genesis 2:1, says,

> It is not for nothing that the throng of creatures is ... called an army (2:1), and that army as Beauchamp puts it 'does not fight, it parades'. The phrase is used commonly of the celestial creation, the angels and the stars (the Lord is the Lord of those armies); they are models of perfect obedience and regular motion ... the word translated 'army' or 'host' designates a diverse totality that is properly arranged, organised and differentiated.[6]

Worship, then, does not begin with human beings as though they alone worship, or as if they are the initiators of worship. Worship begins with God. By virtue of his very being as God, and by virtue of his act of creation, God is the initiator of worship. It begins with God, and it was evident in the celestial and terrestrial creation before human beings were brought into existence. This means that when God created our first parents, they came into a worship-filled creation. By implication their existence was also to be taken up in worship. This is a thought to which we will return shortly.

(2) God's Intention: All is for Worship

Before taking up the thought above, it is worth reflecting on what we have seen so far. In sum, we see that the whole of creation – celestial, terrestrial and human – was built for worship. Why should this be? On the most obvious level we can say that the creation of all things is for the glory of God. The creation, in all of its diversity, displays his glory and evidences his splendour. In Acts 17:24f. Paul says, 'The God who made the world and all things in it, since he is Lord of heaven and earth, does not dwell in temples made with hands, nor is he served by human hands, as though he needed anything, since he himself gives to all life and breath and all things' (NASB)

The action and scope of God's activity is in sharp contrast to the idols, whose ubiquitous presence in Athens provoked Paul to speak in

this way. In the context of condemning the idols and their worship in
1 Corinthians 8:6 he says, 'for us there is one God the Father, from
whom are all things, and we exist for him; and one Lord Jesus Christ,
by whom are all things, and we exist through him' (NASB). Thoughts
like these are echoed in a number of New Testament texts (e.g.
Rom. 11:36; 1 Cor. 11:12; Col. 1:16; Heb. 2:10), and are thoroughly
consistent with the Old Testament theology we have seen expressed
in Psalm 115. God is not just the only God, but he brings all things into
existence to the praise of his own glory.

Passages such as these emphasise two things: firstly, God the Father
is the one who has brought all things into being through the Son (with
the agency of the Spirit), and secondly, they exist for him.[7] In their
existence, and in his sovereignty over all their actions, he is glorified.
Throughout the Scriptures God is shown as the only Creator of heaven
and earth, who is actively sustaining every element of the created
order, and therefore worship is due to him alone.[8]

We should not interpret these things anthropomorphically. God has
not created the world out of a sense of his own interior need, or to
bolster a failing ego. As Irenaeus said long ago, 'in the beginning ...
God form[ed] Adam, not as if He stood in need of any man, but that
He might have [some one] upon whom to confer His benefit.... For
this is the glory of man, to continue and remain permanently in God's
service.'[9] Old Testament commentators now generally recognize that
a deeply polemical purpose is woven throughout the biblical creation
accounts. In this vein, in commenting on the story of creation and its
contrast with similar ancient Mesopotamian cosmologies, Gordon
Wenham states,

> man was made from the dust of the ground, and then God breathed into
> him the breath of life. In Mesopotamian thought, man worked so that the
> gods could rest. Gen. 2 gives no hint of that approach: God worked until
> all man's needs were satisfied. The God of Genesis is totally concerned
> with man's welfare.[10]

As the Westminster *Shorter Catechism* puts it, 'What is the chief
end of man?' 'Man's chief end is to glorify God and *to enjoy him
forever*,' a perception echoed in the *Longer Catechism of the Eastern
Church* (1839), question 120: 'With what design did God create man?'
'With this, that he should know God, love and glorify him, *and so be
happy forever*'.[11]

Worship, as is the case with many aspects of Christian obedience, is often spoken of in the vocabulary of duty: it is our duty to worship and serve God, and our duty to obey him. Such statements, however, often seem to place the concepts of duty and loving response (in which joy is the appropriate motivator) at two opposite poles. The doing of God's will (not least in worshiping him alone, in accordance with the first commandment) is not bare duty, but the thing for which we have been created. It governs human identity and is the arena in which we find our fullness. From the perspective of our relationship to God as our Creator-Father, in whose image we have been made, worship is natural to us. It is only from the fallen perspective of sinful hearts that it becomes a dutiful chore.

To come at this thought from another angle: grammar is that which gives coherence to our language. It is the unspoken paradigm by which sentences are written and conversations held. Ungrammatical statements stand out and declare themselves as being foreign to the structure of the language. They exist, but they do not belong. They have no authentic being. In a similar way, I suggest, the creation has a 'grammar' of worship. This grammar is found in the eternal Triune relationships of the Godhead. It is the grammar of communion, of mutuality, of self-giving, voluntary glorification of the other. It is always doing, being and saying 'for the other', not 'for the self.' This is the essence of *agapē*, the holy love of God, the revelation of which in history is the manifestation of God's glory. We have been made by the Triune God to reflect his internal self-giving love, and to participate in the action of honouring him above all things. After all, God is more interested in seeing that his name is honoured in the universe than we are! And as we, his creatures, share in this God-glorifying life, so we find our home. We live authentic lives, ones that share in the proper grammar of the language of the universe.

The point is this: God did not create because in some sense he needed to be worshiped, but the parameters of worship (the constitutive elements of it) belong to his own being as God. His acts of creation open up the possibility that his creatures may know the ineffable joy and eternal riches of such elements.[12] To put the matter differently, God is to be worshipped, not simply because he demands to be, but because this is the proper destiny of his creation. Anything less dishonours him and disfigures it.

(3) The Creational Necessity of Worship

From what we have seen thus far, it is evident that the creation *must* worship. The non-sentient elements of creation display the glory of God. The earth and all it contains is a manifestation of the glory of the Creator. The sentient elements of creation – celestial beings, as well as humans – are designed for conscious participation in God-glorifying worship. Their existence was also to be taken up in worship, understood in the widest sense of that term. If they would not worship God, they must nonetheless worship someone, or something.

Human beings alone are spoken of as having been made in the image and likeness of God. It is fair to assume that among other things this status gave them vice-regency over the created order. They were not to worship any other element of the creation, whether this was a part of the earthly, visible creation, or part of the invisible, heavenly reality. Angels, for example, were not to be worshipped, nor were any animalistic forms or representations.[13] Instead, human beings were formed in God's image to lead the creation in worship of the God who had created all things.

When we turn more specifically to the early chapters of Genesis, then, we should see humanity as being brought into, and existing in, a matrix of worship. The primal couple did not exist for themselves or by themselves, but they existed for God, at the head of a creation yet to be brought into its full glory. We see that the primal couple was given a mandate, to 'fill' the earth, 'subdue' it and 'rule over' it (Gen. 1:26f.), and a task to 'cultivate and keep' the Garden (Gen. 2:15).

To engage in such tasks and to fulfil the mandate was to be their expression of worship. Their communion with God, the joy of his nearer presence, the offering of praise and adoration to him, were not to be set in some compartmentalised fashion away from their daily activity, but the daily activity was their service to God. Hence Trevor Hart, commenting on that which distinguishes human beings from the rest of the created order, states,

> The particular distinguishing feature I have in mind is the capacity of humans for a conscious relation to God, considered response to him, articulate worship and intercession. So, in the tradition, humans have been deemed priests of creation, gathering up the worship of the whole and offering it to God in a representative act of praise.[14]

(4) Adam as King-Priest in Eden

A number of writers have pointed to the lines of evidence for Adam's priestly function.[15] In part, such a conclusion is drawn from the close relationship between Eden and the later Tabernacle/Temple in Israel. These shared a common symbolism, redolent of Eden at every turn. Such symbolism can be seen in a number of ways. For example, both Eden and the later sanctuaries were entered from the East and were guarded by cherubim (Gen. 3:24; cf. Exod. 25:18-22; 26:31; 1 Kings 6:23-29). God is said to walk in Eden and in the later sanctuaries (Gen. 3:8; cf. Lev. 26:12; Deut. 23:14; 2 Sam. 7:6f.). The rivers flowing out of Eden are matched by the river flowing from Ezekiel's visionary Temple (Gen. 2:10ff.; cf. Ezek. 47:1-12). The menorah (the seven branched candle stick) is fashioned to represent a tree, which may be equated with the Tree of Life (Gen. 2:9; 3:22; cf. Exod. 25:31-35). Eden is portrayed as being (or as being on) a mountain (Gen. 2:10ff. – the rivers flowed *from* Eden to the rest of the world[16]), while the garden imagery of Eden is repeated in the architecture and ornamentation of the later sanctuaries (Gen. 2:8, 10, 15; 3:23f; cf. 1 Kings 6:15-36).

Given these connections, then, it is not surprising to see elements that point to Adam's priestly role over creation. These again are reflected in the later sanctuary worship. The garments of the High Priest represent Edenic symbolism in a number of ways. The garments were to be made of linen (Exod. 28:6), the purpose of which was so that they would not sweat (Ezek. 44:17f.). Sweat is an element of the curse in Genesis 3:18f.; and 'the Priest, as the Restored Man, was required to wear the light material of linen to show the removal of the Curse in salvation'.[17] The gold plate on his forehead was to be inscribed 'Holy to the Lord', thus removing the unholy state of Adam and the curse on his brow. The garments were rich – gold and precious stones which reflect the riches of Eden (Gen. 2:12 cf. Exod. 28:15-30), gold often being associated with the Divine Presence in the Scriptures (see, for example, Exodus 25 compared with Revelation 21).

Moreover, Wenham points out that the terminology of Genesis 2:15 ('to serve' or 'to work/till') is elsewhere used in a religious sense of serving God (e.g. Deut. 4:19), and in particular it is applied to the service of the later Levites (e.g. Num. 3:7-8; 4:23-24, 26 etc.), and therefore forms 'another pointer to the interplay of tabernacle and Eden symbolism'.[18] We see, then, that the whole of Eden was built for worship. Adam was created to be the great leader of the creation in its glorification of God, with Eden as the garden-sanctuary of his communion with the Creator. Worship was never to be an adjunct to Adam's life. All of his life was to express his devotion to God and the glory of his Name, so that if and when Adam were to lift his heart and voice in praise to God it would be praise fully expressive of a whole life of service. While we will later speak of Jesus' role in transforming worship under the new covenant, we should not lose this fully integrated perspective. In a real sense, Jesus' whole salvific mission can be understood as the restitution of the fully integrated nature of worship evident before the Fall.

(5) Jesus: The New Priest-King
While the thrust of the present chapter is to do with the matter of worship in the original creation, we cannot ignore the place of Jesus Christ even here. If he is the Second (Last) Adam, we must refer to him in order to understand the nature and intended destiny of the First Adam. In chapter one we saw that Jesus was anointed to be the new priest and king on the earth, to restore that which had been lost in Adam's fall. Thus, when we see him refuting Satan's temptation in the wilderness, and answering with the words of Scripture that 'you shall worship (*proskynēseis*) the Lord your God and him only shall you serve (*latreuseis*)', he was identifying himself with the normative state of human beings before the fall[19] and indicating what would be the normative state of redeemed humanity in the restoration of a new heavens and earth, namely, conformity with the commandments of God.

The vocabulary Jesus uses in his refutation of Satan in the wilderness is significant. In his reply to Satan's demand for worship, Jesus says that he will not worship or serve anyone but God alone (he adds the adverb 'only', *monos*, to the quotation from Deuteronomy 6:13). In the Greek text, this priority is also reflected by the emphatic placement of the subject in the sentence (lit. 'the Lord your God you shall worship and him alone shall you serve').

Furthermore, Jesus uses the two most important words for worship in the New Testament. The first verb, *proskyneō*, means 'I worship, do obeisance to, prostrate myself', and it is commonly agreed that its most basic meaning is 'to kiss'.[20] In the Greek translation of the Old Testament (the LXX) it is used to translate the Hebrew word *shâchah*, which means to bow down, both before other human beings such as kings and rulers, and before God (or idols) in acts of worship. The second verb, *latreuō*, means 'I serve, I worship'. In the LXX this verb is used to translate the Hebrew *'a'bad*, to serve God (or someone/something else). At the risk of over simplifying the relationship between the two words: the first encompasses outward actions of worship, while the second (though not excluding the outward actions) relates to the disposition of one's heart and life.[21] In answering Satan in this way, by using both words to underline his point, Jesus not only excludes any outward acts of obeisance, but any inward attitude of heart. His whole life, in action and attitude, would be a life of truly constituted worship.

Satan had said to him, 'All these I will give you, if you will fall down and worship (*proskynēsēs*) me' (Matt. 4:9, ESV). His (false) promise was that the kingdoms of this world would be given to Jesus through worship. In a sense he was right. The kingdoms of this world would be given to the Son through worship, but worship rendered to his Father, not to Satan. As the Son of God and Messianic King, Jesus knew that all the kingdoms of the earth were his rightful inheritance (as in Psalm 2). He also knew that the only power the king had was as he stood in submission to God, the Great King, anointed by his Spirit. Moreover, Jesus understood that his whole mission of the redemption and ultimate glorification of his Bride was to restore her to the joy of Edenic worship. He knew that the Father's goal (and therefore willingly his goal also) was to see a new Husband and Bride at the pinnacle of a glorified creation. He, as the Son, was to bring about the glorification of creation through his worship of the Father, and to bring a renewed humanity to participate in its full destiny of worshipping in Spirit and in Truth.

In his office as King-Priest, Jesus not only offered acceptable sacrifice to God on our behalf, but by his current ministry as ascended Priest and reigning Lord he is at work to bring about the glorification of his people and, with them, the renewal of the whole creation (so Romans 8:18ff.). This renewed and glorified creation he then offers as a gift to the Father so that 'he (the Father) might be all in all' (1 Cor. 15:24-28). In contrast to the first Adam, he resisted the beguiling words of Satan, and cast him out of the earth, which is ultimately co-terminal with the Temple. The renewed heaven and earth is not only full of the glory of the Lord, it is full of the *knowledge* of the glory of the Lord. In the end, through the action of the worshipping Son, God is worshipped every where by all things, in every way. In this renewed, glorified and globalized Eden, Satan has no part. The story of the New Testament tell us that Jesus, the new King-Priest, has done (and will do) that which the first one failed to do by guarding the purity of the Edenic Temple and rejecting the false worship of the Serpent.

2. The Fall as a Battle for Worship

(1) God the Creator is Worthy of Worship
One of the implications tucked away in the preceding discussion is that worship is not simply (or even primarily) our response to grace. So often it seems that Christian worship, especially in the evangelical tradition, focuses on the act of redemption. While this is not to be rejected, the Scriptural testimony is much wider than this. The worship and service of God is to be engendered by both creation and redemption, and as much by the former as the latter.

It may be true, theologically, that we cannot see God as Creator without first seeing him as Redeemer, but Jesus' (as with the First Adam's) role was to worship God as his Father, and he stood in no need of redemption. The picture of worship given to us in the Book of the Revelation, especially in chapters 4 and 5, indicates that the worship which is offered in heaven – and which encompasses the whole of creation – is engendered because of God's intrinsic worth and in his action as the Almighty Creator, not simply because of his action as the Gracious Redeemer.

While there are ongoing debates about the exact meaning of the phrase 'image and likeness of God' in Genesis 1:26f., at least one element of it must relate to the fact that Adam was created as a son of God. This is clear from the parallel use of the 'image and likeness' and its link with the idea of sonship in Genesis 5:1-3, which stands at the head of the genealogy that leads to Noah. 'This is the book of the generations of Adam. When God created man, he made him in the likeness of God. Male and female he created them, and he blessed them and named them Man when they were created. When Adam had lived 130 years, he fathered a son in his own likeness, after his image, and named him Seth' (ESV). Just as Seth was Adam's son, 'in his own likeness, after his image', so Adam was the son of God 'in his image and after his likeness'. Thus Adam stands at the head of the Lucan genealogy of which we have made mention in the first chapter: 'Adam the son of God' (Luke 3:38), being the progenitor of the race.

Now it is clear from the Last Adam, who is without doubt the Son of God, that sonship does not consist in status simply, but in active obedience. The temptation brought by Satan in the wilderness to Jesus was a temptation to exercise his sonship on his own terms. Jesus, as the true Son of the Father, replied with his commitment in active obedience to the Father's will. To do anything less would be to betray his very being as Son. All of this means, simply, that worship and sonship are linked, and that to be a true son is to obey the Father. To worship him is to serve him, which is to obey him, which is what sonship is all about. While worship may arise as a response to the gracious action of God in redemption, for example, it actually belongs more fundamentally to the structure of human beings as sons of God. God the Creator is worthy of worship by virtue of his own being, irrespective of any gracious work on his part to redeem fallen humankind. It is this worship for which human beings were created, and it is this which brings added poignancy to the thought that human beings may say to some other, so-called god, 'You are my father' (Jer. 2:27 cf. 3:4, 19).

(2) Satan and the Theft of Worship

In the account of the Fall given to us in Genesis 3, the action of the serpent is really related to his quest for worship. The identity and nature of the serpent have been subject to much adjustment in recent decades. The long-standing tradition that identifies the serpent with Satan, and thus with Lucifer, or the Devil, has been questioned by much recent Old Testament scholarship. It is fairly clear that the primeval prologue of Genesis carries with it a deeply polemical strain. Contemporary exegetes have given due recognition to this polemical purpose, not least in their dealings with the figure of the serpent, a figure widely esteemed in the Ancient Near East. Walton, for example, quotes Sarna: 'Throughout the ancient world, [the serpent] was endowed with divine or semidivine qualities; it was venerated as an emblem of health, fertility, immortality, occult wisdom, and chaotic evil; and it was often worshipped'.[22]

While we would not wish to deny the polemical intention of the material, this strain does not exhaust its meaning. Fretheim points out that in trying to determine the meaning of the serpent we must understand that two different pictures are presented in the chapter. Genesis 3:1 and 3:14 both show that 'the serpent is … simply another animal.' However, 'There are details indicating that [the author] considers the serpent as not *just* another animal'.[23] In particular, Fretheim points to the use of the word 'subtle' (*'arum* = 'crafty' in the NASB and most other translations), 'a word never used elsewhere in the Old Testament for an animal, and used of man almost always in a bad sense.' This word, together with the actions attributed to the creature (seducing man and challenging God), indicates knowledge and intention. Furthermore, the mention of 'the struggle between the seed of the serpent and the seed of the woman (3:15) involves more than the idea that snakes and people do not get along'.[24]

Fretheim's justifiable conclusion is that the serpent represents a 'trans-historical', 'trans-personal' 'representation or personification of evil'. The picture thus painted is quite nuanced. God and his purposes are shown to be opposed by one who stands under him, as a creature, and yet the work of this one is not limited to one age or another. Rather, he stands at the head of a line of opposition (through his seed), which challenges God and his plans.

Moreover, if we move wider afield in the Old Testament, the serpent is used figuratively to denote evil. In Deuteronomy 32:32 the enemies of God's people (which nevertheless are portrayed as fulfilling God's purposes of judgment towards his people) are described. 'Their vine is from the vine of Sodom, and from the fields of Gomorrah; Their grapes are grapes of poison, Their clusters bitter. Their wine is the venom of serpents, And the deadly poison of cobras.' In Isaiah 14:29, Assyria (which in this case had inflicted vengeance on Philistia) is described as a 'serpent' from whose root 'a viper will come out'. In Jeremiah 8:17 the nations bringing judgment (of defeat and exile) are described in terms of 'serpents' and 'adders', for whose bite there is no cure (as contrasted with those bitten in the wilderness). The serpent imagery is notable in the wilderness wanderings, with the fiery serpents of Numbers 21:6-9 manifesting the judgment of God on rebellious Israel. Interestingly enough, 2 Kings 18:4 indicates that the Mosaic serpent pole had become an object of idolatry, and was broken into pieces under Hezekiah's reforms.[25] In Psalm 91:13, the one who trusts in Yahweh is shown to be the one who treads the serpent under foot,[26] while in Psalm 58:4 the wicked are likened to serpents. Other examples could be advanced, but the point is clear that the serpent/ evil connotation of Genesis 3 is part of a tradition widely witnessed to in the Old Testament.

While a polemical element may not be absent from the Old Testament, this need not militate against the more traditional interpretation of the serpent as the embodiment of the Devil. Indeed, there are good reasons for persisting with it, particularly when viewed from the perspective of a canonical biblical theology. Not least among these is the way in which the image is pursued into the New Testament. Paul uses the image of the serpent's temptation of Eve as a warning in 2 Corinthians 11:3, while in Romans 16:20 there seems to be a very clear allusion to Genesis 3:15.[27]

In the Book of Revelation Satan is clearly identified as 'the serpent of old' and 'the devil', who 'deceives the whole world' (12:9; cf. 20:2; 9:19). Here (as elsewhere) the meaning of the names attributed to him is noteworthy. He is called the 'devil' and 'Satan',[28] titles referring to his action as the one who slanders and his role as the adversary of God respectively. He is also notably the one who 'deceives the whole world'; a repeated emphasis in Revelation (13:14; 18:23; 19:20; 20:3, 8, 10) and an ascription of him shared with other New Testament passages (e.g. 2 Cor. 11:3; 2 Thess. 2:9-11; 1 Tim. 2:14; cf. Matt. 24:24; Rom. 16:18; Eph. 4:14).

Taken as a whole, we cannot escape the conclusion that the temptation account in Genesis 3 represents the transpersonal, trans-historical evil of the one known elsewhere as the Devil, or Satan, the chief enemy of both God and man.[29] What, then, is the nature of his temptation?

If we allow the traditional interpretation to stand – that this one is the same as the one elsewhere known as Lucifer – it seems that his desire to usurp the worship due to God alone was at the core of his heavenly rebellion. Isaiah 14:12-14 has been traditionally understood to apply to him:

> How you are fallen from heaven, O Day Star, son of Dawn! How you are cut down to the ground, you who laid the nations low! You said in your heart, 'I will ascend to heaven; above the stars of God I will set my throne on high; I will sit on the mount of assembly in the far reaches of the north; I will ascend above the heights of the clouds; I will make myself like the Most High' (ESV).

Just as Satan sought to usurp the worship due to God in the heavenly realm, so he sought to usurp it in his temptation of Jesus in the wilderness, and so also he sought to usurp it in Eden. His actions in the Garden are part of a deliberate and long-standing manifestation of rebellion, in which he attempts to seize that worship and service which belong to God alone. In the wilderness, Jesus knew that to forego obedience to God at one point was to disobey at all points.[30] For the primal couple, therefore, there could be no 'half way house' of partial obedience to God. They either served him in the hearing and obeying of his word, or they served another through the hearing of his word. The choice was not *whether* they would worship, but *whom* they would worship.

As a result of that act of disobedience, humanity was enslaved to the evil one, and despite universal ignorance of the state of slavery that exists (i.e. men and women do not realise that it is this way, unless their eyes are opened to see it, 2 Cor. 4:1-6 cf. Acts 26:18; Eph. 2:1-3), it is nonetheless real. It is little wonder, then, that idolatry and demonic activity are often very closely linked (e.g. Deut. 32:17; Ps. 106:37; cf. 1 Cor. 10:20f.; Rev. 9:20), a point to which we return later.

The curse that follows the entrance of sin into the Garden, in its several different elements, reveals dislocation at every level. The rest found in God's nearer presence; the communion of intimate fellowship with him and one another; the harmony of the created order; and both the joy of procreation and the ability to rejoice in other elements of the mandate are all affected. The mandate the primal couple had been given now becomes the arena of the curse. The key functions of multiplying and filling, keeping and tilling, ruling and subduing are all accompanied by pain, suffering, hard labour, and ultimately physical death and decay. This leads to a return to the dust from which humanity had been taken, dust which originated outside of Eden, and to which all human beings would now return. Each of the figures in the story is affected: the man, the woman, the serpent and the earth. The consequences of disobedience flow to every area of life, and the primal worship is destroyed as a result.

However, the expulsion of the primal couple from the Garden, as seen in Genesis 3:24, is not completely devoid of hope. As they head out, clothed by God as a sign of his gracious provision for them (3:21), they carry with them the promise of 3:15.[31] From the woman would yet come one who would crush the head of the Serpent (in a killing blow), though this would not be without pain to the victor.[32]

3. Cain and Abel: Conflict and Death in the Context of Worship

(1) Two Different Attitudes in Worship
In the light of the foregoing discussion it is significant that the first record of human violence and murder has worship at its core. The story of Cain and Abel opens up the matter of worship in a very explicit way, and shows the seriousness of its consequences, for good or for ill. It serves to underscore the fundamental difference between two contrasting attitudes in worship.

The basic elements of the story are no doubt well known to us. Cain is shown as the elder of two brothers, and is desribed as a 'tiller of the ground', like Adam his father. Cain's name, the interpretation of which is given to us in Genesis 4:1b,[33] may indicate something of the hope in Eve's heart that this would be the deliverer Seed of Genesis 3:15. Abel, whose name connotes the Hebrew *hebel* ('vanity', 'breath') – perhaps indicating Eve's low regard for this second born, or the brevity of his life – is the younger of the two. He is described as a 'keeper of flocks'.

Each of the sons brought an offering, according to his vocation. Cain's consisted of 'the fruit of the ground', Abel's of the 'firstlings of his flock'. There is no *necessary* difficulty or deficiency associated with the content of the sacrifices each brings, though historically there is a strong tradition that links the sacrifice of Abel with the Old Testament theology of atonement being through the shedding of blood. Later in Israel's worship cultus grain and cereal offerings were acceptable (e.g. Leviticus 2). We also find references to animal sacrifices which were not acceptable to the Lord (eg. Isa. 1:11). In such places, as in the incident in this passage, the emphasis lies on *what* is brought rathar than with *how* it is brought. Abel's sacrifice included the 'fat portions' and 'firstborn', and these indicate that he brought the best, thus revealing the underlying attitude of a thankful heart.[34]

In the text itself the emphasis falls on the person, not the work. 'And the Lord had regard for Abel and his offering; but for Cain and his offering He had no regard' (Gen. 4:4b-5a). The person comes first, then his offering.[35] According to Hebrews 11:4, Abel's offering was given 'by faith', implying that Cain's was not. Philip Hughes quotes Gregory the Great, 'it is obvious that it was not the offerer who received approval because of the offerings, but the offerings because of the offerer.'[36]

This thought is further reinforced by the the way in which John uses the example of Cain in 1 John 3:10-15. Cain is there described as being 'of the evil one' (v. 12), and he stands as a clear illustration of someone whose actions betray his family likeness, in a spiritual sense. His murderous action is shown to be a sign that he has not been 'born of God', i.e. he was not a man of faith. He did not have God's Spirit within him, and thus he belonged to the darkness, not the light, being driven by jealousy and devoid of brotherly love. John's exhortation that 'we should not be like Cain, who was of the evil one and murdered his brother' is matched by the unspoken corollary that we should be like Abel, whose love demonstrated that he belonged to the heavenly Father. In Jude, Cain is used as an example of one of the enemies of the people of God (Jude 11). He is seen to be a rebel, who did not share in the faith of God's people, but rather opposed it.

The New Testament exegesis of the incident, then, leaves us in no doubt that the worship that God accepts is worship offered in faith. Thus Luther says, 'God is not interested in any works, not even those which he himself has commanded, when they are not done in faith.'[37] In his commentary on Genesis 1–5 Luther makes much of the rights of the first-born Cain and the way in which he squandered these to lose his inheritance, for it to pass to righteous Abel.[38] He suggests that Cain, as the first-born son, 'is king and priest', who should have brought acceptable worship to God. This conjunction of first-born status, kingship and priesthood is seen again in Israel (who is both God's first-born son and a nation of king-priests), and in Jesus (who is First-born of heaven and earth, and King-Priest over all creation).

(2) Cainite Worship: Rebellion with a Religious Face

The principle of 'Cainite worship' (to coin a phrase) is one of self-justification. For those who worship according to the line of Cain, worship is a means to an end – the end being one's own blessing, the means being on one's own terms. The later Ba'alism with which Israel had to battle, and in which battle it failed so spectacularly, was built on this principle. If one wanted favour from the gods, one must pull the right strings, go through the right rituals, and establish the right credentials to be heard and answered.

Blocher rightly suggests that 'Cain's reaction shows the profound paganism of his worship. If he was disappointed, it was because by his sacrifice he hoped to build up credit with God.'[39] Cainite worship is not submitted to God in a humble and contrite heart, which looks to him to fulfil his word and keep his promises according to his own sovereign freedom. Rather it seeks to bring God captive to the human will, and exercise dominion over heaven in so doing. Such self-centred false righteousness is condemned throughout the Scriptures, not least by Jesus himself (e.g. the parable of the Pharisee and the tax collector in Luke 18:9-14), and lies at the heart of that type of worship which relies on form rather than on the attitude of the worshipper.[40]

In addition, the incident serves to remind us of the pervasive nature of the effects of faithless worship. The worship of the two brothers is not a compartmentalised affair, which has no effect on the rest of their lives. We have seen already that worship springs from and is related to the core of one's being. It is no peripheral activity. The rage engendered in Cain's heart when he realises that his worship has not been acceptable to God is literally murderous. The first murder in human history relates to the acceptability (or not) of the first recorded act of worship after the Fall. False worship arises in the flesh, breeds jealousy and anger, and ends in death. Anger at God, expressed in a brooding and fallen countenance, is expressed as anger to the brother, who is made in God's image. To kill him is to strike out at God (Gen. 9:5-6). Conversely, where one knows that one's worship is pleasing to God, there is peace and a good conscience (which, of course, is the message of Hebrews in a nutshell), even if this is opposed with violence.

(3) Cain and Abel: Warnings and Examples to Israel
The story in Genesis 4 unfolds in such a way as to let us see the graciousness of God in his dealings with human beings, even with the disgruntled and angry Cain. God approaches him, just as he approached Adam in the Garden.[41] While 4:7 is notoriously difficult to translate,[42] the ESV version reflects the balance of most translations: 'if you do well, will you not be accepted? And if you do not do well, sin is crouching at the door. Its desire is for you, but you must rule over it.' The thrust is clearly twofold: Cain must take responsibility for his sin, and repentance offers a fresh start if he were minded so to do. Even after the murder of his brother, God approaches him, and

questions him 'for the same purpose he queried the man and the woman in the garden (3:9, 11) – not to scold, but to elicit Cain's admission of sin with the view to repentance'.[43] While we know from the narrative that such repentance was not forthcoming, the whole account leaves us in no doubt that the opportunity to repent was there.

The story of Cain and Abel, therefore, stands at the outset of Israel's sacred history and indicates a number of important themes:

* there is worship that is acceptable to God and worship which is unacceptable;
* worship that is acceptable to God is related to the condition of the worshipper, not the external sacrifice *per se*;
* that there would always be a battle over worship, such a battle being severe enough to lead to violence and murder;
* that those who were under God's judgement were nonetheless still graciously approached by him with a view to repentance;
* that refusal to repent led to further judgement;
* that, from the very beginning, there were men and women who offered true worship to God;
* and that there was still a godly line, despite the death of men like Abel, which would continue through Seth, as is made clear in the section of the narrative that follows this story (Gen. 4:26).

4. Worship From Seth to Noah

(1) Abel's Line of Faithful Worship
Genesis 4:25-26, alluded to above, indicates that the godly line of Abel was preserved throughout subsequent generations. 'And Adam knew his wife again, and she bore a son and called his name Seth, for she said, "God has appointed for me another offspring (seed, *zera*') instead of Abel, for Cain killed him." To Seth also a son was born, and he called his name Enosh. At that time people began to call upon the name of the LORD.' Despite the gloomy outlook for humanity because of its sin, and despite the fact that anger born of self-righteousness had already led to murder, there is still hope. We see this in two ways.

Firstly, in Hebrew there is a clever word play relating to Seth's name. 'Seth' (*šet*) connotes the word *šatî* in Eve's statement, 'God has *appointed* for me another offspring instead of Abel,' suggesting that this son was 'appointed' by God as a *replacement* for Abel. This should not be thought of in numerical terms, but in terms of his character. It is probably significant that Seth is described here as Eve's 'seed' (*zera'*), bringing connotations of Genesis 3:15 and the longing for the promised deliverer. Moreover, both his name and the verb come from the root *šat*, which 'can also mean "foundation" [which is] suggestive of Seth's future role in establishing the line of the seed that will crush the serpent's head'.[44]

Secondly, we read that in the time of Enosh, Seth's own son, 'people began to call on the name of the LORD. This phrase has been variously interpreted, but elsewhere in the Old Testament (e.g. Ps. 116:4, 13; Lam. 3:55) it is the equivalent of prayer and praise. In Genesis itself it is linked with the worship of the Patriarchs (e.g. 12:8; 13:4; 16:13; 21:33). The use of the phrase in this context, then, suggests that the true worship of God was never lost from the earth. Despite the downward spiral of human sin, a line of true worshippers was preserved from Seth, through Noah to Abraham and the Patriarchs. Among other things, this would have indicated to Israel that the worship of Yahweh (though it marked them out from the nations round about in specific ways such as in the Temple and its cultus) had always been present in the world through Israel's covenantal ancestors.

(2) Noah as a Faithful Worshipper

One of these true worshippers to come from Seth's line was Noah. Seth's genealogy is found in Genesis 5:6-32, and features not only Noah, with whom it terminates, but the godly figure of Enoch who 'walked with God'. The concept of 'walking with God' connotes a cluster of ideas associated with fellowship and communion with God, obedience to him, pilgrimage with him and the experience of his favour.[45] We have already seen something of the background to this in our comments on the Creation accounts, where God is portrayed as 'walking' in the garden and the later Tabernacle/Temple sanctuaries. It is likely that Enoch's mention here, in the genealogy, serves to underscore the contrast between the character of those who come from Seth's line and those who have been described in Cain's genealogy in Genesis 4:17-24 (where the vengeful and murderous Lamech is featured).

Noah, too is said to be one who 'walked with God' (Gen. 6:9). Throughout the Flood narrative the text emphasises Noah as the obedient hearer of God's word (Gen. 6:22; 7:5, 9, 16, 8:15-18),[46] such obedience being the practical expression of a submitted and worshipful heart. Wherever the idea of walking with God is found it has this connotation (e.g. Gen. 5:24; 17:1; 24:40; 48:15; Mic. 6:8; Mal. 2:6; 1 Thess. 2:12).[47] Those who walk with God are those who respond to him in thankful obedience, which is the essence of true worship.

The fact that Noah is the main focus of Seth's genealogy indicates that Noah is the one in and through whom the plan and purpose of God will be carried forwards. Although Seth's genealogy concludes with Noah, he is given his own 'marker' in the division of the text and thus Genesis 6:9 introduces the next section of the narrative, using Genesis' distinctive *tôledôt* formula.[48]

The setting of the flood narrative is a rising tide of human wickedness and violence, which met with the flood of God's judgement.[49] This tide of evil is portrayed with comprehensive language in Genesis 6, especially in verses 5-7. Alec Motyer comments:

> Without exception, the whole human race is involved in wickedness (6:5), outwardly ('on the earth') and inwardly ('the thoughts of his heart'); equally without exception the whole race has excited divine grief and pain (6:6); and, once more without exception, the race is under judgement of death (6:7). All have sinned; all are alienated from God; all must die. 'But Noah found favour in the eyes of the LORD' (6:8). A new factor operated in this situation of total loss; there was a man named Noah and he 'found favour'.[50]

Motyer goes on to demonstrate that the phrase 'x found favour in the eyes of y' in the Old Testament is one which speaks of the priority of grace in such relationships. Characteristically 'x' has no claim upon 'y', but 'y', 'contrary to merit or deserving, against all odds, acts with "grace".'[51] The narrative leaves us in no doubt that Noah was the object of God's grace and acted accordingly, especially when we bear in mind that Noah's 'righteousness and blamelessness is *in comparison to the people of his time*'.[52] The meaning of Noah's righteousness must therefore be understood in the context of a relationship forged by divine grace.[53] He walks with God, not with the gods of his contemporaries. He hears and obeys God's voice, not that of the wickedness which surrounds him. He builds the Ark, condemns the world and saves his family all by faith (Heb. 11:7). He thus represents the continuation of the faithful line of Abel in word and deed.

In Genesis 8:20 Noah is seen emerging from the Ark (again in obedience to the Lord's word given in 8:15f.), and building an altar for worship. The fact that he takes his offerings from the clean animals and birds already provided in the Ark (Gen. 7:2f.) suggests that the sacrifices here offered were ones which were prepared by God at the outset. The emphasis on Noah's obedience is not lessened here. The building of the altar is tacitly an act of obedience rather than one that lay with Noah's own initiative. He emerges from the Ark, to establish an altar of sacrifice at the dawn of a new world, in obedience to God who had provided clean animals for him in preparation for the offering. Over this new world lies the grace of a sacrifice which God had provided. But what is the nature of the sacrifice Noah offers? Is it simply a sacrifice of thanksgiving? Or is it something more?

The anthropomorphic language of Genesis 8:20 ('The Lord smelled the soothing aroma') 'expresses God's favor and pleasure toward the sacrifice and worshiper (cf. Exod. 29:18; Lev. 1:9; 3:16; Num. 15:3)'[54] and thus indicates that this worship was acceptable to God. There should be no doubt that this is meant as an atoning sacrifice. This is also emphasised in the word play on Noah's name which appears here. 'Noah' comes from a Hebrew word which can be translated 'rest' (*nwh*), the same word used here for 'soothing' or 'restful'.[55] Noah's father, Lamech, had named him in the hope that he would bring rest from the curse (Gen. 5:29). Here Noah offers a 'soothing', 'restful' sacrifice with which God is pleased. Through such a sacrifice there is rest from the curse of God's judgement. By implication, the world had been brought to the destruction of the Flood by its refusal to repent of its violence and wickedness, and thus by its refusal to worship God in repentant faith, as it ought.

(3) Noah's Worship as Warning and Example

The whole account, as with that of Cain and Abel, is designed to stand at the outset of history to mark out for Israel (and through them, the nations) the significance of their worship and to describe its true nature. It does this in a number of ways.

Firstly, why was such an atoning sacrifice needed? It was needed for the very simple reason that Noah, despite being the obedient hearer of the word of God, was still a sinner. In the very verse that speaks of the sacrifice as a 'pleasing aroma' we also hear Yahweh saying, 'I will never again curse the ground because of man, for the intention of man's heart is evil from his youth.' Noah was no exception to this. He had simply become the object of God's saving grace (as Israel was to become, whose primal history had been recorded in the pages of Genesis), and thus he was able to offer up sacrifices that were pleasing to God in worship that God had prepared for him (as was also the case with the later Israel). This was not because the sacrifices were something God needed (as in paganism), but because they were the obedient expression of faith in God's promise of forgiveness to penitent hearts.[56]

Secondly, Israel was to learn repeatedly through the judgements she would undergo that there was no rest for the wicked. In the context of her later history, this wickedness related directly to her rejection of the true worship of Yahweh and the embracing of paganism and idolatry. Often this rejection was through syncretism. Sometimes it was through active attempts to banish the worship of Yahweh from the land (e.g. Ahab and Jezebel). But in whatever form it came, it was fuelled by a promise of rest, peace and prosperity that was based on something other than the system of atonement that God had put in place for them. In this God-given system of worship alone was there rest, for in the atonement that God provided his wrath was removed. Both for Noah and Israel the sacrificial system was not meant to be a religious work, but a gift. Offered in the obedience of faith it brought rest to the worshipper, by his being brought into harmony with God who had given the sacrificial system to make atonement for sin. The Flood story brings home the message that the divine curse cannot be escaped except by grace. Those who do not find favour feel the full weight of judgement, and therefore those who ignore the gift of atonement do so at their peril.

Thirdly, Noah's sacrifice stands at the point of a new beginning. In this new beginning, there is a new mandate, one that is parallel to that given to the primal couple. Here, however, the mandate was (and henceforth will be) under the umbrella of atonement. In the later history of Israel we also see a mandate of sorts given to them regarding the promised land. This land is spoken of in Edenic terms (e.g. Exod. 3:8,)ô17; Num. 13:23-25; Deut. 31:20) and as 'the resting place' (Deut. 12:9 cf. 3:20; 25:19). They were to enter the land, cleansing it from its idolatry, and thus enjoy living in this new place of rest (Deut. 12:28). They would enjoy this rest as they worshipped truly, especially in the matter of the atonement offered at the Temple. Where Israel failed to worship truly, and gave herself to the idols, the mandate in relationship to the promised land was not fulfilled. This is the point of the cycle of judgement and deliverance seen, for example, in Judges 2:10-19:

> And all that generation also were gathered to their fathers. And there arose another generation after them who did not know the LORD or the work that he had done for Israel. And the people of Israel did what was evil in the sight of the LORD and served the Baals. And they abandoned the LORD the God of their fathers, who had brought them out of the land of Egypt. They went after other gods, from among the gods of the peoples who were around them, and bowed down to them. And they provoked the LORD to anger. They abandoned the LORD and served the Baals and the Ashtaroth. So the anger of the LORD was kindled against Israel, and he gave them over to plunderers, who plundered them. And he sold them into the hand of their surrounding enemies, so that they could no longer withstand their enemies. Whenever they marched out, the hand of the LORD was against them for harm, as the LORD had warned, and as the LORD had sworn to them. And they were in terrible distress. Then the LORD raised up judges, who saved them out of the hand of those who plundered them. Yet they did not listen to their judges, for they whored after other gods and bowed down to them. They soon turned aside from the way in which their fathers had walked, who had obeyed the commandments of the LORD and they did not do so. Whenever the LORD raised up judges for them, the LORD was with the judge, and he saved them from the hand of their enemies all the days of the judge. For the LORD was moved to pity by their groaning because of those who afflicted and oppressed them. But whenever the judge died, they turned back and were more corrupt than their fathers, going after other gods, serving them and bowing down to them. They did not drop any of their practices or their stubborn ways.

Fourthly, Noah here stands as the new Adam, looking out on a recreated world. Whereas Adam was the priest over the first creation, Noah stands as a priest over this new creation. But here, in this new creation still marked by the sin of humanity, the fellowship with God that the descendants of this new Adam would enjoy could only be possible through sacrifice. While the gross violence of the world had been removed in the Flood, the problem of sin still remained. For Israel, therefore, Noah was to be a reminder to them that their presence in the land and their access to God who dwelt in their midst were alike acts of his grace. Whereas their sin should banish them from the land, as the primal couple had been banished from the garden, the gracious gift of atoning sacrifice meant that they could enjoy rest in the land because their sin was covered.

Fifthly – and this is a matter to which we will return in more detail later – the presence of sacrifice at the dawning of this new creation prefigures for us the fact that the ultimate new creation is dependent upon another sacrifice. Jesus, who was to undergo a baptism (flood!) of judgement on the cross, would, through this act, bring about a renewal of heaven and earth. He in himself would be a 'soothing aroma' to the Lord, making atonement for sin and thereby ushering in a truly re-created heaven and earth. In this case, however, it would not simply be cleansed from the outward effects of gross violence, but would indeed be the place where only holiness and righteousness would be found. And the constant worship of that new Eden is praise to the Lamb once slain.

5. Worship and the Tower of Babel

(1) The Nations: Unity in Rebellion
The Flood did not end the curse, nor deal finally with the wickedness of humanity. The prologue of Genesis ends with a story of great rebellion, which contains tacit reference to the rebellion of its worship. There are many important Old Testament themes that emerge here, and we cannot do justice to them all. Genesis 11:2 indicates that the eastward journey of exile, begun with Adam and Eve in Genesis 3:24 and intensified with Cain in Genesis 4:16, is still in force. This shows us that humanity is still under the curse, and that it affects every human grouping, all the 'nations'. That the whole of humanity is in view here is plain from two other factors: (1) all speak the same language, and (2) the preceding chapter has listed the 'table of nations', covering the then known world.

The table of nations indicates that all humankind, being descendants of Noah, are to be regarded in some sense as brothers. Despite the diversity of cultures, gifts, talents and destinies displayed in this remarkable piece of literature, human beings are of one substance. The Babel story tells us, however, that the unity of humanity is not neutral. There is a constant anti-God thrust in them, that leads to the co-operative and co-ordinated rebellion of the city/tower building enterprise.

The act of city building has already been linked with murderous Cain (Gen. 4:17), sentenced to wandering even further east of the Garden than his parents. Here the whole of humanity is portrayed as sharing in his rebellion, in an attempt to 'make a name' for themselves 'lest they be scattered abroad' (Gen. 11:4). In the chapters immediately following this episode, through the call of Abram and the promises made to him, we see that the prerogative of making a name for a person or nation lies with God. From one point of view human beings already had a name – 'image of God' – but here we see a rejection of any sense of relatedness to, or dependence upon, the God who had made them. Human autonomy is emphasised at the very centre of their tower building endeavour. 'This city and this society had no room for the God of creation and the garden, who demanded that humans exercise their power as God's vice regents within the limitations of what it means to be human'.[57]

(2) The Tower and the Folly of False Worship
Above and beyond this aspect of human rebellion, the whole story is part of a trenchant Old Testament criticism of Ancient Near Eastern conceptions of power, the mythology and idolatry of the surrounding nations, and the consequent nature of pagan worship. Throughout the narrative we see a repetition of the consonants *n, b, l*, evoking the Hebrew word *nebelah*, meaning 'folly',[58] and representing part of an extended word play on the name 'Babel'. Whereas 'the Babylonians understood Babel to mean "the gate of the god", the Hebrews understood it to mean "mixed up, confused".'[59]

It is significant, then, that the 'tower' is mentioned in addition to the 'city'. Babylon, which throughout the Scriptures symbolises the rebellion and depravity of humanity corporately expressed, has a tower, or ziggurat, at its centre. These were 'an attempt on the part of men to build artificial mountains which could then serve as divine dwelling places'.[60] Walton's discussion on the nature and purpose of ancient ziggurats[61] reinforces this view. 'At the top of the ziggurat was the gate of the gods, the entrance into their heavenly abode. At the bottom was the temple, where hopefully the god would descend to receive the gifts and worship of his people.'[62]

We will have cause later to see the way in which the power of the city of Babylon was linked to its idolatry, and also the way in which the idea of the *city* (as a theological principle) is inextricably bound with its worship. Appearing at this early stage in Genesis, the tower/city connection draws our attention to its importance for later biblical history and theology. Human rebellion is expressed through its worship, which also is built into its systems of security and protection. God is no longer the hiding place and refuge of humanity, but men seek to construct their own refuge, with another worship at its heart, in a deliberate and persistent attempt to avoid doing the will of God. Genesis 11:1-9 'represents in reality a last ditch effort by fallen men to build God out of his world'.[63] It is even stressed that the builders used materials that would be waterproof: baked bricks and bitumen. They did not believe God's covenantal promise and its sign in the rainbow, by which God had assured humanity that he would not act in this sort of judgement again.

In the face of such persistent hostility, God's sovereign power is emphasised. He is not in the least affected by the tower or its builders (as the language of verses 5-7 indicates),[64] and instead God pronounces his judgement on the nations, scattering them to the corners of the earth. While it was always his intention for humanity to spread out from Eden and fill the earth (Gen. 1:28), here the Divine scattering is a judgement on humans' rebellious co-operation. Later, the idea of being scattered amongst the nations on account of idolatry was to become a key theme of Israel's prophetic voices (Deut. 4:25-31 cf. Neh. 1:8-11).

In the next chapter we will see how God's purpose for the nations was to be fulfilled through his calling of one man from their midst, and how through his seed all the nations would be blessed. The substance of this blessing would be the turning of nations from the folly of idolatry to the blessing of true worship.

Chapter 3

The Patriarchs and the Exodus:
Contrast and Conflict

Introduction

At the end of the last chapter we saw that the nations of the Genesis prologue were portrayed in a state of rebellion against God. This rebellion was typified by the building of the tower of Babel. In response to the continuing anarchy of the nations, the reader of Genesis might expect another form of Divine judgement to be revealed. With Abraham, however, a new era is put in place. The covenant God makes with him is with a view to the blessing of the nations. Although Abraham (whilst still known as Abram) is taken *from* the nations (being a resident of Ur of the Babylonians), the covenant God makes with this solitary individual is for the blessings *of* the nations, through Abraham's 'seed'.[1]

1. Abraham, God's Response to the Nations

God's grace towards his rebellious creation is underscored by three main elements in the narrative. The whole episode of Abraham's election; the dimensions of the covenant promises made to him and to his descendants; and the divine intention of God for the nations stressed throughout these events all amplify the compassionate provision of God for the blessing of nations. The idea of 'blessing' that is embedded in the wording of the Abrahamic covenant itself (e.g. Gen. 12:2-3; 17:6), as well as in the narrative surrounding him and the other patriarchal figures (e.g. Gen. 22:17; 26:3; 27 *passim*; 28:3-4), represents a concerted and prolonged echoing of the language of the creation accounts themselves (see Gen. 1:22, 28; 2:3; 5:2; cf. Noah's status as the replacement Adam in 9:2).

If we allow that the concept of blessing embraces the ideas of fertility, authority and dominion, and peace and rest,[2] intrinsic in the creation accounts themselves, then the patriarchs are seen to be the ones through whom the creational blessings are promised to the nations. To be sure, they themselves are the beneficiaries of God's gracious action, but they are not benefactors for their own sakes. Their blessing is for the sake of others. The old motto 'blessed to be a blessing' is indeed true for them, and by implication for their descendants. In particular for our purposes, we note how God's dealings with Abraham have the universal restoration of true worship in view. We see this first in the case of Abraham himself, whose worship is reorientated away from idolatry towards the living God. Then, through his seed, we see it in the restoration of true worship to the nations in the place of their own defiant idolatry.

(1) Abraham the Archetypal Worshipper

The Spirit-empowered preacher, Stephen, begins to recount the history of his own Jewish people with the words, 'Brothers and fathers, hear me. The God of glory appeared to our father Abraham when he was in Mesopotamia, before he lived in Haran' (Acts 7:2). This statement is significant, especially when it is compared with the comment of Joshua: 'Long ago, your fathers lived beyond the Euphrates, Terah, the father of Abraham and of Nahor; and they served other gods' (Josh. 24:2).[3] Abram (as he is named when we first meet him in the narrative) is no different from the rest of the inhabitants of Ur. He and they were all idolaters, following the polytheistic religious practices of the Ancient Near East.

Abraham, however, did not remain as such, for his life was transformed by God's choice of him as the one through whom his purpose would be fulfilled. While we are not told how God appeared to him, it is not unreasonable to assume that this was by way of a theophany, so common in the accounts of Divine calls and commissions in the Old Testament. More importantly, the emphasis lies on the fact that God *spoke* to Abraham (Gen. 12:1, 7) and that Abraham *heard* (i.e. obeyed) him (Gen. 12:4).[4]

The active voice of God is thus the important and transformative element in the narrative, as it was in the original creation accounts. The juxtaposition of 'voice' and 'hearing' marks out the life of Abraham from this point onwards. He stands as the archetypal man of faith – the true hearer of the word of God – who follows the voice of God with whom he walks for the rest of his days. This fundamental predisposition throws his main error into sharper relief. He 'heard' the voice of Sarah (Gen. 16:2) in the matter of her plan for him to raise up an heir through Hagar. The result of this action was the birth of Ishmael. The episode, however, stands out for its difference from his foundational portrayal as the obedient hearer of the voice of God, a foundational attitude tested to the limit in the events of Genesis 22, to which we refer a little later.

It is significant to note that the command to leave the land of his birth is also a command for him to leave his ancestral gods,[5] and to follow the true God into a new land. This God is clearly the God of Israel's later experience in the exodus, and the God who is revealed in the New Testament as the Father of our Lord Jesus Christ.[6] However, at this point the weight falls on the fact that God is not confined to one geographical feature, location or nation. He is the great Creator, who has heaven as his throne and earth as his footstool (e.g. Isa. 66:1), and thus, as Paul says much later, 'The God who made the world and everything in it, being Lord of heaven and earth, does not live in temples made by man, nor is he served by human hands, as though he needed anything, since he himself gives to all mankind life and breath and everything' (Acts 17:24-25). This utterance is in perfect harmony with Old Testament theology, not least with the picture painted in Genesis of God as 'God Most High, the possessor [or creator] of heaven and earth' (Gen. 14:18-23, esp. v. 19). Abraham is free to wander on the face of the earth, without possessing any of it, since the Lord whom he serves and with whom he walks is the maker and owner of all things.

Canonically, Abraham becomes the model of obedient faith, and thus, true worship. Joshua's exhortation, for example, recorded in Joshua 24, uses Abraham as a positive example of one who had put away the foreign gods to which the Israelites still clung. This is given added force by the status Abraham has as the father of the nation. Likewise, Stephen's extended sermon in Acts 7 begins with Abraham as the model of true faith – an obedient faith that differed markedly from so much of the history of Israel – and which certainly stood over and against the stubborn disobedience of his hearers. Paul also uses Abraham as the model of true, faithful obedience who expresses his worship to God in action (e.g. Romans 4 and Galatians 3), while the writer to the Hebrews singles Abraham out for extended treatment as the prime example of obedient faith in Hebrews 11.

Having heard the voice of God, Abraham's life and worship are thus transformed. He becomes a nomad on the earth, but is promised a great inheritance. In this way the covenant formed with Abraham, and his believing response to it, act as implicit and abiding criticisms of the nations' worship, typified in Babel. For the rest of the patriarchal narratives Abraham and his descendants are shown to live as pilgrims and wanderers on the earth, deliberately eschewing the great cities (and their worship centres), related to God by covenant and promise, rather than by location or ritual. The commonly used description of God as 'the God of Abraham, Isaac and Jacob' underscores this focus.

The story of the covenant community of God, beginning with this one man and his immediate family, is traced with unrelenting honesty throughout the narrative. The sins and failures of the characters are not glossed over, and the whole story bears testimony to the faithfulness of God rather than to that of the recipients of the promises. All are shown to fail, in various ways, and to greater or lesser degrees. In addition, the line of inheritance is never straightforward. Age and infirmity, barrenness, or other forms of difficulty seem to stand in the way and threaten the fulfilment of the promise. What remains constant is God's commitment to his promise, and to the fulfilment of the word spoken to the woman in Genesis 3:15 that a 'seed' would come from her who would eventually destroy the serpent and his activities. God is unquestionably shown to be the one who brings this about, despite all expectations to the contrary.

The line of the chosen seed, traced from Seth, to Noah, to Abraham and the other patriarchs, is a line which lives on the fringes of the great cultures and societies of the time. They live outside of the cities, and, for the most part, the city dwellers ignore them. In the eyes of all the great nations, centred on their own worship systems, these few appear as nothing other than a ragtag collection of desert nomads. In reality, this minuscule community is both the guarantee of the nations' blessing, and the assurance that all disobedient worship would be judged and a new worship established. Abraham, in this sense, was merely the first-fruit of a great harvest to come.[7]

(2) Patriarchal Worship as Response to Grace
One of the notable features of the worship actions associated with Abraham (and the other patriarchs) is that these are clearly shown to be *responses* to God's gracious dealings with them. Abraham's worship actions are recorded in Genesis 15:7ff.; 18:1f.; 21:33; 22:1ff. The wording of Genesis 15:7 anticipates that of Exodus 20:2, suggesting that Abraham's experience was equally one of redemption

and liberation. Little is recorded of Isaac's worship, though he was, of course, involved in the worship on Mt. Moriah (about which we say more below) and was clearly a man of faith who inherited the covenant blessings from his father. Jacob has certain experiences of worship (e.g. Gen. 28:10-22; 31:51-54; 35:1-7) that are all significant for him and the confirmation of the covenantal blessings and promises to him. Throughout, 'words of covenant promise and demand lie at the heart of God's encounters with the patriarchs'.[8] In view of this we see that Abraham, Isaac and Jacob

> built altars throughout Canaan to mark the sites where God manifested himself to them under various names ... Sacrifice was not offered at any spot which might happen to be convenient, but only at those sites in particular.... Since heaven was recognized as his actual dwelling-place (e.g. Gn. 11:5; 18:21; 21:17; 22:11; 24:7; 28:12), it was not considered that God was limited to special holy places but that he had simply chosen to manifest his character and will for his people at such sites.[9]

John Currid analyses the main features of the cosmologies of the Ancient Near East,[10] and while not minimising the differences between the Egyptian, Mesopotamian and Canaanite systems, he gives a succinct summary of their similarities. All three cultures were polytheistic; the gods themselves were self-generated or generated by other gods in the pantheon; magic was the real power of the universe; and throughout 'humans were basically viewed as insignificant'.[11]

On every score, the worship associated with the patriarchs is contradictory to the prevailing cosmologies. In this way, the narratives were to serve as both foundational to Israel's subsequent worship, and exemplary of the way in which God keeps his covenant promises. Throughout, Israel could see that their separation from the nations and their gods was due to the divine choice of Yahweh, the true Creator of heaven and earth.

They could also see that their relationship to him did not depend on their ability to manipulate a response from him by the use of magic or other elements of polytheistic worship. Though these lessons should have been transparent to the subsequent generations, they were not. One of the battles that Israel faced when settling in the land, some 400 years after the promises were given to Abraham, was that of fertility rites. Would they fall back on the magical practices associated with Baalism, or trust Yahweh at his word? The history recorded in the former prophets tells us: they refused to trust, and with a few notable exceptions, such as the worship reforms of kings such as Asa and Josiah, the whole of their national history bore testimony to the failure to worship God alone.

(3) Abraham and Isaac at Mt. Moriah

Space precludes a detailed discussion of the various accounts of patriarchal worship mentioned above. However, one incident stands out as being of singular importance, both for the principles of worship embodied within it, and for its abiding significance for the subsequent generations of Israelites, and thence for the rest of the biblical narrative. This is the account of Abraham's worship on Mt. Moriah, recorded in Genesis 22.

The incident is clearly portrayed as a deliberate testing (*nasah*) of Abraham's obedient faith. The idea of God testing individuals and peoples is well attested (e.g. Exod. 15:25; 16:4; Deut. 8:2; Judg. 2:22; 3:1-4), and indicates 'Yahweh's desire both to evaluate specific aspects of his people's character as well as to influence and shape them'.[12] In particular, the testing here is seen to relate to the idea of 'fearing God' (as affirmed in its outcome in verse 12).

First and foremost, Abraham is shown to be a hearer of God's voice, with all that this implies about being an obedient servant of the one who speaks.[13] God addresses him, calling his name, and he immediately responds with willingness: 'Here I am' (Gen. 22:1). In this response he stands as a contrast to Adam, who heard the voice of God calling his name in the garden, and who hid himself from the presence of the Lord. He stands also as a contrast to Cain, to the people of Noah's generation, and to the builders of the tower, all of whom had shown themselves to be inveterately opposed to the voice and commands of God.

The pattern of obedient hearing seen here is reflected in other places. Moses is shown to respond in almost identical words (Exod. 3:4), as is Samuel (1 Sam. 3:3-10) and Isaiah the prophet (Isa. 6:8), and into the New Testament, of course, the supreme obedient hearer is Jesus Christ himself. Here, in Genesis, the testing of Abraham is shown to have revealed the integrity of the old man's faith (Gen. 22:12), and in view of this God affirms his covenantal promises to him (Gen. 22:15-18).

The command that God gives him in Genesis 22:2 is direct and shocking: 'take your son, your only son Isaac, whom you love, and go to the land of Moriah, and offer him there as a burnt offering on one of the mountains of which I shall tell you.' The emphasis is twofold. The account reflects the natural affection that Abraham has for his son, but it also reflects Isaac's role as the bearer of the covenantal promises. This is particularly clear in the timing of the passage in the narrative, since God's choice of Isaac has been so strongly emphasised in the preceding chapter, where Hagar and Ishmael have been sent away and Yahweh had affirmed his covenantal commitment to Isaac (Gen. 21:12). The testing involves a journey, picking up the theme of Abraham's life from Genesis 12 onwards. Here he is to set out yet again, to a mountain in Moriah that the Lord would show him, and for an event that would seem to spell the end of all the promises entailed in the long years of pilgrimage with God up until this point.

Although Genesis 22:2 speaks of the 'land of Moriah', it is likely that the 'Mount Moriah' of later Old Testament worship was regarded as identical with the place of Abraham and Isaac's testing.[14] According to 2 Chronicles 3:1 (cf. 2 Sam. 24:16-25), this was the place on which Solomon built the temple, and thus the theological importance of the site was preserved throughout the history of Israel's worship in the Temple (and on into this day, since both Jews and Muslims regard it is a sacred site because of its associations with this event).

The command to render up Isaac as a burnt offering is startling, not just because of the natural revulsion one feels at the prospect, but also given the theological significance of the term in the Old Testament. A burnt offering ('*ōlâh*) is later shown to make 'a pleasing aroma to the LORD' (e.g. Lev. 1:9, 13 etc.), a phrase that parallels Noah's burnt offerings which were 'a soothing aroma to the LORD' (Gen. 8:20-21). The discussion of this phrase seen earlier, when we were considering Noah's worship, has indicated that this was indeed seen as an atoning sacrifice, and throughout the later Old Testament cultus burnt offerings formed the central feature of the whole system of substitutionary sacrifice that lay at the heart of Israel's worship.

From a canonical perspective, Abraham's sacrifice here was clearly aligned with the theological implications of the whole of the Old Testament sacrificial system. Basic to the burnt offering 'was its gift character; something was brought and offered to the Lord for and on behalf of the worshiper',[15] and since it was offered to God in accordance with the conditions he had prescribed, it was seen as a provision from him for continuing atonement to be made for the sins of his people.[16]

The narrative leaves us in no doubt about the remarkable nature of Abraham's faith: despite the natural counter indications (his beloved son, the one through whom the promises would be fulfilled, the shocking prospect of offering him as a burnt sacrifice), Abraham obeys. 'So Abraham rose early in the morning, saddled his donkey, and took two of his young men with him, and his son Isaac. And he cut the wood for the burnt offering and arose and went to the place of which God had told him' (Gen. 22:3). His preparations are shown to be detailed, complete and willing. Indeed, his unquestioning obedience is almost as dramatic to the reader as the command he obeys. He heads off, 'to the place which God had told him,' and thus stands in utter contrast to Cain, the tower builders and other such figures who decide to 'dig in' where they were, and thus mark out their existence as being antagonistic to God and his plans.

Having arrived at the appointed site after three days' journey,[17] Abraham instructs the young men with him to stay behind while he and Isaac go ahead to offer worship. He seems assured of God's purpose being fulfilled, both in the worship and in the ongoing provision of the promised seed through Isaac, saying that 'we will worship and return to you' (Gen. 22:5). For the reader, who expects the death and the destruction of Isaac, this statement seems astounding. However, the narrative has already drawn attention to the miraculous nature of Isaac's conception and birth in a manner that uses both barrenness and old age to accentuate the impossibility of his generation by natural means alone (Gen. 11:30; 16:1 cf. 17:15-21; 18:9-15; 21:1-7). So incredulous had Abraham and Sarah been that at various points both had laughed in the face of the divine promise and its messengers. The incident with Hagar and Ishmael, having been brought to its conclusion in the preceding chapter, has further served to underscore the unique nature of Isaac as the inheritor of the covenant promises and the absolutely miraculous nature of Isaac's existence.

In the New Testament, Paul highlights both the age of Abraham and the barrenness of Sarah (Rom. 4:19) as natural barriers to the fulfilment of the word of promise, so that 'in hope, against hope, [Abraham] believed'. Not only was his own body 'as good as dead', being nearly 100 years old (Rom. 4:19), but Sarah's womb was also closed due to her inherent barrenness and to her own advanced age. In the light of the insurmountable difficulties thus faced, Abraham's faith is characterised as being placed in 'God, who gives life to the dead and calls into existence the things that do not exist' (Rom. 4:17). Likewise, the writer to the Hebrews sees Abraham as a man 'as good as dead' (Heb. 11:12), and similarly emphasises not only Abraham's age, but the age and barrenness of Sarah (Heb. 11:11). He then goes on to speak about the fact that Abraham 'considered that God was able even to raise [Isaac] from the dead, from which, figuratively speaking, he did receive him back' (Heb. 11:19). On this verse Calvin aptly comments:

> The death of Isaac ... was like the destruction of all the promises; and Isaac is not to be thought of as simply one of the common company of men, but as one who contained Christ in himself.... Abraham ascribed to God the honour of being able to raise his son from the dead. Therefore he did not reject the promise given to him, but extended its power and truth beyond the life of his son by refusing to limit the power of God to such narrow limits that it could be confined or extinguished by the death of Isaac.[18]

The themes of death and resurrection are thus woven throughout the New Testament's interpretation of Abraham's relationship to Isaac on a number of levels. In this light, it is not unreasonable to see that Abraham understood the principle of resurrection from his own experience of Isaac's birth, and that his expectation of returning with him after worshipping on the mountain was built on the bedrock of God's commitment to his word. Nothing would stop the fulfilment of the plan that God revealed to him: not even offering up his son as a '*ōlâh*.

The account unfolds with sombre reverence, as we read that 'Abraham took the wood of the burnt offering and laid it on Isaac his son. And he took in his hand the fire and the knife. So they went both of them together' (Gen. 22:6). While the emphasis throughout lies on Abraham, Isaac's part in the proceedings should not be overlooked. Here, and with increasing clarity as the account progresses through verses 7-10, Isaac is shown to be a willing participant in the action, submitting himself to Abraham's leadership and trusting him in the unfolding drama, even when its inevitable outcome seems too plain to ignore. There is no doubt that he could have overpowered the old man and ran away. Instead he allows himself to be bound, to be stretched out on the altar, and there to await the blow that would end his life. What the whole event meant for his subsequent experience and expression of worship cannot be estimated, but it is notable that the accounts of his and Rebekah's life together are remarkably free of the idolatry that troubled Abraham's grandchildren and their descendants.

At the very point of the sacrifice, the word of the LORD again resounds in Abraham's ear, with the same willing response being shown. As he raises the knife to slay[19] his son, 'the angel of the LORD called to him from heaven and said, "Abraham, Abraham!" And he said, "Here am I"' (Gen. 22:11). Here, even at this point of extreme testing, Abraham is seen to be the true, obedient hearer of God's word. While standing ready to go through with the command, he also stands ready to hear the voice of God. While it may be that he had hoped for some sort of intervention (e.g. as implied in Genesis 22:8, that God himself would provide a lamb), the interpretation of the event in Hebrews 11 stresses his expectation of an even more dramatic intervention of God: through resurrection if necessary.

This passage is important for a number of reasons:

Embedded within it is clear testimony to the principle of animal sacrifice, and in particular the atoning sacrifice of a lamb (Gen. 22:7b, 8), which indicates that Israel could see the foundations of its later Temple worship laid in its earliest history.

Furthermore, it gives clear testimony to the principle underpinning the entire system of Old Testament tabernacle and temple worship: God both provides (and accepts!) an animal sacrifice in place of the life of men and women. The lamb here is clearly a substitute for Isaac, and thus Israel always knew that the system of worship it had been given (rather than developed) was built on the principle of substitution.

One of the consequences of this is that Israel for ever should have shunned the practice of human sacrifice, and the principles of magic on which such sacrifices were based. Unfortunately this was not always the case, and the worst excesses of pagan worship were also adopted in Israel at times of its greatest religious (and thus moral) degradation (Deut. 12:31 cf. Jer. 7:31; 19:5; 32:35; 2 Chron. 33:6).

Additionally, the incident furnishes the most eloquent example in the whole of the Old Testament of the true nature of spiritual obedience i.e. 'the one who fears God, that is, the faithful worshiper, will obediently surrender to God whatever he asks, trusting in God's promises of provision and blessing.'[20]

And of course this passage stands as one of the great typological passages of the Old Testament, prefiguring in so many ways the matter of obedience, substitution and resurrection seen in the sacrificial death of Jesus Christ, *the* Seed of the promise. He indeed was the '*ōlâh* who 'gave himself up for us, a fragrant offering and sacrifice to God' (Eph. 5:2).[21]

(4) The Subsequent Patterns of Patriarchal Worship

Both in Abraham's case and in the cases of Isaac and Jacob, it is plain that the patriarchs operated as father/priests over their households. We have already commented on the fact that most frequently their acts of worship are tied to the *revelation* of God, and hence the establishment, reiteration or confirmation of the covenant promises. Their recorded actions of worship are all shown to be actions in response to grace, and therefore they typify the underlying theme of biblical worship: it is initiated by God, rather than by human beings. It is thus the appropriate response of human beings who become objects of God's love and gracious care. Furthermore, it reminds us of the fundamental place of covenant in biblical worship. Throughout the Old Testament and into the New, all true worship takes place within a covenantal structure and is expressive of a covenantal relationship. This removes from the equation any idiosyncratic worship and relates the actions of the worshippers to the great themes of God's character as the covenant making and keeping God. It also properly shows up idolatry for what it truly is: adultery against one's covenant partner.

The patriarchs set up altars and other markers which persisted long into Israel's subsequent history at significant sites (e.g. Shechem, Bethel, Hebron), but they established no centralised, institutionalised religious worship system. Throughout, they remained as pilgrims on the fringes of the great nations, and their worship rested on the continued hearing of the word of God. The inroads of idolatry already evident in Jacob's family[22] persisted throughout Israel's subsequent history, as we have seen, but overall the worship of the patriarchs was marked out by its simplicity and its non-idolatrous character. However, it is clear that had not God kept on speaking to them, working in and through them – even wrestling with them as in the case of Jacob – their natural proclivities would have led them away from true worship of God, and they would have been affected by the worship of the nations surrounding them, and out of which, in Abraham, they had been chosen.

2. The Exodus as a Battle for Worship

The story of Genesis ends with Joseph's father, Jacob, and his family coming to Egypt to find respite from famine. Readers will no doubt be familiar with the narrative, and the themes of electing choice, sovereign providence, and human fidelity and foolishness that interweave throughout the chapters. The whole narrative serves to magnify God's faithfulness to the covenantal promises made to Abraham (and then reaffirmed to Isaac and Jacob) and to demonstrate the workings of his providential will, turning evil to good in the accomplishing of his purposes so that his promises may go on being fulfilled.[23]

The opening chapters of Exodus, however, tell us of a changing situation. Israel had been in the land for over 400 years and had multiplied under the blessing of God. The Egyptians' good will towards them was based on the memory of Joseph and his central role in the preservation of the nation from destruction through unprecedented famine. The narrative quickly moves on, however, to indicate that this comfortable situation was to move rapidly in a different direction, as 'a new king, who did not know about Joseph, came to power in Egypt' (Exod. 1:8, NIV). It is not our purpose to go into the development of the narrative, charting Israel's descent into abject slavery, the rise of Moses and the hardheartedness of the Pharaoh who refused to let Israel go. What is of particular importance for our theme is the nature of the exodus event as one with worship at its heart.

(1) The Exodus as Judgement on the Gods of Egypt

There are three Old Testament passages in which this interpretation of the exodus event is made particularly plain. Exodus 12:12 reads: 'I will pass through the land of Egypt that night, and I will strike all the firstborn in the land of Egypt, both man and beast; and on all the gods of Egypt I will execute judgments: I am the LORD.' The thought is echoed in Numbers 33:3-4:

They set out from Rameses in the first month, on the fifteenth day of the first month. On the day after the Passover, the people of Israel went out triumphantly in the sight of all the Egyptians, while the Egyptians were burying all their firstborn, whom the LORD had struck down among them. On their gods also the LORD executed judgments.

and it is reiterated in 2 Samuel 7:23-24, in the context of David's prayer of thanksgiving for the covenant God had made with him:

And who is like your people Israel, the one nation on earth whom God went to redeem to be his people, making himself a name and doing for them great and awesome things by driving out before your people, whom you redeemed for yourself from Egypt, a nation and its gods? And you established for yourself your people Israel to be your people forever. And you, O LORD became their God.

In what way was the exodus event a judgment on the gods of Egypt? On one level it is possible to see a correlation between various plagues and some of the multiplied deities Egypt's pantheon. Enns, for example, comments that 'the Nile was personified and worshiped as a god in Egypt'[24] and draws attention to the frog-headed god Heqet, and the sun god, Re[25] whose likenesses were parodied or functions frustrated in the plagues of the frogs and darkness respectively. However, there is another level of meaning to the event, involving the main player in Egypt's history, Pharaoh himself.

Currid's analysis of the exodus event is particularly helpful at this point. He comments (approvingly) on the widely held view that the exodus event is depicted as 'a second creation. It was a new conquest of chaos, another prevailing over the waters of the deep, and a redemptive creation of the people of Israel.'[26] What he goes on to show, however, is that means by which this creative-redemptive event took place was 'an ironic undoing or destruction of the creation order in the land of Egypt'.[27] Central to Egypt's worship was the concept of *ma'at*, which he says 'may be simply defined as universal order'[28] and which governed all aspects of life and death. It is even reflected in the way in which one was judged in the afterlife.[29]

At the same time we must bear in mind that the Pharaoh was not simply (or even primarily) a political figure, but a divine god-king. Pharaoh 'was a god by office ... responsible for the welfare of Egypt, including the Nile'[30] and, of course, for maintaining *maat*.[31] Currid comments, therefore, that 'the importance of *maat* for Egyptian kingship should not be underestimated' and that 'when Yahweh assailed Egypt with the ten plagues, he was casting the universal order of creation (*maat*) into chaos. This was a direct challenge to the power and sovereignty of Pharaoh: could he maintain *maat* or could he not?'[32] In the face of Yahweh, the maker of heaven and earth, Pharaoh's real status is exposed. His lack of divine power shows 'that he is no god, or at least no god like Yahweh'.[33]

The defeat of the whole spiritual system that undergirded Egypt's life thus lies at the very heart of the account of the exodus, and reminds us of the comments we made in the first chapter regarding the nexus between worship and power. This was no mere political or social liberation, but is deeply spiritual in its meaning, in which the victory of the Divine Warrior is seen very clearly.[34] The nature of this victory is specially to be noticed. Yahweh is seen to exercise his might on behalf of his people, in faithful remembrance of his covenant with Abraham. He is the Liberator-God, who acts in power to bring his people out from the power of the spiritual forces behind the idols, so that his people could be freed for true worship. Their power for true life and blessing would continue to rest in their worship, so that were they to turn from God towards the idols he would fight against them and bring them to judgment. Their enjoyment of the blessing of rest in the land that he would give them, and the associated states of blessing and fruitfulness, would hinge on their fidelity in the matter of worship.

For Israel, the events of the exodus became the defining feature of their identity as the people of God. It formed part of the fabric of their national and religious memory, and the events were preserved at the hub of their worship through their psalmody (e.g. Pss. 78; 105; 106; 136) and through the cultus itself.[35] Passover was cemented into the bedrock of Israel's worship, and the whole tabernacle/temple cultus was a testimony to the worship which God gave them at Mt. Sinai, in the context of the Mosaic covenant and the giving of the Law.

(2) The Exodus as Deliverance for Worship
The passages from Exodus, Numbers and 2 Samuel quoted above all imply another aspect of the exodus event that is important for our theme. If the exodus was a judgment on the gods of Egypt, it was also an event which was designed to establish true worship in Israel, as a nation. The end point was not simply deliverance *from* spiritual

bondage, but liberation *for* true worship. This is made plain in the accounts themselves.

It is foundational to God's call and commissioning of Moses: 'And God said, "I will be with you. And this will be the sign to you that it is I who have sent you: When you have brought the people out of Egypt, you will worship God on this mountain"' (Exod. 3:12) and it is theme repeated throughout the encounters between Moses and Pharaoh. It is spoken of in terms of service, 'Let my son go that he may serve me' (Exod. 4:23; cf. 7:16), but also in terms of holding feasts to Yahweh in the wilderness (e.g. 5:1), and most commonly, of offering sacrifice to him there (e.g. 3:18; 5:3, 8; 8:27). Pharaoh himself calls this service 'sacrifice' (Exod. 5:17; 8:8, 25, 28), indicating that he understood that the issue involved their worship. His reluctance to let Israel go may not therefore have been simply for reasons of lost productivity (as Exodus 5:1-9 may be read), but more because of the threat that such worship posed to his status within Egypt.

It is not inconsequential, then, that this first encounter between Moses and Aaron, and Pharaoh (i.e. in Exod. 5:1-9) contrasts two issues: work under Pharaoh as servitude and worship in the wilderness as rest. From Pharaoh's point of view, as one who does not know Yahweh or recognise his name,[36] he sees the request for the Israelites to go out for the purpose of worship as a plea prompted by laziness. The 'rest' theme is developed further in the next chapter, where the Lord assures Moses that his purpose is to bring Israel out from under the 'burdens' and 'bondage' of the Egyptians (Exod. 6:6-7) and to bring them into the land (6:8), which is later called 'the resting place' (Deut. 12:9). This resting place is marked by liberty in the worship of Yahweh (Deut. 12:11), and the fidelity of that worship in accordance with his command (Deut. 12:13-14).

Moreover, in the giving of the Law at Mt. Sinai, Yahweh commands that rest be a pivotal part of Israel's weekly life (Exod. 20:9-11; cf. Deut. 5:12-15). Indeed the whole of Israelite economic and social activity was built around the weekly sabbaths, sabbatical years, and jubilee years. Rest was integral to the life of Israel, and at the very outset of their nation-forming and identity-forging exodus, it is seen to be central to God's purposes of deliverance. Without doubt, given the divine status of Pharaoh mentioned above, it is clear that the natures of two different 'gods' are being contrasted. Pharaoh is the god whose service is slavery. Yahweh is the God whose service is rest.[37]

God's purpose in the exodus event is to establish his presence amongst his people (as seen in Exodus 25:8, for example), and to forge them into a priestly nation (as in Exodus 19:5-6), holy to the Lord, for his service. Given the theological themes connecting the various books of the Pentateuch, there should be no doubt that we should see the whole exodus episode – together with the entry into the land flowing with milk and honey as the intended resting place for his people – as redolent of creation.[38] Despite Israel's continual rebellion, God's purpose is to re-establish in his people that royal priestly role that was abandoned in the rebellion of Genesis 3, and to form a new worshipping community of king-priests who would enjoy his communion and rest under his blessing, all guaranteed by his presence. Worship in the context of covenant is the climax of the book.

> Worship at the mountain of God (19:1–40:38) includes arrival at Sinai, and preparation to receive the words of the covenant (19), the giving of the Ten Commandments (20:1-20), the Book of the Covenant (20:21–24:18), the instructions for worship and the building of the tabernacle (25:1-31:18; 35–40:33), the breaking of the covenant and construction of the golden calf and covenant renewal (32–34); God's descent upon the tabernacle (40:34-38).[39]

The movement from Egypt to Sinai is thus a movement towards the worship of the true God, and the book of Exodus culminates with the presence of God gloriously dwelling in the midst of his people, as his glory fills the tabernacle. This blessed outcome of the exodus events, however, was hotly contested along the way: not from the armies of Pharaoh (who are dispensed with in chapter 14), but from within the camp itself.

(3) The Golden Calf

The account of Israel's alternative worship at Sinai is found in Exodus 32. While the 'male calf or young bull was a popular symbol of both power and fecundity throughout the ancient Near Eastern world'[40] it is most likely that the formative influence for this particular event was the worship of similar gods in Egypt itself.[41] There were a number of bull cults in Egypt (e.g. the Apis; Buchis and Mnevis cults) and the fact that the Israelites built the idols in the shape of this particular animal is not to be marvelled at, given the past 400 years or so spent in Egypt, surrounded by its religion and culture.

It is frequently assumed that the worship of the golden calf was associated with fertility, but Janzen has argued persuasively that the main clues in the narrative present the calf 'as an intended symbol of God the divine warrior and protector who leads the people to their restful habitation'.[42] Certainly the introductory verse to the event (Exod. 32:1) stresses the fact of Moses' delay, thus implying that the Israelites thought that they did not have anyone to lead them further. There may well be some hint of menace in their approach to Aaron[43] and there is no doubt that their statement is full of scorn for Moses: 'Up, make us gods who shall go before us. As for this Moses, the man who brought us up out of the land of Egypt, we do not know what has become of him' (Exod. 32:1).

Significantly, there is no mention of Yahweh here. The people seem to have attributed the deliverance from Egypt to Moses himself, rather than to Yahweh who had sent Moses to them and in whose name he had spoken. Now that Moses seemed to have disappeared off the face of the earth, they needed access to some other divine powers to lead them on. It is also telling to observe that the events of Exodus 24 have included two ringing affirmations of the people's faithfulness: 'All the words that the LORD has spoken we will do' (Exod. 24:3, 7). 'The *next* time the people speak it is in Exodus 32:1,'[44] which is their demand for other gods to lead them on/go with them. The contrast between their avowed faithfulness and actual conduct could not be more stark, and it indicates the recalcitrant rebellion of the Lord's people that led both Moses (Deut. 31:24-29) and Joshua (Josh. 24:19-28) to speak of such avowals as being witnessing *against* the nation.

The commentary on the golden calf incident given by Psalm 106:19-21 is blunt: 'They made a calf in Horeb and worshiped a metal image. They exchanged the glory of God for the image of an ox that eats grass. They forgot God their Saviour, who had done great things in Egypt.' In the New Testament, Stephen uses the incident to illustrate the point that 'our fathers refused to obey him [Moses], but thrust him aside, and in their hearts they turned to Egypt' (Acts 7:39). There can be no thought, therefore, that this was an excusable action or a naive misunderstanding. It was rebellion pure and simple, the direct repudiation of their vows to covenant faithfulness expressed in Exodus 24:1-8. Moses' absence was not an extenuating circumstance, but the illegitimate excuse for spiritual and moral anarchy.

The actual link between the bull image and the god it represented (or with which it was associated) in ancient Near Eastern observance is not straightforward. Sometimes the bulls were seen as the incarnation of one of the gods (e.g. the Apis cult regarded the sacred bull as an incarnation of Horus). On other occasions (as in the Buchis cult) the bull represented the power and might of a god (in this case, Montu the war god with whom the Buchis bull was closely associated), or the figure could stand as the carrier of the invisible god's majesty or presence (as seemed to be the case in Canaanite Baalism). The options are not mutually exclusive.

What was actually in the minds of the Israelites at the time of their worship of the calf is not clear from the narrative, nor does it much matter. What is clear is that they regarded the figure as a replacement for both Moses and Yahweh. 'The people demand a substitute for Yahweh himself ... [and] are portrayed ... as apostate and polytheistic from the outset.'[45] Aaron makes an altar and declares a feast day, and all this takes place while Moses is in the closest possible communion with God himself, hearing his voice on the top of the mountain, receiving the instructions for the building of the Tabernacle: the facility which would be the dwelling place of God in the midst of his people.

The most generous interpretation of Aaron's response is that it is an attempt to make the best out of a tragic situation. He knows that the command he and Moses delivered to Pharaoh involved a feast in the wilderness (Exod. 5:1), and so declares that 'tomorrow will be a feast day to the LORD', thereby at least reintroducing the name of Yahweh to the narrative. Even if this were the case, however, the outcome is no less wicked, since it tacitly approves of the action and adds the extra complication of identifying Yahweh's name with idolatrous worship practices that – in the minds of the rest of the people at least – are designed to replace Yahweh with another god or gods. In any case, he and the seventy elders had already participated in a true feast in Yahweh's presence (Exod. 24:9-11), so he must have known that the suggestion was disingenuous at best. The feast had already been held to celebrate the sealing of the covenant.[46] Now one would be held that would mark its infraction, and Aaron could not be accounted blameless for letting the people get out of control (Exod. 32:25).

The aftermath of these events is beyond our scope to consider here. The narrative goes on to recount Moses' entreaty that God would not destroy the people; his breaking of the tablets of the Law in his anger; the destruction of the calf; the punishment meted out by the Levites at Moses' instruction; the further intercession of Moses; and the construction of the tent of meeting.[47] Eventually the two tablets of the Law are replaced and the whole of Israel is engaged in a covenant renewal ceremony, at Yahweh's initiative. While these are all important elements of the unfolding Exodus narrative, the most significant thing for our purposes is to note the location of the calf incident in relation to the preceding events and the aftermath and its consequences.

In Exodus 25–31, the chapters immediately following the initial covenant affirmation of chapter 24, Moses is engaged in receiving instructions about the Tabernacle and the cultus to be observed in it. The events following the calf incident eventually lead to the resumption of the journey and the building of the Tabernacle itself. It is not only striking that the incident occurs in the very midst of the section in which Yahweh is engaged in giving the gift of true worship to his people, but it is also noteworthy that it is given such extensive coverage. The calf incident 'forms the heart of a lengthy unit of three chapters ... right in the middle of the divine instructions at Sinai. It produces a rupture of enormous proportions and stands as a threat to the covenant from the beginning.'[48] The location of the event within the narrative, and the attention devoted to it and its consequences, both serve to concentrate the awareness of the reader to the terrible menace of illegitimate worship.

It is self-evident, then, that the incident stands as a demonstration of the terrible reality evident in the ensuing biblical drama: that idolatry infects the life of God's covenant people at the very root of their existence. The wonderful gift of the Law – with its clear prohibitions of idolatry and the ringing moral integrity related to having no other God but Yahweh – would not, of itself, prevent transgression. Even the Tabernacle and later Temple were not proof against the inroads of the idols, and God's people would for ever stand in need of a Mediator, of whom Moses was a stunning prefigurement.[49] The incident also underscores the costly nature of forgiveness, and the necessity of Divine judgment on sin. If there were to be a new worship, in which idolatry were cleansed once and for all, this could only come about through the necessary judgment being borne through a greater and more perfect Mediator.

In, through and behind all these comments, however, stands another issue. The incident highlights the real nature of idolatry in terms of its personal affront to God, and its demeaning effect on human beings as his covenant partners. The whole section of Exodus in which the incident is found is governed by the words of God in Exodus 19:3-8:

> Thus you shall say to the house of Jacob, and tell the people of Israel: 'You yourselves have seen what I did to the Egyptians, and how I bore you on eagles' wings and brought you to myself. Now therefore, if you will indeed obey my voice and keep my covenant, you shall be my treasured possession among all peoples, for all the earth is mine; and you shall be to me a kingdom of priests and a holy nation. These are the words that you shall speak to the people of Israel.' So Moses came and called the elders of the people and set before them all these words that the LORD had commanded him. All the people answered together and said, 'All that the LORD has spoken we will do.' And Moses reported the words of the people to the LORD.

Here the matter is brought into sharp relief: God's mighty deeds in the exodus were performed so that his redeemed people could be brought into more direct relationship with himself, as verse 4 makes plain. To be 'lifted up on eagles' wings' connotes God's strength and the soaring ease of his victory over the gods of Egypt, and yet it also implies his tender care of his own brood, his covenant children.[50] God's purpose in bringing Abraham's offspring out of the land of Egypt – and thereby demonstrating his fidelity to his covenant with Abraham (see Gen. 15:12-14; cf. Exod. 3:7-14; 6:2-5) – was so that they could walk with him, as Abraham had, and as had Adam in the original Edenic sanctuary. His purpose was to restore the communion fractured by human sin, and to establish the worship that is the necessary foundation for the glorification of the cosmos, and to do all this with this particular group of people: his own possession out all the nations of the earth. The focal point of the narrative is the *personal* action of God in redemption for a *personal* communion with his people.

This personal communion is emphasised by other terms such as God's desire to 'dwell' with his people (e.g. Exod. 25:8; 29:45-46; Ps. 68:16; Zech. 2:10) or to 'walk' with them (e.g. Lev. 26:12; Deut. 23:14; cf. Gen. 3:8). We should bear such images in mind when interpreting covenantal concepts and the place of the Law (*torah*). The Law was given to a redeemed people at Mt. Sinai, in conjunction with the gift of a complete sacrificial cultus centred on the Tabernacle, so that this communion could be maintained (rather than established). Obedience to the *torah* was really obedience to Yahweh, since the *torah* was his personal instruction for his chosen people with whom he wished to share his presence.

In the light of these considerations it is clear why the Law equates idolatry with the hatred of God. In Exodus 20:4-6 we read:

> You shall not make for yourself a carved image, or any likeness of anything that is in heaven above, or that is in the earth beneath, or that is in the water under the earth. You shall not bow down to them or serve them, for I the LORD your God am a jealous God, visiting the iniquity of the fathers on the children to the third and the fourth generation of those who hate me, but showing steadfast love to thousands of those who love me and keep my commandments.

Here it is clear that idolatry is tantamount to expressing hatred of God, who had constituted himself as Israel's covenant Father. He had acted towards them in faithful love, rescuing them by his own action, so that they might share in the blessing of his nearer presence and that, through them, the seed might come to reverse the effects of the Fall. In and through God's own personal communion with his people, the full blessing of the creational Sabbath-rest was to come to the nations. To engage in idolatry is thus a deep expression of hatred to the One who is love, and who has expressed that love in holy, redeeming action.

There are three terms used in Exodus 19:4-6 to describe God's people. They are his 'treasured possession' (*segullah*), a 'kingdom of priests' (*mamleket kōh^{a}nîm*) and a 'holy nation' (*gôy qâdôš*). These terms all accentuate the unique nature of Israel, defined by her relationship to God.[51] In the first chapter we saw how worship forms and shapes character. Here, Israel, as God's elected, covenant people, are to serve God so that they will bear his likeness in the midst of the nations. They are terms which indicate clearly the principle seen throughout the Old Testament: 'You shall be holy to me, for I the LORD am holy and have separated you from the peoples, that you should be mine' (Lev. 20:26). They are employed to signify not only Israel's status *among* the nations, but her new role *as* a nation, under the kingship of Yahweh.

No longer does she belong merely to a general community of peoples, from whom she can only with difficulty be differentiated. She now has been elevated into a distinct entity and endowed with special privileges.... She will provide, under the direct divine rule which the covenant contemplates, the paradigm of the theocentric rule which is to be the biblical aim for the whole world.[52]

The word *segullah* is not common in the Old Testament. While it could be used to refer to one's personal property (1 Chron. 29:3; Eccl. 2:8), its most significant meaning attaches to God's direct claim on Israel's allegiance. They, out all the nations, are his *'am segullah* (chosen people, special possession, treasured nation). Here, in Exodus 19:5, it is clear that their status as such was dependent upon their obedience to the God who had declared himself to be their God, and whose worship was thereby demanded. Other Old Testament usage reinforces this connection. In Deuteronomy 7:6 they would demonstrate that they were his *'am segullah* by rejecting idolatry. In Deuteronomy 14:2 they would reject any associations with pagan mourning rites and their connotations with the death of fertility,[53] since they were 'sons of the Lord, your God' and thus his *'am segullah*. In Deuteronomy 26:18 they were to prove themselves to be his *'am segullah* by their total obedience to him, not least in their worship as celebrated in the great pilgrimage feasts of life in the land they were being given. The other ascriptions of Israel as God's 'kingdom of priests' and 'holy nation' have a similar force. Israel was 'dedicated to God's service among the nations as priests function with a society' and the life of Israel 'shall be commensurate with the holiness of the covenant God. The covenant responsibility encompasses her whole life, defining her relation to God and to her neighbors, and the quality of her existence.'[54]

It is clear, therefore, that the blessings of being God's *'am segullah* were dependent upon the integrity of Israel's worship and their consonant rejection of idolatry. If they did live in true worship and its consequent moral and ethical obedience to the Law of God they would be 'set high above all the nations of the earth' (Deut. 28:1). Where they refused to live in the worship for which they were created, they would come under the covenant curses instead of the covenant blessings, as enunciated in Deuteronomy 28:15-68. Indeed, there would be a reversal of the exodus, as the sequence of divine judgment spelled out through the curses makes plain.

Speaking directly to Israel, God says, 'I will bring upon you again all the diseases of Egypt, of which you were afraid, and they shall cling to you' (Deut. 28:60), and 'whereas you were as numerous as the stars of heaven, you shall be left few in number, because you did not obey the voice of the LORD your God' (Deut. 28:62). Instead of dwelling at rest in the land, they would be scattered to the nations, to serve their gods *in situ* where 'you shall find no respite, and there shall be no resting place for the sole of your foot' (Deut. 28:64-65), so that at the end, 'the LORD will bring you back in ships to Egypt, a journey that I promised that you should never make again; and there you shall offer yourselves for sale to your enemies as male and female slaves, but there will be no buyer' (Deut. 28:68).

The calf incident thus exemplifies a theme that is taken up extensively in the rest of the Old Testament. Israel is shown to be a faithless covenant partner, whose transgression is not just an infraction of the Law of God, but a rejection of him as their faithful creator, deliverer and redeeming husband. The calf incident is a specific example of a general trend, spoken against repeatedly by the later prophets.

By way of faithless response to God's redeeming grace, Israel forgot him 'days without measure' (Jer. 2:32), and in so doing exchanged him for the lie of idolatry (so Jer. 13:25), constituting themselves haters of God. Here, as always, the action of idolatry is a deliberate forsaking of God, not a mere transgression of some written code (Jer. 2:13; 5:7, 19). 'Therefore thus says the Lord GOD: Because you have forgotten me and cast me behind your back, you yourself must bear the consequences of your lewdness and whoring' (Ezek. 23:35). This is the real nature of idolatry: it is adultery against God, and brings Israel into a status of 'covenant breaker', where all the curses of the fractured covenant come into terrible play. This, indeed, is what we see played out in the rest of Israel's history, even in the good land that the Lord was giving them to be their resting place. What is abundantly clear even at this point, however, is that 'Israel's future as Yahweh's people will depend ultimately not on their ability to obey, but on the character of Israel's God.'[55]

Chapter 4

Worship in the New Land

Introduction

At the end of the previous chapter we saw that the people of Israel were prey to idolatry, even at the very occasion of Yahweh's gracious gift of the Law and the worship at Mt. Sinai. We thus are given to understand something of the power and pull of illicit worship, and find in the incident of the golden calf a litmus test revealing the stubborn-heartedness of the people whom God had called to himself. The biblical narrative leaves us in no doubt that the Israelites would find the same propensity to idolatry to be a great test of their faithfulness to God, even in the very land which God had promised them. Indeed, it proves to be the greatest test of all, and ends in the failure of the nation to abide in the covenantal faithfulness to which they had been called. In thus renouncing the blessing of being God's *'am segullah* (his treasured people) they find that the curses of the broken covenant lead to expulsion from the land and a scattering amongst the nations that is representative both of God's loving discipline and their disobedience.

1. Worship Under the Judges and Kings of Israel

(1) Joshua: leading the people in a time of transition

Moses, and Joshua after him, were used by the Lord to lead and guide Israel, not just in terms of their military conquests, but more importantly in terms of the allegiance to Yahweh upon which any of their successes were built. While Israel had these great figures in place, the people lived in greater faithfulness to the Lord, and in greater conformity to his Law, but there are many indications of Israel's underlying tendency to abandon the worship of God (or at least syncretise it with some other worship) at any opportunity. The episode of the golden calf stands at the head of a theme that runs like a river through the pages of the Old Testament.

We have already mentioned the closing chapter of Joshua in the preceding chapter, with reference to the worship of Abraham and his removal from Ur of the Chaldees. It is clear that Israel had still kept some connection with the ancient gods of Mesopotamia (Josh. 24:14-15), and that Joshua knew they would be drawn to serve the gods of the Amorites among whom they were now living (Josh. 24:15). It is notable that in this passage Joshua gives voice to a principle that we have already noted: there is no vacuum of non-worship. The people are given a choice of sorts. They may serve the ancient gods from beyond the River, or they may serve the gods of the Amorites.

While they should serve Yahweh, Joshua is very clearly of the opinion that they will not (Josh. 24:19-22), and when they come to the act of covenant renewal the narrative is pointedly silent regarding the extent of their repentance. There is no mention of the destruction of the gods which Joshua has said must be put away (Josh. 24:23), but only a verbal declaration from the people that they would indeed be faithful to Yahweh (Josh. 24:24). Joshua's statement of verse 22, 'You are witnesses against yourselves that you have chosen the LORD, to serve him,' is sombre. He knows the true nature of the people and the consequences for covenant transgression, and sees their avowal of sincerity as being the prelude to culpable disobedience. He also knows that the people must worship: and if they will not worship God, they must worship something or someone else.

The key transition point is the entry into the land. This had been promised to Abraham for his descendants, and is described in terms deliberately chosen to reflect Edenic categories. It is thus depicted as the resting place for God's people (Exod. 33:14; Deut. 9:12; cf. 1 Kings 8:56; 1 Chron. 23:25); as an area of God's special care, watched and tended as a gardener might care for his garden (Deut. 11:10-12); a place of abundance: flowing with milk and honey (e.g. Exod. 3:8, 17; Num. 13:27; Deut. 6:3); and the place where God would dwell with his people and walk among them (e.g. Exod. 25:8; 29:45; Lev. 26:11-12; Deut. 23:14). There is a conditional element to all of this paradisaical imagery, however, just as there was in the first Eden. If Israel were to refuse to walk in the ways of God, then they would not be able to enjoy his fellowship of blessing (e.g. Lev. 20:22-24; 26:3-4; Deut. 31:20-21), and the land would vomit them out (Lev. 18:28; 20:22).[1] Just as Adam had been expelled from the garden, Israel would be expelled from their resting place to serve the other nations in hard labour and under judgment.

(2) The Judges' Cycle

The death of Joshua ushers Israel into the consequences of this time of transition. They were now no longer slaves in Egypt nor nomads in the wilderness. They were dwellers in the land. During this transitional phase, as also would be the case when they had become more deeply settled there, the central place of worship is accentuated. Joshua had brought them in, through his faithfulness to the Lord. How would they manage when he had gone? The pattern is set out very clearly for us in the text of Judges 2:7-23:

> And the people served the LORD all the days of Joshua, and all the days of the elders who outlived Joshua, who had seen all the great work that the LORD had done for Israel. And Joshua the son of Nun, the servant of the LORD, died at the age of 110 years. And they buried him within the boundaries of his inheritance in Timnath-heres, in the hill country of Ephraim, north of the mountain of Gaash. And all that generation also were gathered to their fathers. And there arose another generation after them who did not know the LORD or the work that he had done for Israel. And the people of Israel did what was evil in the sight of the LORD and served the Baals. And they abandoned the LORD, the God of their fathers, who had brought them out of the land of Egypt. They went after other gods, from among the gods of the peoples who were around them, and bowed down to them. And they provoked the LORD to anger. They abandoned the LORD and served the Baals and the Ashtaroth. So the anger of the LORD was kindled against Israel, and he gave them over to plunderers, who plundered them. And he sold them into the hand of their surrounding enemies, so that they could no longer withstand their enemies. Whenever they marched out, the hand of the LORD was against them for harm, as the LORD had warned, and as the LORD had sworn to them. And they were in terrible distress. Then the LORD raised up judges, who saved them out of the hand of those who plundered them. Yet they did not listen to their judges, for they whored after other gods and bowed down to them. They soon turned aside from the way in which their fathers had walked, who had obeyed the commandments of the LORD, and they did not do so. Whenever the LORD raised up judges for them, the LORD was with the judge, and he saved them from the hand of their enemies all the days of the judge. For the LORD was moved to pity by their groaning because of those who afflicted and oppressed them. But whenever the judge died, they turned back and were more corrupt than their fathers, going after other gods, serving them and bowing down to them. They did not drop any of their practices or their stubborn ways. So the anger of the LORD was kindled against Israel, and he said, 'Because this people have

transgressed my covenant that I commanded their fathers and have not
obeyed my voice, I will no longer drive out before them any of the nations
that Joshua left when he died, in order to test Israel by them, whether
they will take care to walk in the way of the LORD as their fathers did, or
not.'

This passage highlights the shallow nature of Israel's covenant
renewal described in Joshua 24. It also acts as a theological preface
to (and framework for) the rest of the narrative in Judges, while the
principle enunciated here is also played out in a variety of ways
throughout the rest of the Old Testament, leading ultimately to the
judgment of the exile. A number of points are worthy of note in the
passing, almost all of which we have seen in principle already.

Firstly, we see that the idea of 'knowing the Lord' (v. 10) is still of
vital importance. We have seen that this theme pervades the exodus
narrative, and it is prominent throughout the ensuing drama at Sinai
and in the wilderness wanderings. Whether it be in the gift of the
Law; the gracious provision of the tabernacle and its cultus; the
command to teach the knowledge of God and his deeds from one
generation to the next (connected, for example, with the feast of the
Passover); or the repeated emphasis on 'remembering' the deeds
and words of God; *knowing* God was always to be the central feature
of Israel's life.

Secondly, the lapses into idolatry are depicted as being blameworthy
actions and expressive of an intentional rejection of Yahweh. They
are thus 'evil' acts (v. 11), described as abandoning or forsaking God
(vv. 12, 13), for which the people must be held accountable, and which
provoke the Lord to anger (vv. 12, 14).

Thirdly, their action in discarding God in this way is, in fact, adultery
or harlotry against their true covenant partner/divine husband (v. 17).
It is thus not simply an action of disobedience, but one of disloyalty
and one which underscores Israel's lack of love for God himself.

Finally, we notice the action of God's wrath being emphasised,
chiefly in the way in which he gives them over to the hands of the
enemies (vv. 14, 20). This theme emerges repeatedly in the Old
Testament account of God's dealings with Israel, and informs the
New Testament understanding of the nature of God's wrath, as seen,
for example, in Romans 1:18-32 (where significantly the wrath is
expressed from heaven against the suppression of the truth through
idolatry). Here there is a deep irony. The worship of idols, particularly

as seen in the later history of the kings, is deeply linked with the desire for power. Often this was to come through the concomitant creation of political alliances, but it would lead, inevitably, to the status of powerlessness brought about by defeat. God's people could ever only have one source of power, and to abandon him would render them powerless, even if, for a time, it rendered them (seemingly) more politically secure.

It is also plain that the exchange of worship involved the resident Canaanite gods (v. 12), here described as the Baals and the Ashteroth (vv. 11, 13). In its most basic sense the word *baal* means a lord, master or owner, and thus (from the perspective of the ancient Near East), husband. It is regularly found in compound expressions, in place names, for example, 'often on or near mountains,'[2] and as a title (i.e. lord or master) it 'is used as an appellative for many gods in the ancient world'.[3] These elements reflect the ancient understanding that gods were lords of particular areas or sites, who were to be worshipped in that location, often on a 'high place'. Here, however, the name is more specific, and refers to

> the storm/weather god, who in the Canaanite mythological literature goes by the name Hadad and several other titles.... Baal was one of the seventy offspring of El and Asherah, along with his opposite, Mot, the god of death and the netherworld, and Yam, the god of the sea. When the plural form *baālîm* occurs, the reference is not to a multiplicity of gods, but to numerous manifestations of the one weather god, on whose blessing the fertility of the land was thought to depend.[4]

The Ashteroth (*aštārôt*) is a plural form of Astarte, a title that may be used as a general term for a goddess,[5] but is commonly recognised as the specific figure widely worshipped in the ancient world as 'the goddess of love and war. In the Canaanite literature Anath usually functions as Baal's consort. Astarte also appears as Baal's spouse, however, which agrees with the broader ancient Near Eastern world reflected in the Old Testament.'[6] We also read of Asherah, which may be the physical pole/tree/grove representing the unseen Astarte (e.g. Deut. 16:21; Judg. 6:25-30; 1 Kings 15:13) as well as other deities such as Molech (e.g. Lev. 20:1-5; 1 Kings 11:7; 2 Kings 23:10; Jer. 32:35) and Chemosh (e.g. Judg. 11:24; 1 Kings 11:7, 33; 2 Kings 23:13; Jer. 48:7), whose worship became particularly infamous amongst some of the later kings of Israel and Judah.

Created For Worship

The intricacies of Canaanite worship practices are almost impossible to reconstruct at this distance. It seems clear, however, that at the centre of the cultic practices lay a celebration of Baal's cycles of death and resurrection as he battled with Mot the destroyer through the seasons[7] and to the role of the female consort deity or deities with whom he copulated.

Biblical descriptions of Canaanite worship practices are mixed. Deuteronomy 18:10-14 describes various practices including human sacrifice, necromancy, spiritism etc., which are associated with the nations that are to be driven out of the land. 1 Kings 18:25-29 describes blood sacrifices, self-mutilation, wild dancing and loud wailing/crying out. Numbers 25:1-5 describes the Israelites being seduced by the worship of Baal-Peor (literally 'the lord of the opening'), and this title, together with the emphasis on the role of the 'daughters of Moab' (Num. 25:1) in association with the terms 'harlotry' (25:1) and the Israelite men who 'joined themselves to Baal of Peor' (25:3, 5), seems to indicate either ritual prostitution or other illicit sexual activity.[8] The 'high places' are commonly understood to be locations of Baal/Ashteroth worship (as in 1 Kings 14:23). They are associated with child sacrifice, incense burning (2 Kings 16:3-4),[9] male cult prostitution (1 Kings 14:23-24) and other forbidden practices.

The summary statement of 2 Kings 17:9-11 is representative of the whole: 'And the people of Israel did secretly against the LORD their God things that were not right. They built for themselves high places in all their towns, from watchtower to fortified city. They set up for themselves pillars and Asherim on every high hill and under every green tree, and there they made offerings on all the high places, as the nations did whom the LORD carried away before them. And they did wicked things, provoking the LORD to anger.'

Whatever else the complexities of Canaanite worship may have been, they were expressive of the longing for and need of fertility. The whole Canaanite system was linked to the cycle of the seasons and to the productivity of land, crops and animals. This is significant, especially in view of Israel's immediate and long term history, before her entry into the land. For over four hundred years they had been in the land of Egypt, at the centre of which lay the Nile. Moses had to instruct the people about the fundamental difference between Egypt and the land to which they were being taken by the Lord:

> For the land that you are entering to take possession of it is not like the land of Egypt, from which you have come, where you sowed your seed and irrigated it, like a garden of vegetables. But the land that you are going over to possess is a land of hills and valleys, which drinks water by the rain from heaven, a land that the LORD your God cares for. The eyes of the LORD your God are always upon it, from the beginning of the year to the end of the year (Deut. 11:10-12).

This is a significant shift. No longer would the Israelites have a ready supply of water on the doorstep, and no longer would they be able to grow vegetables simply by moving the abundant water from one place to the next – watering the land 'with their feet' as some translations express the idea of irrigation in verse 10. No longer would they be able to rely on the annual flooding cycle of the Nile delta. After four hundred years they needed to learn a completely new way of going about providing for their daily food needs. And they needed to do this in a land where there were no significant supplies of permanent surface water. They needed, then, to trust Yahweh, and to see that the guarantee of fruitfulness belonged to their God.

The mode of expression of verses 11 and 12 indicate the depth of his care of the land. 'The land literally "drinks" the heavenly water supply, suggesting both ease and plenty. The relationship between Yahweh and his land is at its most intimate here as he "cares for" it, watching it all the year round to ensure that the watering is adequate to keep it fruitful.'[10] This, of course, necessitated a response of obedient faith on Israel's part. They needed to hear Yahweh's word, and live in conformity with it, in order to share in the blessings of his care, as the preceding verses make plain (Deut. 11:8-9) and the subsequent verses reiterate (Deut. 11:13-17). If they were to 'turn aside and serve other gods and worship them' (11:16), then 'the anger of the LORD will be kindled ... and he will shut up the heavens, so that there will be no rain, and the land will yield no fruit, and you will perish quickly off the good land that the LORD is giving you' (11:17).

When Israel entered the land, therefore, the matter of its continued fertility was a prominent testing point for them. Israel had already seen the power, providence and grace of God. The people should have had confidence in him to provide the necessary harvests, rain and increase of flocks, but they did not. While the worship of the idols was doubtless very seductive (and thus appealing to the baser instincts of human fleshliness), at its core the battle for worship was related to

Israel's faith in God as their covenantal Lord. Would he act according to his promises? If they relied on him alone, would the land prosper? The Baals and Ashteroth seem to have served the needs of the local population quite well, so perhaps they have had the right approach? May we not have faith in Yahweh *and* faith in the local gods, just by way of insurance? Are Yahweh and the local gods that different in any case?

The battle for worship in Israel at the time of their entry into the land had the issue of Yahweh's very nature at its centre. He had entered into covenant relationship with his people, who therefore had to trust him solely on the basis of who he had revealed himself to be. Yahweh would not be bribed by magic, as were the idols. His worshippers had no control over him, as the worshippers of the idols mistakenly thought they had over their gods.[11] They simply had to live by faith in his Word, and the reality of that faith would be demonstrated in their obedience to his commands, and the rejection of idolatry.

The quotation from Judges 2, with which this section began, describes the outcome. The people abandoned the worship of God, and did so with alacrity. The deities of Canaan, and the practices that seem to be associated with Canaanite worship, were just too appealing. The generation that took over from Joshua was 'unable to resist the attractions of the prevailing religious system, even for a little while. It is as if they could hardly wait to get into the land so they could attach themselves to these exciting gods.'[12] How could this situation be remedied?

(3) Kings Instead of Judges?

The book of Judges ends with the comment that 'in those days there was no king in Israel. Everyone did what was right in his own eyes.' (Judg. 21:25). This has become a repeated refrain in the latter part of the book (Judg. 17:6; 18:1; 19:1 as well as 21:25), as it closes out with descriptions of terrible incidents of apostasy and degradation. Micah's idolatry (chapter 17); the Danites' search for territory, their destruction of the people of Laish, their theft of Micah's idols and their establishment at an idolatrous tribal worship centre at Dan (chapter 18); the gang rape and terrible abuse of a Levite's concubine, and the deliberate parallels with the actions of the Sodomites preceding this event (chapter 19); the vengeful, bloody civil war between the

Israelites and Benjaminites which resulted in the wholesale destruction of the Benjaminites' women (chapter 20); and the subsequent theft of women from the remaining tribes (chapter 21) are all described in brutal detail.

None of these things is described with approval. Indeed, the opposite is the case, as each one on its own, let alone all of them together, demonstrates how deeply degraded the people of God had become. Is the writer therefore saying that human kingship in Israel is the answer? If only they had a king, all these things, including the worship, would be put in order?

This appears not to be the case. Dumbrell points to the anti-kingship polemic that runs throughout the book and its emphasis on Yahweh as Israel's true, sovereign ruler, so that the real model of government commended in Judges is a theocracy.[13] Rather than approving the establishment of earthly kingship, Judges 21:25 should be taken another way. Dumbrell rightly suggests that it seems to be a comment on the

> remarkable persistence of Israel, notwithstanding her sustained apostasy and her continued attempts to undo herself. It is remarkable that, after such a chaotic period, when the people did what was right in their own eyes and when social abuses were so glaring, Yahweh was still not prepared to give up on Israel. But just as during the preceding period, it would be Yahweh – and he alone – who would account for Israel's continuance.[14]

It is clear that Israel had abandoned their allegiance to their true King, Yahweh, and that their character was deeply affected for ill because of this. Human kingship would be no answer to this problem, as the narrative of the books of Samuel, Kings and Chronicles will go on to show.

(4) Kingship and Worship

The biblical narrative gives only qualified recognition of the success of kingship in Israel. The initial establishment of kingship in 1 Samuel 8-12 is described in ambivalent terms, reflecting the innate contradiction that exists in Israel's request for a king, one who would be a monarch 'like the other nations' (1 Sam. 8:5, 19-20). 'The basic difficulty is the nature of kingship the elders have in view. Kingship like that of other nations would be dynastic, bureaucratic [and] tightly regulated ... [and] carries with it a virtual unilateral withdrawal from the Sinai covenant, which mandated Israel's difference from the world'.[15] Indeed, in wanting a king who would function as the kings of the surrounding nations, Israel's action is clearly delineated as rejecting the kingship of Yahweh. God's word to Samuel is both a comfort to him and an explanation of the real motive behind the people's request: 'obey the voice of the people in all that they say to you, for they have not rejected you, but they have rejected me from being king over them' (1 Sam. 8:7), which in the New Testament finds its terrible culmination in the crucifixion of the Son of God (John 19:15).

However, as Samuel's speech to Israel in 1 Samuel 12 goes on to show, the appointment of a king ought not to have lessened Israel's covenantal obedience. Fundamental to any analysis of the issues is the fact that Yahweh was already the King of Israel, *de jure* (1 Sam. 12:12). So – despite the fact that Israel had requested a visible earthly king and all that this demand implied regarding their rejection of Yahweh – the earthly king can be spoken of as having been 'set over' Israel by Yahweh himself (1 Sam. 12:13).

Since Yahweh was their true King, by right and not by Israel's choice, the undeniable consequence was that both king and people ought to have served God, and that the covenant blessings and curses applied both to king and nation: 'If you will fear the LORD and serve him and obey his voice and not rebel against the commandment of the LORD and if both you and the king who reigns over you will follow the LORD your God, it will be well. But if you will not obey the voice of the LORD, but rebel against the commandment of the LORD, then the hand of the LORD will be against you and your king' (1 Sam. 12:14-15).

The theology of kingship in the Old Testament is complex, being linked with wider themes such as sonship, vice-regency and servanthood, among others. These, in turn, are creational categories, so that the king in Israel was meant to function as the obedient hearer of God's word, just as Adam was to be the royal, vice-regal, servant and son of God in Eden. Thus, in Psalm 23, the shepherd-king of Israel is seen as one who has Yahweh as his shepherd over him. Nowhere in the Old Testament is any credence given to kingship that does not share in the character of obedient sonship, whether this be in the Psalms or the wider Old Testament theology of kingship. This means that the actions of the king with reference to worship would have profound effects, for good or ill, on the entire nation.

His kingship was to be a servant kingship in two ways. Firstly, the king was to live as a loving and responsive servant/worshipper of Yahweh. By the means of such covenantally faithful worship, he was to be a servant-king in the second sense: by bringing the blessings of the covenant to bear on the nation. If the king were to refuse to serve/worship Yahweh, he would not only damage himself, but lead the nation into the arena of covenant curse. Conversely, if he were to walk before God in integrity of heart and obedience to his will, he would lead the nation in receiving the blessings of covenantal faithfulness. At core, then, the king in Israel was meant to be the servant of Yahweh *par excellence*, thus modelling for the whole nation what it was to be Israel's adopted son and servant. It is thus no exaggeration to say that the destiny of the nation hinged on the worship of the king. Linked with this was the way in which the king used his authority to defend the true worship of Yahweh.

This reality is reflected in the links between kingship and worship that are developed in the rest of the former prophets. Saul is shown to be a man who had an attachment to the outward worship of Yahweh, but whose heart was not fully submitted to the Lord who had set him as king over Israel. Samuel rebukes him for his disobedience in dealing with the Amalekites and the booty of war, but sees the particular incident as an expression of the fundamental principle: 'Has the LORD as great delight in burnt offerings and sacrifices, as in obeying the voice of the LORD? Behold, to obey is better than sacrifice, and to listen than the fat of rams. For rebellion is as the sin of divination, and presumption is as iniquity and idolatry. Because you have rejected the word of the LORD, he has also rejected you from being king' (1 Sam. 15:22-23).

The link between worship and obedience of heart is plain. Outward acts of devotion are worthless without a submitted spirit. Indeed, where there is no obedience of heart, nascent idolatry already exists. If Saul's action here can be attributed to greed (which is entirely defensible), he becomes an Old Testament example of the Pauline principle that greed amounts to idolatry (Col. 3:5). He thus stands condemned as one who rejected God, and who was therefore justly rejected by God. In effect, Saul 'disqualified himself from kingship in Israel. He ... refused to defer to the divine king.'[16]

By way of contrast, David is shown to be the one who best illustrates the model of submitted kingship. He is presented as a man who shepherded Israel through the integrity of his heart, and who was thus able to guide them with skilful hands (Ps. 78:72); as one who walked obediently before the Lord (1 Kings 9:4); whose heart was like God's own heart (1 Sam. 13:14 cf. Acts 13:22), and who was 'wholly true to the LORD' (1 Kings 15:3). To walk in such integrity of heart is innately connected with the rejection of idolatry, as the parallelism of Psalm 24:4 makes clear where 'he who has clean hands and a pure heart' is the one 'who does not lift up his soul to an idol or swear by what is false' (NIV).

The sins and shortcomings of the man are not glossed over, especially in the matter of Bathsheba and Uriah the Hittite, but the penitential psalm which David penned at the time of his deepest conviction of sin (Ps. 51) portrays a man of wholly different spiritual substance when compared to Saul. When confronted with the voice of God in the words of Nathan the prophet, David did not seek to hide from the presence of his King (and therefore Judge), or to justify his actions with lame excuses. He recognised that his sin was against God himself (ever before it was against Bathsheba and Uriah) and he cried out to God in penitential faith for mercy. Throughout the account of his reign two things are emphasised: his willingness to hear and obey the voice of God, and his integrity of heart. Even when he is seen in the full horror of sinful action his quickness to repent is evidence of a man who lived his life before the face of God.

One of the remarkable observations concerning his reign is his singular devotion to the worship of Yahweh. The greatest repository of his spirituality in this regard are the many psalms penned by him, and the evident encouragement he gave to the true worship of the Lord (e.g. in the return of the ark of Yahweh to Jerusalem, and in the provision for priestly praises and service in 1 Chronicles 15; in his actions in 1 Chronicles 23 regarding the administration of the Levitical priests and the provision of instruments for their praise; and in the lasting legacy they provided in the nation as seen in 2 Chronicles 29:25-26).

The psalms bear eloquent and enduring testimony to a king who led his people in true worship, and they reflect the kind of gloriously unobstructed communion that God desired for all his people. In joy, lament, antiphonal praise, penitential prayer, intercession, cries for help and deliverance: in all these and others Yahweh is the focus of David's spiritual expressions. The theology of the psalms is extensive, covering God's role as creator, redeemer, deliverer, sustainer, healer, lawgiver, judge, avenger, and faithful covenant maker and keeper. Many of the psalms have the kingship theme at their heart, some are clearly 'wisdom' psalms, and others outpourings of deep personal anguish. All, however, have Yahweh as their focus. In and through the whole of the narrative we see David (unconsciously?) fulfilling the role of the king-priesthood of Melchizedek, not supplanting the Levitical priesthood, but offering to the nation an overall leadership in the matter of worship that preserved true devotion to Yahweh.

2 Samuel 7 is instructive at this point. David's own desire was to build a temple for the dwelling place of the ark of God. From the preceding material in chapter 6 (where the ark of the covenant is virtually equated with the presence of God) and the material in chapter 7 (especially in terms of Yahweh's response in verses 5-7), it seems that David's desire in building the temple was to provide a dwelling place for God himself. The narrative makes it clear that this desire was an expression of gratitude to God. Yahweh had given David a house for himself and he had granted him (and thus the kingdom) rest on every side from his enemies (2 Sam. 7:1). David did not take any of this for granted. He knew that both who he was, and what he been able to achieve, were manifestations of God's gracious choice and empowerment, to which thanksgiving was the proper response. In a very real way, David stands as the representative worshipper at this point. The spiritual condition of his heart as expressed in his desire to honour the Lord in this way, should have been the response echoed in all Israel.[17]

Having given voice to this ambition, David received initial approval from Nathan the prophet (2 Sam. 7:1-3), but that very night, Nathan received a direct word from God that this was not to be the case (2 Sam. 7:5-7).[18] Instead, God says that he would build a house for David and for his descendants, and the Lord gives David the promise that his son would build a house for the dwelling place of God's name (2 Sam. 7:13). While this has its immediate fulfilment in the person of Solomon, we will later see that the real accomplishment of this goal in all its glory would belong to someone greater than Solomon, who comes to build something greater than the (physical) temple (Matt. 12:6, 42) in Jerusalem.

David prepared many of the materials for the temple and purchased the site, but it was his son Solomon who was the builder. This is shown to be in accordance with Nathan's prophetic statement in 2 Samuel 7:12-15, so that the narrative describes Solomon's actions in terms that deliberately reflect the language of that chapter and underscore the obedient nature of the action. Thus, in his alliance with King Hiram of Tyre, the text recounts Solomon's words: 'but now the LORD my God has given me rest on every side. There is neither adversary nor misfortune. And so I intend to build a house for the name of the LORD my God, as the LORD said to David my father, "Your son, whom I will set on your throne in your place, shall build the house for my name"' (1 Kings 5:4-5). The timber of Lebanon is thus dedicated to the building of the temple, and the labour is put in place by both Solomon and Hiram in appropriate numbers for the immense building project to be taken forward apace (1 Kings 5:13-17).[19]

The account of the building work is found in 1 Kings 6–7, while 1 Kings 8 describes the bringing of the ark of the covenant into the newly completed edifice, God's appearance in the cloud of his glory there, and Solomon's prayer of dedication and benediction. We will discuss the theology of the temple and the meaning of these events below. However, at this point the matter of main significance to note is the role of the king in the establishment of true worship. Through Solomon, God has now put in place a permanent centre of worship where his name might dwell, and where the people of his royal priestly nation might have access to him day and night. The temple centralised worship in the land that they had entered in a way that was hitherto impossible, and it provided in the centre of the capital a visual testimony to the presence of God with his people and a living exhibition of his character as the holy, covenant making God.

Solomon's reign does not receive unadulterated praise, however. Fundamental to the Old Testament theology of kingship was the fact that in Israel the role and responsibilities of the king were circumscribed by the Deuteronomic code, a reality clearly understood by David, and given prominence by his dying words of commissioning to Solomon in 1 Kings 2:2-4:

> I am about to go the way of all the earth. Be strong, and show yourself a man, and keep the charge of the LORD your God, walking in his ways and keeping his statutes, his commandments, his rules, and his testimonies, as it is written in the Law of Moses, that you may prosper in all that you do and wherever you turn, that the LORD may establish his word that he spoke concerning me, saying, 'If your sons pay close attention to their

way, to walk before me in faithfulness with all their heart and with all their soul, you shall not lack a man on the throne of Israel.'

The teaching of Moses included the laws concerning kingship in Deuteronomy 17:14-20 which are of special importance for our later discussion, but the general principles of the Torah as embodied in Deuteronomy's teaching applied to the king also, since he was still a member of the covenant community and therefore subject to God as the Covenant-Maker. Kingship in Israel was thus evaluated on the basis of its alignment with the Torah in general and the law regarding the monarchy in particular.

According to the Torah, power was to be distributed among a variety of institutions such as 'local courts (Deut. 16:18: 17:2-7), a central court (17:8-13), a king (17:14-20), a levitical priesthood (18:1-8), and prophets (18:15-22)'. Within this division of powers 'the monarchy is the only social institution whose existence is deemed to be optional'.[20] In particular, the kingship law prohibited certain things. The king 'shall not multiply horses for himself, nor shall he cause the people to return to Egypt to multiply horses' (Deut. 17:16); neither shall he 'multiply wives for himself, or else his heart will turn away; nor shall he greatly increase silver and gold for himself' (Deut. 17:17).

In addition, the king in Israel was to be one of the members of Israel, a 'brother' who was to 'write for himself a copy of this law on a scroll in the presence of the Levitical priests. It shall be with him and he shall read it all the days of his life, that he may learn to fear the LORD his God, by carefully observing all the words of this law and these statutes' (Deut 17:18b-19). Through the conscious submission of his reign to Yahweh via Torah and priesthood he was to ensure 'that his heart may not be lifted up above his brothers, and that he may not turn aside from the commandment, either to the right hand or to the left, so that he may continue long in his kingdom, he and his children, in Israel' (Deut. 17:20).

The picture of kingship in Deuteronomy 17 thus 'differs enormously from that of the usual ancient Near Eastern concept of the king as the chief executive in all aspects of the nation's life'.[21] Indeed, as far as the ancient Near East is concerned the teaching of Deuteronomy 'redesigns the notions of God, people and king', enshrining in Israel's national identity an anti-totalitarian ethos, 'rejecting the state as its own justification' as was the situation in both Egypt and Canaan.[22]

Deuteronomy does this by subjecting all aspects of the nation's life, including that of the king and his court, to the rule of Yahweh, the great sovereign King.

Miller rightly argues that Deuteronomy operates on two great axes: the Shema and the Decalogue. 'A theological structure is thereby given to the covenantal community [that] continues throughout its life … the relation of faith and love or obedience, as succinctly set forth in the Shema, and the relationship to God and others embodied in the Ten Commandments' constantly demonstrates 'what matters most for those who live under and with this God'.[23]

Both king and people stand under the one God: Israel as God's chosen servant/son, and the king as God's appointed son/ruler. The king, along with all his brothers in Israel, was to be subservient to the word and will of Yahweh. In a very real sense, therefore, Israel and the king were to stand as models for the surrounding nations of the difference between life in thrall to Yahweh and that dominated by the idols. The greatness of both Israel and her king lay in the acknowledgement of their status as God's servant.[24] In Israel, kings were to serve God by serving his chosen people. He was to be the servant king of the servant nation of Yahweh.

This perspective is seen very clearly in the account of the dissolution of the kingdom after the death of Solomon. However sound Solomon's reign had been to begin with, there are clear indications in the text that he transgressed the law of kingship in the Deuteronomic code, and that his reign developed along lines similar to the ethos of kingship evident in the surrounding nations. The positive connotations of Yahweh's approval at his accession to the throne and his request for wisdom are somewhat overshadowed by other elements of his reign. 1 Kings highlights the very things that the Deuteronomic kingship code prohibits. Great wealth, polygamy, trade in horses and links with Egypt are integral to the description of Solomon's reign, and may well carry an implied criticism. These are somewhat muted in the first part of his reign (e.g. the writer of 1 Kings simply juxtaposes without comment the fact that Solomon spent seven years building the house of God, but almost double this time on his own house in 6:38 cf. 7:1), but by the time the reader comes to 1 Kings 11 the criticisms become more overt.

By this stage in Solomon's reign a number of severe and damaging compromises have become evident. His action demonstrates transgression of the Torah on a number of levels. It ignores the law on intermarriage with other nations, applicable to all Israelites, king included (e.g. Deut. 7:3-4; cf. Exod. 34:15-16 and 1 Kings 3:1-14; 6:11-13); it expressly runs contrary to the kingship code of Deuteronomy 17:17; it disregards the restriction on making alliances with other nations (implied in Deut. 7:2, and condemned in many places in Kings, Chronicles and the prophets: e.g. Hosea 7:10-13; 9:9-10; Isa. 20:14-28; 30:1-5; Jer. 2:14-19) and above all it leads to idolatry, in transgression of the first two commandments. 'Solomon's sin may have begun small. It may have developed in stages over time. However it started, however it was fuelled, it began a national disintegration that was at times slowed, but never completely halted.'[25]

The history of the northern tribes following the split after Solomon's death is recounted in wholly negative terms. The 'sin of Jeroboam the son of Nebat who caused Israel to sin' is repeated as a refrain throughout the record of the northern kingship, so that the whole landscape seems to be dominated by illicit worship. The illegitimate nature of the northern worship was multifaceted. Not only was the worship instituted by Jeroboam in the wrong place (i.e. not in the divinely approved central sanctuary in Jerusalem), but it was worship in the wrong way, being inherently syncretistic. Indeed, the text of 1 Kings 12:28 connotes the worship of the golden calf recounted in Exodus 32: 'So the king took counsel and made two calves of gold. And he said to the people, "You have gone up to Jerusalem long enough. Behold your gods, O Israel, who brought you up out of the land of Egypt." '

In effect, this action institutionalised idolatry in the north by giving regal approval to a new form of religion.[26] In so doing, the northern tribes were predisposed to the inroads of idolatry from the very beginning, with the outcome that the conduct of the northern kings receives unremitting prophetic denunciation throughout the narrative. The conduct of the kings attracts the ire of the prophets not only for the continuation of Jeroboam's worship centres, but also for the elaboration of this syncretistic worship through the royal patronage of the prophets and priests of Baal. It goes without saying that the moral and ethical climate of the north deteriorated along with its worship, and the northern tribes came to necessary judgment (under the hand of the Assyrians) approximately 150 years before the southern exile.

Perhaps the acme of northern kingship (or its nadir, if one is looking from the perspective of prophets such as Elijah) was the rule of Ahab and his queen Jezebel, daughter of Ethbaal king of Tyre. Doubtless this was a cunning economic and political alliance from Ahab's point of view, but it opened the floodgates to rank idolatry in the land, the like and extent of which could only be matched by so great a figure as Elijah the prophet. The description is blunt: After marrying Jezebel, Ahab 'went and served Baal and worshipped him. He erected an altar for Baal in the house of Baal, which he built in Samaria. And Ahab made an Asherah. Ahab did more to provoke the LORD, the God of Israel, to anger than all the kings of Israel who were before him' (1 Kings 16:31-33).

Not only did this step legitimise the worship of Baal, but the problem was further compounded by Jezebel's passionate opposition to the covenant religion of Israel. As Ahab's queen she exercised enormous power, which she used in a determined effort to extirpate the worship of Yahweh from the land. She launched a bloody and systematic *pogrom* against the prophets of Yahweh (1 Kings 18:4, 13; 19:2; cf. 2 Kings 9:7), while giving royal favours to the prophets of Baal (1 Kings 18:19), with the result that she became the object of the most terrible and specific judgment of God against her (2 Kings 9). Despite the great victory that Elijah was granted over the prophets of Baal in the epic encounter on Mt. Carmel (1 Kings 18:20-46), and regardless of the drastic actions of Jehu, who was anointed as king over Israel by Elisha (2 Kings 9:1-13) and who acted as the avenger of Yahweh against the corrupt house of Ahab/Jezebel and its institutionalised Baalism,[27] the die was cast.

Jehu did not undo the original problem of institutionalised illegitimate worship. He 'did not turn aside from the sins of Jeroboam the son of Nebat, which he made Israel to sin – that is, the golden calves that were in Bethel and in Dan' and despite the promise that there would be four generations of his descendants on the throne, the overall assessment given of him by the narrator is negative (2 Kings 10:29-35). The subsequent history of the northern tribes continues on its downward spiral until the axe of divine judgment finally falls on the kingdom in the person of the king of Assyria.[28]

When we turn our attention to Judah, the situation in the south is less bleak, but not resoundingly so. The line of southern kings is punctuated by reforming monarchs whose actions are commended by the narrators of Kings and Chronicles. Rulers such as Asa, Jehoshaphat, Hezekiah and Josiah stand out as beacons of light in the midst of conditions of gross apostasy. In and through their reforms idolatry was cleansed from the land and the temple to varying degrees, but the 'high places' continued to exercise their enervating spiritual effects like a running sore in Judah. While there may be some tentative amelioration offered in the narrative before the temple was constructed (1 Kings 3:2-3), the Torah was clear in its teaching (e.g. Num. 33:52; Deut. 12:2) and the destruction of the high places becomes a benchmark for the extent and success of the various kings' reforms (e.g. 1 Kings 15:14; 22:43; 2 Kings 12:3; 14:4; 15:4, 35).

Josiah's reforms were the most thorough in this respect (e.g. 2 Kings 23:19-24 cf. 23:25), but both the extent of reform needed and the fact that this was carried out only after Hilkiah the priest discovered the book of the law in the temple archives (the book which was supposed to be copied out personally by the king and used as his daily guide, according to Deut. 17:18-20) serve as powerful illustration of how far king and nation lived habitually in a backslidden state. The best efforts of godly kings, prophets and priests notwithstanding, the southern tribes followed the downward spiral of idolatry and its associated ethical and moral decay, making the enactment of the covenant curses inevitable.

Before turning from this matter, however, it is important to note that in and through all these events the continued rebellion of God's covenant people is matched by God's continued faithfulness to his covenant promises. The poignant portrayal of his faithfulness given to us in Hosea, for example, indicates that, even in the state of gross degeneracy that characterised the very people who should have been his *'am segullah*, God was still *their* God even if they did not wish to acknowledge that they were his people.

In the opening chapter we discussed briefly the teaching of Psalm 115: that those who worship idols become like them. Indeed, because of the pervasive influence of the gods of the land and the worship accorded to them, God's people had become like the idols they served: deaf to his word, blind to his actions and dumb in regard to his praise. However, even in the north God sent many unnamed prophets, as well as the great figures of Elijah and Elisha, and in the south he persisted too, with the great writing prophets such as Isaiah, Jeremiah and Ezekiel. Even in the situation where the temple was ultimately destroyed, God is still shown as being faithful to his character and promises.

The overall picture, from the time of the worship of the golden calf in Exodus 32 to the exile to Babylon almost a thousand years later, makes one point with great force: the preservation of faithful worship in the earth was only possible because of God's continued intervention. Left to themselves, even his covenant people would revert to rank idolatry and the terrible social ills that accompanied it, and they would do so with eagerness. Of themselves, God's gracious gifts of the Law and the worship – bestowed as the substance of the Mosaic covenant on Mt. Sinai where God had brought his enslaved people to himself for liberated service – could not secure undistracted devotion to the Lord.

This, of course, is the point taken up by so much New Testament theology, not least in the writing of the apostle Paul. The covenant at Sinai was in force 'until the seed would come, to whom the promise had been made' (Gal. 3:19). It was provisional, demonstrating beyond any doubt, over centuries of history, that the human heart was desperately wicked. The graciousness of God in the giving of these covenant markers (of Law and worship) amplified the continued rebellion of his people, and served to accentuate the point that the covenant so lightly entered into by Israel at Sinai and so regularly broken could not secure undevoted service to Yahweh. The fault lay not with God, but with his people.

An honest reading of Israel's history would tell that a new covenant was needed, and indeed the promise of such is embedded within the Old Testament's prophetic testimony itself. Passages such as Jeremiah 31:31-33 and Ezekiel 11:18-20 (cf. 36:24-27), to name two of the most obvious ones, indicate a new situation would eventually obtain where worship would be empowered by the renewal of the hearts and minds of a revived people of God. Such passages should not be treated in isolated, proof text fashion, for we should not fail to keep in mind the great themes of hope evident in the Old Testament prophetic corpus that tend in the one direction.

The dominant messianic expectation linked with a true fulfilment of the Davidic covenant; the promised outpouring of the Holy Spirit; the imagery associated with a renewed Edenic resting place for the people of God; the repeated portrait of God as the divine husband of his people, who *would* have a pure people for his glory and their blessing, no matter what; the promise that God himself would be the shepherd of his flock and presence himself amongst them and provide for them in true faithfulness; the replacement of barrenness and wilderness images with pledges of fruitfulness and abundance; the indications of a coming, cleansing fire of holy, restorative judgement; not to mention the great image of a restored temple to which the nations would come and from which the blessing of God's river would flow to the ends of the earth; all of these and many others are themes which pave the way for the great transformation of worship that would come about through the epiphany of the Son of God.

2. Worship in Tabernacle and Temple

Before moving on to consider the transformation of worship brought about by the incarnation, death and resurrection of Jesus Christ, however, it is necessary that we consider the role and function of the tabernacle and the later temple in Israel. It goes without saying that a comprehensive treatment of this theme is not in view here. Entire volumes could be (and have been) devoted to the description of these great worship centres, to the discussion of the typology associated with their structure and contents, and to the nature and variety of the sacrifices so pivotal to the cultus. Later we will consider the theology of worship provided for us in the New Testament book of Hebrews, to which many of these matters are relevant, but for now we must consider some of the main historical and theological issues relating to the tabernacle/temple theme in the Old Testament.

(1) Tabernacle and Temple: Similarities and Differences

The tabernacle was essentially a portable worship centre, the description of which takes up most of the second half of the book of Exodus.[29] The word 'tabernacle' (Heb. *miškân*, translated in the LXX by *skēnē*) means simply 'tent', and thus 'dwelling place', from the root *škn* 'to dwell'. Thus the same word could be used of the dwelling places (tents) of God's nomadic people (e.g. Num. 16:24), as it is sometimes used in parallel with *'ōhel* the other common word for a tent dwelling (e.g. Num. 24:5).[30] The over-riding meaning of the tabernacle was that it was a sign of God's presence with his people (e.g. Exod. 24:16; 25:8; 29:45-46; 40:35), as was emphasised in the visible sign of the glory-cloud (e.g. Exod. 13:21; 14:19, 20, 24; 16:10; 19:9, 16). For readers of the New Testament, however, the statement that the Word of God literally 'tabernacled' (from the verb *skēnoō*) among humans (John 1:14) would have been replete with Old Testament allusion.[31]

The tabernacle was entered from the east, and the first sight (and smell) greeting the worshipper would have been the altar of burnt offering, which stood in the outer court. To the west of this was the large bronze basin full of water used by the priests alone for their ritual cleansing. The sanctuary proper was further west again, entered from the east. The outer part of this two-part sanctuary was also called the holy place, and it contained the golden, seven-branched candle stick, the table of showbread and the altar of incense. Beyond this altar was the most holy place, or the holy of holies. It contained the ark of the covenant, with the mercy seat atop it, where the high priest entered annually to make atonement for the sins of all Israel.

We should remove from our minds any connotation of quiet, contemplative cathedralesque stillness. This was a place of action. It was full of noise, not least the sound of the bleating and lowing animals about to be sacrificed. It was full of colour and continual movement. The altar of holocaust, the incense used daily to represent the prayers of the people, as well as the burning lamps and candles providing both light and smoke, meant that one's sense of smell as much as one's sight and hearing were all immersed in the experience of worship at the tabernacle. These things were no less so in the temple, and in fact were magnified due to its larger scale of operation and sheer physical size.

Exodus 25:9 and 25:40 indicate that the tabernacle and its contents were fashioned according to the divine pattern revealed to Moses on the mountain. This indicates that it was not to be understood as a manifestation of a form of worship that had its origins with the people themselves.[32] Rather, it was bestowed on the covenant nation by God himself, and thus had the imprimatur of divine authority, standing on earth as a representation of an existing reality in heaven.[33] The tabernacle is sometimes also called 'the tent of meeting' (*ōhel mô'ēd*, e.g. Exod. 28:43; 29:44; 40:34),[34] emphasising its function as the designated meeting place of God and his people; or 'the tent of testimony' (*miškan hâ'ēdut*, e.g. Exod. 38:21; Num. 9:15; 17:7-8; 18:2) emphasising its role as the repository of the ark of the covenant, which is called 'the testimony' in many places (e.g. Exod. 27:21; 30:26, 36; Num. 7:89), since it bears testimony to the covenant at Sinai and all that this reveals of the character of God.

In another sense this acted as a testimony against Israel, since they had bound themselves by the obligations of the Sinai covenant, and now had in their midst a permanent testimony of their pledges, made in response to God's gracious deliverance of them from slavery in Egypt. Any transgression of these pledges or offence against the Torah of the covenant would thus render them liable to be treated as covenant breakers, subject to the terms of the broken covenant. Even here, however, the curses were curses *of the covenant*. Even in their rebellion and the necessary judgment that this brought upon them, God remained their God. Israel's sin, therefore, was always against the knowledge of God that they had been given, and for this reason is all the more reprehensible (which is the point Paul makes in Romans 2-3).

The task of the construction of the tabernacle is described in terms of the ministry of the Spirit, especially in relation to Bezalel the son of Uri (see Exod. 31:1-12; 35:30-36:1). The Lord says of him, 'I have filled him with the Spirit of God, with ability and intelligence, with knowledge and all craftsmanship' (Exod. 31:3), indicating that the task of the building itself was under God's direction as much as the giving of the original pattern on the mountain.[35] The book of Leviticus is largely devoted to the laws regarding priesthood and sacrifice, all under the main themes of holiness and purity. In the first chapter we commented on the Edenic imagery evident within the tabernacle, and this bears on its fundamental purpose: to function as the appointed sanctuary-meeting place of God and his people. It is axiomatic that such divine communion could only be possible through the maintenance of the space as 'holy' and through the necessary purity that the presence of God demanded.

The relative dimensions of the tabernacle[36] as well as the items associated with the cultus, were all preserved in the construction of the temple. It is possible to argue that Solomon appears here as the wise (and by implication, Spirit-anointed) master builder, the new Bezalel appointed for the construction of the replacement for the tabernacle.[37] The temple, however, was no portable worship centre! The descriptions of Solomon's temple found in 1 Kings 6–7 and 2 Chronicles 3–5 are replete with references to the splendour of its internal beauty and the lavishness of the wealth associated with its construction. They also emphasise the substantial nature of the building's stonework and supporting timbers. This was a formidable construction in every way, which dominated the city of Jerusalem and was the central focus of the nation's life.

The three great pilgrimage feasts of Passover, Pentecost and Tabernacles all terminated there, and the whole edifice embodied in a physical structure the main elements of Israel's knowledge of God. As in the tabernacle, every item declared to Israel the character of God and the way in which he had dealt with Israel as his covenant people. Such great esteem was given to this edifice, that the false trust placed in its presence became part of the reason for the ultimate judgment of the Babylonian exile (Jer. 7:4).

Following the destruction of the original Solomonic temple by the armies of Babylon, there seemed to be no hope for the nation. The people had been removed from the land, and had lost not only their earthly king, but also the central sanctuary and its cultus. However, God intervened in mercy to raise up Cyrus, in order to bring his people back into the land after 70 years of exile, as he had spoken through the word of Jeremiah.

The account of the return of the exiles and the re-building of the temple under Zerubbabel can be found in the books of Ezra and Nehemiah. The resettlement and rebuilding programmes did not proceed without difficulty, and the returning exiles had to deal with local and official opposition, as well as the demotivating effects of despair. They proceeded with the task in fits and starts, and at some points it looked as though it would be abandoned midstream. The work was spurred on to great effect by the prophets Haggai and Zechariah, and not least through their ministries of encouragement the building was erected. The prophet's word to Zerubbabel, 'not by might, nor by power, but by my Spirit, says the LORD of hosts' (Zech. 4:6), in fact encompasses the principle of all true action. Nothing of good in Israel's history had been accomplished in any other way. In 516 B.C. this second temple was dedicated.

Zerubbabel's reconstructed temple stood all the way through to the final destruction of the temple in A.D. 70 (though not without being somewhat battered during the time of the Maccabees), when the Roman armies which had laid siege to Jerusalem under Trajan laid waste the city and razed the temple to the ground. By this time, of course, it had been greatly expanded by Herod the Great, who had modified and extended it into a physical structure of overwhelming magnificence and wealth. Jews and Jewish proselytes from all corners of the known world flocked to it during the great pilgrimage feasts, thronging its courts by the thousands, as did the local populace throughout the year.

It was, however, only a temporary structure despite its size and splendour – as the Roman army's actions made plain. The false trust placed in the physical presence of the building that characterised Jeremiah's day was not absent from Jesus' contemporaries (as John 2:20 might be taken to imply), but by the time of the destruction of this physical building the new temple of which Jesus spoke (John 2:19) was already spreading out to cover the earth, as representatives from all the nations were being brought into it through the proclamation of the gospel.

(2) Underlying theology
Just as there is an underlying unity between the physical structures of the tabernacle and the temple, there is an underlying unity of theological themes.[38] Again, we cannot do these justice here, though there is some fine work currently being undertaken that indicates the importance of them.[39] In the first chapter we drew attention to the Edenic imagery evident within the tabernacle and temple, and we commented on the importance of this there. Edenic imagery is not the only motif to be seen in these great worship structures, however.

The description of the tabernacle with its royal colours, as well as that of its furnishings, indicate that this was indeed intended to represent the royal tent of the divine King,[40] who dwelt with his people and who led them on. The people were not in control of their destiny in this respect. They moved when the King moved, following the glorious fire/cloud of his presence, as they had done in the events of the exodus itself (Exod. 13:21-11; 14:24; cf. 40:34-38; Num. 14:14). The matter of God's presence was crucial, for Moses understood that unless God went with the people, they would have no hope or future (Exod. 33:15-16).[41]

The exodus had been brought about by the presence of God, who through Moses is seen to be acting on behalf of his enslaved people.[42] This presence not only led them out as the great Shepherd of the Flock (Exod. 13:21; cf. Pss. 77:20; 78:52; 80:1, etc.), but also protected them along the way (e.g. Exod. 14:13-20) and provided water and sustenance during the journey. The concepts of 'presence' and 'exodus' are two sides of the one reality,[43] so that it is little to be marvelled at that the greatest exodus of all – that of the New Covenant – is brought about by the one who is Immanuel: God with us.

Bearing in mind the liberating nature of the presence of God, and how vital this was for Israel's self understanding, the idea of God's abiding presence (not just on the journey, but in the settlement) was 'absolutely vital to Israel being God's people.... It was the *sine qua non*: no presence of God, no people of God.'[44] The sovereign King who had made the promise of the land to Abraham would be the one to lead his people through the wilderness to it, and go ahead of them to enter it, settling the people around him as he caused his name to dwell in the central sanctuary of the temple.

By the very presence of God with them (both in exodus and settlement), Israel was declared to be Yahweh's royal priest-nation to the surrounding nations. As the inheritors of the covenant promises, they were the nation-seed through whom the other nations would ultimately be blessed. Their presence in the midst of the nations, with the presence of God among them, bore testimony to his plans and purposes for the nations themselves. Hence, when we read that God's word to Moses had been 'let them make me a sanctuary, that I may dwell in their midst' (Exod. 25:8), we should understand the dynamic nature of the abiding presence thus indicated. Such dwelling was no passive presence. God was actively with and among his people for the furtherance of his plans and purposes for them, and thus for the nations.

In the temple, the theme of God's dwelling in the midst of his people is no less pronounced than in the tabernacle narratives. This can be seen, for example, in the way in which the concept is woven throughout Solomon's prayer of dedication and benediction at the dedication of the temple in 1 Kings 8, a chapter about which we say a little more below. God's dwelling with his people is a repeated Old Testament motif (e.g. Exod. 29:45; 1 Kings 6:13; Isa. 12:6; Zech. 2:10; 8:3), which of course finds its great culmination in the incarnation of the Son of God (John 1:14) and the subsequent eschatological restoration of all things (Rev. 21:3). In a very real sense, therefore, the tabernacle and later temple were a visible representation of God's purposes in salvation history. These centres of worship with their detailed cultuses proclaimed the same message: the holy Edenic communion forfeited through Adamic rebellion is restored by God's gracious action of providing holy access to him through the gift of his atoning sacrifice.

The theme of God's dwelling with his people is emphasised by another aspect of tabernacle and temple stories, namely, the fact that both were filled with visible manifestation of the glory of God. The majesty and power of the event, which first took place at the time of the dedication of the tabernacle, is described in Exodus 40:34-38. The elements inherent in this description are repeated in directly parallel terms at the time of the dedication of the temple (1 Kgs 8:10-11). In Exodus 29:43 the Lord had said to Moses, 'There [at the tent of meeting] I will meet with the people of Israel, and it shall be sanctified by my glory,' such glory being virtually equated with God's personal presence (as the remaining verses of Exodus 29 indicate). This took the experience that had been given uniquely to Moses in his own 'tent of meeting' (e.g. Exod. 33:7-11) and expanded it to include all of Israel.

The sanctifying glory of God was seen in the overt revelation of the *shekinah*: the visible glory cloud of the divine presence, before whose weighty splendour none could stand. This was the glory of the heavenly temple come to earth. Kline suggests that this filling is 'the invisible heavenly temple brought into a veiled pre-consummation form of visibility', so that the *shekinah* 'enthroned above the cherubim in the holy of holies was the clearest possible manifestation of the fact that the tabernacle had been designed as a symbolic reproduction of the heavenly temple where the God of Glory is enthroned in the midst of the angelic divine council.'[45] The tabernacle was indeed made after the pattern of heaven, though not so much by way of a blueprint, as a living representation of the dynamic nature of the heavenly realm and God's ruling presence there.

As is clear in the revelation of the glory given to Moses on Mt. Sinai (recorded in Exodus 33:17–34:9), the true weight of this glory lay in its association with the divine Name. When Moses asked to see the glory of God (Exod. 33:18), God graciously granted him the privilege of seeing it in part (Exod. 33:20-23). However the *content* of the revelation lies in the declaration of the divine Name. This is made plain both in God's description of what he is about to show Moses:

And he said, 'I will make all my goodness pass before you and will proclaim before you my name "The LORD." And I will be gracious to whom I will be gracious, and will show mercy on whom I will show mercy' (Exod. 33:19);

and in what God actually proclaimed to him:

> The Lord descended in the cloud and stood with him there, and proclaimed the name of the Lord. The Lord passed before him and proclaimed, 'The Lord, the Lord, a God merciful and gracious, slow to anger, and abounding in steadfast love and faithfulness, keeping steadfast love for thousands, forgiving iniquity and transgression and sin, but who will by no means clear the guilty, visiting the iniquity of the fathers on the children and the children's children, to the third and the fourth generation' (Exod. 34:5-7).

Doubtless the *event* of seeing the *shekinah* would have been awe inspiring (though it seems the Israelites became quite accustomed to it in the wilderness!), but its real substance lay in the moral glory[46] that it represented. The cloud was the shimmering, vibrant, overt, representation of God's moral nature: pure, holy, and abounding in lovingkindness and truth. It is the declaration of his Name in the ancient sense of the phrase: it is the revelation of his character.

Without the verbalised revelation of God's Name to accompany the visible representation of his presence, the *shekinah* fire/cloud itself could not have communicated the fullness of God's character. The power for this lies in the communication of his word to his people, to which the glory cloud was a fittingly magnificent adjunct. However, if there were no word, the glory would have remained meaningless, or at least subject to mere pagan interpretation. This, of course, provides an important link with the New Testament, where the Word becomes flesh, with the result that we behold the glory of God in the face of his Son, who is the Word himself. In him we see the fullest revelation of the Name/Character of God that is possible (so Heb. 1:1-4), but in ways impossible even for the likes of Moses. He could only see the 'back' of God (Exod. 33:23), but in the Glory-Son who is Jesus Christ we see him face to face (so John 1:14).

This revelation of God's Name in conjunction with his glory also reveals a paradoxical aspect of the dwelling/presence motif. The glory of the Great King who was the maker of heaven and earth dwelt with the people in the tabernacle/temple. So closely associated is the glory with his presence that it can be said that God himself is now dwelling amongst them (e.g. Exod. 29:45). Yet it is clear that the God who has the earth as his footstool could never be contained in the structure that he had filled with his glory. He dwelt with his people in the tabernacle, but he was not limited to it. There could be no thought, therefore, of God being in any sense 'captive' in the edifice he had graciously ordained as his 'tent' on the earth (no matter how large or magnificent it was). His immanence in no way contradicted or compromised his transcendence, a line of thought that is very evident in the dedication of Solomon's temple in 1 Kings 8.

In 1 Kings 8 the ark is brought into the completed temple (about which we say more below); the whole structure is sanctified by the glory cloud of God's presence; Solomon addresses the assembly of Israel; leads them in prayer; pronounces a benediction on them; and then joins with the multitude in offering sacrifices before God. In a very real sense it is the high point of the tabernacle/temple motif in the Old Testament, for from the end of Solomon's reign onwards there is never again such a pure and powerful manifestation of the corporate worship of the nation. The temple is referred to as the place where God has caused his Name to be, to dwell or to rest, a designation which runs through the chapter in verse after verse (e.g. 1 Kings 8:16, 17, 18, 19, 20, 29). This, in turn, acts as a reprise of a theme that was inherent in the Lord's teaching to Israel through Moses (e.g. Exod. 20:24-25; cf. Deut. 12:5, 12, 21; 14:23-24; 16:2), and is also picked up in the promise of the Davidic covenant (2 Sam. 7:13). The Name is associated with God's effective presence and the declaration of his character, both ancient features attested to in literature elsewhere in the ancient Near East.[47]

The deliberate repetition of the theme of the temple as the dwelling place of the Name of God in this chapter thus indicates that this event is the culmination of one of the threads of salvation history, as God is now shown to be fulfilling that which he promised so many years before. The passages in Deuteronomy draw a contrast between the dwelling place of God's Name and the removal of the names of the idols (see, for example, Deut. 12:2-3; cf. v. 5), and thus imply that the 'true place of worship is one that is known to belong wholly and unequivocally to Yahweh'.[48] This place was to be dedicated to him, and thus representative of his character as Yahweh, the eternal Creator-King of the heavens and the earth, whose moral nature had been revealed so clearly in his covenantal relationship with Israel, and whose presence was now made manifest in the glory cloud.

In some senses this event was a recapitulation of the glories of Mt. Sinai, but where the audible voice of God proclaimed his Name to Moses in the midst of the glory cloud, now the physical structure of the temple proclaimed his Name to the people: both in terms of the splendour of its form and in terms of the salvation history it encapsulated within its cultus and accoutrements, the moral glory of God was continually being revealed. Whereas the tabernacle may have been seen as 'a sort of moveable Sinai'[49], the temple was a fixed presence on the mountain of Moriah in the heart of Jerusalem (God's holy mountain-city). It could be argued that through its associations with the sombre and magnificent events of Genesis 22, it explicated the Name of God more fully than the tabernacle did, and was thus its fitting replacement.

It is no surprise, therefore, to see the themes of immanence and transcendence woven throughout the Solomonic speeches and prayers. The temple is 'an exalted house, a place for [the LORD] to dwell in forever' (1 Kings 8:13), but it is also inescapable that 'heaven and the highest heaven cannot contain you; how much less this house that I have built!' (1 Kings 8:27). Thus it follows that the people might come to the house to make their prayers known, but God hears 'from heaven' (1 Kings 8:33-34), a phrase which runs like a refrain throughout the prayer of dedication. Why? Because even though God has placed his presence in the Temple, heaven is his real dwelling place (1 Kings 8:43). He cannot be said to live in a Temple made with human hands, even one that is built according to his will to reflect the pattern shown to Moses on the mountain. Thus we see that 'God is lofty, holy, and mysterious, yet approachable at the same time. The Temple [serves] as the physical symbol of these divine realities. Here the unapproachable Lord becomes approachable and ready to help those who worship, sacrifice and pray.'[50]

Above we made brief mention of the link between the descent of the glory-cloud onto (and into) the temple, and the ascent of the ark of the covenant through Jerusalem to be placed in the holy of holies. The centrality of the ark of the covenant to the meaning of the temple and tabernacle is inescapable, and it acts as a strong reinforcer of the Sinai connections mentioned immediately above. In the dedication of Solomon's temple, the whole narrative leads up to the event in which the ark is brought into the temple (1 Kings 8:1-9), and at this very point, in harmony with the culminating nature of the action, the glory-cloud of Yahweh filled the temple (1 Kings 8:10-11). Solomon refers to the temple as the house of God (e.g. 1 Kings 8:13, 17-20), but this, too, finds its real locus in the presence of the ark of the covenant.

Thus Solomon concludes his speech to the people with the words:

> Now the LORD has fulfilled his promise that he made. For I have risen in the place of David my father, and sit on the throne of Israel, as the LORD promised, and I have built the house for the name of the LORD, the God of Israel. And there I have provided a place for the ark, in which is the covenant of the LORD that he made with our fathers, when he brought them out of the land of Egypt (1 Kings 8:20-21).

The temple is thus, pre-eminently, 'a place for the ark', which both in the symbolism of its presence and in the nature of its contents governed not only the whole cultus, but also the entire life of the nation. Solomon (as the representative king) was dedicating a temple that was the dwelling place of the very Torah to which he was subject. The holiness of God's nature reflected in the Law necessitated the atoning sacrificial cultus that surrounded the ark, and the descent of the glory-cloud of the presence reinforced that fact that this Law was indeed the expression of the will of the Great King. It also established beyond any doubt that both king and nation could be held accountable for their actions – especially in terms of their worship – in accordance with the obligations of the Sinai covenant. The gracious gift of the Law of life bore testimony to the true way of living in God's creation as his holy nation, and at the same time it rendered his people without excuse for any subsequent apostasy. Neither king nor people were above this Law, and neither could spurn it with impunity. On the other hand both king and people could be assured of the protecting, guiding and sustaining presence of God were they to continue in obedience to him and maintain faithful worship in his house.

In the following chapter we will be drawing attention to the powerful New Testament connections with the temple theme, but perhaps at this juncture it is worth drawing attention to one passage. In his speech to the Athenian philosophers, Paul states that 'the God who made the world and everything in it, being Lord of heaven and earth, does not live in temples made by man, nor is he served by human hands, as though he needed anything, since he himself gives to all mankind life and breath and everything' (Acts 17:24-25). The socio/religious context of Paul's statement in Acts 17 is important. Coming as it does in the midst of the extended Areopagus speech, which has the idolatry of Athens as its immediate background (Acts 17:16; cf. 17:22), Paul's criticism of the idolatry of the city is based on his exposition of God's nature as the Creator-Father of all humanity. In effect, he argues that idolatry is wrong because it is God the Father who gives life to all things, and it is he whose children we are. He alone, therefore, is the fitting object of our worship. Paul's discourse is thus entirely congruent with the Old Testament, particularly the message of Jeremiah. In Jeremiah 2:27, for example, the shame of Israel is revealed in the actions of the kings, priests, princes and prophets, 'Who say to a tree, "You are my father," and to a stone, "You gave me birth." For they have turned their back to me and not their face.' They are thus 'faithless sons' (Jer. 3:14) who have not obeyed the voice of God.[51] God's purpose, however, is to lead them through repentance to know him as Father again (cf. Hosea 1:10). He says to them, 'You shall call me Father, and not turn away from following me' (Jer. 3:19).[52] Sonship, therefore, is a matter of relationship and obedience, and this secured through redemption, not simply through natural birth or creation.[53] The presence of the temple in Israel was, by its very existence, the witness of the futility and heinous nature of Israel's idolatry as rebellion against the nation's Covenant Father. For this reason, even the presence of the temple was no talisman against the necessary judgment on the sin of idolatry, and it is thus entirely fitting that the prophets take up a stand in many of their oracles against formalism and false trust in the temple and its presence.

(3) Prophetic Critique of False Trust in the Temple
The peril of placing false trust in temple, and God's willingness to forsake it as his dwelling place if there was no fidelity to him in the hearts of his people, had been foreshadowed in the Lord's words to Solomon as recorded in 2 Chronicles 7:12-22.

> Then the LORD appeared to Solomon in the night and said to him: 'I have heard your prayer and have chosen this place for myself as a house of sacrifice. When I shut up the heavens so that there is no rain, or command the locust to devour the land, or send pestilence among my people, if my people who are called by my name humble themselves, and pray and seek my face and turn from their wicked ways, then I will hear from heaven and will forgive their sin and heal their land. Now my eyes will be open and my ears attentive to the prayer that is made in this place. For now I have chosen and consecrated this house that my name may be there forever. My eyes and my heart will be there for all time. And as for you, if you will walk before me as David your father walked, doing according to all that I

have commanded you and keeping my statutes and my rules, then I will establish your royal throne, as I covenanted with David your father, saying, "You shall not lack a man to rule Israel." But if you turn aside and forsake my statutes and my commandments that I have set before you, and go and serve other gods and worship them, then I will pluck you up from my land that I have given you, and this house that I have consecrated for my name, I will cast out of my sight, and I will make it a proverb and a byword among all peoples. And at this house, which was exalted, everyone passing by will be astonished and say, "Why has the LORD done thus to this land and to this house?" Then they will say, "Because they abandoned the LORD, the God of their fathers who brought them out of the land of Egypt and laid hold on other gods and worshiped them and served them. Therefore he has brought all this disaster on them." '

The themes within this passage are familiar to us from the preceding material in this chapter. What is of singular importance at this juncture, however, is to notice that despite the fact that the temple is here designated as the place to which God's eyes are open and ears attentive (v. 15) and that his eyes and heart will be there perpetually (v. 16),[54] there is no inevitable commitment to preserve the building as an institution, come what may. In addition, the accent lies on the imitation of David's obedience (v. 17) and the necessity of this obedience to be continued in David's line in order for the blessings accorded to him to be continued (v. 18). While the words recorded in this passage are addressed to Solomon in the first instance, it quickly becomes evident that the whole nation is being addressed, as the plural pronouns in verses 19-22 indicate. The whole nation is bound by the same necessity for obedience as is the king. And, as we have seen above, the king in particular had a special responsibility to lead the nation in the true worship of Yahweh.

Comments such as these articulate with a theme that runs through the book of Deuteronomy: that of the necessity to have a truly circumcised heart towards God (Deut. 10:16; cf. 30:6). The provision of physical circumcision had marked Israel out as God's nation, and was the particular sign of the great covenant made with the patriarch Abraham (Gen. 17), their father. Circumcision was not a means to *make* covenant (as though the initiative lay on the human side), but a *sign* of a covenant already made, the initiative for which was wholly divine.

Just as Abraham was a man who 'walked with God' (given all the connotations that this phrase has with the concepts of divine-human communion and responsive human obedience), so Israel as a whole nation was to walk with God after the pattern set by Abraham. In the passage we have been considering above, Solomon was to walk with the Lord in the pattern set by David, and the whole nation was to walk with God in the full obedience of their hearts towards him. The injunction that they must not abandon him (v. 22) means that they had been created to be *with* him, or, to use Jeremiah's words, to *cling* to the Lord, 'as closely as a loincloth clings to the loins of a man' (Jer. 13:11).

The idea of having a circumcised heart means two reciprocal things. On the positive side it was to indicate that the nation lived in whole-hearted love towards God (e.g. Deut. 6:5-6; 10:12), while on the negative side is was to indicate that the nation had been separated from the mores of the surrounding nations, especially in the matter of worship (e.g. Deut. 11:13; cf. 11:16). Whole-hearted love would be expressed in the joy of keeping the Law, at the head of which lay the prohibitions on idolatry, as expressed in the first two commandments (Deut. 5:7-10). There is thus a command for Israel to have a circumcised heart (Deut. 10:16) – which is fitting given their status as God's beloved, chosen people – and also an indication that they will not, in fact, have one, so that the Lord promises he will provide this for them (Deut. 30:6). It is this promise that lies behind the provisions of a new covenant in the later prophets (e.g. Jer. 31:31-34; Ezek. 11:19; 36:26), but this does not lessen the obligation on the people to live in congruence with the status of royal sonship they had been given. In Leviticus 26:41, therefore, an uncircumcised heart is equated with rebellion against God, while Jeremiah 4:4 makes it clear that the circumcision of heart of which the prophet was speaking was in fact the rejection of idolatry (cf. Jer. 4:1).

All of this assists us to grasp the message of the prophets in their oracles against formalism in religion and superstitious trust in the temple. These are not two distinct matters, but two sides of one coin. False trust in the temple's presence went hand in glove with a rejection of the real matters of the law in favour of outward observance. The matter is made exceedingly plain in the following passage from Jeremiah:

> Do not trust in these deceptive words: 'This is the temple of the LORD, the temple of the LORD, the temple of the LORD.' For if you truly amend your ways and your deeds, if you truly execute justice one with another, if you do not oppress the sojourner, the fatherless, or the widow, or shed innocent blood in this place, and if you do not go after other gods to your

own harm, then I will let you dwell in this place, in the land that I gave of old to your fathers forever. Behold, you trust in deceptive words to no avail. Will you steal, murder, commit adultery, swear falsely, make offerings to Baal, and go after other gods that you have not known, and then come and stand before me in this house, which is called by my name, and say, 'We are delivered!' – only to go on doing all these abominations? Has this house, which is called by my name, become a den of robbers in your eyes? Behold, I myself have seen it, declares the LORD. Go now to my place that was in Shiloh, where I made my name dwell at first, and see what I did to it because of the evil of my people Israel. And now, because you have done all these things, declares the LORD, and when I spoke to you persistently you did not listen, and when I called you, you did not answer, therefore I will do to the house that is called by my name, and in which you trust, and to the place that I gave to you and to your fathers, as I did to Shiloh. And I will cast you out of my sight, as I cast out all your kinsmen, all the offspring of Ephraim (Jer. 7:4-15).

The interweaving of moral and ethical disobedience with the spiritual disobedience of idolatry has been a well observed pattern in our studies. In this passage the temple itself has virtually become an idol, since the true trust that should have been placed in the Lord was placed in the institution itself (v.14). Moreover, God here uses the example of Shiloh (vv. 12-14) to indicate that he has no *a priori* connection with any holy place, and thus his presence cannot be presumed upon. The blessings of his presence (v. 7) could not be guaranteed by physical structures (v. 4) or by outwardly pious acts of devotion (v. 10), but by having a heart that was truly devoted to him as expressed in love for him (by rejection of idols, vv. 6b, 9b), and love for his people (by living in true justice and mercy, vv. 5, 9a).

A quick glance through the rest of the Old Testament prophetic corpus will reveal that Jeremiah is not alone in his views (e.g. Isa. 1:23; Ezek. 13:19; 22:12; Mic. 3:11; Zeph. 3:3; Mal. 1:10), and underscore the fact that Jesus was acting in line with the true prophetic tradition when he cleansed the temple from its nascent idolatry at the outset and conclusion of his earthly ministry (Jer. 7:11; cf. John 2:16; Matt. 21:13). Indeed, one greater than Solomon would build a more glorious temple than his ever could have been: one which – by virtue of its very union with Christ himself – could never be invaded by the idols again, and which would become the true and eternal dwelling place of God in the Spirit.

Chapter 5

Jesus and the Transformation of Worship

Introduction

The previous chapter concluded with some comments about Jesus as the new Solomon, who had come to build a new temple, but one which transcended the old in both nature and scope. This statement implies a transformation in many aspects of worship, but it also denotes a deep sense of continuity. Many of the themes that we have seen thus far are taken up in the New Testament account of Jesus' life and teaching and in the apostolic interpretation, expressed in the New Testament documents, of the significance of his death, resurrection and ascension for the theology of worship. What is clear is that the coming of Jesus Christ is crucial to the transformation that takes place.[1] In this chapter we will be considering three key areas: Jesus' relation to the temple and to the history of Old Testament worship (which we will access by considering two salient passages from John's Gospel); the paradox that Jesus is both the true worshipper of God and the one to whom worship is accorded; and the promise of Trinitarian worship that he both declares and effects.

1. Jesus, the Temple and Old Testament Worship

(1) A New Temple to be Raised Up (John 2:13-22)
The cleansing of the temple in John's Gospel stands at the outset of Jesus' public ministry.[2] However, the material in the first part of John 2 is a significant element of the context of this event, as are the many Old Testament motifs evident in John 1. Before we can direct our attention to the events of the cleansing, therefore, it is important that we set them in this wider literary and theological context.

Immediately preceding the account of the cleansing we have been told of the miraculous sign of turning the water into wine. This sign was performed in secret to ease the distress and deep social embarrassment of the hosts of a family wedding when the feast was in danger of failing (it was possibly one of Jesus' cousins who was being married). When they had run out of wine Jesus provided for them, in abundance, by turning water set aside for ritual cleansing into wine. Not only was the quantity ample, but the quality of this wine was superb. Indeed, the best wine had been kept till the last (2:10)!

This event, which took place in Cana of Galilee in the far north of the country (and thus at a very remote location from Jerusalem), is the first of the special 'signs' recorded in John's Gospel. John's use of these signs indicates that they were not just 'miracles' (though they were undoubtedly miraculous), but actions full of meaning that, like all other signs, needed to be read in order to penetrate their significance. They were not just works of power, but actions which declared who Jesus was and what he had come to do. They are placed at important junctures in the first eleven chapters of John, and are often linked with extended discourses which serve to unpack their meaning. Even when such discourses are not immediately present, the literary location of the signs in relation to the surrounding material is significant.

In conformity with John's purpose in using these specially selected signs (see 20:30-31) the miraculous provision of wine is as freighted with meaning as any of the others. It sees an interweaving of the themes of Jesus' presence, his actions and his glory (e.g. 2:11) and also describes Jesus' ministry in terms of replacement and fulfilment. The water that was turned to wine is clearly described. It came from 'six stone water jars' that were there 'for the Jewish rites of purification, each holding twenty or thirty gallons' (2:6). The Messiah is here shown to be the one who brings about a transformation of the categories of thought and action. That which was once associated with the old covenant rites and rituals (in this case for attaining ritual purity, not just the physical cleansing away of dirt) is now completely transformed and pressed into the service of the King, as he provides for the family's wedding banquet.

The wedding banquet/feast in itself was an image rich in Old Testament allusion to the coming banquet/feast of the Lord so prevalent in the teaching of the prophets (e.g. Isa. 25:6-9; 55:1-2; Jer. 31:12-13; Zech. 9:16) and which marked the experience of Israel when they knew God to be present with them (e.g. Exod. 24:9-11). Wherever it appears with reference to God and his people, the banquet imagery is always associated with the direct action of God in which he himself is the host of the feast. The provisions are from the *abundance* of his household, so that Psalm 36:8-9 can be taken as the classic expression of the fulsome nature of God's supply: 'they feast on the abundance of your house, and you give them drink from the river of your delights. For with you is the fountain of life; in your light do we see light.' The theme of God's bountiful provision is often taken up in the Old Testament, both with reference to his gifts to humankind generally, and also to the special nature of his provision for his people.[3] In providing for them in this way, the twin concepts of the divine presence and the abundance of provision for his household were redolent of Eden. Thus, the eschatological vision of the prophets is taken up in the Book of Revelation to depict the garden-sanctuary of the presence of God, containing a plenitude of fruit and water, where God names and owns his people fully, and they own him (e.g. Rev. 22:1-4).

In relation to the wedding imagery itself, Jesus was very specific in his own self-understanding as the bridegroom of his people (e.g. 3:29; cf. Matt. 9:15; 25:1-10; Luke 5:34-35), hereby drawing in many Old Testament images of God as the divine husband (e.g. Ezek. 16). He also indicated that the feast begun with his people on earth would be culminated in the eschaton at the great banquet feast of the kingdom (e.g. Matt. 26:29). It is no coincidence that this latter reference is found in the context of Jesus' description of his actions in inaugurating the New Covenant, to which we have alluded elsewhere. This covenant would be sealed in his blood, but it would not be culminated until the last day, when, finally, all his people would be 'saved to sin no more'.[4]

In the light of these observations, it is no surprise that the theme of the divine marriage and associated heavenly provision is developed in other parts of the New Testament. In Ephesians 5:25-33 Christ is depicted as the husband of his church, who is his bride. He 'nourishes and cherishes' his bride (Eph. 5:29) because she and he are 'one flesh' (Eph. 5:31-32). Later, the wedding feast motif is used to depict the eschatological glory of God's presence with his people (e.g. Rev. 19:7; 21:2, 9), and such imagery is entirely of a piece with the whole of the biblical witness regarding the plan and purpose of God for the creation and for his redeemed humanity.

In the wedding of Cana of Galilee, Jesus is portrayed as the secret host of the feast, who by his intervening presence redeems it from its otherwise inevitable failure. While it may well be that Jesus' action was motived by his compassion for the hosts of the wedding – stirred by the risk of their very public embarrassment and consequent social exclusion – we should not limit the meaning of the actions to this. John's Gospel is replete with layers of meaning and there is hardly a passage that does not pick up on central Old Testament motifs in one way or another. We are justified, therefore, in seeing at the core of this sign a testimony to the mission of Jesus to bring about a transformation from the necessary, but limited and obsolete, provisions of the old covenant to the fulfillment of the promises of abundance and Messianic banqueting associated with the new.

The theme of transformative action embedded in the first of the signs is taken to a very public arena in the account of the temple-cleansing that follows hard on the heels of Jesus' gracious action in the north of the country. There the deed was done quietly, here the action takes place on the most public stage available: in Jerusalem, some 70 or more miles to the south of Cana in Galilee, in the full gaze of the multitudes. Jesus' action in cleansing the temple could not have been more dramatic or public, yet it is as much a sign of transformation as the quiet 'domestic' miracle at the wedding.

One of the first things that strikes us when reading the account of the temple cleansing is its direct association with Passover. The time reference at the beginning of the account (2:13) is echoed at the end of the account (2:23), and these serve as an emphatic *inclusio* for the action. The reader is meant to understand that the cleansing took place at *this* time specifically. This is important for at least two reasons. Firstly, the Passover designation would have alerted the first century reader to the exceedingly visible nature of the event. Passover was the first of the three great pilgrimage feasts held annually in Israel. It thus led to a dramatic increase in the population of Jerusalem in general and to the thronging of the temple and its environs in particular. Jesus' action here was not being done in a corner!

Secondly, the Passover festival ties in with themes already given prominence in John's Gospel. The entire focus of the Passover festival lay in the events of the exodus, in which the Lord 'passed over' the houses of the Israelites in Egypt and in which, in the culmination of his great and terrible works of power, he caused all the firstborn in Egypt to die. The Israelites were protected by the sign of the blood of the Passover lamb, sprinkled on the doorposts and lintels of their houses, there sheltered from the consuming judgment of God. There they had light in the midst of the deep darkness that cloaked the nation, and there they engaged in a solemn feast, forged as a memorial of the events and as a testimony to the character of God thus revealed, to be observed throughout all the subsequent generations of Israel. Associated with the happenings of the exodus were the presence of the glory-cloud and the giving of the gift of the Law and the worship on Mt. Sinai. It was here that the structure of the tabernacle was laid out for Moses, and where God's presence was so clearly manifest to his people, about which we have commented previously. The actual Passover festival thus recalled the deliverance from Egypt, but it had inevitable and wider connotations. The deliverance itself acted as the necessary precursor to the dwelling of God with his people, the obligations of which were enshrined in the Sinai covenant, which was the goal of the exodus. Israel was brought *out* of Egypt to be brought *to* God in worship. Their release from bondage was for his glory.

When we turn to the opening chapters of John's Gospel, we see that these themes are recapitulated in the language and imagery John uses to describe the coming of the Word into the world. The Word is identified as the eternal, true Light which shines in the darkness and of which John the Baptist bore testimony (1:4-5; cf. 1:6-9) – a theme taken up and developed further in Jesus' direct teaching about himself and his mission recorded in other places in John (e.g. 8:12; 9:5: 12:46). Moreover, Jesus, as the incarnate Son of God, is nothing less than God himself 'tabernacling' amongst us (1:14), here shown first to come to his own people (1:11), just as God had tabernacled amongst the Israelites in the wilderness.

Again the theme of God's presence with his people in the person of Jesus (and its counterpart: the non-recognition of this presence by those who should have understood it) pervades the Gospel. Furthermore Jesus is the one who, as the new Moses, makes the Father known (1:18), and does so 'full of grace and truth' (1:17). Moses brought the Law to Israel from God, but he could not bring the full revelation of the Father. The incarnate Son alone could bring this, since he and he alone is the enfleshed Word, who has been the Son of the Father from eternity. No matter how great Moses was, he was still the servant of this Son (whose Spirit-words had filled him and all the other true prophets in Israel), of whom alone it can be said that he dwells 'in the bosom of the Father'.

This theme of the Son as the one who reveals the Father in word and deed is ubiquitous in John's Gospel, and given added power when we see that Jesus' mission in the world was to gather his bride to be with him, 'so that where I am, you may be also' (14:3). His revelation of God is not static (a portrayal of God in tableau form that may or may not be appreciated if one cares to) but active: through it he actually accomplishes his mission and brings about the relational union of his people with himself. He brings his people into union with God, the knowledge of whom is eternal life (17:3), and his prayer is 'that they may all be one, just as you, Father, are in me, and I in you, that they also may be in us, so that the world may believe that you have sent me' (17:21; cf. vv. 23, 26). The oneness of the Father's children congruent with the oneness of the Father and the Son: a perichoretic union[5] in which each is in the other, and therefore gives to and receives from the other.

In addition to these things, Jesus is the one in whom we see the glory of God (1:14) and who reveals that glory to his disciples (2:11). Later, the implications of his sharing in the divine glory are even further spelled out where Jesus himself lays claim to his divine nature (17:5, 24), but we also see that his glory is in fact shared with his disciples, as he gives them this glory in order to sanctify them in the world (17:12). We have commented earlier on the link between the glory-cloud of the divine presence and the revelation of the character of God in the exodus/wilderness events. This connection is given added substance when we note that in the context of Jesus' comments about his glory, he is also able to declare that he has made God's *name* known to his followers (17:6, 11, 12, 26). Whereas the glory-cloud of the Old Testament could bear but mute testimony to the character of God, Jesus as the embodiment of the *shekinah*-presence of God reveals the name of God in every word and deed, in living flesh and blood.

Along with all of these things, Jesus is also spoken of as the Lamb of God (1:29; 2:36), clearly identifying him as the Passover's sacrificial victim, a motif again addressed later in the Gospel (e.g. 10:15). This identification does not negate the other line of reasoning that could be applied: the lamb as the atoning sacrifice for sin that lay at the heart of the Old Testament cultus. It is not so much a case of 'either/or' as 'both/and', since the characteristics of the lamb in either case (e.g. its spotlessness) and the outcome of the sacrifice (deliverance/

forgiveness) are mutually interpretive categories. For the first century reader, familiar with the profound weight of Old Testament allusion embedded within the opening pages of John, the identification of Jesus as the Lamb in this way would have meant one inescapable outcome: the death of the Lamb as the means of bringing about a new exodus through the forgiveness of sins.

While there are other exodus/wilderness motifs evident elsewhere in the Gospel (e.g. the comparison and contrast between Jesus as the bread of heaven and the manna in the wilderness in John 6; the imagery of the rock in the wilderness and Jesus as the source of divine water in John 7), it is clear enough from what has been said that the various descriptions of Jesus in the opening pages of John all connote exodus motifs that allow for development in the later parts of the Gospel. These lines of development show both continuity and discontinuity with the Old Testament itself. The Old Testament referents are of a piece with the New Testament developments, but are related to them as the precursor is related to the main event, or shadow to substance (to anticipate the contents of the next chapter). The substance, however, is Jesus Christ himself.

All of the above reflections on the Old Testament connections in the first two chapters of John help us to take a closer look at the temple cleansing itself. In the first chapter of this book we made some comments on the conflict for worship that took place in the wilderness temptations, where Jesus was directly tested by Satan in the matter of his worship and service of God. In particular, we saw the import of this temptation in the light of his preceding baptism and its accompanying events. There, in the bestowal of the Spirit and the baptismal declaration by the Father, we saw the empowerment of Jesus as the great Prophet, Priest and King; raised up by the will of God and anointed with the Holy Spirit for the fulfillment of these exalted offices.

If we bear in mind what we have said earlier about the exodus as a battle for worship, and how the Israelites were delivered from the gods of Egypt in order to be worshippers of the Lord alone (e.g. Exod. 12:12), then these things are not insignificant. God had indeed brought Israel out 'on eagles' wings', but not simply to be 'brought out'. He had brought them to *himself*. They were to be his people and he their God, so that the future of the nation was bound up with the gracious gift of his presence and the fellowship afforded to them in the worship system he had ordained at Sinai. Communion with him lay at the very heart of Israel's identity: 'Know that the LORD, he is God! It is he who made us, and we are his; we are his people, and the sheep of his pasture' (Ps. 100:3). This was Israel's self-understanding in almost creedal form, summarising the knowledge of their own nature by reference to God and his choice of them in order to be with them as the Great Shepherd.

The kings, prophets and priests of Israel were all meant to hold this reality to their hearts in order for it to become the motive force for their actions. Just as the great kings in Israel's past had demonstrated their love for God and for his people in addressing the matter of idolatry, so Jesus – as the newly anointed King, crowned with the Spirit for his royal ministry – is bound by his love of God to cleanse his Father's house and remove the nascent idolatry displayed there (as evidenced in the greed of those who served in the temple and in the undue boasting in the splendour of its construction). Likewise, standing in union with the line of the true prophets of Israel, Jesus knew that his appointed task was to speak the word of God to enable the people of God to come to repentance and fill them with hope.

We have already commented on the false trust in the temple of Jeremiah's day, and the echoes of this in Jesus' own time. As the great, eternal Son of God he has stood in the Lord's council like none other, and so has heard the voice of God to bring to the people of God. He thus comes as a true prophet should, full of love for God and directly commissioned by him, with the effect that he cannot allow the name of God to be abused. It is necessary, therefore, for the dwelling place of the name of God to be cleansed of all that is not congruent with his character. Likewise, as the true Priest, Jesus comes to offer service to God that is not tainted by the sins, transgressions and selfish infidelities of many of the priests of past days. Indeed, bearing in mind our comments from the first chapter, he has come to establish and confirm priesthood of a new order: the royal priesthood of the order of Melchizedek.

On all these counts, then, the action of the cleansing is his obedient response to the anointing of God for his threefold office, and in every way he is shown to act as the prophets, priests and kings of the Old Testament should have acted. Indeed, the ones who fulfilled their roles properly did act rightly in this matter, but even then we must consider their actions with due recognition of the transient nature of their office and the sinful limitations of their own flesh.

While we should not collapse the categories prophet, priest and king into one another (they did have specific callings and distinct areas of responsibility even if, in some senses, these were overlapping) the outcome of the three ministries (as was also the case with the other main group mentioned in the Old Testament: the sages/wise men) was always dependent upon their own worship and it was always meant to lead to the establishment and preservation of true worship for the nation. We have seen, for example, that the kings of Israel were to be bound by the Torah and were to be single-hearted in their devotion to the Lord so that they could lead the nation in covenantal faithfulness. Where the kings compromised their worship and service of Yahweh, the nation suffered. Where they maintained integrity in this area, then they were rightly able to bring blessing to the nation by reforming its worship and leading in the proper cleansing from its gross idolatry.

The principle applies across the board. Where the prophets worshipped the Lord and thus served him by obeying his voice, they were empowered to be a blessing to the people, even if their obedience necessitated strong words of warning to be uttered in faith, looking for the fruit of repentance. Where they departed from the worship of God they could not hear his voice, so had nothing to bring but a 'vision of their own imagination' (Jer. 23:16).

Jesus' action in the cleansing of the temple is the necessary and inevitable consequence of his own obedient worship of the Father. He could not be the true servant of the One who had sent him, unless he acted to maintain the glory of his name in the place where God had caused his name to dwell. This place needed to be cleansed in order that it might be used properly for the purpose for which it had been originally sanctified by the divine glory. In this way, then, we may see Jesus, the physical embodiment of the glory of God and the true representative of God's name, here bringing about a renewed sanctification of the earthly temple through his words and actions. Later, in an event corresponding to the descent of the glory-cloud filling the first tabernacle and first temple, he would send the Holy Spirit in tongues of fire on the new temple he had built through his death and resurrection. Already he has this new temple in view (2:21), but his actions towards the physical temple are completely natural for the role he fills as the bearer of the divine glory.

Nor is his identification as the Lamb of God (with all its exodus and Old Testament cultus connotations) incidental to all this. It was through the sacrifice of the Lamb that Old Testament Israel was protected so that it might be brought out from under the gods of Egypt to worship the living God. It was through the continual sacrifice of the lambs in the tabernacle and temple that atonement was provided, so that the fellowship God had purposed for his people could be maintained. It is thus entirely fitting that the one so signally marked out as the Lamb of God in the opening chapter of John should come to cleanse the very place where all the actions of the cultus, and all the testimony to God's salvation history embedded in its structure and accoutrements, should actually bear witness to him. He knew that he was the Lamb to which all the multiplied sacrifices pointed. He was the fulfilment of Passover and of the Day of Atonement, as well as the morning and evening sacrifices and all that happened in between. The greed of the traders in the temple and all the moral and spiritual decline that they represented obscured the temple's witness to himself.

We are told plainly that the house of Jesus' Father had become a 'house of trade' (2:16). This was diametrically opposed to its original purpose. The original tabernacle and later temple were instituted in part to remind Israel that the God of heaven and earth had chosen them to be his people and that they were thus his special possession out of all the nations on the earth. One of the corollaries of this was that Israel should have recognised that nothing was in fact theirs, as Exodus 19:5-6 so clearly denotes: 'now therefore, if you will indeed obey my voice and keep my covenant, you shall be my treasured possession among all peoples, *for all the earth is mine* and you shall be to me a kingdom of priests and a holy nation.' The reality of the Lord's sovereign ownership of all the creation is emphasised in many places (e.g. Exod. 9:29; Deut. 10:14; Job 14:11; Ps. 24:1; Dan. 4:34-35).

What is striking about the range of such references are the manifold implications drawn from the simple reality that the whole earth is the Lord's. This same truth is applied to the demonstration of his power to humble kings, as much as to the necessity for his praise amongst his people, as to the need for simple humility before him. In particular, the idea of wealth in Israel was never to be tied to one's own strength and ingenuity, but to the gracious and abundant provision of God (as Deuteronomy 8 makes so very clear). Given this background, the presence of the temple, was (among other things) to remind Israel of the fact that he, not they, was the one who owned all things – even the land on which they were living – and that he, not they, was the one who made their ways to prosper. To turn the temple into a means of personal wealth creation by making profit on the sale of sacrificial animals, money changing and other merchandising activities was utterly irreconcilable with the very meaning of the temple's presence in Israel.

Having said all of these things, however, it is clear that the main weight of the narrative lies in its reference to the transformation of worship that Jesus is shown to be bringing about. Jesus has necessary and due regard for the temple as the dwelling place of the name of God, but he also knows that his purpose was to fulfil in actuality all that the temple pointed to in type, and to build spiritually all that the temple represented in its physical structure. Jesus is thus able to speak of the destruction and rebuilding of the temple, but with these words he was speaking of a greater meaning beyond that which his hearers understood. The temple had been necessary, but now the holy presence of God was in the midst of his people in flesh and blood, and this meant that the whole notion of a centralised physical temple needed to be revised. The building had been necessary, but with the advent of the Messiah 'something greater than the temple is here' (Matt. 12:6). Jesus himself was nothing less than the tabernacle/temple of God bearing the glory and name of God in the midst of the nations.

Central to this glorious revelation of the character of God would be his own crucifixion, which would enact in real and substantial terms all that the Old Testament cultus foreshadowed. Thus, when Jesus would be crucified as the sacrificial Lamb *this* temple of his body, not the glorious edifice of gold-plated bricks and mortar, would be raised up (2:19-21). Neither the ones questioning Jesus about his authority (2:18) nor the disciples themselves understood this, but we are told that later, after the resurrection, 'his disciples remembered that he had said this, and they believed the Scripture and the word that Jesus had spoken' (2:22).

The way in which other New Testament writers spoke about the temple indicates that they recognised this was a transformative utterance. While Jesus was speaking about raising up his body as the temple, it is also clear that he was speaking about more than his own resurrection. He was speaking of a new temple, raised up in and through his own resurrection. This is borne out by the way in which Peter, James and John (and Paul, who wrote in the same apostolic spirit) use the language and vocabulary of temple and cultus in their writings.[6] From the point of Pentecost onwards, when the disciples fully understood all that Jesus' life and mission had been about, the whole New Testament corpus bears witness to an understanding of temple and worship that is entirely transformed. The temple as physical presence is no longer necessary to the equation. It could be torn down (and was), without in the least threatening the integrity and power of the new worship that Jesus had come to establish.

In view of these things it is possible to read John's use of Psalm 69:9 in John 2:17 in two ways. After describing the action of the cleansing (2:15-16) John writes that 'his disciples remembered that it was written, "Zeal for your house will consume me".' The immediate context is that of the physical cleansing of the precincts of the temple. Jesus had exercised some force in this event. He had taken the time to make a 'whip' (*phragellion*) and had used it with the full moral authority of his innate holiness to drive out all the beasts and those who were selling them. This is indeed an action of righteous 'zeal', and it is fully in line with the earlier prophetic oracles against the greed of God's people, especially in using the temple as a means of profit (Jer. 7:11). Later, Jesus' statements about the temple are misrepresented at his trial (Matt. 26:61) and become part of the taunts taken up by those who watch his crucifixion (Matt. 27:40). On one level, then, his zeal for the temple as his Father's house led to his crucifixion and thus consumed him.

However, I believe that the wider theology of the temple in the New Testament, and not least the transformative nature of Jesus' words and actions, allow us to take a second layer of meaning from the verse. While Jesus was full of zeal for the Jerusalem temple as the dwelling place of his Father's name, that which ultimately consumes him is the passion for the new, spiritual temple which would become 'the dwelling of God in the Spirit' (Eph. 5:22). The zeal for this temple would take him to the cross as the atoning Lamb of God,[7] there to make a once-for-all sacrifice for sin to seal the new covenant in his blood. The new covenant would have a new temple, made of living stones built together in Christ himself.

The New Testament imagery relating the church is multi-layered. The redeemed people of God are spoken of in a variety of ways, none of which is mutually exclusive of the others. They are the body of Christ, the household of God, the family of the Father, the bride of the Son, the branches of the vine, and so on. Of particular note, however, is that they are repeatedly called the temple of God or the temple of the Spirit (e.g. 1 Cor. 3:16-17; 6:19; 2 Cor. 6:16; Eph. 2:21-22; 2 Thess. 2:4; 1 Peter 2:4-10; Rev. 3:12). It is zeal for this house which consumed the Son of God, and which took him to the cross for its construction. Moreover, 'the church as the temple of God stands under his special protection. He will destroy anybody who tries to destroy his church (1 Cor. 3:17).... Thus the continuing life of the church is guaranteed. There is no possibility that it will cease to exist.'[8]

(2) Neither Jerusalem nor Samaria (John 4:7-30)
The next main passage we wish to consider is that involving Jesus' conversation with the Samaritan woman at the well in Sychar. The setting is well known. Jesus was passing through Samaria with his disciples on his way back to Galilee (4:1-4) and stopped about midday for a rest by a well (4:6), the history of which went all the way back to Jacob (4:5). He was there by himself as the disciples had gone away to buy food (4:8), deep in territory that was normally hostile to Jews, and to which they were normally antagonistic. The Samaritans were partly related to the Jews, and so also traced their inheritance back to Jacob (hence the woman's comment in 4:12 that this was the well of her ancestor, Jacob), though the Samaritans and the Jews were separated by many centuries of deep hostility. Indeed they had no dealings with one another, as John explains (4:9b), and their interactions had led to bloodshed and abiding hatred.[9]

The response of the disciples recorded in Luke 9:5 more typically reflects the prevailing nature of the relationship: 'Lord, do you want us to tell fire to come down from heaven and consume them?' In response to the fact that Jesus, a Jewish man, spoke to her at all, the woman's amazement is clear. 'The Samaritan woman said to him, "How is it that you, a Jew, ask for a drink from me, a woman of Samaria?"' (4:9). She may well have been aware of the fact that Jesus was risking ritual defilement in this action,[10] and she certainly would have been aware that any acts of kindness between Jews and Samaritans were so rare as to be virtually non-existent.[11] This Jewish man was different, and he drew her into conversation like none other before.

The fact that this is a Jewish/Samaritan interaction that is not filled with either hatred or deep distrust is not the only unusual feature of the account. The woman comes to the well in the middle of the day, and for those first century readers familiar with the daily necessity of drawing water from the village well, this detail would have immediately rung alarm bells. This was no ordinary situation, since the normal time for drawing water was in the early hours of the morning, before the heat of the day built up. Moreover, it was a profoundly important social occasion, in which all the women of the village would have exchanged news and engaged in the sort of interaction that makes for day by day social cohesion amongst small communities. This woman was coming at the wrong time (midday) and in the wrong way (alone). She was not, therefore, part of the accepted social fabric, and the timing and manner of her coming to the well testify to her social exclusion.

The reason for this exclusion is not hard to find. As the conversation unfolds, it becomes clear that she has had numerous liaisons with the men of the village, and that therefore she had become an object of approbation to the women of the community.[12] Jesus recognised the deep thirst to which her actions bore testimony, and in order to draw her out to face the necessity of repentance in the light of his grace, he asks her to bring her husband.

> Jesus said to her, 'Go, call your husband, and come here.' The woman answered him, 'I have no husband.' Jesus said to her, 'You are right in saying, "I have no husband"; for you have had five husbands, and the one you now have is not your husband. What you have said is true.' The woman said to him, 'Sir, I perceive that you are a prophet. Our fathers worshipped on this mountain, but you say that in Jerusalem is the place where people ought to worship' (4:16-20).

The jump from the statement about Jesus' nature as a prophet (v. 19) to the comment the woman makes about worship (v. 20) is important and not as incongruous as it might first appear. The matter of worship lay at the heart of the Samaritan/Jewish problem, and traced its history all the way back to the split between the northern and southern tribes under Jeroboam and Rehoboam respectively.[13] The Samaritans had built their own temple on Mt. Gerizim, where they offered sacrifices according to their understanding of the Law,[14] and the woman draws attention to the long-standing tradition behind their practices inherited from the fathers of her people (4:20a). In other words, they believed that they had access to a means of acceptable sacrifice, validated by a long historical tradition, which gave them a legitimate claim on the God of Israel. From a Jewish perspective, this worship could never have been correct under any circumstances. From the Samaritan point of view, they saw their worship as providing them with the blessings of the appointed means of sacrificial atonement as much as that which took place in Jerusalem. This background is noteworthy when we consider what was actually happening in the conversation. We must bear in mind that the whole exchange is part of the process of the woman coming to new birth. Later in the narrative she becomes, in effect, an early (if not the first) Christian evangelist whose work brings about a great harvest of belief in Jesus as the Messiah (4:28-30, 40-43). The question regarding worship is part of the woman's response to the reality confronting her. If this man, whom she later comes to know as the promised Christ,[15] could read her heart and mind in order to expose her deepest secrets, could he not answer this question about worship, the one which had separated Jews and Samaritans from the very beginning? And is it not exceedingly important that the question be answered? If she had guilt and shame exposed before the eyes of one who was, at the very least, a prophet and who may be the Messiah himself, what hope would she have if her worship had not been correct? Where could she find atonement for her sins if the Samaritan worship were deficient? Could there be any forgiveness for her, or must she abandon all and become a Jew? And could she do this? And what difference would it make, since the Jewish women along with the Gentiles were excluded from the central part of the Jerusalem temple? The question about the worship, therefore, is an understandable response of one in whom the conviction of sin is at work. She must know if she can and should continue to worship as she has done in the past, since if that worship was wrong her hope for atonement was gone.

Jesus deals with the question of worship in some detail and in doing so he makes a number of significant statements. He implies that Samaritan worship had indeed been deficient, and that the Jews had been right in insisting on the necessity to worship at Jerusalem: 'You [Samaritans] worship what you do not know; we worship what we know, for salvation is from the Jews' (4:22). The Samaritans 'stand outside the stream of God's revelation, so that what they worship cannot possibly be characterized by truth and knowledge'.[16] This matches with all that we have seen regarding the establishment of the central sanctuary in Jerusalem as being in accordance with God's plan and purpose to have a place for his name to dwell, where true sacrifice could be made and true worship thus effected and empowered.

The alternative worship centres set up in the north had never been proper and, indeed, they did not reveal the character of God. The Samaritans thus did not know who or what they worshipped (4:22a), whereas the Jews had received the revelation of God in the covenants and the associated, divinely sanctioned worship centre at Jerusalem. However poorly they lived in accordance with this privilege, the fact that it was granted to them remains (cf. Romans 9:1-5). Neither does Jesus' statement rule out Jewish synagogue worship (which he himself attended and in which he taught, e.g. John 6:59) since the synagogues preserved the reading and teaching of the whole of the Jewish scriptures and thus carried in their worship the complete testimony to the nature of God who had revealed himself in his covenant dealings with Israel throughout their history.

The recognition of the priority and correctness of Jewish worship is not the end of the story, however. Jesus indicates that, if the worship of the Samaritans had been deficient, the worship of the Jews had been provisional. Now that form of worship itself was passing away. 'Jesus said to her, "Woman, believe me, the hour is coming when neither on this mountain nor in Jerusalem will you worship the Father"' (4:21). Worship was no longer a matter of location related to one's racial history. Jews and Samaritans both were now in a situation where they could come to know the Father, and this transformation was already taking place: 'But the hour is coming, and is now here, when the true worshippers will worship the Father in spirit and truth, for the Father is seeking such people to worship him. God is spirit, and those who worship him must worship in spirit and truth' (4:23-24). I believe that Jesus could already see what was happening in the life of this woman. I think that he saw the light go on in her eyes, even as he was speaking, so that 'even now' she was becoming a true worshipper of the Father. It is a most remarkable event, especially given the history of the two people groups, that this marginalised and sinful woman should become the first to hear and believe the proclamation of the Father from the lips of Jesus. This new covenant and its new worship was for all races to share in, and for sinful women as much as for 'righteous' Pharisees, for Samaritans as much as Jews.

Jesus' words in verse 23 keep us mindful of the situation that has obtained all the way through our discussion. From the creation, through the fall, to the accounts of God's dealings with the patriarchs, and through the long years of Israel's subsequent history, God has been the one to take the initiative. He created humanity for worship, and when that creational state was rejected in the fall, he kept taking the initiative to establish true worship and to maintain communion with his people. God has always been the one who seeks out worshippers. Left to themselves, they would never come. And Jesus knew that he had been sent from the Father to seek them out, even among the Samaritans, in the middle of the day near a well!

Moreover, Jesus stresses (twice, in verse 23 and 24) that this new worship of the Father is 'in spirit and truth'. The theme of water is obviously central to this passage and must be given some attention. The imagery associated with water here in John 4 ties in with what we have seen previously, and also looks ahead to later developments in John's Gospel. Just as the incident at the wedding feast of Cana in Galilee demonstrated that Jesus had come to transform the old categories of rite and ritual, so here there is an implicit transformation of family ties. The woman comes to the well of her ancestral father Jacob, to draw water. There she meets a man who promises her a different sort of water from a different well, relating her to a different Father. Instead of drawing physical water from the well of her ancestors, Jesus is inviting her to draw spiritual water from the well of his own Father, so that she might know him as her Father also, and thus come to worship him. 'To know God wholly as a person can know him is the very essence of true life. It is from such knowledge that true worship issues.'[17]

The water of which he speaks is nothing less than the Holy Spirit. Jesus is the one on whom the Spirit rests and he knows himself to be the one through whom the Spirit will be poured out in a baptism greater than that of John the Baptist's water baptism (1:32-34). Thus all who will come to Jesus and drink will not only be satisfied, but also they will have a fountain of the Spirit welling up from their innermost being (7:37-39), as they receive the Spirit from him. The promise of the Spirit's coming is reiterated in Jesus' discourse in the upper room (John 13–16) where it is the major theme of his teaching, and where it is clear that he asks for and receives the Spirit from the Father in order to be sent upon his followers. We will consider some elements of the teaching contained in the upper room discourse a little later, but for now the main point is that Jesus knows himself to be the incarnate embodiment of the source of the river of God's Spirit.

The well/water/river/fountain imagery of the Old Testament is quite extensive and beyond full examination here. A few salient points follow. The theme of the river of life that flows from the presence of God is well attested in the Old Testament (e.g. Ps. 36:8-9; cf. Ps. 46:4; Isa. 8:6-7), while the concept of God being (or providing) waters that refresh and satisfy is also seen in many places (e.g. Ps. 23:2; Jer. 2:13; 17:13; 18:14). There are no doubt Edenic allusions underpinning all such references, as Eden was the place of abundant water *par excellence* (Gen. 2:10-14), flowing from the place of God's presence.[18]

Perhaps one of the most notable Old Testament references for our discussion is the extended image found in Ezekiel's vision of the restored temple (Ezek. 47:1-12). There it is clear that the water that flows from the temple brings life to the furthest regions of the promised land, transforming those with whom it comes in contact, affecting the very creation itself. While it starts out very small, as but a trickle, it grows into a river so mighty that no man may cross it. So also it is with the Son of God and his distribution of the Spirit. In a very real sense, he is the spring/fountain head of the river (as the imagery is preserved in John 4:14; 7:37). He, as the living flesh and blood tabernacle of God, is the one from whom the river flows, but now it over-spills the borders of Judaism to touch the ends of the earth (cf. Revelation 21:6; 22:1, 17). And here, the river flowing out of his own heart touches and transforms the life of a Samaritan woman who comes looking for water in the heat of the day. As it flows out, it transforms. As it transforms, it brings about a new worship. This woman is just the first of a great harvest; the shallow headwaters of what will become a universal torrent spreading out to cover the earth.

2. The Worship of Jesus Christ

In the above passages we have seen that Jesus' own ministry was transformative in the matter of worship. He saw himself to be the one who had the authority to declare both the destruction of the old temple and the building of a new one, of which he was the founder. He saw that his coming, as the long promised Messiah, replaced both deficient worship (as in the case of the Samaritans) and correct, but provisional, worship (as was the case with the Jews). He knew, therefore, that what he had come to do was utterly unique.

As God incarnate, he could do that which no one else could: reconfigure the whole understanding of acceptable worship and establish the new covenant on which it was based. Yet, as we have already seen in the first chapter of this book, Jesus was truly man as well as fully God, and as such he needed to render acceptable worship to God. This matter lay at the very core of the temptations in the wilderness. In response, Jesus' reply sets out what is the normative position for human beings: to worship the Lord their God and to serve him only (Matt. 4:10).

A consideration of the New Testament documents thus reveals two complementary pictures. On the one hand, Jesus is shown to be the true and faithful worshipper of God his Father, and on the other he is shown to be the one to whom worship is offered. In this section we aim to see how both of these elements play their role in the transformative nature of Jesus' person and work by which the matter of worship is reconfigured.

(1) The Worship which Christ Offers

Jesus' statement in Matthew 4:10, alluded to above, has already been the subject of some consideration in the first chapter of this book. There we saw that 'to worship' and 'to serve' were two sides of the one concept. We serve what we worship, and we worship in our serving. We have seen the connections between Jesus and Israel and Jesus and Adam. He stood as the new Adam to offer acceptable worship to God, and as the new Israel to offer true covenantal service to God and thus to bring his blessings to the nations. As the second Adam and as the representative of the true Israel of God, Jesus succeeded where all others had failed. He triumphed in resisting the tempter and walked in continual obedience to God. At this point we simply need to comment on the various ways in which Jesus is depicted as the true worshipper of God. None will be developed extensively, neither have I drawn attention to all the parallel references in the synoptic Gospels, unless there is a particular point to be made by the comparison. All together they paint an inescapable picture of a life dedicated to bringing glory to God.

First and foremost, we note the continual emphasis on Jesus' obedience to his Father. This is evident in a variety of ways. In John in particular there is a strong emphasis on Jesus being the one *sent* from his Father (e.g. 3:17, 34; 4:34; 5:23, 24, 30, 36-37; 6:29) and the fact that this status means that Jesus did not come to do his own will, but the will of the one who had sent him. His whole mission is thus an expression of his service to God, to whom he renders filial obedience and thus worship. Elsewhere we note the stress that Jesus places on the single-hearted devotion to God (e.g. in Matthew 6:24, it is God or money, not both!), and the fact that as the true servant of God 'he did not come to be served but to serve and to give his life as a ransom for many' (Matt. 20:28). This latter thought embraces much material that will be considered in the next chapter, but for now we can simply note that the supreme purpose of Jesus' incarnation was the redemption of sinners through sacrificial atonement. This, pre-eminently, was the manifestation of his worship to God.

We also note Jesus' teaching about, and personal devotion to, prayer. Again it is a repeated theme. We note, for example, the extended teaching on the subject that Jesus gives to his disciples in the first half of Matthew 6, including the pattern of prayer encapsulated in what has come to be known as the Lord's Prayer and the contrast that this pattern of prayer made with that of the surrounding religious culture. We see his own personal prayer in solitary places at key times in his ministry (e.g. Matt. 14:23), perhaps most poignantly in Gethsemane (Matt. 26:36), but we cannot escape the impression that these were typical of his manner of life as he walked with God, rather than emergency actions reserved for times of deep trial (e.g. Luke 5:15-16). He gives thanks to God for the daily provisions of food and drink (Matt. 15:36; cf. 26:27) and prays for the children who are brought to him to bless (Matt. 19:13). His habit of prayer lies behind his power over demonic forces (Mark 9:29) and he knows that the ongoing mission of the people of God is linked to prayer, particularly for God to send out workers into his harvest (Luke 10:2). Thus he taught that prayer should be the normative state of his people and that they should not lose heart in times of trial (Luke 18:1).

In addition, there are occasions where Jesus himself is shown to be rejoicing in praise to God (Luke 10:21; Matt. 11:25-26) and encouraging his followers to enter into his joy in all its fullness (Luke 10:20; John 15:11; 17:13), even in the midst of their suffering for the sake of the kingdom (Luke 6:23). Jesus' actions lead to the glorification of God and to outbursts of praise and worship (Matt. 15:13;

Luke 18:43; 19:37), and he encourages his disciples to see that in their obedience to the Father, glory will likewise be directed to him by virtue of their witness (Matt. 5:16). In Jesus' high priestly prayer in John 17 one of the consistent themes is that of glory: not just that Jesus will be glorified with his own eternal glory, but that he has glorified the Father on earth in his words and deeds, making his Father's name known to his disciples.

The things on which we have commented so far are those which relate to Jesus' attitudes and actions towards God as the manifestation of his own devoted service to him. The matrix of Jesus' life is also shown to be related to the matter of worship. Everywhere, Jesus is shown to be a fully righteous Israelite in the matter of his public worship of God. He is often pictured teaching and preaching in synagogues (e.g. Matt. 12:9; 13:54; Mark 1:21), which was clearly his normal custom (Luke 4:16) – though he taught with much greater authority than those who normally occupied the teacher's chair! He went to the temple at the time of the appointed feasts (e.g. John 2:13) and he taught in its precincts (Mark 14:49; John 8:2) and was clearly at home in the place which was his Father's house from an early age (Luke 2:46).

All of this material has been drawn from the four gospels. In the next chapter we will consider in more detail the matter of Jesus' high priestly ministry, and how the resurrection and ascension confirm (rather than conclude) this office. At the risk of pre-empting the material to follow, we can simply point forward to some of the essential content. The book of the Acts and the various New Testament letters portray a raised and glorified Jesus who continues to serve God as the man in heaven, and to lead creation in its praise. The extensive Christological material in the rest of the New Testament will not let us assume that his worship was just an incarnational 'phase', as though it did not belong to the ontological nature of his humanity.

In heaven, the Son is *still* the incarnate one.[19] He did not put off his human nature in the process of the resurrection and ascension, but brought it to its full glory so that in his human nature he might be the true King-Priest over the whole of the household of God and over the creation itself. In his resurrected and glorified humanity we see the guarantee of ours, and the assurance that all who are united with him by grace through faith would in fact become in eternity what they already are in time: a kingdom of priests to rule with him (so Rev. 1:6; 5:10; 22:5).

Though we have not 'unpacked' any of this material, it is self-evident that Jesus' entire earthly life was one of obedient service of God, worshipping him through every word and deed so that his Father would be glorified. In his continuing heavenly role, Jesus remains as the leader of the worship in heaven, bringing the creation to glory so that it unites in praise to God. In Jesus, we see the worship for which human beings were created operating at its full pitch, enabling him to effect the works of God with power and purity unhindered by the curse of idolatry. He is the great Servant-King who is thus able to bring the full blessings of God down on the heads of his people, and thus to effect the release of the whole of the creation from its bondage to decay. In and through him a new exodus would be accomplished, affecting not just one nation, but all the nations of the earth. The peoples of the world would be released from the bondage of death and the power of the evil one who rules through it (so Hebrews 2:14f.). In this way, Jesus is the fulfilment of the great Old Testament promises of deliverance, preserved in such magnificent passages as Isaiah 25:6-10:

> On this mountain the LORD of hosts will make for all peoples a feast of rich food, a feast of well-aged wine, of rich food full of marrow, of aged wine well refined. And he will swallow up on this mountain the covering that is cast over all peoples, the veil that is spread over all nations. He will swallow up death forever; and the Lord GOD will wipe away tears from all faces, and the reproach of his people he will take away from all the earth, for the LORD has spoken. It will be said on that day, 'Behold, this is our God; we have waited for him, that he might save us. This is the LORD; we have waited for him; let us be glad and rejoice in his salvation.'

(2) The Worship Offered to Jesus[20]

Having set out all the material above, we must now turn to the complementary side of the issue: the fact that the New Testament bears abundant witness to the worship that is offered *to* Jesus Christ, not just that which is offered *by* him. While we might expect this from the New Testament letters (particularly in those passages speaking of his ascended glory) or the Apocalypse, the fact is that it is evident in the synoptics (most plainly in Matthew) and also in John (particularly by association with the divine name I AM). There is a consistent thread of testimony to the matter, so that the worship that is offered to the glorified Son in heaven is all of a piece with that offered to him even in his earthly life.

There are two issues here, neither of which we can address in any depth. The first is what this means for our understanding of the *person* of Christ, the second is what it does for our understanding of God as *Triune*. In relation to the first issue, Jesus is clearly and universally attested to in the New Testament as God incarnate. In particular (in terms of the later theology of the Church), he is the second person of the Trinity become flesh. It is not our purpose to expound the theology relating to the deity of Christ, as the evidence for it is assumed as part of the biblical witness and is enshrined in the great historic creeds and confessions of the Church. Our purpose is simply to give indications of where and how the worship of Jesus is expressed without being drawn into a discussion of the consequent theological issues relating to his person (e.g. the two natures of Christ and their relationship to one another).

However, the matter is important for the second reason named above. The worship of Jesus Christ – in the sense of that which is offered to him – is a 'given' in the New Testament that opens up the development of the later, formal expressions of the doctrine of the Trinity. Again, we do not intend to defend this doctrine, which to any honest reader of the New Testament must appear as self evident, but it is important to note that we could have no real knowledge of the three persons of the Trinity without the revelation of Jesus Christ.

This latter point relates to another theme in systematic theology: that of progressive revelation. Hebrews 1:1-3 sets out the principle: 'Long ago, at many times and in many ways, God spoke to our fathers by the prophets, but in these last days he has spoken to us by his Son, whom he appointed the heir of all things, through whom also he created the world. He is the radiance of the glory of God and the exact imprint of his nature, and he upholds the universe by the word of his power.' We will give some attention to this passage in the next chapter, but we simply note at this point that there is something definitive, unrepeatable and final about the appearing of Jesus Christ. The incarnate Son does not bring a new God into the scene, but a new *knowledge* of God, which was not possible before.

It is clear, then, that the revelation of the Triune being of God could not have come about in all its fullness until the second person of the Trinity took human nature to himself in the incarnation. This event opens up for New Testament believers worship of God in a way not possible before. It is not that the Old Testament saints were worshipping a different God, but that they were worshipping a God who had not yet revealed himself as fully and completely as he has done in the Son's coming. New Testament believers worship the same God as the people of Israel did, but they worship him in the fuller knowledge of his being. We will turn to some of the implications of this in the last part of the chapter, but for now we simply need to note that the New Testament documents do not give a systematic defence of these things because it was the assumed, common experience of all believers. Having said all of this, we now turn to some of the places in which the worship offered to Jesus is recorded, and then move on to see what this means for our experience of Triune worship.

In Matthew's Gospel the theme is evident from the outset. The very first verse identifies key markers to Jesus' identity. He is 'Jesus Christ [Messiah], the son of David, the son of Abraham' (Matt. 1:1). In this short statement Matthew encapsulates identity markers that dominate the themes of the Gospel as it unfolds. Jesus is the promised Messiah, the anointed one who is the heir of the promises made to David and Abraham in the covenants that bear their names. As we have seen in earlier chapters, both covenants involve the destiny of the nations, and both picture the emergence of a royal seed (descendant) to rule over the nations under the sovereign appointment of God. Matthew's Gospel therefore shows how it is that the one commonly believed to be the lowly son of Joseph is in fact the promised Messiah-King, and by way of consequence, how the nations are to be blessed by his reign. The place of his suffering is not incidental to this destiny. Although misunderstood even by his own disciples (and mistakenly taken by his adversaries as a sign of his defeat and rejection by God) Jesus is shown to be the true king, even at the point of his crucifixion, which is demonstrably an event that happens according to the eternal plan and purpose of God. This truth does not exculpate his own people, who were the descendants of Abraham and David, and who should have recognised the time of their visitation.

Given this very brief sketch of some of the theological themes of Matthew's Gospel it is not to be wondered at that we see representatives of the nations worshipping him almost at the outset. In Matthew 2:1-12 the wise men from the east come to worship the new born king, while Herod, the 'king' of the Jews, secretly plots to murder him, using the subterfuge of his desire to 'worship' him as a means to lure them and the infant Jesus to destruction. In

Matthew 14:33, after he comes walking to them on the water in the midst of a storm and after he had rescued Peter (who had wanted to share in the action, but then found his eyes drawn to the waves rather than the Son of God), the disciples fall down and worship Jesus in the boat. In Matthew 21:15-16 the young children cry out in praise and worship of Jesus (much to the disgust of the religious authorities), and they do so in the midst of the temple: the dwelling place of the name, which Jesus himself embodied in their midst. At the time of the crucifixion it is only a Roman centurion and his fellow soldiers who recognise that this man was the Son of God (Matt. 27:54). In Matthew 28:9 the women who come to the tomb on the first Easter morning are met by the resurrected Christ (having been told by angelic messengers of the reason for the empty tomb) and they, too, worship him. The eleven (for by this time Judas had taken his own life) are also shown to worship the risen Jesus immediately before the commission he gives them to take the gospel to the ends of the earth (Matt. 28:17; cf. Luke 24:52).

What is notable in this collection of references is that the bulk of the populace, and as far as we can see almost the entirety of the religious elite, did not bow to him. Those whose voices did not count (the women and the children), and that peculiar band of followers chosen by him to be his disciples (whose voices were likewise rejected) are shown to be the ones granted insight. Representatives of the nations (wise men and a centurion) acknowledge him for who he is, while the rulers of his own nation reject him. None of this, however, undermines his true identity nor detracts from his divinely appointed purpose. He is the Son of God, whether recognised or not, and he does have all authority over the nations granted to him (Matt. 28:18ff.) to send out his followers in his power to bring the nations to share in his worship.

In addition to the explicit material from Matthew mentioned above, there is also an important testimony to the divinity of Jesus (and thus to the legitimacy of worship offered to him) in the Gospel of John. There is no need to expand this here, as it is self evident from the very first verses of John's Gospel, where we see that the man Jesus is in fact the eternal Word of God become flesh. In his free use of the I AM formula (see for, example, John 8:58), as well as his self-consciousness as the one who had pre-existed with the Father in eternity (e.g. John 17:5, 24), the divinity of the Son is clearly portrayed.

In John 12 there is a tacit, but clear, identification made between Jesus and Yahweh, which is significant for the theme. In John, the public ministry of the Messiah concludes in chapter 12. The discourse that takes place in the upper room from John 13–16 is for the disciples' ears only, and the deeply moving prayer of John 17 is Jesus' high priestly intercession for them and for those who would believe through their testimony. John 18 and 19 describe the betrayal, arrest and trials of the Son (in both senses of the word) leading to his crucifixion. The events surrounding the empty tomb are recounted in John 20, and then, at the end of that chapter and into chapter 21 we see Jesus again with the disciples, with a particular focus on his relationship with and commissioning of Peter (who had denied him three times).

John 12 thus stands at a transitional point in the Gospel. The public actions of the seven signs and their associated discourses has ended. The 'hour', which had been anticipated all the way through the narrative (John 2:4; 7:30; 8:20) has now come (John 12:23, 27; 13:1). Moreover we should note the connection here: this hour is the hour of his glory, but it is also the hour of his suffering. He does not just come *through* the cross *to* glory (in the resurrection and beyond), but *in* the cross his glory is displayed, and he himself glories in that declaration of the divine name seen there. Given the connections between the glory of God and his Name that we have examined in the Old Testament, and to which we have referred earlier in this chapter, this should not come as a surprise. God's glory is seen in his actions, which reveal his character. The glory of God revealed to Moses on the mountain was accompanied by the proclamation of the meaning of God's Name:

> The LORD passed before him and proclaimed, 'The LORD, the LORD, a God merciful and gracious, slow to anger, and abounding in steadfast love and faithfulness, keeping steadfast love for thousands, forgiving iniquity and transgression and sin, but who will by no means clear the guilty, visiting the iniquity of the fathers on the children and the children's children, to the third and the fourth generation' (Exod. 34:6-7)[21]

In the cross and its aftermath we see the divine name clearly revealed. In the action of the crucifixion, God has declared his mercy, love, faithfulness and forgiveness of sins by providing the sacrificial Lamb for the sins of the world. And he has not left the guilty unpunished. For those who have faith in Christ, the cross *is* the punishment for their sins (as in Isaiah 53:4-9). For those who refuse and reject the offer of the crucified Lamb, there is punishment for that rejection, and for the sins which they thus retain to themselves.

In Israel's history, the rejection of the Son and the message of his apostles led to the destruction of the city of Jerusalem and the tearing down of the physical temple in which they had taken so much pride, and in the name of which they had crucified the Son of God. They did not recognise the day of their visitation (in grace), so there would be another visitation (in judgment).[22] For all men and women, however, the real fruit of either repentant faith or stubborn unbelief is seen in eternity, a fact which makes the proclamation of the word of God a sobering business. For those who refuse to heed the words of the one sent from God, the wrath of God abides on them (John 3:36).

In John, then, the cross is *the* great hour of God's glory being revealed in Jesus. The signs of the first eleven chapters need to be read, and through them the glory of his name is revealed, to a certain extent, to those who have eyes to see. They all lead up to this great revelation, however, in which the glorious name of God is laid bare in the red timbers of the cross, on which the Lamb of God was slaughtered as the one, great sin offering and Passover sacrifice of all time. This recognition is given added power when we recall the fact that Jesus claimed authority to lay down his life and to take it up again, such authority having been given to him by his Father so that there might be one new flock in the world (John 10:16-18). The cross was no historical accident or event which lay outside of Jesus' power. His status as the 'sent one' all devolved to this point, at which he would *willingly* lay down his life for those who were estranged from God. To echo Paul's words from Romans 12:1-2 (to which we will return later), Jesus is the one who presents his body as a living sacrifice to God on behalf of others, as his reasonable worship to the Father. His love for the brothers for whom he dies, is, ultimately, the expression of his love for God in all his holy purity.

What becomes plain in John 12 is that the ministry of the Son up until this point had not led to an opening of eyes, but rather to a hardening of hearts. The general response to him and to his message had been one of puzzlement, or unbelief, or opposition, or all three. Thus, after his last public utterance to the crowds in verses 35-36 we are told that 'when Jesus had said these things, he departed and hid himself from them. Though he had done so many signs before them, they still did not believe in him' (vv. 36b-37).

It is in this context that John picks up the wording of Isaiah 6, where the call of the prophet is given in the environment of the continued unbelief of Israel. Isaiah had been called to preach, but in the knowledge that the multitudes would have hardened hearts towards his message, and towards the God who had sent him. John's use of Isaiah 6 in this passage (he alludes to or quotes from it in 12:38, 39, 40 and 41) is important.[23] Not only does it underscore the reason for the unbelief of the multitudes, but it forms the setting for a quite remarkable statement. We are told that 'Isaiah said these things because he saw his glory and spoke of him' (John 12:41). In the original passage the 'him' refers to the one Isaiah saw lifted up on the throne, whose glory filled heaven and earth. Here the 'him' refers to Jesus.

> The verbs that have God as their subject in Isaiah are taken here as referring to Jesus.... For the glory of God revealed in Jesus is the self-sacrificing love evident in the Suffering Servant. The scandal of the arm of the Lord revealed in the Suffering Servant corresponds to the scandal of the love of God revealed in Jesus. And as the revelation of the arm of the Lord produced mute disbelief in Isaiah 52:12-53:1, so the glory of the Lord revealed in Jesus has produced disbelief.[24]

The implications of this use of Isaiah in John 12 are considerable. It means that disbelief in Jesus is the same as disbelief in God. It equates the glory of God revealed in Isaiah 6 with the glory revealed in the Son, and it means that the one whom Isaiah saw in that vision was none other than the pre-existent Son, now incarnate in the man Jesus. The wording in John 12:41 is quite strong: Isaiah said what he did *because* he saw his glory.[25] And the glory he saw there is now revealed in the incarnate one, who is on the way to the cross to display that glory in all its holy power through his own bloody sacrifice. For this reason the glorified *Lamb* (together with the one who sits on the throne) becomes the object of the exalted worship of heaven and which draws forth praise from the whole of the creation (Rev. 5).

Given the fact that Jesus is none other than God incarnate, it is not surprising to see doxological material addressed to him elsewhere in the New Testament. The two most unambiguous expressions of this are 2 Peter 3:18 and Revelation 1:5-6. In addition, it is most likely that Romans 9:5 should be taken to refer to him also. In 2 Timothy 4:18

the doxology may be addressed to Christ or the Father (the syntax is uncertain) and while Hebrews 13:20-21 may be capable of another interpretation it is most likely that it attaches to Jesus Christ himself. As well as this, there are passages elsewhere that are addressed jointly to the Father and the Son (e.g. Rev. 5:13; 7:10). Moreover, there are prayers recorded to Jesus, as seen in Acts 7:59-60; 2 Corinthians 12:8-9; 1 Thessalonians 3:11,12 and 2 Thessalonians 3:5, 16 (taking the word 'Lord' here to refer to Jesus, which is its most common New Testament usage), and the whole book of the Revelation bears testimony to the worship of the Son in heaven and on the earth, in time as well as in eternity.[26] It is this new actuality that governs the shape of early Christian worship and opens up for us the reality of the Triune worship and service of God.

3. Jesus and the Inauguration of Trinitarian Worship

The Trinitarian nature of God is revealed to us in the coming of the Son, from the Father, in the power of the Holy Spirit. The events of Jesus' baptism, and all his subsequent teaching about the nature of the Father and the gift of the Spirit, not to mention his own self-awareness as the Son of God in human flesh (as we have reflected on above), all make the matter of the Trinity inescapable in the New Testament. What is clear, however, is that the New Testament writers took the Trinitarian revelation of God as a 'given' so that they did not make it the subject of extended theological reflection in and of itself. This task fell to the theologians of the early centuries of the Church, particularly because of challenges to the biblical witness presented by various groups and sects such as the Gnostics, Sabellians, Docetists, Arians and others. The nature of the person of Christ was central to the development of the doctrine of the Trinity and was the epicentre around which all the main doctrinal developments moved.

The early councils of the Church (e.g. at Nicea, Constantinople, Ephesus and Chalcedon) met to discuss the issues and settle disputes, and from these the credal statements of the Church were developed which enshrined the orthodox position. All the Creeds accepted by the universal Church (e.g. the Apostles', Nicene and Athanasian creeds) and other statements (e.g. the Chalcedonian Definition) have an explicit Trinitarian pattern, and the worship of Father, Son, and Holy Spirit has been enshrined in the worship of the Church from the earliest liturgies onwards.

The study of the history and development of liturgy in the various branches of the Church is an enormous field. Likewise studies of the various creeds and confessions adopted by diverse branches of the Church are important. Both areas have many good resources to which one can turn.[27] Such studies are valuable, particularly for allowing us to trace the lines of doctrinal development and their impact on the public assemblies of the worshipping communities that use the relevant liturgies, as well as the creedal and confessional statements that express the theological convictions and tradition of a particular community. This means that the pattern of Trinitarian worship remains unique to Christianity, and that it could not have emerged without the revelation of Jesus the Son. He has thus inaugurated a new pattern of public worship, which, whatever it might owe to the worship of God's Old Testament people – for example in the use of the Psalms; the reading and exposition of the Hebrew Scriptures; the patterns shaped by Jewish synagogue worship – could not be equated with any of its precursors. Any worship of God that is not fully Trinitarian is not fully Christian.

However, debates about the person of Christ and the nature of the Trinity should not lull us into thinking that the transformation which Jesus came to bring was simply in the liturgy and wording of public assemblies. The New Testament expressions of the Trinitarian framework are more organic than systematic. They relate to the life of the people of God in their experience of community, more than to their life as an expression of the academy. In the New Testament, Trinitarian statements (or at least threefold patterns of reference to God) are found to be pastorally and personally related, and express the matter of worship in terms that are less formal than the way in which they have been enshrined in subsequent liturgies. While not denying that there may be hymnic or liturgical language embedded in the New Testament documents, the context in which they are used indicates that the import was more applied to day to day life and relationships than to the public assemblies as such. We will consider some of the implications of these statements later, particularly when we come to examine the use of cultic language in the Pauline corpus. However at this point we wish to notice two main things.

Firstly, we notice the prevalence of passages that have a threefold pattern in reference to God, if not fully orbed Trinitarian statements. For example, Matthew 28:19; Acts 20:28; Romans 14:17-18; 15:16, 30; 2 Thessalonians 2:13-14; 1 Corinthians 12:4-6; 2 Corinthians 1:21-22;

3:3; 13:14; Galatians 3:11-14 and 4:6; Philippians 3:3; Colossians 1:6-8; Ephesians 1; 2:18, 20-22; 3:14-16; 1 Peter 1:2; 4:14; Titus 3:4-6; Hebrews 10:29; Jude 20, 21; and Revelation 1:4-5 (and this list is not exhaustive) all reflect a clear threefold pattern or use the names of the three persons of the Godhead.

Secondly, we notice that the contexts of such uses are primarily pastoral or relational. The baptismal formula of Matthew 28:19 appears in the context of the commissioning of the disciples for the task of proclamation. The utterance comes from the lips of the risen Jesus, and relates to the task of the disciples to make disciples of the nations to which they are being sent. As they go, they are to be busy 'baptising in (lit. *into*) the name of the Father, and the Son and the Holy Spirit', and in so doing to be assured of Jesus' power, presence and authority accompanying them on the way. In Acts 20:28 the threefold pattern occurs in Paul's strong exhortation to the Ephesian elders who have been appointed by the Spirit to shepherd the flock of God which he purchased with the blood of his own Son. They are therefore to regard the flock as precious, and to love and care for it with all the love and integrity that such self-sacrifice on the part of God demands.

In Ephesians the repeated allusions to the threefold pattern are the underpinning to the whole theme of the letter: the unity of the church and the great inheritance it has in the plan of God. In the Corinthian situation, the gifts and ministries of the people of God are not theirs, but those of the Triune God given for the good of the whole body and for the building up of each part in love. What emerges is a dynamic (and organic) understanding of the nature and implications of Triune worship: not just liturgy, but the action of life as service in and through the Triune God. It is this worship that Jesus came to inaugurate, and which the apostles encouraged among the new churches formed by the proclamation of the word. It is this to which we will return in the last chapter of this book.

Chapter 6

Worship in *Hebrews*

Introduction

In the previous chapter we saw something of the transformation of worship brought about by Jesus Christ. By virtue of his office as the mediator of the new covenant, the things he could do and say with regard to the Temple and the system of worship embodied there were unique. He alone could bring about the transformation of worship inherent in the new covenant promises by virtue of who he is (his Person) and by virtue of what he has come to do (his Work). We saw that Jesus therefore stood as the terminus of worship under the old covenant, and the inaugurator of the worship of the new, in which a new situation obtains. In particular, he has come to usher the church into the blessing of fully orbed Trinitarian worship, and all that this means for their life and relationships.

The letter to the Hebrews was written to a group of people who were still coming to grips with this new reality. They were new covenant worshippers, but for various reasons were deeply tested in their adherence to the new situation into which they had been brought, and were sorely tempted to retreat to the patterns more familiar to them under the old covenant. The letter becomes the object of our attention here since it emphasises most fully the outmoded nature of the cultus associated with the old covenant, and demonstrates how this old covenant cultus had been fulfilled, and therefore rendered obsolete, in and by Jesus Christ. It also has a bearing on the other dimension of the transformation which we discussed in the previous chapter: the paradox of worship offered by and to Jesus Christ and the way in which this releases new covenant worshippers into the full liberty of service in and of the Triune God.

I suspect that *Hebrews*[1] is a book much neglected in the church today. Its vocabulary, context, concepts and themes seem strange to our ears. While it still holds much interest in academic circles,[2] my pastoral experience indicates that for many contemporary Christians it is more or less a closed book. It demands too much, both intellectually and morally, and assumes too much familiarity with the Old Testament to be very 'user friendly' to today's Christian consumer culture.

It is my conviction, however, that *Hebrews* is important for today, and for a number of reasons. It presents a view of the Christian life that takes the issue of suffering seriously and provides an enduring pastoral response, one that is embedded in a wider discussion about the nature of worship in the new covenant. It focuses our eyes on the inseparable concepts of faith and hope and reinforces their eschatological orientation in an age that has relegated such to the discard pile in favour of the immediacy of personal fulfilment in the present. It teaches us about the relationship between the covenants, in an age in which the church is often (in practical terms) Marcionite in its view of the Hebrew Scriptures.[3] And for the theme of this book in particular, it is important for the contribution it makes to our understanding of the development of early Christian worship and the implications of this for the theology and practice of worship today.

1. The centrality of Jesus Christ in *Hebrews*
The most obvious and inescapable feature of the book is the centrality of Jesus Christ. *Hebrews* has the theme of worship at its core because it has the person and work of Jesus Christ at its heart. He is the one who is shown to be both the offerer of perfect worship to God, and the one through whom God may be worshipped by his people. Jesus ushers in a transition from the old to the new, replacing the worship of Israel by fulfilling it. Peterson comments:

> The idea that Jesus' life was the expression of perfect worship, culminating in his sacrificial death for others, [is seen] in the gospels and the writings of Paul. More fully than in any of these other sources, the ministry of Christ – past, present and future – is portrayed in Hebrews as the only basis on which we can relate to God and offer him acceptable worship. What others mention briefly, Hebrews makes central to its message.[4]

The essential argument of the author is that Jesus Christ has ushered in a new era, the era of the new covenant, and that this epoch has already been experienced by the people to whom he is writing. This covenant was promised in the Old Testament (in particular in chapter 8, the author points to Jeremiah 31:31-34), and this promise is the hermeneutical key to unlock the significance of both the Old Testament system of worship and the person and work of Jesus Christ. The author tells us that the worship and accoutrements of the old covenant were given by God to foreshadow the new and that this new covenant has been inaugurated by the sacrificial offering of the new high priest, Jesus. The writer thus sees a direct link between the two covenants, but not direct continuity. As with the transformation of worship of which we spoke in the previous chapter, there is both continuity and discontinuity. The relationship is rather one of shadow to substance. The substance of the present, confirmed and guaranteed by the person and work of Jesus Christ, transcends the shadow of the past. Indeed, the old covenant, with all its cultus, is 'obsolete ... growing old ... ready to vanish away' (Heb. 8:13).

The pastoral setting of *Hebrews* has been much debated. What is clear is that the central issue facing the readers[5] of the letter is suffering, and in particular the suffering of persecution. In the face of such suffering the people to whom *Hebrews* is addressed seem to be in danger of turning back, away from the new, in favour of the familiarity and safety of the old. Lane argues that, 'The purpose of *Hebrews* is to strengthen, encourage, and exhort the tired and weary members of a house church to respond with courage and vitality to the prospect of renewed suffering in view of the gifts and resources God has lavished upon them.'[6] Whether his assessment of *Hebrews* being addressed to a house church is defensible or not,[7] the inescapable pastoral issue faced by them is the suffering of persecution brought on by their Christian confession.

The central place accorded to Jesus Christ in *Hebrews*, then, is not because of an academic interest in his person and work or his relationship to God, but because of a pastoral conviction. Lane rightly suggests that the exalted Christology of *Hebrews* is the author's pastoral response to the crisis faced by his readers. Indeed, 'to be more precise, the readers' lethargy derives from their failure to grasp the full significance of Christ. They were prepared to abandon their confession because they had lost the realisation of its significance.'[8]

The writer's point throughout *Hebrews* is that the appearing of Jesus Christ has rendered such a reversionist abandonment of their confession essentially impossible. They might be Hebrews, but they could not go back to that which lay at the centre of Hebrew identity, namely, Jewish worship and the Sinai covenant with which it was attached. His readers might well go back to the *form* of the old covenant and to its worship,[9] but the point remains that, through Jesus, God has rendered this whole system null and void.

From the very outset of *Hebrews*, therefore, Jesus is 'centre stage'. He is indeed God's final and definitive word (Heb. 1:1-4), and as such he eclipses all other media and modes of revelation used in the past. Because of who he is (as son of God) and because of what he has done (as high priest of the new covenant), Jesus is better than all that has gone before. He is superior to all angelic beings and their ministry, he is superior to Moses, to Aaron, and to the whole Old Testament cultus. He is a better priest, who offers a better sacrifice, and who now intercedes for his people in a better tabernacle.

Moreover, he is a better priest because he, foreshadowed by the figure of Melchizedek, is the great, eternal King-Priest, the Son who rules at the Father's side. For this reason he is able to lead his people to a better city than Jerusalem, to a more holy mountain than Sinai, and to a more perfect and complete rest than Joshua or David.[10] He is indeed the great shepherd of the sheep, brought up from the dead by the blood of the eternal covenant, to cleanse and sanctify his people and present them to God his Father. All this has been done while still being the brother of his people, having assumed flesh and blood to give help to the Father's children.

In short, then, if we take Christ out of *Hebrews*, we are left with nothing. He is the substance of the book and without him the whole reality of the new covenant and the life of Christian belief and worship collapses. The writer, then, does not spare his readers the glory of Christ's person and work nor the demands this places upon them. There is no 'laid back religion' in *Hebrews*. The author expects his addressees to attend to what is being said with diligence and urgency. The change of worship brought about through Christ is irreversible, and its consequences are inevitably pressing.

2. The Worship of Jesus Christ in *Hebrews*

The title of this section is deliberately ambiguous, for *Hebrews* gives us grounds for reading 'of Jesus Christ' as both an objective and subjective genitive. Jesus Christ is at once the one who is worshipped and one who offers worship. The dual character of this identification is implicit in the Christology of the book, and is fully in keeping with the themes we have developed in the previous chapter.

(1) Jesus Christ: The Object of Worship

It has become a truism in New Testament theology to speak of the 'high Christology' of *Hebrews*. Walmark comments, 'The theological epicenter of the Epistle to the Hebrews may be summed up in one word: Christology. No biblical document outside of the four Gospels focuses as totally and forcefully on the person and redemptive achievement of Jesus.'[11] I trust that the link between Jesus' person and work implicit in Walmark's statement will become obvious in what follows, but it is already inherent in what we have seen up to this point. Jesus could only do *what* he did (and does) by virtue of *who* he is. The person and redemptive achievement of the great King-Priest are the centre of gravity for the book, and therefore inform the theology of worship to be drawn from it.

The high Christology is evident from the very outset. In Hebrews 1:1-4, Jesus is described in terms that magnify his status as divine Son of God. The anarthrous use of the noun (i.e. lacking the definite article) *huios* has been much commented upon, but in brief it indicates that he is a new and definitive category, not one son of many. It is a qualitative term, distinguishing him from all that has gone before. Westcott thus says 'the absence of the article fixes attention upon the nature...of the Mediator of the new revelation. God spake to us in one who has this character that He is Son.'[12]

The qualitative use of the noun is emphasised in the statements that are made about him in these verses. He, and he alone, is the 'heir of all things' and the one 'through whom [God] created the world'. Of him alone can it be said that he is 'the radiance of [God's] glory and the exact imprint of his nature', and because he is clearly one with God, of him alone can it be said that he 'upholds the universe by the word of his power'. Whether we follow the argument of Lane that in the opening verses the writer is deliberately couching his description of Jesus in terms of the wisdom tradition of Hellenistic diaspora Judaism,[13] or that of more conservative scholars who see these phrases against a purely Old Testament background of categories and concepts, the end point is the same: the writer affirms the consubstantiality of the Son with the Father. Hughes' work is replete with the comments of the early church Fathers, indicating that this pre-existent, consubstantial view of Christ implicit in these verses has held sway ever since the beginning of the church.[14]

Furthermore, throughout *Hebrews* 1, the writer uses a number of Old Testament passages to underline the divine nature of Jesus, whose person and work lie at the heart of the letter. These emphasise his divine pre-eminence, his eternal reign, and his divine actions and accomplishments. Thus, throughout *Hebrews* 1, 'the Son performs functions which are the prerogatives of God as well as being the perfect means for making him known.'[15] Moreover, as *Hebrews* unfolds, the Son is shown repeatedly to share in divine characteristics. He is described as 'the author of salvation' and the 'one who sanctifies' (2:10, 11); the 'builder of ... all things, [who is] God' (3:3, 4); the one who abides forever (e.g. 6:20; 7:24, 25) or lives 'perpetually' because he is the Son of God (7:3); who shares in the power of an indestructible life (7:16, 25); against whom the sin of apostasy can be committed (6:6; 10:29); who in himself 'is the same, yesterday, today and forever' (13:8); and who is worthy to receive glory for ever and ever (13:21).

Given the themes that we have seen in the chapters devoted to the worship of God in the Old Testament, it should be self-evident that these things could only be said of the one who is, himself, divine. Because of his divine nature, it is fitting, therefore that Jesus be the object of worship. The angels of God are said to worship him (Heb. 1:6), and they are his ministering spirits (1:14). Believers are urged to cry out to him in their hour of need (4:15ff.), and to make him the object of their faith and devotion (12:2), while recognising that his place at the right hand of God and his divine nature/title of 'Son' makes his priesthood not only sympathetic to their needs, but divinely powerful to meet them.

In Larry Hurtado's fine book, *At the Origins of Christian Worship*, we are reminded of the remarkable character of early Christian devotion. The book draws on the full range of the New Testament documents to build its argument, and demonstrates the remarkable consistency of the earliest Christians' devotion to Christ. Across the immense diversity of races, religious backgrounds, geographical locations and historical situations of the early Christian communities, their worship was distinctive. This distinction had to do specifically with the devotion offered to Christ, without compromising the monotheism fundamental to the Old Testament. What applies to the New Testament as a whole applies no less to Hebrews:

what we have is a binitarian, exclusivist monotheism, able to accommodate Jesus, but disdainful of any other god or lord as rightful recipient of devotion.... This full cultic reverence which may be described as 'worship' is given to Jesus, not because early Christians felt at liberty to do so, but because they felt required to do so by God. They reverenced Jesus in observance of God's exaltation of him and in obedience to God's revealed will.[16]

(2) Jesus Christ: The Offerer of Worship

Despite the exalted position and person of the Son evident in the above comments, the writer does not leave Jesus divorced from humanity. It is significant that this Son (un-named all the way through the writer's first chapter) is first identified as *Jesus* in *Hebrews* 2:9, and with some emphasis:[17] 'But we see him who for a little while was made lower than the angels, namely Jesus, crowned with glory and honour because of the suffering of death, so that by the grace of God he might taste death for everyone.'

This one verse alludes to the wider themes of the Son's incarnation, vicarious suffering and death, resurrection (by implication) and exaltation to the place of glory, and is one of the most compact theological statements in the New Testament. Moreover, this verse appears immediately after the discussion of Psalm 8 in *Hebrews* 2:5-8, which is used by the author to affirm Jesus as the True Man, fulfilling the glory ascribed to humanity in Psalm 8, but which had been abrogated through sin and disobedience. It thus confirms that 'the sovereignty which man has proved unable to exercise thus far is already wielded on man's behalf by the true Son of Man; his suffering and triumph constitute the pledge of his eternal kingdom'.[18]

Hebrews 2:11 is significant, then in this context: 'for he who sanctifies and those who are sanctified all have one origin. That is why he is not ashamed to call them brothers.' The verse implies both the Son's humanity and his divinity. He is one with his brothers, but he is also the one who sanctifies. This phrase ('he who sanctifies') in the Old Testament is characteristic of God's self-identification (e.g. Exod. 31:13; Lev. 20:8; 21:15; 22:9, 16, 32; cf. Ezek. 20:12; 37:28). But this very one is 'not ashamed' to call those his 'brothers' who are suffering under the tyranny of sin and pain of death. This is not a metaphorical description of them, but an actual one, for the Son, who is of right 'higher than the angels', is made lower than them for a season, joining the 'children' in whose 'flesh and blood' he came to share (Heb. 2:14). This action was so that 'through death he might destroy the one who has the power of death, that is, the devil, and deliver all those who through fear of death were subject to lifelong slavery' (Heb. 2:14-15). In order to render such help 'he had to be made like his brothers in every respect, so that he might become a merciful and faithful high priest in the service of God, to make propitiation for the sins of the people' (Heb. 2:17). It is not difficult to pick up the resonances with the events of the exodus here, whereby the Son becomes the new deliverer of his people from the heel of the spiritual Pharaoh, the devil himself. He does so by making atonement in his own flesh (fully in accord with the role of the Lamb we discussed in the previous chapter), while the entire context of *Hebrews* indicates that he has done all this in order to bring his people to a new place of worship. Indeed, the exodus imagery is pressed into service to make this very point in *Hebrews* 12:18-24, where the mountain to which the Old Testament people were brought to worship God is contrasted with the new. They have not come to Mt. Sinai, but to Mt. Zion, spiritually understood.

The one who brings about this mighty deliverance is indeed Yahweh, but embodied in the person of Jesus. The humanity of Jesus is clearly emphasised throughout the book. His humanity is subject to temptation (2:18; 4:15) and such was the force of the testing (in the Garden of Gethsemane?) that he offered up prayers 'with loud cries and tears, and he was heard because of his reverence' (5:7). He learned obedience through suffering and is made perfect (i.e. fitted for the task of being the intercessory High Priest) through them (2:10; 5:8-9), and knew also that he would die as a sacrifice for sin (2:9, 14). He knew, therefore, the problem of mortality, and in particular the problem of judgement. The human body of Jesus had been specially prepared for this purpose (10:10), and he offered himself up through the eternal Spirit to God (9:14, 26). Jesus is thus one with his people (2:14), and shares in the fellowship of temptation and suffering (4:14ff.; 5:8ff). Thus, 'although *Hebrews* stresses the unique supremacy of Jesus, he does not do so at the expense of his solidarity with the rest of humanity.'[19]

We should note, therefore, the strategic nature of the first mention of the title 'high priest', in *Hebrews* 2:17. It is important that we note the delay in the introduction of this important term. It governs so much of the theology of the book that we might have expected it to appear in the very opening chapter. However, Jesus is identified as such only after we have seen his divine Sonship and also after we have been reminded of his incarnation, ministry, death, resurrection and glorification. He is the divine Son become man, to give help to his brothers, *and such help could only come by virtue of him being high priest*. That is the weight behind the term's location.[20]

From this point onwards the author unfolds the cultic imagery of the Old Testament in every aspect of his discussion. In the Old Testament the high priest represented the whole of Israel, the elect nation of God's covenant. The new high priest Jesus stands as the representative of a new elect people of God, and offers worship acceptable to God on their behalf, in the context of a new covenant inaugurated through him. Because of who he is, as Son of God and also one with his brothers, he is able to fully and completely fulfil the role of mediating high priest, representing God to the people, and the people to God.

How does he do this? The writer affirms a number of points about the high priestly ministry of Jesus, about which we comment briefly in the following paragraphs. In essence, however, the entire treatment of Jesus' high priestly ministry is an exposition of the two adjectives 'merciful' and 'faithful', first used of him in *Hebrews* 2:17. Throughout the whole, the writer shows that via Jesus' identification with his people, his sacrificial death, and his ongoing intercession in the heavenly tabernacle he (and the God who has sent him as apostle and high priest) has been merciful to sinners, and faithful to his covenantal promises. The character of God seen in Jesus is summed up in these two adjectives.

Fundamental to the writer's argument is the conviction stated in *Hebrews* 7:12 that 'when there is a change in the priesthood, there is necessarily a change in the law as well'. In *Hebrews* a whole cluster of concepts are inextricably related. Covenant, law, worship, priesthood, tabernacle and resting place all belong together, and in maintaining the integral cohesion of this constellation of ideas the writer is entirely at one with the Old Testament. One cannot have a change of covenant without a change in the system of worship. One cannot have this, without a new order of priesthood. This, in turn, cannot come about without a change in the 'venue' of priestly ministry, and with an appropriate change in the nature of the sacrifice the priest offers. The sacrifice itself, because of what it is (the sacrifice of the Son of God), is truly effective for the cleansing of the conscience.

This means, then, that the eternal resting place of the new people of God must be of an order fitting for the eternal communion such cleansed sinners have with God, brought about by such a wonderful and efficacious sacrifice. Thus the arena of priestly worship is moved from earth to heaven, which is the goal and resting place of the new redeemed community.

The interconnections mentioned in the above paragraph are worthy of a greatly extended treatment of the writer's theology, to which we cannot give attention here, but from what we have seen in the earlier chapters of the book they are thematically intertwined. The point of mentioning them so briefly here, however, is that the worship of the new covenant community *lies totally within this new arrangement and all its new connections.* This is why any reversionist tendency must be resisted and why the eschatological character of the new community of faith is so powerfully emphasised throughout *Hebrews.* We will say more about the eschatological orientation a little later, but we simply note at this point that such an orientation is entirely appropriate to the change which the merciful and faithful high priest Jesus has brought about.

The identification of Jesus as a high priest after the order of Melchizedek (Heb. 5:4-6, 10; 6:20; 7:11, 17), then, does not simply arise from the necessity to counter the objection that Jesus was not of the Levitical line, but is inescapable, given what he has come to accomplish. The Levitical priesthood related to a particular covenant, with a particular worship, to be conducted in a particular earthly arena (the Tabernacle/Temple), which by its very nature was limited in what it could accomplish.

By contrast, the blood of the new high priest actually removes sin once and for all (9:12-14, 15-22; 10:19, 29; 12:24; 13:12), precisely because he was the unblemished sacrifice for sin that alone is effective (so 7:27; 9:14, 28). He is a priest of a new order, a King-Priest who is also a Priest-Sacrifice, and for this reason his atoning death is unrepeatable (7:27; 9:24-28; 10:10-14). And because he shares in the power of an indestructible life he lives forever to intercede for his people at God's right hand. This place, being the very place of absolute power, also guarantees his ability to come to the aid of his people in the midst of their suffering. He is able not simply to sympathise with them, but to intervene effectively for them in a way that no earthly high priest could or can.

J. B. Torrance is one who has made much of the high priestly mediation of Christ. Indeed it is the dominant theme in all his work. The article appearing in *Theological Foundations for Ministry* (which was itself a reprint of the article first published in 1970) is reworked and expanded into *Worship, Communion and the Triune God of Grace*, which has this theme at its heart. It is also evident in the work of T. F. Torrance, most accessibly in *The Mediation of Christ*. In short, the emphasis in these writers is on the vicarious humanity of Jesus. J. B. Torrance thus suggests,

In the language of the Epistle to the Hebrews, Jesus is the mediator of the New Covenant (8:6; 12:14). As High Priest, Jesus Christ *represents God to men and represents men to God* in his own person. The Epistle to the Hebrews, which says so much about worship, is significant in that in its High-Priest Christology, it lays such stress on the vicarious role of the humanity of Jesus in worship, ministry, sacrifice and prayer, while always seeing this as the ministry of the Incarnate Son of God.[21] (his italics)

Now while affirming wholeheartedly the description of the role of the High Priest, the concept is flawed by the introduction of the idea of his 'vicarious humanity'. A wider reading of Torrance indicates his (their) view that Jesus took on fallen human nature, and that he did so as the representative for all people for all time, and that this act of incarnational union redeems fallen humanity, exalting it ultimately to the right hand of God. Atonement is brought about by virtue of union with his person.[22] His repentance is our repentance, his baptism is our baptism, his communion is our communion and his worship is our worship, and so on.[23] Thus T. F. Torrance suggests, 'Since in Jesus Christ God himself has come into our human being and united our human nature to his own, then atoning reconciliation takes place in the personal Being of the Mediator.... Thus we must not forget that the incarnational union was an atoning union, in and through which our lost and damned humanity is redeemed, healed and sanctified by Jesus Christ.'[24]

The reason for mentioning these views here is simply that much of the argumentation for their position (especially in the work of J. B. Torrance) is taken from *Hebrews*. For the writer to the *Hebrews*, however, the effectiveness of Jesus' High Priesthood lies not simply in his person alone, but what this enables him to accomplish on our behalf. In *Hebrews* 2:17 we read that his taking on human nature was so that 'he might become a merciful and faithful high priest in things pertaining to God, to make propitiation for the sins of the people'. Both purpose clauses are related. He could not be the merciful and faithful high priest he has come to be without making propitiation for sins.

This concept inevitably implies atoning sacrifice, imbued fully with the Old Testament concept of substitution. His high priesthood 'is not achieved as it were *ex opere operato*, by his act of incarnation'.[25] It needs the sacrifice for sin that took place alone on the cross, where he bore God's wrath (allowing *hilaskomai*, the word translated in 2:17 as 'propitiation', to have its full weight) on the sin of 'the people'. The abiding image of the effectiveness of Christ's priesthood in *Hebrews* relates to the Day of Atonement. There can be no restoration of communion with God without the vicarious sacrifice for sin made on Calvary, where Jesus suffered outside the camp and ushered in a new covenant, at the same time condemning the old forever. The weight of *Hebrews*, then, lies on the vicarious sacrifice of the High Priest, rather than on his vicarious humanity.

Having said all of this, however, we must affirm the emphasis on the ongoing and active ministry of Christ on our behalf, which is also evident within the Torrancian view. Jesus abides as a priest forever in the presence of God, there to represent the new elect people and to lead them in their worship. This latter concept is particularly evident in *Hebrews* 2:12-13, where the author takes up a number of Old Testament quotations and interprets them Christologically.

In verse 12, quoting from Psalm 22:22, Jesus is shown as proclaiming the name of God to the brothers he has redeemed. The context of the Psalm is significant, for the suffering of the abandonment in the earlier section of Psalm 22 is past, with the joyful psalmist exalting in the Lord's deliverance. His proclamation of the name of God (in particular his character as deliverer) takes place in the midst of the assembly (*ekklēsia*), this being the LXX translation of *qahal*. Given the pastoral context of *Hebrews*, however, Attridge is surely right in commenting that 'although the author says little explicitly about the church, he is clearly concerned that his addressees remain faithful to their community of faith. Hence, the ordinary Christian connotation of *ekklēsia* should not be ignored.'[26]

The other quotations in this section, from Isaiah 8:17 and 18 (found in *Hebrews* 2:13), are again significant in their original context, which is that of a believing remnant who wait on the Lord. The writer is surely affirming that the believing Hebrews are the spiritual heirs of that past generation and its prophet who put their trust in God in the midst of their suffering. What is significant, however, is that Jesus is shown to be present with the congregation, bearing testimony to his own trust in God on the one hand, and his identification with his people on the other.

Calvin makes much of this, especially in the face of the battles with erroneous concepts of 'priesthood' that lay at the heart of the reform of the church. 'Moreover,' he says, 'we must notice the functions that Christ takes on Himself, namely, those of declaring the Name of God, which began to be done in the preaching of the Gospel, and continues daily in the pastoral ministry…. This ought to add not a little to our respect for the Gospel, that we must think of it as told not so much by men themselves as by Christ with their lips.' A little later in the same place he says that Christ not only 'heeds our praise', but also is 'chief Conductor of our worship'.[27]

The writer to the Hebrews, then, presents us with a view of worship tied to the transition from one covenant to the next, which is centrally and inescapably related to the transition of priesthood. In the new covenant community there are no piacular sacrifices, for Jesus has been the one eternal, efficacious Sacrifice for his people. There is no sacerdotal priesthood among men on the earth, for Jesus is the one, great High Priest who abides forever to intercede at the right hand of the Majesty on high. There is no earthly temple, for it has been superseded by the work of Christ, who has fulfilled all its symbolic actions once and for all. This is the new worship of the new era into which the Hebrews have been ushered. The implications of turning away from the worship of the new covenant are more serious than turning away from the worship associated with the old. That turning, at least, had its own biblical logic: the old needed to be left behind when the new had come. To turn from the new in favour of the old, however, would not only be the manifestation of gross ingratitude in the face of all that God has done in Jesus Christ, but it would inevitably leave them in no other position than that of being under the judgment of God. Outside of a relationship with Christ there is no refuge from the wrath to come.

3. The Form of Worship Implied by *Hebrews*
The first feature of the theology of *Hebrews* we noted was the centrality of Jesus Christ. The second feature we noted was the high Christology of the book, which informs the writer's understanding of the efficacy of Jesus' High-Priesthood. It is the centrality of Jesus and the efficacy of his ministry that lies at the heart of the transition from one covenant to the next. We have already noted, however, that for the author of *Hebrews*, there can be no change of covenant without a change of priesthood, and this cannot happen without affecting the shape of worship. The question thus arises, 'What shape did the worship of the new covenant community addressed by the latter take?'

On the surface it seems as though we are told little directly about the worship of the Hebrews who received the letter.[28] Certainly *Hebrews* is silent on issues such as the Lord's Supper,[29] the Lord's Day, the order of the Christian meetings and their contents. There is a possible allusion to Christian baptism in *Hebrews* 10:22, but no elaboration. Perhaps, on the face of it, it is surprising that a book so concerned with questions of worship should make so little of the shape of the worship of the new community.

This, however, would be to misread the intention of the author and the context of his addressees. The writer has no need to write an instruction manual on early Christian worship practice, but only has to affirm the validity of existing arrangements in the face of the pressure to return to the old. The emphasis must be, therefore, on the futility of such a path, rather than on instruction regarding their current and accepted practice. What needs to be demonstrated, however, is the futility of the old cultus and the effectiveness of the new, which being bound up with the person and work of Christ, is by its very nature heavenly rather than earthly. For this reason the theology underlying the lack of Christian cultic activity must be emphasised, and this the writer does to great effect.

There are, however, a number of passages in *Hebrews* in which worship vocabulary occurs, and we need to look at these before coming to a conclusion about the shape of the community's worship.

(a) *Hebrews* 10:23-25
In this passage the author urges his addressees to continue in their regular meetings together: 'not neglecting to meet together, as is the habit of some, but encouraging one another, and all the more as you

see the Day drawing near' (v. 25). This statement is couched in the context of the eschatological hope that fuses together much of the Christological and pastoral material in the book: 'Let us hold fast the confession of our hope without wavering, for he who promised is faithful' (v. 23), while constantly considering 'how to stir up one another to love and good works' (v. 24).

There are a number of immediate observations that can be drawn. Firstly, the writer assumes that regular assembling of the people of the new covenant community for worship is not only normative but important. Indeed, some commentators suggest that the whole purpose of the letter is to encourage this small house group/church to resume attendance at the larger assemblies of the people of God. There is an unusual noun used in the first part of *Hebrews* 10:25 *tēn episunagōgēn* (the meeting, assembling, gathering), which is used in only one other place in the New Testament in this form, where its context is also eschatological: 'Now concerning the coming of our Lord Jesus Christ and our being gathered (*hēmōn episunagēgôs) together* to him' (2 Thess. 2:1). The verbal form of the word can be found in a number of places (e.g. Matthew 23:37; 24:31; Luke 17:37) where it refers to the act of crowds gathering or being gathered together. Attridge suggests that 'it is likely that the author has particularly in mind the assembly of his addressees as a worshipping community',[30] a line also taken by Hughes. Hughes has a special note on the meaning of *episunagōgēn* in which he concludes that the term 'should be understood as simply the regular gathering together of Christian believers for worship and exhortation in a particular place – a practice that first took place daily (Acts 2:46), but subsequently weekly, on the first day of the week (Acts 20:7; 1 Cor. 16:2). The JB [Jerusalem Bible] captures the sense.... Do not stay away from the meetings of the community.'[31]

Secondly, the emphasis on eschatological considerations is inescapable. We will say more on this below, but for now we simply note that the assemblies of the new covenant community as portrayed in these verses were living in the light of the 'end'. The new covenant community does not belong to this world, hence it cannot find its home in this world. The fact that they are strangers and aliens on the earth places them in the line of the people of faith from Abel onwards, and confirms the pilgrim status of all of God's people in the current age. Their gathering together as the worshipping community of the new covenant, therefore, is very much aligned with them maintaining their identity as the community of the age to come, about which the author has been speaking all the way through (*Heb.* 2:5). Their life in the present, particularly in relation to their suffering, must be understood in the light of the goal to which they have been called: the participation in the eschatological rest of God. Just as Old Testament worship was connected to the resting place that God had given to his people in the land, New Testament worship is connected with the eschatological resting place that they have been granted in and through the ministry of the Son.

The structure of the early chapters is significant in this regard. The first chapter introduces the Christ in his person, leading to the identification of Jesus as Messiah in chapter 2. The latter part of chapter 2 is steeped in exodus imagery (especially obvious is 2:14ff., on which we have commented), and then the discussion moves on to consider the importance of the divine rest promised to God's people. In the development of the work the author has retained a direct connection with the sequence of the Old Testament narrative. The exodus itself led people to the brink of the resting place of the land. Rebellion based on unbelief had prevented the people from entering. Now, in a new exodus, the new and better rest is made available to the people of God. Indeed, from one point of view they have already entered it (e.g. 4:3). However, it still remains to be entered eschatologically. It lies in the realm of eternity, and so the entrance to that resting place is, by its very nature, one which transcends any physical location or geographic site. It is entered by faith, expressed in hope. To turn back from this resting place is to forsake the reality to which the earthly resting place of the land was a type. For the Hebrews, such turning back would be an expression of unbelief. In particular it would be an expression of unbelief in the once-and-for-all sacrifice of the Son, and of unbelief in his continued ministry as their merciful and faithful high priest. Any reversion to the Old Testament cultus would be to repeat, in principle, the sin of the old covenant community who failed to enter their resting place.

This means, therefore, that the gathering of the people of God was always with the hope of the future in view. We will give attention to some matters related to this in the following chapter, but it would be fair to say that one of the main purposes of New Testament worship was to assure the believing community of their hope in Christ and confirm them in the faith and love that were the necessary accompaniments to such hope. This was especially significant for them since the appearances of things in the present tended to push them to another conclusion. Where their eyes were drawn to the suffering that accompanied their walk with Christ, and where they were sorely tempted to resile from the marginalisation into which their profession of faith ushered them, they needed to be assured of the hope that was set before them.

With no temple, no priesthood or clerical hierarchy, no (visible) sacrifices, none of the outward accoutrements of formal worship that accompanied all other religions, no visible god and no future (as far as the world's estimate of things was concerned), the importance of eternal hope cannot be overstated. Hope was the life of the community of God's people, and its natural accompaniments (at least in the realm of the Spirit) are faith and love. The worship of the community thus acted as the focal point of hope's sustaining power in the midst of a hostile world.

Thirdly, we must note the emphasis on relationships within the believing community. This is a consistent theme of the various New Testament writers, and about which we say considerably more in the next chapter. The issue is one of congruence. The external acts of worship must be matched by true personal devotion to Christ, shown in love for one's brother or sister.[32] In these passages the positive injunction to 'stimulate one another to love and good deeds' is as important as the negative injunction not to forsake assembling together for public worship. Indeed the two are related, and we see a similar juxtaposition of ideas in the passage we next consider.

On the problem of not assembling together Hughes comments: 'such unconcern for one's fellow believers argues unconcern for Christ himself and portends the danger of apostasy, concerning which our author is about to issue another earnest warning.... It is important, therefore, that the reality of Christian love should be demonstrated in the personal relationships and mutual concerns of the Christian community.'[33] These are not two unrelated items: the gathering together for worship is the gathering of a worshipping *community*. Where the community does not live in the love which formed it, and which will be fully consummated in the eschaton, it is denying its real nature as the people of God.

(b) *Hebrews* 12:28-29; 13:1

The eschatological context of this passage is even more pronounced than that noted above. It comes at the end of an extended discussion of the pilgrimage motif that is so prominently developed throughout chapters eleven and twelve, and which is concluded by the climactic description of the new and eternal Mount Zion/Jerusalem/Covenant/ Kingdom to which the Hebrews have come. The point is made that this kingdom, though unseen, is in fact the more substantial and lasting one. It is the reality which is the genesis of their hope and the basis of their faith. They belong to an eternal kingdom, though for now they inhabit the world that is passing away. In this world the powers and rulers of this age seem to hold sway. In it, those who belong to the old covenant worship structures seem to be secure.

By contrast, the small band of new covenant worshippers seems to have little power and no prospects for a stable future. In fact, the opposite is the case. Their future is the one that is secured, and the testimony of the great heroes of faith (as seen in chapter 11) has shown that the greatest power in life is to look unswervingly at the promises of God. Such hope in his promises empowers the people of faith to be sustained beyond the sufferings of the present in the light of the future. Thus the writer urges them, 'Therefore, since we receive a kingdom which cannot be shaken, let us show gratitude, by which we may offer to God an acceptable service with reverence and awe; for our God is a consuming fire' (12:28-29).

The verse embeds an important term, perhaps better seen if we alter the word order: '... by which *we may offer service/worship* to God, acceptable'. The words in italics translate the one word *latreuōmen*, from the verb *latreuō*, which we have seen earlier in this book to be one of the key terms to describe biblical worship. Worship is the service of God.

Various forms of *latreuō* have appeared elsewhere in *Hebrews,* mainly to describe the ministry of the Levitical priests under the old covenant (8:5; 9:9; 10:2; 13:10). It is also used to describe Christ's cleansing of the worshipper's conscience (9:14). This latter use is important, since it underlines what we have said above regarding Christ's sacrifice of himself being his highest expression of his worship/ service of God. In shedding his blood as the one, eternal and effective sacrifice for sin he is able to cleanse the guilt that obstructs the worshipper's conscience. Jesus' worship thus allows the believer to worship truly, with a conscience cleansed from its attempts to bring before God dead works as a means of appeasement. Christ is the true and lasting High Priest who has offered himself once and for all, who thereby renders all other sacrifices obsolete.

Here, in 12:28, however, *latreuō* is used of Christian worship, and it is characterised as being pleasing (acceptable) to God. This implies that there is a new priesthood, but one now not restricted to a priestly class. The whole community is worshipping, serving God acceptably, especially in the matter of showing thankfulness to God. In the first chapter we commented on the necessary place of thankfulness to human existence and to the heart of worship. Conscious thankfulness to God is the mark of a worshipful heart (as unthankfulness is the mark of an idolatrous one; e.g. Pss. 50:14-15, 23; 86:12; cf. Rom. 1:21-23).

Elsewhere true Christian worship is characterised by thanksgiving and gratitude (e.g. 2 Cor. 9:15; Eph. 5:20; Col. 3:15-17; 1 Thess. 5:18). Here the community is marked out as the community that gives thanks to God, and thus serves him with true reverence and awe. The NASB's 'let us show gratitude' is a good translation of the idiomatic *echōmen charin*, though we would not want to minimise the importance of the concept of grace (*charis*) implicit in the phrase. All true worship, throughout both Testaments, is offered from thankful hearts as a response to the grace and love of God. 'To the grace of God the proper response is a grateful heart, and the words and actions that flow from a grateful heart are the sacrifices in which God takes delight.'[34]

The worship that the thankful community brings is pleasing or 'acceptable' to God. This is a significant point. We have seen how great a thing this is: even to the point where Cain murdered his brother Abel since the latter's worship was acceptable to God and Cain's was not. There are many Old Testament passages that highlight the importance of worship being acceptable to God (e.g. Ps. 19:14; Isa. 56:7), and how one could not presume that because the external form was in place that one's physical sacrifices were *ipso facto* pleasing to God. It all depended on the attitude of the worshipper (e.g. Isa. 1:10-20; 66:1-6). In a real sense, this is the very issue faced by the woman at the well of Sychar: is my worship (in Samaria) acceptable to God? Here the great assurance is that those who have received the eternal kingdom of the new covenant brought into play by the Son are able to bring pleasing worship to God as they continue in thankfulness to him for the gifts, blessings and promises afforded to them in the new covenant.

Should they depart from these, and abandon the great High Priest of this covenant, there is no chance of them offering acceptable worship under the conditions of the old cultus. Abandoning faith in the Son would be the greatest possible expression of unthankfulness. In their current setting there would have been an inescapable pressure to see that the old covenant worship preserved in the cultus was acceptable to God. It had the status of a *religio licita* (a religion accepted by the state) in the Roman world. By contrast, the people of the Way – as Christians were also called, see Acts 9:2; 19:9 – were a small and insignificant group, often marked out for hostile attention. This hostility came not least from the Jewish community who saw the new form of worship of Jesus as Messiah to be extremely heretical (e.g. Acts 9:23; 13:50; 20:3; cf. 2 Cor. 11:26). The fact that their worship was acceptable to God could only be known by faith, and faith rooted and grounded in the finished work of Jesus Christ.

While *Hebrews* 13:1 begins a new chapter in our translations, there is a thematic link between this verse and the preceding ones. In effect, what we see in the material which follows in *Hebrews* 13:1, beginning with 'Let brotherly love continue', is a description of the works of faith that are pleasing to God. The Hebrews' 'choice of the Christian way has consequences for daily living, in love and mutual support, and faithfulness in marriage. This is what it means to be the people of the new covenant, and to allow God to work his perfect will in the midst of his people.'[35]

In this way the teaching of *Hebrews* is consonant with that of both Paul and James. True faith in Christ must result in works of service, such works being seen first and foremost in the deeds of true love. In this respect the writer is completely at one with the call to good works which emerges as a consistent theme of the New Testament (e.g. Matt. 5:16; 26:10; John 10:32; Rom. 12:17; 2 Cor. 8:21; Eph. 2:10; 2 Tim. 5:10, 25; 6:18; Titus 2:7, 14; 3:8, 14; 1 Peter 2:12), and is expressing the wider theology of worship embraced within it. The way in which one serves one's neighbour is counted as a measure of one's service to God. Our worship for him is expressed in our love for them.

What is implicit here is made more explicit in the passage that follows, namely, that the manner of thankful living appropriate to the worshipping people of the new covenant affects the whole of life, sanctifying every aspect of it. The teaching can be summed up as: 'Let us live a life of thankfulness...and by doing so let us worship God. Giving thanks in word and deed and worshipping God are two sides of the one coin. Worship is not limited to a formal worship service on Sunday.'[36]

(c) *Hebrews* 13:15-17

In these verses the writer urges his addressees to 'continually offer up a sacrifice of praise to God, that is the fruit of lips that give thanks to his name'. This is to be done 'though him' (Jesus), and it is immediately connected with the injunction, 'do not neglect doing good and sharing; for with such sacrifices God is pleased.' The following injunction to 'obey your leaders and submit to them' is of slightly less relevance to our discussion, but it does tell us implicitly something of the nature of this early Christian community. They were well ordered and had a clear line of pastoral and leadership responsibility governing their gatherings and their daily life. The shepherding ministry of the elders is an important theme in many of the New Testament letters, and this prominence, together with the role of elders described in places such as Acts 20, both serve to indicate the normative nature of eldership in the new covenant communities.

The sacrifices are described in terms of praise to God and service to one's brother. Hughes refers to the General Thanksgiving in the *Book of Common Prayer*, 'not only with our lips, but in our lives,' and draws our attention to the Heidelberg Catechism, where the whole section dealing with the theme of the Christian life is covered by the heading 'Gratitude'.[37]

Such worship is described as a 'continual (*dia pantos*) offering (*anapherōmen*)'. The latter term is used at 7:27 and 9:28, in each case with reference to Christ. The idea of a 'sacrifice of praise' is found in the Psalms in particular (e.g. 50:14, 23; 107:22), and links with the attitude of responsive thanksgiving we have noted above. This is also true of the related concept of the 'fruit of the lips' (cf. Prov. 18:20; 31:31; Hosea 14:2 especially). Thus the overall thought here accords with that of Psalm 50:23, 'He who brings thanksgiving as his sacrifice honours me.' Thus, the rites of the old covenant cultus were to indicate the reality of a thankful heart expressing praise to the Lord of the covenant. 'God wanted thanksgiving, for that in turn emerged from human lives full of joy; it was the joyful lives of the covenant members, expressed so vividly in the sacrifices and words of the ceremony, which fulfilled in God the richness of relationship which he had given to his people.'[38]

Such passages highlight the profound continuity that obtains regarding the spirit of true worship across both Testaments. It also emphasises why the prophetic oracles against mere formalism and falsely placed trust in the temple (on which we have made comments earlier) were so trenchant: they cut to the heart of the matter of deficient worship by exposing the ingratitude of God's people that lay at its foundation. By way of consequence it also indicates that the issue is one of pride, since pride and thankfulness cannot dwell together. Thankfulness, by its very nature, implies humble submission. Importantly, the thanksgiving offering in 13:15 is to be continual, literally 'through all things' (*dia pantos*), leaving no aspect of life outside the orbit of Christian devotion. A thankful heart is one that expresses itself in worship of God in all aspects of life, for all is seen as coming from the hand of God.

This emphasis is further magnified in verse 16: 'Do not neglect to do good and to share what you have, for such sacrifices are pleasing to God', on which Attridge comments:

> The 'offering' of v15, though not a bloody sacrifice, was still an act of worship. At this point it is the non-cultic activities of mutual love and service that are designated 'sacrifices'…. That God is thereby 'pleased' … recalls the faith, exemplified by Enoch, that was said to be the *sine qua non* of pleasing God (11:5-6). It more immediately recalls the remark about the pleasing service of 12:28. The motif of being 'outside the camp' has now gained another layer of significance. The new covenant community has a cult that is quite outside the realm of the cultic.[39]

We will return to Attridge's comment about the cult of the new covenant community shortly, but note at this juncture that the emphasis on worship in the community of faith is congruent with the transformed cultic language we find elsewhere in the New Testament, for example in Romans 12:1-2; 15:15-16; Philippians 2:17; 4:18 and 1 Peter 2:5, and to which we give more attention in the next chapter. On purely exegetical grounds, I find myself agreeing with the view of Lane, who regards verses 15-16 as 'the theological and practical synthesis of Hebrews', suggesting that

Authentic worship consists in the praise of God and in a shared life of love. It provides the context for the response desired by God to the commandments to love God completely and to love one's neighbour fully.... Every impediment to worship has been permanently and decisively removed. The community has been consecrated to the service of God (13:12) and is fully qualified to approach God in worship. The response of praise to God and the commended works of love are now the only appropriate sacrifices remaining to the redeemed community.[40]

While we have noted elements of continuity with the acceptable worship of the Old Testament, the verses we have been considering in this section are also expressive of a deep discontinuity with old covenant worship. This is clear when we note their surrounding context. The writer has been emphasising that the new covenant community should not become bound up with the dietary laws that have now been superseded by Christ's advent and the subsequent inclusion of the Gentiles into the new covenant community (Heb. 13:9), and that the altar that the Christians have at the centre of their worship is different from that of the old covenant cultus (Heb. 13:10).[41]

Christ, as both Priest and Offering, has fulfilled all that the Old Testament '*ōlâh* (burnt offering) represented, and has thus removed its significance once and for all. The discontinuity is further accentuated in the verses that follow, for the believers are instructed to see their position is now 'outside the camp' relative to the worshippers under the old covenant system (13:11-13). They are, in fact, *not* outside the camp (representing the holy ground sanctified by the presence of God) since they have *already* been brought into God's presence through the sacrifice of the Son, and through him offer up sacrifices to God. However, *from the point of view of their contemporaries*, they are considered to be outside the camp, and there the writer urges them to go, not being ashamed or afraid to bear the humiliation of rejection that this implies.

We would be wrong, however, to assume from all this that the writer to the Hebrews has no interest in the form of the assembly's gatherings for worship, or that the new covenant community is completely a-cultic. To be sure, there is none of the accoutrements of the old tabernacle/temple worship, and no earthly priesthood acting as an intermediary between God and the people, but we would be wrong in assuming that the New Testament congregations did not gather for corporate acts of praise and thanksgiving, confession, prayer, fellowship, and the public reading and preaching of the word of God. We get glimpses of various New Testament communities at worship elsewhere (e.g. 1 Cor. 11; 12-14; Col. 3:12ff.; Eph. 5:18ff.) and we can discern something of the forms of their worship from these passages about which we will say more in the chapter that follows. What about in *Hebrews*? Is Motyer right in his suggestion that '"Worship" is ... remarkably *absent* from Hebrews. There is no clear reference to the eucharist, and the 'meeting together' which they are urged not to neglect is for the purpose of mutual encouragement rather than 'worship'"?[42]

Richard Longenecker has recently argued for widespread evidence of confessional material in the New Testament documents. In *New Wind Into Fresh Wineskins: Contextualizing the Early Christian Confessions*, he argues that the New Testament gospel proclamation (often expressed by the earliest Christians in the form of confessions) was contextualized by the New Testament writers as they needed to deal with specific pastoral situations. They thus drew into their argument material familiar to the worshippers to deal with particular theological aberrations or to address the mind-sets of particular groups. Longenecker's line is in accord with the approach of Wu, who argues that 'creedal confession in the early Christian communities are all Christocentric and are designed for the presentation, identification and defence of this new faith'.[43]

Longenecker uses modified and expanded form criticism criteria[44] to identify such confessional elements. Using this approach, he argues for confessional material being directly incorporated into *Hebrews* 1:3 and 5:7-9, with possible echoes of confessional material in 4:12-13. While suggesting that it is now impossible to reconstruct the 'precise contents' of the confession(s) or the 'original social setting' in which the confessions were made (i.e. the form of the community's worship), Attridge suggests that the writer 'bases his Christology on the proclaimed faith of the community addressed. This proclaimed faith would probably have included the affirmations found in the first two chapters of Hebrews.'[45]

In addition, we cannot ignore the nature of the document itself. We have already commented briefly on the genre of *Hebrews*, which does not neatly fit into the category of an epistle and identifies itself as a 'word of exhortation' (13:22). It seems, however, that the word of exhortation has been completed at 13:17, (or possibly 13:19) and then finalised by the magnificent benediction in 13:20-21. What is implicit here is a pattern of worship. The congregation, it seems, was assembled to hear this document read out. The writer expected them to be gathered, and expected, as would have been the case had he been there in person, to announce the benediction over them. In addition, the genre of the book emphasises the particular power of the spoken word of God.

> The writer expressly declares in Heb. 13:22 that his 'word of exhortation' has been reduced to writing. As such, it is available for study to a modern reader, taking on a life of its own independent of the audience for whom it was written. But it is clear that this was not the writer's intention. It is also clear that the writer would have preferred to have spoken directly with the men and women he addressed (Heb. 13:19, 23). In the realm of oral speech, the speaker and the auditors are bound together in a dynamic relationship within a world of sound. Although forced by geographical distance and a sense of urgency to reduce his homily to writing, the writer of Hebrews never loses sight of the power of the spoken word.[46]

The emphasis on the power of the word is also evident in the writer's use of Scripture. This, of course, has a long history of analysis, and all of the commentators devote sections to it. My purpose is not to defend or analyse the specific use of the LXX and the author's exegetical methods, nor to draw conclusions as to what these might say about the author and his hearers, but simply to note the fundamental assumption. The Word of God written is the equivalent of the word of God spoken.

For the writer of Hebrews, the Scriptures are the word of God (cf. 1:1, 4:12-13) or of God's Holy Spirit (cf. 3:6, 13-15; 4:3, 7, 13; 12:5-7). In keeping with the high Christology of the book, we also note the attribution (in 2:14 and 10:5-10) of Old Testament quotations as the words of Jesus, and the wider fact that for the writer, 'the belief in Jesus as the Christ provides the hermeneutical framework within which the interpretation of the Old Testament proceeds.'[47] The assembly for the hearing of the word, therefore, was particularly important, and an obedient response of faith to the hearing is identified with acceptable worship (as is seen in the discussion of Psalm 95 in chapters 3 and 4). The significance of the connection between hearing God's word and standing in his presence is taken up by Motyer, who argues that 'Hebrews bursts out of those [Old Testament images] and attains a status never enjoyed by Israel: we are 'partakers of the Holy Spirit', we *all* hear the voice of God, and we *all* stand in his presence.'[48]

From the above discussion it seems that, for the Hebrew Christians, their public assemblies of worship were occasions for corporate confession of their faith, mutual edification and encouragement, the reading and hearing of the Word of God, and the receiving of the benediction belonging to Christ but brought to them in and through the Word. Hurtado is right when he says that 'we cannot appreciate early Christian worship unless we keep before our eyes the fact that for Gentile Christians it represented a replacement cultus. It was at one and the same time both a religious commitment and a renunciation.'[49] Though this comment is made in a context other than that of a discussion of *Hebrews*, it is none the less true if applied to the book. Christian worship in *Hebrews* is nothing if not a replacement cultus, by which these Hebrew believers are both expressing the nature of their devotion to God through Christ in the power of the Spirit, and renouncing all alternatives, old covenant worship included.

All of this, however, can only be properly understood if seen in the context of the eschatological framework of thought which governed the writer's approach and which was also shared by the other New Testament writers. We have already made some comments on this in relation to specific passages above, but it is worth drawing out some of the thematic elements of this for the whole of *Hebrews*, since we will then be able to compare this with what we find elsewhere.

4. The Eschatological Context of Worship in Hebrews

The whole of *Hebrews* is constructed in the face of the unresolved eschatological tension of the new era. The theme of pilgrimage is central to the identity of the church, which 'is viewed almost entirely in terms of the wandering people of God'.[50] In this current age – the time between the first and second appearings of the Son of God – the characteristic words the writer uses to describe the Christian life are significant: obedience (3:18; 4:11; 5:8), patience and endurance (10:32, 39; 12:2-3, 7), faith (4:1-11; 10:22; 11:1-12:2; 13:7), hope (6:11, 18; 7:19; 10:23) and love (6:10; 10:24; 13:1). These are characteristics of the Christian life that here and elsewhere in the New Testament (e.g. 1 Cor. 13) are associated with life in the Kingdom of God and with the expectation of that Kingdom's consummation.

In *Hebrews*, the community of believers is at the one time an assembly of 'aliens and sojourners' in the earth (11:18-16; 12:22; 13:14), and God's own household (3:2-6). This community has no lasting city here, nor any lasting place of worship on the earth. Thus, 'The people of God must pass through the wilderness, not seek refuge within the supposedly safe enclaves of an earlier generation's sacred territory. The goal of their pilgrimage is nothing less than the reign of God, which Jesus now shares, and which he holds out to his followers as their inheritance.'[51]

In this time of pilgrimage wandering Gordon identifies what he calls 'cultic deprivation' as a key pastoral issue. In response to this disconnectedness to the cultic worship of their heritage, *Hebrews* affirms the things they possess as members of the new covenant community:

> In Christ the 'Hebrews' have a 'great high priest' (4:14), and as those who have fled to take hold of God's proffered hope they have this hope as an anchor to the soul (6:19). In 8:1 it is again asserted that they have a high priest, now described as 'seated at the right hand of the throne of the Majesty in the heavens.' According to 10:19 they have confidence 'to enter the sanctuary' – by which is meant the objective right of access – on the basis of Christ's self offering, while in 10:34 they have something better and more durable than the temporal belongings lost because they had been victimised as Christians. Even 12:1, in saying that they have a great cloud of witnesses surrounding them ... may be said to contribute to the theme. The final statement as to what the 'addressees' have calls for special attention, because it not only claims that they 'have an altar' but also asserts that access to this altar is denied those who 'officiate at the tent' (13:10). Having made this much of the idea of possession, and even of non-possession, the author makes a final assertion that explains the need for the others, namely that in this world Christians *do not have* a 'lasting city' (13:14).[52]

The new covenant community is not to find its identity and security, then, through the concepts of sacred space and time as they belong to the old covenant. In *Hebrews* these concepts have not been obliterated, but relocated.[53] The holy place is now in heaven, to which the pilgrim community is heading. The holy time is the eschatological rest of *Hebrews* 3 and 4, which remains for them to enter, incipiently now, and fully at the time of the *telos*. Thus, 'Jesus is shown to have gained access to the only sacred space worth having – heaven. That space is superior to any previously gained through entry into the promised land or into the inner sanctum of the cult place. Trusting in this, his readers should not hanker after the lost Jerusalem.'[54]

5. Implications of Hebrews for Worship Today

In what follows I offer only some brief comments, acknowledging the inadequacy of their depth, but highlighting areas which are of fundamental importance for our approach to worship. It would be a very useful and profitable task to tease these out at more length and develop from them some criteria by which we may be able to evaluate much of the material being generated in the current 'worship wars' debates which are proving so divisive in some circles of the church, and this may be strengthened by what follows in the next chapter. However, at this point I want to draw out some of the elements which seem self evident from all that has gone before, and to at least give some indication of the lines forward for our approach to Christian worship in the contemporary setting.

Firstly, *Hebrews* will not let us develop any form of Christian worship that is not rooted and grounded in the person and work of Jesus Christ. This means that we must be diligent to instruct our people in the height and depth of his person and work, in all his offices, but particularly in his office as the great King-Priest over the household of God. We must go beyond the sentimental and emotional devotion to Jesus that characterises much contemporary Christian worship and press instead for a fully rooted and grounded mature faith in Jesus. We must be as rigorous as the author of *Hebrews* himself in presenting Christ to our people, and not let them be unaware of the eternal consequences implicit in either hearing or rejecting his Word. We must present Christ in all his fullness, so that our people are not held captive to a culturally bound and idolatrous image of him, but so that instead they are liberated into the full obedience of life lived under his Lordship.

Secondly, we must press home the implications of Jesus' uniqueness, both in terms of his person and his work. This is crucial in a postmodern, pluralistic age, in which devotion to Christ is one of many options. While the historical situation facing the original recipients of the letter is unique, the principle behind it is unchanged. The true worship of Jesus Christ is a renunciation of every other attempt to approach God. Through him, and through him alone, is access granted to the Father, and this access is granted solely on his terms. This is particularly important for an age in which the cult of the 'Self' and its consumerist approach to life is inherently syncretistic.

Thirdly, and this point is immediately related to the ones above, we must both affirm that the Christology of *Hebrews* undoes forever all earthly notions of priesthood and mediation. This, while obviously having implications for our view of ordained ministry, is also important for other forms of Christian ministry, counselling not least among them. It is my observation that men and women are increasingly taking on themselves mediatorial functions in his name that do not enhance but inhibit faith in Christ. Men and women must not be cast back upon themselves, their own resources, or those of another human being on whom they become dependent. Instead they must be directed to Christ in all his fullness.

Fourthly, the Christology of *Hebrews* also undoes forever any notion of mystical communion with God. By this, I mean that communion which bypasses Christ to have a direct experience of divine enlightenment, or some numinous spiritual feeling. This is important when we see many contemporary worship songs, activities and approaches which emphasise the inner psychological/emotional state of the worshipper and use it as the criterion to decide if worship has been effective or not. *Hebrews* will not let us replace the mediation of Christ with the mediation of the worship leader who is able to engender an affective response, which is then interpreted as direct communion with God.

Fifthly, we must do all we can in our worship services to emphasise the eschatological tension in which we live. The church is still a pilgrim people, but in many instances it does not realise this. *Hebrews* will never let us be satisfied with an approach to life and worship which seeks to make this world our home and to live in it as comfortably as possible. Where such a climate develops, the deeds of faith, hope and love, and the obedience of faith of which these speak, are all diminished. Only in the light of such a sustained and insistent eschatological orientation as *Hebrews* has, can the church really find its identity and develop the spiritual maturity needed to cope with the sufferings of life.

Sixthly, we must take seriously the gathering together of the people of God and the incredible power of the Word revealed in our midst. We have commented on the connection between worship and power in other places, but in *Hebrews* the matter is brought into its full pastoral focus. The people of God are empowered to endure the sufferings that are brought upon them by their identification with Christ in their worship of Christ. They are strengthened to bear the world's hostility against God and his people in the context of worship of God the Father in the Spirit. In their assembling for worship, Christ is in the midst of his people to draw their eyes and hearts to the throne of grace, where needy, sinful and suffering people may find mercy and grace to help in time of need. It is only with this fundamental conviction that we are able to proceed with the necessary task of contextualising the confession of our faith in each age and location. Without this foundation, however, contextualisation too easily gives way to syncretistic compromise, where the uniqueness of Christ is lost because of the shame of owning his Name.

Finally, we must press for the same congruence between public worship and private life that is evident in *Hebrews* and elsewhere in the New Testament. We must enable our people to see that the New Testament category of worship does extend beyond the gatherings of God's people for formal acts of worship, but without minimising the power and importance of those corporate acts of worship. The recognition of this congruence and the acknowledgement of the inter-relationship between the two spheres of worship is missing from much that has been written on worship recently, from all sides. Without its reinstatement we will be forever condemned to debating issues of pragmatics on the one hand or style on the other. Neither of these, however, figure in *Hebrews* at all, where the substance has replaced the shadow, and the eternal has replaced the trivial.

Chapter 7

Worship in the Letters of Paul and Peter

Introduction

Over the course of the last two chapters we have traced a path through some of the issues associated with the transformation of worship brought about by Jesus Christ, and in the Book of *Hebrews* we have seen how this transformation affected one of the early Christian communities. In that letter in particular the accent fell on the necessary transformation of worship brought about by Christ, as he was seen to be the fulfilment of all the Old Testament types embedded in the tabernacle/temple and associated cultus. In fulfilling them, he transcended them, rendering them obsolete, and establishing a community of new covenant worshippers. 'Jesus' saving death gives an entirely new meaning to sacrifice as a consequence of his resurrection and the sending of the Holy Spirit. He opened up a new dimension of reality. As a result, sacrifice is reduced to its core from which ethical consequences can be drawn for Christian life and faith.'[1]

In establishing a new community, he established a new empowerment for that community in the indwelling presence of the Spirit and in their spiritual union with him, through whom they could worship the Father.

This community had real continuity with all the true worshippers of God from time immemorial, through their attitudes of faith and obedience. The worshippers addressed by the writer to the Hebrews were encouraged to see themselves as inheritors of that faith evidenced in Abel, Abraham, Isaac, Jacob, Moses and other great Old Testament figures who truly worshipped God. They were thus one with the true people of God through the ages. However, their experience also drew attention to areas of profound discontinuity with the worship of the Old Testament, in that all aspects of the newly formed Christian community's worship had been de-ritualised. All outward accoutrements associated with the Jewish worship practices of millennia had been removed, and replaced by an approach to worship that entirely transformed cultic language to focus on relational categories (e.g. love for one's neighbour), and attitudes of heart (e.g. thankfulness in praise to God). The priesthood, tabernacle, altar and sacrifices of the new covenant community were (and remain) fundamentally spiritual in their form and function. This non-cultic worship brought upon them the opprobrium of their kinsmen, which in turn formed the pastoral setting of the book and which provided real pressure upon them to revert to the worship systems associated with their Jewish heritage.

In this chapter we will turn to the New Testament letters of Paul and Peter to see in what ways these lines are evident within other writers' theologies of worship, and to comment on the pastoral significance of their approach to the believing communities under their care. In particular we will be focusing on those passages which adopt cultic terminology and which use this to express a transformed understanding of worship.[2] Of necessity, the treatments will not be exhaustive. However, the material will be indicative of the normative position of the apostolic authors and their followers, and by establishing the normative position for them we will be able to see more readily some of the consequences for our understanding and practice of worship.

1. Worship in the Pauline Corpus

(1) Worship in Romans

In the first chapter of this book we drew attention to Romans 1:18-32. This is one of the most significant passages in Paul's letters, not just because of its implications for the matter of worship, but for the way in which its fundamental presuppositions influence the whole of Paul's soteriology. Paul's gospel makes sense only in view of the categories of sin and wrath evident in the opening chapter of Romans. Significantly for our current study, Paul's theology of worship is fundamental to his understanding of the human predicament before God and its resolution. The issues that are addressed in Romans 1:18-32 are 'worship' issues. The suppression of the truth spoken of there, and the exchange of that truth for a lie, are alike descriptions of human activities that have illicit worship at their core. They are expressions of the fact that human beings have not given thanks or glory to God as they ought. In view of this rejection the human heart has become darkened, and the characteristic state of fallen humanity is one of 'foolishness' – allowing the term all the moral weight associated with it in the Old Testament. While we do not need to repeat all that we said in that first chapter, it is clear that for Paul there is no possibility of redemption that does not address the matter of worship.

The theological counterpoint to the opening chapter of Romans, with its emphasis on illicit worship and the moral degradation brought about by idolatry, is Romans 12. Whereas in Romans 1 we are given a picture of illegitimate worship that leads to the moral breakdown of every kind of social relationship, in Romans 12 we are given a picture of the integrating effects of true worship, in which the whole of the new covenant community delivered from the power of the idols and brought out from under the wrath of God which such idolatry merits – expresses its worship through love.

The opening verse of Romans 12 recapitulates the whole theme of the letter: 'I appeal to you therefore, brothers, by the mercies of God, to present your bodies as a living sacrifice, holy and acceptable to God, which is your spiritual worship.' The mercies of God are the substance of the preceding chapters. The utter hopelessness of the human situation is portrayed with abiding power in Romans 1:18-3:20, and in response to this wretched and helpless state, the mercies of God are proclaimed in the rest of the letter. Romans 3:21-26 is the theological nub of the epistle, giving a densely packed account of the matter of redemption, which is entirely attributed to the free grace of God and received by faith without reference to one's own merits.

In effect, the rest of the letter unpacks this theological mother lode, indicating that the issues of which Paul speaks are in fact in line with the Law and the Prophets, and showing how they have been the way of life of the people of faith from Abraham onwards. Moreover, this merciful and free redemption is for all: the Jew as well as the Gentile, so that it places both groups into one, new, unified community before God. It is the shared life of this new community, and their response to the world in which they live, that are in view in Romans 12 and the chapters that follow.

By the mercies of God, this new covenant community has been released from the darkness and foolishness of illicit worship to serve the living God in spirit and truth. In a very real sense this is the goal of the process of redemption, just as it was in the Old Testament exodus. God brought Israel out from the bondage of Egypt that they might serve/worship him. Here, God's mercies have brought this new humanity out from the bondage of its idolatry, legalism, guilt, fear, and the judgment of God's wrath, to serve him in a new and living way.

Where both Greek (in pagan worship) and Jew (in temple worship) would have brought dead animal sacrifices to offer, now they, in their own bodies, are living sacrifices with which God is pleased. The force of the allusion is somewhat lost on those of us who do not come from a sacrifice-saturated culture.

By contrast, the culture of the first century Graeco-Roman world was brim full of opportunities to make sacrifices to a variety of gods in a variety of ways. But irrespective of whether the sacrifices were licit (as in the ordained cultus in the Jerusalem temple) or illicit (as in the countless pagan and idolatrous sanctuaries and shrines), the principle would have been immediately recognised. One brought an offering of the appointed type to sacrifice on one's behalf and to entreat the favour of the deity represented in the idol's form. Here the *presenting of one's own body* is the sacrifice. This leaves no place for externalised, or merely formal, acts of worship. That worship that is acceptable to God flows from his mercy, is a response to it, and is manifest in wholehearted devotion to doing his will in the present age.

While the thematic, linguistic and theological links between Romans 1 and Romans 12 are worthy of a much expanded discussion, I believe that it is possible to argue for a direct continuity between them. Paul's purpose, as an apostle to the nations, was to bring about 'the obedience of faith among the Gentiles' (see Romans 1:5; cf. 15:18). Such obedience is manifest in true worship, and is the goal of life itself. We have seen that we have been created to worship God, and anything less than this both demeans us as the creatures who bear his image and belittles the glory due to his name. Here, Paul gives voice to the nature of this new worshipful community: one made up of Jews and Gentiles, who give glory to God in their lives day by day, and who through their bodies engage in worship that is pleasing to him.

Thus, this new worship, though spiritual, is not disembodied. Indeed, the opposite is the case: the spiritual service to God that this community offers is in and through their bodies. 'The bodies are yielded to God as his possession.... This originates a new sacrifice that could not previously be brought to God, for this sacrifice is living and not marked as God's possession by being killed.... They present the body, by means of which they live and act, as a gift to God.'[3] The realm of the service of God is what one does with one's body. This is all encompassing. One ought not do with one's body that which is not in keeping with its new status as the living offering of a life to God. Rather, the believer's body is to be employed as the living, breathing expression of the grateful response of a life lived under the recognition of the expansive mercies of God. It is appropriate to do with one's body, in any and every sphere of life, that which will honour God and bring glory to his holy name. Paul thus takes formal cultic language and redefines it so that 'the sacrifice of which Paul writes demands not the destruction but the full energy of life. It is positive and dynamic.'[4]

The emphasis on the 'living' nature of the sacrifice also connotes the new status believers have been given by virtue of their union with Christ. Once they had lived (or at least, existed!) under the reign and rule of death, which held sway over all men and women by virtue of sin, until the coming of the second Adam (so Rom. 5:12-21). Now they have been transferred into the realm of life, having been brought up from the dead in the resurrection of Jesus Christ who died and rose again on their behalf. Thus, in Romans 6:13 Paul has urged his readers, 'Do not present your members to sin as instruments for unrighteousness, but present yourselves to God as those who have been brought from death to life, and your members to God as instruments for righteousness.'

Here, in Romans 12, that submission to God is characterised as their worship and, to use the terminology from earlier in this book, it is the victorious outcome of the battle for worship. The slavery of sin and its link to the idols have been broken through the death and resurrection of Christ, so that in union with him a new humanity might be raised up to glorify God in their lives, just as he did (and does) in his. Their living sacrifice is made possible because he has rendered himself as the sacrificial Lamb. His life has been poured out to death on their behalf, so that they might live to God in him.

The means by which this re-orientated worship is expressed and the nature of its outcomes are made plain in the rest of the chapter. Romans 12:2, in which Paul urges that his readers 'not be conformed to this world, but be transformed (*metamorphousthē*) by the renewal of your mind', sets the pattern. There is a transformation taking place, one that Murray terms a 'metamorphosis in the seat of consciousness',[5] helpfully preserving the underlying Greek verb. This process has already begun in them and will be completed in the last day, when the adoptive sons of God are all alike conformed to the image of the Son himself (Rom. 8:29).

We have already seen the eschatological context of new covenant worship emphasised in the passages we considered from Hebrews. Here the same situation applies. The 'world' of which Paul speaks here is not the earth, but the age (*aiōn*) in which the church lives. Elsewhere it is the aeon that stands in contrast to the things of God and is the realm of hostile action against the people of God (e.g. 1 Cor. 2:20, 2:6, 8; Gal. 1:4; Eph. 2:2; 1 Tim. 6:17). Paul's point in Romans 12:2 is that this aeon is constantly applying pressure to the new covenant people to be conformed to its ethical, social and moral mores.

Behind all of these stands the power of the 'god of this age' (2 Cor. 4:4), who blinds the eyes of men and women so that they do not see the glory of God in Christ. Central amongst his armoury in this deceitful action are the idols, by whose seductive power he lures men and women into the morass of illicit worship, with all its concomitant immorality. Here the newly formed worshipping community is urged to be aware of their context: they are not 'at home' in this age. They belong to the age to come, and the present age is not to be embraced as their resting place (to use the image so powerfully employed in *Hebrews*). They are in a time of transition.

Until the time of the *telos* (God's goal for the whole creation), there is a constant battle waged against the people of God, the object of which is to deflect them from living in accordance with the new status and standing they have been given in the Son. In this current age, they need continually to learn how to walk by faith in him. At the core of this lies the necessity to have their minds renewed in meditation on the truth of the gospel by the power of the Spirit. There is warfare going on, and one of the prime means that the enemy of God's people employs is disinformation. The world, the flesh, and the devil work in league to misinform, deceive, mislead and misrepresent the people of God, and by all and every means subvert their worship. But 'since the life, death and resurrection of Jesus, "this age" can no longer be the regulative principle of life for those who have died and been raised with Jesus (vi.3ff.)'.[6] The regulative principle for their life must be the age to come, the nature of which has already been revealed in Christ, and the power of which has already been loosed in their hearts by virtue of their union with him.

In this age, therefore, the renewal of the mind leads to transformed actions by which God is acceptably worshipped. Whereas in

Romans 1:18-32 the exchange was negative: the truth for a lie; here it is positive. Whereas that first, sinful, exchange of worship led to darkness of mind and heart, so that 'professing to be wise, they became fools', here the new transformation has the opposite effect: believers may now know 'the will of God, what is good and acceptable and perfect' (Rom. 12:2; cf. Eph. 5:17). They have had the scales lifted from their eyes, and their minds have been opened by the mercies of God to see, and to long to do, the will of God. What follows is the detailed advice and instruction on what this will is and what believers are to do as members of the new covenant, worshipping community.[7] The injunctions contained here are the substance of true worship since they are the expression of the love of God in action in the world. The emphasis in the rest of Romans 12 is on the actions of love that mark out the obedient community of God, and which lead to the edification of God's household. Whether it be the use of the various gifts of the Spirit in the body (12:3-8), or the unfeigned simplicity of love and its generosity (12:9-13), or the treatment of one's enemies (12:14-21), each and all are to use their bodies in these various situations to bring glory to God in their worship of him.

The transformed cultic terminology of Romans 12:1 is echoed with some force in Romans 15:16. Here Paul describes his own mission and commissioning: 'to be a minister (*leitourgos*) of Christ Jesus to the Gentiles in the priestly service (*hierourgounta*) of the gospel of God, so that the offering (*prosphora*) of the Gentiles may be acceptable, sanctified (*hēgiasmenē*) by the Holy Spirit.' Schreiner speaks of the 'piling up of cultic terms' that cannot but be deliberate,[8] and which would have been confronting to both Jews and Gentiles in their respective understandings of worship. Universally, men and women went to sacred places to offer worship.

Here, Paul's ministry as an apostle – especially his commission to bring the once ostracised Gentiles into the family of God – *is* his worship to God. Not only was his priestly ministry 'radically different because it was conducted in the world, rather than in some sacred place', but also it is clear that 'the breaking down of the distinction between the sacred and the profane was part of the breaking down of the division between those two groups within humanity'.[9] In and through the ministry of the apostolic gospel, the barrier of division that had stood physically between the Gentiles and the Jews in the temple precincts had been totally removed (see Eph. 2:11-22). The Jews had been brought out from the holy space of the temple, and the Gentiles had been liberated from the exile of the outer courts, and both had been brought into the very presence of God by virtue of their union with the Son in whom they had come to believe. It is truly appropriate that priestly language be used to describe this holy task of redemption and reconciliation.

The comments we have made above should not be misinterpreted to mean that the gathering together of the people of God in public assembly is not important. Neither Paul nor the writer to the Hebrews would countenance such decontextualised individualism! However, the above material does press forcibly the point that the New Testament radically altered the language and categories of worship to orientate them along lines that are both personal and relational.[10] This is what the Lord had come to establish: a temple of *living* stones, where each is organically united to the other. The new temple, itself, worships God. The people of God in the New Testament do not *go to* the house of God to worship, they *are* the house of God at worship. And as they present their bodies as living sacrifices in the loving service of brother (and enemy!) day by day, praise ascends to God through them.

(2) 2 Corinthians 9:12

This verse falls within a larger discussion about Christian giving. In the chapter immediately preceding this one, Paul has been speaking to the Corinthian Christians about the abounding generosity of another congregation (the Macedonians) whom Paul uses by way of an illustration of the practical outflow of the grace of God in caring for the needs of others. Of the Macedonians he says that 'in a severe test of affliction, their abundance of joy and their extreme poverty have overflowed in a wealth of generosity on their part' (2 Cor. 8:2). Here he is referring to the immense generosity shown by the Macedonian believers in their desire to help the impoverished and famine-stricken church in Jerusalem. Despite their own, not inconsiderable, suffering for the sake of the gospel, they were 'begging us [i.e. Paul and his companions] earnestly for the favor of taking part in the relief (lit. 'service' *diakonia*) of the saints' (2 Cor. 8:4).

Such a spirit of generosity was all the more commendable because of its source. Says Paul, 'they gave themselves first to the Lord and then by the will of God to us' (2 Cor. 8:5). The point of this description is to urge the Corinthian believers to continue in the task that they had also begun in terms of contributing to the needs of the poorer, Jerusalem congregation (2 Cor. 8:6ff.). The ultimate example for such giving, however, is not another congregation, but the Lord himself: 'For you know the grace of our Lord Jesus Christ, that though he was rich, yet for your sake he became poor, so that you by his poverty might become rich' (2 Cor. 8:9). The initial work had been alluded to in 1 Corinthians 16:1ff., and now that Titus had been sent to the Corinthian congregation the matter needed to be revived (2 Cor. 8:6).

There is a network of allusions and references in other parts of the New Testament to the commonly shared task of caring for the poor, especially other poor believers and impoverished congregations. The congregation at Jerusalem was among the most needy, and it is clear that gifts had been taken to them on other occasions (e.g. the assistance taken by Paul and Barnabas to Jerusalem from the Christians at Antioch, as seen in Acts 11:27ff.). Many years later we read that Paul desires to take contributions from the believers in Macedonia and Achaia to Jerusalem (Rom. 15:25ff.; cf. Acts 24:17), so that the activity does not seem to be a 'one-off' event, but part of the habitual life of the various congregations founded by Paul on his journeys.[11] The extended treatment given to the subject in 2 Corinthians 8–9 indicates not only the delicacy with which the matter needed to be approached, but also its importance. Paul saw the completion of this task as a vital part of the Corinthians' ministry to the whole body of Christ, and as an appropriate expression of their love.

It is not our purpose here to trace the structure of Paul's argument, nor to comment on the theological premises he brings to bear on the discussion. However, what is significant for our purpose is the fact that the task is spoken of in terms of worship: 'For the ministry (*diakonia*) of this service (*leitourgia*) is not only supplying the needs of the saints, but is also overflowing in many thanksgivings (*eucharisita*) to God' (2 Cor. 9:12). What is clear is that the action of giving to support the poor results in thanksgiving to God. 'Many thanksgivings' rise up to him: from those who receive the gifts; from Paul, the other apostles and those with them; and from those who give. The gifts lead to expressions of praise and worship. However, the giving of the gifts themselves is also worship (service) to God. 'Unfeigned charity is in its very nature a sacrifice of praise to God – the answer of our love to His; and it has its best effect when it evokes the thanksgivings to God of those who receive it. Where love is, He must be the first and last.'[12]

The pattern seen here is of a life lived for the good of others. The 'other person centredness' of the Trinity, about which we spoke in the first chapter, is the normative expression of Christian love and service. Paul here urges congruence with the new situation in which the Corinthians find themselves. When they were bound to the idols they were, by nature, self-centred and covetous. Now that they had been set free from them, he urges them to live in accordance with the liberal generosity of God's grace, of which they have so lavishly received. To live in step with such grace is to worship God in deed.

(3) 1 Corinthians 11:17-34

This passage is the *locus classicus* of Paul's treatment of the Lord's Supper. Two things are especially important to note: the context of his comments, and the normative understanding of the nature of Christian assemblies that the discussion implies.

The context is doubtless well known. Paul was writing to the Corinthian church about a number of matters which formed part of their on-going exchange of correspondence.[13] He was also forced to address pressing pastoral issues that had been brought to his attention by 'Chloe's people', i.e. 'members of the Corinthian congregation who [had] first hand knowledge of the situation'.[14] Pre-eminent among the difficulties that Paul had to address was the issue of factionalism. The congregation was fissured on a number of levels (e.g. over which teacher various ones liked the best; who had which gifts of the Spirit; who had the better position in terms of wealth and social standing), but each of these is symptomatic of a deeper spiritual immaturity, in which the Corinthians were being deeply influenced by the culture (and worship) of the world around. While it is difficult, if not impossible, to get at the exact make-up of the Corinthian community and the direct influences upon it, 'what can be said with confidence is that the root of the problem was the Corinthian addiction to the power, prestige and pride represented in the Hellenistic rhetorical tradition, with its emphasis on the glory of human wisdom and its attainment and its corresponding flagrant and flamboyant lifestyle'.[15]

What makes this fissuring even more problematic is the relative size of the congregation(s) involved. There were no large church buildings in the first century, and most activities were carried out in the homes of the church members. Not just in Corinth, but throughout the ancient world, the church met in groups in such homes, with the wealthier families providing space for other members to gather under the one roof. In Romans 16:5, for example, Paul sends not only greetings to his co-workers Prisca and Aquila (16:2), but also to 'the church in their house'. This seems to be one of at least five such 'house churches' represented in the chapter.[16] In 1 Corinthians 14:23 Paul speaks of the 'whole church' meeting together, which seems to imply that there were occasions when the house churches of a city came together for worship. While we do not know how many house churches existed in Corinth, we can assume that even in the largest of houses the number that could be accommodated would have been only in the tens,[17] so that even a gathering of a number of these would not have made an enormous congregation.[18] The raft of divisions evident in the Corinthian correspondence is therefore a manifestation of 'close quarter' relational difficulty.

We are given no exact indication of where or when this gathering together would occur, but it is not unreasonable to suggest that the assembling for the Lord's Supper on the first day of the week was the normative pattern (Acts 20:7; cf. 1 Cor. 16:2). Certainly, this was the order that was continued in the very early history of the post-apostolic church and which has continued to this day. On the basis of parallelism in the language between 1 Corinthians 14:23 and 11:17-22, where the emphasis falls on them 'coming together' in an action that seems to include the whole church, it is likely that the setting of Paul's teaching on the Lord's Supper is the regular assembly of the whole congregation of the city. In such gatherings (as also in the house churches) all social groups would have been represented, with perhaps the bulk of the membership coming from the less well-off members of society (based on Paul's comments in 1 Corinthians 1:26-29), though clearly with a few more affluent members amongst them.[19]

If we turn to what this gathering tells us about the normative nature of the assemblies, we find that the idea of fellowship (*koinōnia*) lay at their heart. In Acts we see the depth and dimensions of the fellowship of the Jerusalem congregation expressed in their self-giving love for one another, as they shared all things for the good of each member of the congregation (Acts 2:41-47; 4:32-37). *Koinōnia* was both supported by prayer and the apostles' teaching (the other elements mentioned in Acts 4:42), but also itself reinforced the power of these things. Prayer and teaching are inspiringly dynamic in the context of true *koinōnia*, where the things prayed for are 'with one voice' and the things heard are embraced readily by the whole community. In this lively context of love, then, 'the breaking of bread' took place (Acts 2:42, 46; cf. 20:7, 11). The 'breaking of bread', which was most likely Luke's term for the Lord's Supper,[20] took place in the context of a shared meal, in which teaching would also have occurred, together with acts of prayer, thanksgiving and praise.

Paul uses the word *koinōnia* frequently in a variety of contexts. For example, it is used of the believers' relationship to Christ (1 Cor. 1:9) or the Spirit (2 Cor. 13:13; Phil. 2:1) as well as to describe the shared action of the ministry of the gospel (Phil. 1:5). Significantly, given our earlier discussion, it is used to speak of sharing in the contribution needed to support the materially poor Jerusalem congregation (e.g. Rom. 15:26; 2 Cor. 8:4; 9:13). This, together with Paul's manner of life as he travelled with his co-workers (as seen, for example in 1 Thessalonians 2:1-13 and Acts 20:17-38) and his continual teaching on the primacy of love (e.g. 1 Corinthians 13), indicates that the normative expectation of Paul and the apostles was to see the depth of the Christian communities' love expressed in concrete forms of *koinōnia*. The love of God expressed in such depth of fellowship was both the goal and the means of the apostolic ministry, for it is the goal and means of the redeeming work of God himself, who *is* love.

It would thus seem that the normal pattern of assembly was a shared fellowship meal or 'love feast' (Jude 12) which was 'the focal point of the common life of the Christian community'[21] and the place in which the *koinōnia* of the community was most commonly expressed. All members of the Christian church would share together in the action of the breaking of bread, the hearing of the word, and the prayer for the communities' needs.

In the light of these considerations, then, we can understand the vehemence with which Paul wrote regarding this issue in Corinth. When the Corinthian Christians were coming together they were, in their actions, denying the very meaning of the assembly in which they were engaged. Paul says that they were not celebrating the Lord's Supper at all, no matter what they thought they were doing (1 Cor. 11:20), for their actions were based on gluttony and greed: 'in eating, each one goes ahead with his own meal. One goes hungry, another gets drunk. What! Do you not have houses to eat and drink in? Or do you despise the church of God and humiliate those who have nothing? What shall I say to you? Shall I commend you in this? No, I will not' (1 Cor. 11:21-22). He reminds them of the divine provenance of the Lord's Supper: it comes from the *Lord* himself, who gave it to his people as a sign of the new covenant inaugurated in his death, and which acts therefore as a 'rembrancer' of him (1 Cor. 11:24, 25).[22] The Lord's Supper also maintained the eschatological focus of the community, lifting their eyes to the event of Christ's return, proclaiming the meaning of his death in the current age (1 Cor. 11:26). The whole event was a proclamation of the nature of the gospel and the grace of God, where in Christ we see that he 'did not come to be served but to serve and to give his life as a ransom for many' (Mark 10:45).

For this reason the Corinthian's gluttonous feasts were the complete antithesis of what the Lord's Supper really signified. The consequences of continual transgression in this matter are severe to the point of death (1 Cor. 11:29-32), and for this reason one must pay close attention to all the members of Christ's body (1 Cor. 11:29). The church is not another social institution, and it is most certainly not a pagan temple where the baser elements of one's appetites might be given expression. It is indeed the body of the Lord, in which each member has his or her vital place according to the various gifts and callings of God the Spirit. Therefore, Paul says 'so then, my brothers, when you come together to eat, wait for one another – if anyone is hungry, let him eat at home – so that when you come together it will not be for judgment' (1 Cor. 11:33-34). Any other practice 'violates both the principle of identification with the Christ crucified "for you" and the participatory sharing in the "one bread" (11:24-25; 10:16-17)'.[23] So great are the issues at stake that the Lord himself visits his people with judgment where the love of the fellowship is jeopardised.[24]

While there is much that can be said about this passage we note the following as particularly significant for our theme. Firstly, the whole section here hinges on the relational nature of the life of the church. Issues of 'formal worship' (as in the congregation gathering together for the purpose of observing the Lord's Supper) cannot be separated from the dynamic love of the community. Indeed, we undertake such separation at our peril, since the whole purpose of the Supper is to 'remember' Christ so that the *koinōnia* of the body might be both recognised and further strengthened in acts of real love. The power and meaning of the Lord's Supper is not preserved in it being ritualised (which was the mistake in the post-apostolic church), but by its innermost meaning being enacted in the life of the believing community.

Secondly (and by way of consequence), there ought to be no separation in our thinking between acts of formal worship and those deeds of love by which we serve our brother. The former are of no value without the latter. This is a theme that we have seen emerging elsewhere, but which is portrayed here with exceptional power.

Thirdly, we notice the radical nature of this de-ritualised emphasis within Paul's cultural setting. This seems to be part of the problem at Corinth. Because the gatherings of the community did not take place in temples or other sacred spaces, the people seemed to assume that the gatherings could be like other feasts that they may have held in their homes. However, his teaching brings us back to the fundamental connection we saw in the first chapter: worship and character formation are integrally related. The Lord's purpose for his people is that they would bear his character, and thus the whole matter of the shape of their worship needed to be the real and active expression of the love of God himself. They were to be marked out by the spirit of grace, patience, mercy, other-person centredness and self-giving love that the Supper itself proclaimed in their midst.

Before we leave this section of Corinthians, however, there is one other observation to be made. The Lord's Supper was an expression of the participation or sharing of the community in the life of Christ. Paul's words in 1 Corinthians 10:16, are taken as a 'given' throughout the subsequent discussion: 'the cup of blessing that we bless, is it not a participation (*koinōnia*) in the blood of Christ? The bread that we break, is it not a participation (*koinōnia*) in the body of Christ?' In other words, the Lord's Supper is a communal expression of the unity of the people of God with Christ, their covenant mediator. The communal aspect is further emphasised in the verse immediately following (10:17), where the symbolism of the bread is applied to the body of believers: 'because there is one bread, we who are many are one body, for we all partake of the one bread.'

There is a causative aspect here: the unity of the body is only possible because of the meaning indicated by the bread. However, what stands out is that the *whole community* belongs to Christ, and therefore to one another (as also seen in Romans 5:4-5, 'members one of another and all together members of Christ'). To be united to Christ is to be united to his people in an organic union where all share in the life of Christ himself, by virtue of their common reception of the Spirit.

The location of Paul's comments here, however, indicate that he is using the shared understanding of what the Lord's Supper represented as a powerful argument against idolatrous worship. In 1 Corinthians 11 he speaks of the relationships *within* the body of Christ around the Lord's Supper, but in 1 Corinthians 10 he is speaking of the relationships *between* the body of Christ and the world, and what the Lord's Supper means for these. In the first instance, the Supper is inclusive in its action: all in Christ must be embraced with genuine hospitality. In the second case it is exclusive: all in Christ must not embrace fellowship with the powers of evil that do not belong to Christ. In particular, he focuses on the matter of idols and their worship.

Paul's attitude to idolatry is highly nuanced, though it is revealed to us as part of his response to specific questions raised by the Corinthians regarding the matter, rather than in a discussion he initiates. He turns to their question in 1 Corinthians 8:1 – 'now concerning food offered to idols'. The situation was pressed on the Corinthian congregation by virtue of their cultural setting. The whole of the ancient world was awash with idols and their various shrines and temples, and Corinth was no exception to this. Some of the most notable shrines in Roman Corinth were those devoted to Aphrodite, Asklepios, Hera Argaea, Apollo, Tyche, Demeter and the cult of the Emperor,[25] though this list is indicative rather than exhaustive. Each had its own priesthood and associated cultus, with the outcome that virtually all meat on sale in the market place had originally been offered through the slaughter house/temples of paganism. In addition, the idol temples themselves were places of social (and sometimes sexual) intercourse, and frequently included the ancient equivalent of a restaurant as part of their complex of buildings.[26]

Paul, repeatedly in this section (8:1; 4, 7, 10; 10:19),[27] refers to the matter of meat offered to, or associated with idols (*eidōlothuton*),[28] and since it was raised by the Corinthians themselves it was clearly an important issue to them. The matter is further complicated by the social connotations related to the discussion. Meat eating was not for all, at least not all of the time. For the most part the rich only would eat meat regularly, and certainly they alone would have been able to afford the luxury of dining out in a pagan temple. They were the ones, it seems, who were purchasing meat (an item generally not within reach of the masses) in the market place and who were also eating at idol shrines and encouraging others to do so, perhaps by hosting them. Thus, '1 Corinthians 8-10 provides further evidence that there were some well-to-do members of Paul's congregation in Corinth, as is shown by their meat eating in home and temple, and that they were causing Paul no end of trouble.'[29]

This wealthy group in the church were robust in their pursuit of liberty, even if they were not well informed about the nature of Christian freedom. From one point of view, they were right. Paul says, 'as to the eating of food offered to idols, we know that "an idol has no real existence," and that "there is no God but one"' (1 Cor. 8:4). It is possible that Paul is here quoting some of their own catch-phrases in his reply, or alluding to some of the statements recorded in the Corinthians' letter to him. Whatever the case, this is in line with his teaching here and elsewhere that idols are in fact non-entities (e.g. in 1 Corinthians 10:19; and from implication in Acts 19:26). In this, Paul is at one with the Old Testament polemic against the idols as vain, empty, inanimate and foolish objects (e.g. Deut. 32:21; Ps. 115:4-8; Isa. 41:24, 29; 44:8-9; Jer. 10:14; 55:17-18; Hab. 2:19-20). The theological reality is that there is only *one* God, and therefore every other so-called god must be a sham deity.

For this underlying theological reason one should give no thought to the origin of meat purchased from the market place or even if eaten in the home of an unbeliever (1 Cor. 10:27). Meat is meat, and part of God's provision for the body to be received with thankfulness (1 Cor. 10:30; cf. Rom. 14:6). Whether it has been sacrificed to an idol or not is irrelevant, so far as its fundamental nature is concerned. The idols thus exercise no influence over the material nature of the sacrifices they have received, and there should be no superstitious attitude adopted towards them or the meat that once formed a portion of their offerings. One cannot pollute one's self by eating meat that has been offered to them, nor can one jeopardise one's holy status by so eating. If there is to be an avoidance of meat-eating (in this context at least), it is only associated with issues of conscience (1 Cor. 10:28-29). Both here, and in Romans 14, the issue is that of love: the one with whom you eat may be offended in their conscience, so prefer them in love, and forego for their sake that which is part of your legitimate freedom. In Christ you are so free that you need not insist even on your freedom!

However, this is not the end of the matter, since Paul also warns against the danger of giving worth to these charlatan gods in acts of worship to them. The idols themselves may be non-entities, but the power behind them is nothing less than demonic. Thus says Paul, 'that what pagans sacrifice they offer to demons and not to God. I do not want you to be participants with demons. You cannot drink the cup of the Lord and the cup of demons. You cannot partake of the table of the Lord and the table of demons' (1 Cor. 10:20-21). Again here Paul is entirely in line with Old Testament theology, where the spiritual powers that energise the idols and their worship are a 'given' (e.g. Deut. 32:17; Lev. 17:7; Ps. 106:37). This does not contradict Paul's comments about the nature of meat and the freedom one has to eat it. Rather, the focus falls on the venue and implications of the eating. What is in view in 1 Corinthians 10:20-21 is the participation in pagan feasts in the very temples of the idols, knowing what this would mean for the associated moral and spiritual entrapment that the demonic powers exercise in such settings.

As in ancient Israel, where the worship of God was exclusive of all else, so it was to be in the new covenant community. He alone is worthy to be worshipped (for he alone is God), and only the worship of God will bring blessing to the people of God (since false worship buys into a spiritual system of destructive evil). God's purpose, from the fall onwards, has been to liberate his people from such bondage, and in Christ he has brought about the great exodus, where, once and for all, his new humanity has been brought out of spiritual bondage to serve him in spirit and in truth. How incongruous, then, to want to have one's communion with God polluted by continuing the connection with idol worship. This is not liberty, but a return to bondage! And it is certainly not the demonstration of liberty when one takes the weaker (and poorer) brother by the scruff of the neck and forces him to eat *eidōlothuton* against his conscience, or so demonstrate one's liberty that one shares in the worship of idols. Such behaviour is clearly not that associated with the self-giving love of God seen in the Lord's Supper, nor in the exclusive right that he has to be worshipped as God. 'There is a fundamental incompatibility between eating and drinking at the table of demons, sharing activities and benefits with them, and doing so with the Lord. These are mutually exclusive fellowships.'[30]

The prime reason for this is that church *is* the temple of God (1 Cor. 6:9), which is the sign of his dwelling with men and women on the earth. In fact, in the terms of the new covenant, the church is the temple because of God's *indwelling* of men and women by virtue of their union with Christ. As in the Old Testament narrative, where God brought out a people to be his own, special possession on the earth, so here in the New. This special possession is in fact possessed by him, so it should give no place for fellowship with the evil and darkness from which it has been delivered.

(4) Ephesians 2:11-24
In this passage Paul[31] takes up the language and imagery of the Jerusalem temple in order to further his argument about the essential unity of the church. The image that underpins this passage is that of the existing temple with which his readers would have been familiar, and the discussion about the enmity between Gentile and Jew is founded upon the separation of these groups in their worship. To move from the end of the passage backwards: the end point of the plan and purpose of the Father is the formation of a new, spiritual temple. This is consistent with the wider New Testament teaching on which we have commented that sees the physical temple in Israel as being replaced by the temple of Christ's body (as in John 2:13-22), and the subsequent transformation of Old Testament cultic language into relational categories. The fullness of the Spirit in the new people/ temple of God is linked to the actions and attitudes of love (Eph. 4:30 in context, cf. 5:1ff.), which in turn is linked to walking with God (Eph. 5:17ff.).[32]

Those who do not walk with God (e.g. the Gentiles who have not submitted to the gospel, Eph. 5:17f.) do not share in this worship, but rather have hardened hearts and darkened minds, characteristic of idolatry (by comparison with Romans 1:18-32). Just as everything that took place in the Old Testament temple was regulated by the Law of God (expressed in the Sinai covenant), so now all worship in the New Testament temple is regulated by the Law of the New Covenant. This is the real and more substantial regulatory principle that governs New Testament worship. Clearly the worship of the New Testament temple is not a free for all, but is expressive of the Love-Law of God who has created the church as his dwelling place, to be his image bearer in the earth.

In Ephesians 2:19ff. the apostle indicates that Jew and Gentile in the church are being built into the dwelling place of God (as was the tabernacle/temple in the Old Testament), and although he does not use the language of 'living stones' the relational reality and unity of the situation is plain. The church *is* the temple: one that is not made by human hands in which God dwells (cf. Acts 17:24). This building of the stones together is through the initiative of God the Father, to whom all have access in the Spirit, by virtue of the sacrifice of reconciliation made by Christ the Son. The question of access to God through the Jerusalem temple was a hallmark of all that separated Jews from Gentiles. To say that now both have free and unhindered access in Christ (Eph. 2:18) is to make a statement of momentous dimensions, flying in the face of multiplied centuries of division. All of Paul's comments, however, focus on Christ, who is the cornerstone of this new temple. The ministry of apostles and prophets is consequentially essential to the growth of the church, being expository of the person and work of the Cornerstone. The defining feature of the temple is the spiritual union with Christ, in whom all growth and edification takes place (Eph. 2:21, 22).

That which provided the difficulty between Jew and Gentile at the temple, but which represented all the other social, religious and historical differences, was 'the barrier of the dividing wall' (Eph. 2:14). The image here probably refers to the wall that separated the court of the Gentiles from the court of the house of Israel. According to one of the pillars of this wall unearthed in 1871, the warning inscription ran: 'No man of another race is to enter within the fence and enclosure around the temple. Whoever is caught will have only himself to thank for the death which follows.'[33] The real nature of this barrier, however, was spiritual rather than physical. The barrier wall represented the gulf between Jew and Gentile as embodied in the covenant(s), law and its associated worship. The epithets 'circumcision' and 'uncircumcision' (2:11) operated as short hand titles to indicate the vast chasm that stood between Gentile and Jew.[34]

While the plan and purpose of God has been orientated to all the nations from the beginning, it is clear that Old Testament Israel was God's chosen people of the earth, as his *'am segullah*. In being the object of his gracious choice, Israel possessed gifts and a status not shared by the rest of the nations (Eph. 2:12; cf. Rom. 9:4-5). There was a vast difference between Jew and Gentile, as is clearly spelled out in Ephesians 2:12. The very act of circumcision indicated that Israel shared in the promises made to Abraham. The Gentiles' position ('the uncircumcised') is expressed in the bleakest terms, which serve to emphasize the contrast with their current situation in the church.

Of all the elements of Israel's life and worship that separated them from the Gentiles, perhaps none was of more significance than the Old Testament cultus. The Gentiles had no access to God, since they could not share in Israel's sacrificial system. They had to stay behind the barrier, while sacrifices were offered by and for the people of Israel. Now, the Gentiles in the church are urged to remember their former position (Eph. 2:11), and see that they have been brought near in Jesus Christ (Eph. 2:13). Where once they had been far off (Eph. 2:13; cf. Mic. 4:3; Isa. 5:26; 49:1) they had now been brought near to God in the work of Jesus on their behalf. Indeed, the one who is designated as the Prince of Peace in Isaiah 9:2 is the One who himself is our peace (Eph. 2:14). He and he alone is shown to be active in bringing about peace between estranged, unreconciled (and un-reconcilable) communities. Both Jew and Gentile have been given the gift of peace, proclaimed to them by Christ himself (as in Isaiah 57:19, quoted in Ephesians 2:17).

How has this remarkable state been brought about? The answer lies in the nature of Christ's work. They Gentiles have been brought near 'by (in) the blood of Christ (*en tō hamarti tou Christou*)' (Eph. 2:13b). For Paul this phrase connotes many things. Through 'the blood of Christ' comes redemption and forgiveness of sins (Eph. 1:7); propitiation, justification and redemption (Rom. 3:23ff.); justification, deliverance from wrath and reconciliation (Rom. 5:9-10); and, by association with these concepts, adoption and the gift of the Spirit (Gal. 4:1-6). In short, without the shedding of Christ's blood, there can be no unification with him, or with one another. The end point of the sacrificial action of Christ is that he 'might reconcile us both to God in one body through the cross, thereby killing the hostility' (Eph. 2:16). There are both vertical (in relation to God) and horizontal (in relation to one another) dimensions to this action.

The language of blood sacrifice indicates that *both* groups needed reconciliation with God. The Jews may have been nearer by virtue of their covenantal status and heritage, but they too needed this atoning sacrifice to be made for them, and they too have only come into the new community by believing the message preached to them (Eph. 2:17). Through this action there is a horizontal reconciliation brought about also. The enmity of the law has been taken away, as

Christ in his body bore its curse and suffered God's just judgment for its transgression. This means that the Gentiles and Jews together were brought into a completely new relationship with God and with one another. The Gentiles did not have to become Jews (this was the error that Paul had to fight in Galatians), but neither did the Jews have to become Gentiles. The new community was one in which a 'cultural meltdown' had taken place to forge a new entity in the earth. In this it stands as the witness of God, as his eschatological community. 'If the church in Ephesians 2 stands for the overcoming of that fundamental division of humanity into either Jews or Gentile, it stands for the overcoming of all divisions caused by tradition, class, color, nation, or groups of nations. Anything less would be a denial of that nature of the church which [Paul] takes as axiomatic.'[35]

So, how does the shedding of Christ's blood effect this new unification? The answer lies in Ephesians 2:14-15. Through this action, 'the barrier of the dividing wall is broken down'. This refers not to the physical removal of the Temple's restrictions (which was probably still standing at the time), but to the removal of the spiritual barrier that it represented. In Christ's flesh (Eph. 2:15a, here standing as a parallel to 'the blood', as a comment on the cross rather than the Incarnation)[36] the Old Testament distinctions which separated Jew from Gentile had been taken out of the way, and the enmity had been destroyed. The 'enmity' (both in Eph. 2:15a and 2:16c) is only removed in the cross. That which Christ there removes is not simply the hostility of xenophobia, but the nature of the Law as an instrument of separation between Israel and the nations. The (believing) Gentiles have now undergone a true circumcision (cf. Col. 2:11ff.) to bring them into full covenant membership, but not into membership of the restricted Sinaitic covenant with Israel. Through faith in Christ, Jews and Gentiles become members of a 'new man', which may also be described as 'one body' i.e. the church.

> The new 'man' is Christ insofar as he represents and realizes the church in himself. Christ and the church are not thereby identical; the church is grounded 'in him' and should grow into him (2:21; 4:13, 15) and Christ, the Head of the Body (1:22; 4:15; 5:23) remains her basis (2:30), the source of her growth (4:16) and her inner life through the Spirit (2:18, 22; 4:4a). In that he leads the two formerly separated groups of Jews and Gentiles in his own person to a new, indissoluble unity, he establishes ultimate peace between them.[37]

The above discussion reinforces all that we have seen earlier about the mission of Jesus Christ in building a new temple, with a new priesthood and worship at its heart. Here, the dimensions of that temple are universal in scope. It transcends the nationalism of Israel and embraces the nations of the world so that all believers of whatever ethnic background may offer spiritual sacrifices to God. We note, too, the Triune pattern of this temple's worship. It is the dwelling place of God the Spirit, united with God the Son and one in its worship of God the Father. This is not just worship *of* the Triune God but *in* the Triune God. As this new temple of living stones serves one another in love in the power of the Spirit it is transformed ever more into the likeness of the one who created it.

None of this is possible without the powerful action of the grace of God. The temple does not build itself, and the living members of the structure are not united to one another by their own efforts at creating *koinōnia*. They *are* one with each other by virtue of their gracious union with Christ, whom the Father has constituted as the head of the body and the cornerstone of the temple. What they express in the deeds of love and service (which are their worship to God) is the inherent nature of their unity. The works of love do not make the church one, but are the manifestation of the oneness that it has been granted as a gift by the Triune God. So great is the love of God for his people that he not only dwells among them, but *within* them, so that the unity for which they have been created might truly be effected according to the might of his power that works inside of them. For the church that he has thus formed, it is important that love flows unhindered, for this is the matrix of their worship. Thus, the grieving of the Spirit is primarily relational in its expression:

> Be angry and do not sin; do not let the sun go down on your anger, and give no opportunity to the devil. Let the thief no longer steal, but rather let him labor, doing honest work with his own hands, so that he may have something to share with anyone in need. Let no corrupting talk come out of your mouths, but only such as is good for building up, as fits the occasion, that it may give grace to those who hear. And do not grieve the Holy Spirit of God, by whom you were sealed for the day of redemption. Let all bitterness and wrath and anger and clamor and slander be put away from you, along with all malice. Be kind to one another, tenderhearted, forgiving one another, as God in Christ forgave you (Eph. 4:26-32).

(5) Ephesians 5:1-2

The thought of this passage is of a piece with all that we have said above. Ephesians 5:1-2 in fact forms the conclusion of the paragraph from which we have just quoted, which in turn begins at Ephesians 4:25. Throughout, Paul has been speaking of the relational unity of the people of God, and indicates that the grieving of the Holy Spirit occurs when such relationships are not maintained in love and integrity. The implication of this is that should the people of God grieve the Spirit by their lack of love they would not know the full power and depth of *koinōnia*. But this is not all. Old Testament parallels suggest that the concept is associated with judgment falling on God's people (e.g. Ps. 78:40; Isa. 63:10; cf. Ezek. 16:13; Isa. 43:24), and reflects a stubborn heart that is displeasing to him (e.g. Ps. 95:10; cf. Acts 7:51).

Paul's summary of the injunctions is simply expressed, but profound in its implications: 'Therefore be imitators of God, as beloved children. And walk in love (*agapē*), as Christ loved us and gave himself up for us, a fragrant offering *(prosphora)* and sacrifice *(thysia)* to God' (Eph. 5:1-2). *prosphora* and *thysia* are habitually used to describe the offerings in the temple (e.g. Acts 21:26; 24:17; Heb. 10:5, 18),[38] and reinforce what we have seen elsewhere: the self-sacrifice of Jesus on the cross was the ultimate expression of his worship to God, and thus the greatest expression of divine love (*agapē*) possible. What is of particular importance for our theme at this point, is that Paul commands his readers to share in this same spirit of self-giving love, with the implication that this is *their* worship to God. Indeed we have already seen the terms *prosphera* and *thysia* become standard in their use to refer to acts of Christian love and service (e.g. see above on Romans 12:1; 15:16; and below on Philippians 2:17; 4:18 and 1 Peter 2:5).

The other matter of significance here is the concept of 'imitation' (*mimeomai*) that forms the focus of the injunction in these two verses. Paul uses this specific word elsewhere on a number of occasions (e.g. 1 Cor. 4:16; 11:1; Phil. 3:17; 1 Thess. 1:6-7; 2:14; 2 Thess. 3:7-9), and in other places he commonly uses the concept without using this particular word (e.g. in the extended use of the churches of Macedonia as an example to be emulated by the Corinthians in 1 Corinthians 8-9; his exhortation to the Ephesian elders in Acts 20 is based on his own manner of ministry; he urges the leaders of the various congregations to be examples to the flock in Titus 2:7 and 1 Timothy 4:12; and so on). The theme of imitation in Paul is worthy of much more attention, but even from a brief glance at the passages mentioned, and taking into account those which use related concepts, it is evident that it is a powerful part of his apostolic pastoral method. One might be tempted to think that this was because of his unique calling as an apostle. This might explain his readiness to ask people to imitate him, but it does not explain the fact that he praises churches for imitating one another, or puts forward other individuals as worthy examples for imitation. There is no doubt that for Paul, imitation was a fundamental category of pastoral care and leadership. He uses both positive and negative examples, thus providing foundations for both admonishment and encouragement. There can be no doubt, however, that the prime one to imitate is Christ himself, and that any calls to imitate others are subsumed under the headship of Christ. He alone is the one into whose image all believers are being conformed, so he alone is the one true model for imitation.

For Paul, the issue of imitation is linked to living a cruciform life[39] (i.e. one forged by the cross, and shaped into its pattern of self-giving love). This applies both to the suffering that the cross brings, and also the self-giving life that marks true ethical living in Paul's theology. Having considered the principle imitation and example texts in Paul, Andrew Clarke comments:

> What, then, is Paul's model of leadership? This can be viewed from three perspectives; first in one sense Paul's model of leadership (the model to which he turns) is Christ, supremely depicted as the servant of the Philippian Christ-hymn; secondly, Paul's model of leadership (the model or example which he sets) is his own, albeit imperfect, 'imitation of Christ'; and thirdly, Paul's model of leadership (the model which he teaches) is that, in their own imitation of Christ leaders should direct all believers to imitation of Christ, in contrast to the secular models of Corinth, or the *politeia*-dominated practice of the Philippians.[40]

Ephesians 5:1 is unique in that it is the only occasion in which Paul urges believers to 'imitate God'. The imitation thus called for is the action of gracious forgiveness and love, and in some ways parallels the Lord's teaching as found in Matthew 5:43-48. The imitation is set within the familial relationship of believers to God as their heavenly Father. The Ephesians are not simply to be imitators of God, but to do so 'as beloved children' indicating that they are to bear the family likeness. In this case: like (heavenly) Father, like (earthly) sons. Lincoln comments:

> The readers' forgiving of one another, just as God in Christ forgave them, entails their becoming imitators of God. They are to make God's activity the pattern for their lives … It would be incongruous to be God's dearly loved child and not to want to become like one's loving Father. In fact, the new child-Father relationship not only requires, but also enables imitation to take place, as the children live their lives out of the love they have already experienced from their Father.[41]

This is the true evidence of worship: character formation in the image of the God and Father we adore, who has given us his Son that we might be one with him and all his people, and that we might live in such unity by the power of the Spirit he has poured into the hearts of his people. The initiative for all of this lies with God himself, the God of all grace, who desires us to be conformed to the image of his Son (who is the image of God), and sends this same Son into the world to bear the disfigurement of sinners. These sinners, saved by the sovereign grace of God, are then called to be transformed in their daily living to show forth to the world the character of their holy Father.

(6) Philippians 2:17

Without needing to enter into debates about the date of Paul's martyrdom, it seems clear that in writing to the Philippian Christians, Paul saw himself as being near to the end of his earthly life, having run the race that God had set before him, now facing the prospect of his own death as a martyr. Against this background he says to his Philippian friends in this verse: 'even if I am to be poured out as a drink offering upon the sacrificial offering of your faith, I am glad and rejoice with you all.' This verse is replete with the vocabulary of the Old Testament cultus, the frequency of which is better preserved in the NASB's translation: 'But even if I am being poured out as a drink offering (*spendomai*) upon the sacrifice (*thysia*) and service (*leitourgia*) of your faith, I rejoice and share my joy with you all.' The verse is important for what it portrays in terms of Paul's relationship to this congregation, to whom he had given so much spiritually, and from whom he had received both spiritual and material support. He sees his own life (and his impending death) in terms of service for others in the ministry of the gospel, and has no hesitation in applying a fulsome range of worship words to this action. We have met both *thysia* and *leitourgia* before in similar contexts, but the only other place that *spendomai* occurs in Paul is in 2 Timothy 4:6, where the phrasing is almost identical: 'I am already being poured out as a drink offering, and the time of my departure has come.' The Greek *spendō* in the LXX is used to translate the Hebrew *nâsak* and in the Old Testament was the 'technical term for offering libations (of wine).... [These] were not, like the blood sacrifices, an atoning offering, but an expression of dedication to God.'[42] In both places Paul sees his imminent death as an expression of the fact that he has expended his life as an apostle in the worship of God, by serving the Lord's people. His death is not the end of his worship, but an expression of it.

The self-giving love that Paul speaks of, therefore, is not idealistic. He, in his very life (and death) did pour himself out for the people of God. The worship he offers with his body is full and complete, not restraining the service he offers because of the inconvenience it might bring, or to avoid the suffering it might evince. This helps us see that Paul's reorientated worship language is practical in the extreme. It is not worship by good intentions, or by spiritually uplifting feelings, but by the practical actions of self-giving love. In so doing, he knows himself to be sharing in the life of the Son of God, with whom he was spiritually united, and whose power working within him allowed such worship to be offered. This is not worship arising out of Paul's strength of commitment, but that which arises out of the constraint of love (cf. 2 Cor. 5:14). The former is more a characteristic of pagan worship; the latter is uniquely Christian, since it arises from the love and grace of God, and issues in thanksgiving and joy by way of response. It is this worship that had gripped Paul, and for which he expended all his energy that others might be constrained by the boundless love of God also.

(7) Philippians 3:3

This verse appears in the context of a passionate warning (see Phil. 2:2!), and contrasts the believing community with unbelieving Judaizers who seem to have come into the situation to undermine Paul's apostolic ministry and draw the believers away from the word of grace.[43] In contrast to the troublemakers who based their message on the law rather than the gospel, Paul says: 'For we are the real circumcision, who worship (*latreuontes*) by the Spirit of God and glory in Christ Jesus and put no confidence in the flesh.' There is a threefold appellation in Philippians 3:2 ('dogs', 'evildoers', 'those who mutilate the flesh') which seems to stand in antithetical parallel to the threefold appellation in 3:3 ('real circumcision', who 'worship by the Spirit of God', and who 'glory in Christ Jesus'). The emphasis in this verse on worship according to the Spirit corresponds with what we have seen in John 4, in Jesus' discussion with the Samaritan woman.[44] It also ties into the wider framework of Paul's theology, where Flesh and Spirit operate as two opposing forces, the nature and mode of whose operations are mutually exclusive (e.g. Gal. 5:17; Rom. 8:5, 13).

In this section, Paul is stating that the worship of believers is truly spiritual, and therefore acceptable to God, because it is Spirit worship (by grace) rather than Fleshly worship (on the basis of law). The Old Testament background that links circumcision with the state of one's heart before God is not hard to find (see Deut. 10:16; 30:6; cf. Jer. 4:4; 9:26; Ezek. 11:19), and this was clearly a well known element of Paul's preaching and teaching. In Romans 2:28-29, for example, Paul states (as though it were a common way of summarising his gospel), 'For no one is a Jew who is merely one outwardly, nor is circumcision outward and physical. But a Jew is one inwardly, and circumcision is a matter of the heart, by the Spirit, not by the letter. His praise is not from man but from God.' Likewise, in Colossians 2:11-15 Paul equates this true circumcision with believing union with Christ (expressed in baptism), and in which one is launched into a new, resurrection life in which the works of the law have no place.

It is significant that, in the Old Testament, the idea of having a circumcised heart is closely associated with true love for God, expressed in obedience to his law. In particular (as seen for example, in Ezekiel's exposition of the theme in Ezekiel 11:19 and 36:25-27), the matter relates to the rejection of idols and single-hearted devotion to Yahweh. Thus, the promise of the new covenant embedded in the Old Testament looked forward to the day when God would do that which his people had shown themselves incapable of doing: loving him from the heart and worshipping him alone. Philippians 3:3 thus stands in solidarity with this Old Testament line of promise, and indicates that its fulfilment is found in union with Christ, in whom believers are filled with the Spirit of God to enable true worship. Thus, 'the Spirit promised by the prophets ... dwelling within the Christian, gives to the Christian life and power to love so that he can offer to God true and acceptable worship from the heart (John 4:23-24; Rom. 12:1; 1 Peter 2:5).'[45] In the wider context of Philippians, such worship is expressed in self-giving love for others, and robust rejection of anything that would hinder the liberty of grace in the life of the believing community.

(8) Philippians 4:18
We have already mentioned the mutual giving and receiving in financial matters that went on among the congregations of the New Testament. This was not simply inter-congregational, but intra-congregational, as members of congregations willingly gave to those who ministered amongst them. Paul himself habitually worked to provide for his own needs, and frequently also supported those who were with him (e.g. Acts 20:34; cf. 18:3; 1 Cor. 4:12; 1 Thess. 2:9; 2 Thess. 3:8-9). While recognising that he or others could be supported by gifts from congregations where the situation allowed it (e.g. 1 Cor. 9:9, in its context; 2 Cor. 11:8-9; 2 Tim. 5:17-18) it is clear that for many, small, newly formed congregations such expectation of support was impossible. His self-employment was therefore part of his service to God, by thus allowing the gospel to be preached without price and by ensuring that there could be no charge of selfish greed brought against him which would tarnish the gospel itself.

It is clear that the Philippians had a history of contributing to his needs in support of the gospel (Phil. 4:14-16), and here Paul describes such on-going support as he has just received from them while in prison in worship terms: 'I have received full payment, and more. I am well supplied, having received from Epaphroditus the gifts you sent, a fragrant offering (*osmēn euōdias*), a sacrifice (*thysian*) acceptable and pleasing to God' (Phil. 4:18). The 'fragrant offering' language alludes to the incense offerings in the temple, and is seen in other places in the New Testament in this transformed sense, both applying to the sacrifice of Christ (e.g. Eph. 5:2), and the ministry of his servants (e.g. 2 Cor. 5:15f.). *Thysian* we have already encountered in the preceding passages, and together the terms reiterated the force of the relational and practical understanding of worship that was normative amongst the congregations. Not only does Paul use these terms, but the context and manner of use here and elsewhere seem to point to a shared understanding of the transformed nature of worship in all the Pauline congregations. It is hard to imagine what a contrast this must have been, for in every other situation worship would have been most naturally associated with holy places, acts, times, seasons and physical sacrifice. Such a new understanding of worship as the gospel unleashed on the world was indeed counter-cultural. It was not just transformed, but transformative.

(9) Colossians 3:17 (cf. Eph. 3:20)
This verse acts as a concluding statement to a longer paragraph in which Paul has been speaking about the manner of life appropriate to the new covenant community in Colossae. In it Paul indicates that the whole of life acts as the matrix for one's thanksgiving and praise to God: 'and whatever you do, in word or deed, do everything in the name of the Lord Jesus, giving thanks to God the Father through him.' The statement at the one time sums up the teaching that precedes it (see more below), but also connects with all that follows it. In effect, the rest of chapter 3 and the first part of chapter 4 give examples of how whatever one does in word or deed is an expression of thanks to God (e.g. in the relationship between wives and husbands in 3:18-19; children and parents in 3:20-21; slaves and masters 3:22-4:1). 'In becoming a Christian the believer calls on Jesus as Lord (Rom. 10:9, 10) and comes under the authority of Christ. He belongs wholly to him; thus everything he says or does ought to be in the light of the fact that Jesus is his Lord.'[46] The whole of one's life is thus the appropriate arena for expressing one's service to the Lord, by living in obedience to him.

Chapter 3 is given over to exhortations and injunctions regarding the new manner of life into which the believers at Colossae have been brought by virtue of their union with Christ. 3:1-4 acts as a theological bridge between Paul's teaching on the person and work of Christ in chapters 1 and 2, and the consequences for the church in chapters 3 and 4. Since believers have been raised up with Christ to a new life and have had their entire destiny sealed through union with him (3:1-4), it is necessary now to live in congruence with their new identity. It is not who and what they were that matters, but who and what they are as redeemed people that counts. They must, in effect, be in deed what God has already made them by his grace. The life of Christ is now their life, and this requires that certain things be put to death or put off (3:5, 8), and other things must be brought to life or put on (3:12, 14). This is only possible because they have in fact *already* put off the old humanity and put on the new humanity by virtue of their incorporation into Christ (as the tenses of 3:9-10 indicate). Thus, how they live is the manifestation in the present of the new status that they have already been granted through God's action on their behalf.

In this, context, then, Paul speaks about the essential unity of the people of God (3:11) and how, as God's elect people, they are to live in a manner in keeping with their chosen status:

> Put on then, as God's chosen ones, holy and beloved, compassion, kindness, humility, meekness, and patience, bearing with one another and, if one has a complaint against another, forgiving each other; as the Lord has forgiven you, so you also must forgive. And above all these put on love, which binds everything together in perfect harmony. And let the peace of Christ rule in your hearts, to which indeed you were called in one body. And be thankful. Let the word of Christ dwell in you richly, teaching and admonishing one another in all wisdom, singing psalms and hymns and spiritual songs, with thankfulness in your hearts to God. And whatever you do, in word or deed, do everything in the name of the Lord Jesus, giving thanks to God the Father through him (Col. 3:12-17).

This passage is almost identical in theme and content to Ephesians 5:18-21, where Paul uses the same pastoral method (moving from theological discussion to pastoral application) to make very similar comments. The Ephesian passage likewise links to a section dealing with domestic relationships (especially the nature and meaning of marriage), and thus gives an indication of what it means to worship God in every sphere of one's existence:

> And do not get drunk with wine, for that is debauchery, but be filled with the Spirit, addressing one another in psalms and hymns and spiritual songs, singing and making melody to the Lord with all your heart, giving thanks always and for everything to God the Father in the name of our Lord Jesus Christ, submitting to one another out of reverence for Christ (Eph. 5:18-21).

It is not unreasonable to suggest that these are common threads in Pauline theology since they were the common issues with which the various New Testament congregations needed to become acquainted. In effect these passages continue to spell out the principle that we have seen in Romans 12:1ff., that the whole of a believer's life is the *embodiment* of his worship. There are a number of points here that recapitulate many of our earlier comments. For example, we see the issue of congruence: who believers are in action is to be commensurate with who they are in terms of their status. They are to forgive as they have been forgiven, love as they have been loved, and show kindness, patience and compassion to one another as they have received these things from God, and so on. How they dealt with one another was a direct reflection of the way in which they understood how God had dealt with them.

In addition, we also see that the actions of their public worship assemblies were for the edification of one another as they gave praise to God. This was the spiritual expression of the *koinōnia* they had in Christ, as their sharing of material blessings was the expression of such fellowship in other ways. As Peterson points out, 'the God-directed ministry of prayer and praise and the notion of edification are intimately linked in the New Testament ... even "psalms and hymns and spiritual songs" (RSV), which are expressions of faith and thankfulness to God, are to be considered simultaneously as the means of teaching and admonishing one another.'[47] Thus, when we gather together in the dynamic power of Word and Spirit, we sing our praises to God and at the same time sing the truth into our hearts. As we share in the public and corporate thanksgiving of such vocal praise, we edify our souls and those with whom we worship. The whole pattern reflects the self-giving life of the Triune God, which forms what earlier we called the grammar of our worship. In passages such as these we see the whole community worshipping in and through the gracious action of the Triune God, and bearing more fully his image in the context of their self-giving service of one another.

What is particularly evident within Paul's theology in passages like these is the emphasis on thanksgiving (Col. 3: 15, 16, 17; Eph. 5:20), the frequency of which theme sets Paul's writings apart in the ancient world,[48] and which we have already seen lies at the heart of true worship. Indeed, the giving of thanks is the mark of the new covenant community that sets it apart from the world: 'Let there be no filthiness nor foolish talk nor crude joking, which are out of place, but instead let there be thanksgiving' (Eph. 5:4). The new covenant community is the community that gives thanks to God, not just for all he has done in the redeeming work of Calvary, but for all that he gives in every sphere of life. Such thanksgiving, the essence of worship, is made possible by the work of God himself. The thanksgiving ascends to God (the Father) through the Son as mediator, enabled by the ministry of the Spirit. The Triune God himself brings his redeemed people into the blessing of true worship by his own grace. This worship is corporate, but not confined to specific acts, times or places, however much these may be means of its valid expression. The one reinforces the other, and both lead to the glory of God in all aspects of life.

(10) The Pastoral Epistles
The letters to Timothy and Titus are called the 'Pastoral Epistles' (following the lead of Berdot in 1703)[49] because they are addressed to named individuals who were in pastoral care of congregations in Ephesus and Crete respectively. The authorship of these documents has been much debated, with respected scholars arriving at different conclusions.[50] The view taken here is that the books are Pauline, but no momentous issues for our theme hinge on acceptance of this opinion. What is clear is that Timothy and Titus had been appointed to oversee the churches established in these locations, and the letters therefore give us not only an indication of the way in which they were to go about their functions, but an insight into the normative structure of Christian leadership at the time.[51] What is clear is that the appointment and function of elders was a 'given' in each situation (Titus 1:5-10; 1 Tim. 3; cf. Acts 14:23) and that these men had a particular responsibility for preaching and teaching in the congregation (1 Tim. 3:22; Tim. 2:2, 24; Titus 1:9).

Preaching and teaching are themes that run throughout these letters (1 Tim. 1:3; 4:11; 6:2; 2 Tim. 4:2; Titus 2:1, 3), and they are concepts closely linked with the ideas of admonishment, exhortation and even rebuke (1 Tim. 5:20; 2 Tim. 4:2; Titus 1:9, 13; 2:15). The other side of this emphasis is that the letters portray a deep interest in the effects of poor or heretical teaching, and the way in which such deficient ministry leads to ethical and moral degradation amongst the congregations (1 Tim. 1:3-7; 4:1-10; 6:3f.; 2 Tim. 2:14-19; 3:1-9; 4:3-5; Titus 1:10-16; 3:8-11). Timothy and Titus are thus those who have to guard the gospel (both in terms of content and acceptable conduct) and pass the apostolic deposit of truth on to others.

There is no specific cultic language involved in this, but the letters do paint a picture for us that is entirely in keeping with what we have seen above. The life of the new covenant communities over whom Timothy and Titus have pastoral responsibility was essentially the life of *koinōnia*. The aim of the teaching ministry (not just in its content, but also in the way in which it was to be conducted) was love (1 Tim. 1:5) and the expected outcome was to be good works amongst God's people (1 Tim. 2:10; 5:10, 25; 6:18; Titus 1:16; 2:7, 14; 3:8, 14), which is entirely consistent with what we have seen elsewhere (e.g. Heb. 10:24). Prayer was a central focus of the assemblies, especially for the peaceful existence of the church: 'I urge that supplications, prayers, intercessions, and thanksgivings be made for all people, for kings and all who are in high positions, that we may lead a peaceful and quiet life, godly and dignified in every way' (1 Tim. 2:1-2). All this was to be done in decent order. What emerges is a portrait of worshipping communities whose public assemblies and communal relationships formed a seamless robe of service to God.[52] As Cranfield has said, 'any divorce between worship in the sense of church services, private prayers etc. and worship in the sense of the whole offerings of our lives to God is intolerable.'[53]

2. Worship in Peter's Letters
There are two clear passages in Peter in which transformed worship vocabulary occurs, both of which pick up themes on which we have commented above.

(1) 1 Peter 2:5 (cf. 2:9)
The passage in which these verses are embedded is one in which the characteristic descriptions of God's Old Testament covenant community are applied to the New Testament community of God's believing people. The new covenant people of God are thus called 'a *chosen race*, a *royal priesthood*, a *holy nation*, a *people for his own possession*, that you may proclaim the excellencies of him who called you out of darkness into his marvelous light' (1 Peter 2:9). The terms that Peter uses (here indicated in italics) have a rich Old Testament provenance and either directly adopt Old Testament usage, or allude to passages demonstrating a thematic union with them (e.g. Exod. 19:6; Deut. 4:20; 7:6; 10:15; Isa. 14:2; 43:20-2; 61:6; 66:21). Likewise, the mission of the redeemed people in proclaiming the glory of God picks up on Old Testament images, particularly in Isaiah (e.g. 42:8, 12; 43:7). There can be no doubt that Peter sees the new covenant

community of God as the inheritors of the titles, functions and associated divine commissioning attributed to Israel in the Old Testament, and in this he is at one with Paul and the writer to the Hebrews.[54]

Whereas the people of Israel were rooted in the land of the covenant promise made to Abraham, this new elect people of God is scattered abroad, dispersed throughout the world (1 Peter 1:1-3). Where Israel's identity was bound up in the physical realities of land, temple, kingship and so on, the identity of the new covenant people is fully bound up with their elect status and faith in Jesus as the Christ (1 Peter 1:3-9). They are indeed the heirs of the great salvation of which the Old Testament prophets spoke (1 Peter 1:10-12), who live in the present world but look for the eschatological revelation of the world to come (1 Peter 1:12, 13). All of this accentuates the fact that they are indeed God's holy people, who are to reflect God's own holiness (1 Peter 1:14-15). Through faith in the word preached to them, they have been given hope and been born again of God's own imperishable seed (1 Peter 1:17-25). All of Peter's ensuing paraenetic instruction is based on this new identity which both sets them apart from the world in which they live, and accounts for their suffering in it.

It is this group of scattered people, who on the surface view of things seem to be so disintegrated, that are actually the *one* temple/house of God on the earth. Peter says of them 'you yourselves like living stones are being built up as a spiritual house (*oikos pnuematikos*), to be a holy priesthood (*hierateuma hagion*), to offer spiritual sacrifices (*pneumatikas thysia*) acceptable to God through Jesus Christ' (1 Peter 2:5). Whereas much of Israel's identity was bound up with the worship centred on the temple in their midst, the new covenant community *are* the temple of God and priesthood at the one time. Just as the one who built that temple was rejected (1 Peter 2:4, 6-8), so they will experience suffering and rejection (the main pastoral elements addressed in the letter). Jesus Christ is the cornerstone of the temple he has built, and believers in him are as choice and precious in the sight of God as he. The tenses of 1 Peter 2:4-5 may be translated in various ways, but Grudem is probably right in suggesting the sense (preserved in the NASB), 'As you continually come to Christ (in initial faith, then in worship and prayer) you yourselves are being built into a spiritual house.'[55] What they offer is spiritual: sacrifices of praise, prayer, good works, holy living and deeds of love – as we have seen throughout this and the previous chapter. That what they offer is acceptable is because they are offered through Jesus Christ who is *the* priest in the temple of God, and who has provided the perfect sacrifice in his own blood (as in 1 Peter 1:18-19). Despite the fact that the new covenant people has no visible cultus, no geographical centre and no earthly priesthood the suffering believers to whom Peter writes should have no doubt that their day-by-day worship is fully pleasing to God.

(2) 1 Peter 4:10-11

These verses reflect many of the characteristics of the new communities' corporate assemblies seen earlier in this chapter. While they may apply to the attitudes and actions of love that should mark the people of God in their daily lives, the principle of love and self-giving service was also to mark the assembly of God's people for worship. There should be no difference between the attitudes and actions of the assembled community and those when it is scattered abroad during the normal round of weekly activities that are demanded by work, family and business. Thus, 'As each has received a gift (*charisma*), use it to serve one another, as good stewards of God's varied grace: whoever speaks, as one who speaks oracles of God; whoever serves, as one who serves by the strength that God supplies – in order that in everything God may be glorified through Jesus Christ. To him belong glory and dominion forever and ever. Amen.' (1 Peter 2:10-11). There is not much that needs to be added by way of comment, for we have seen the principle of self-giving service that is enshrined here throughout our discussion to this point. The main point to note is simply this: God is glorified when the church lives in the power of the gifts he supplies and uses them to serve one another. The glorification of God, (which is the goal and content of all true worship, is brought about by the mutual service of his people.

3. Conclusion

There can be no doubt that the New Testament evidence we have examined supports a totally transformed understanding of the nature of worship. The worship language used of and by the new covenant congregations was in a very real sense counter cultural. It took the old worship categories of the temple, and metamorphosed them into relational and personal categories, where the self-giving, other person centredness of the life of God was reflected in the lives of his people. What we see is worship not just *of* the Triune God, but *in* the Triune God, enabled by his grace. Whatever debt the new covenant communities might have owed to the old covenant categories, their worship was of a different order. While, in the 'public assembly' sense, their worship may have owed something to the basic features of synagogue worship,[56] it is not the worship of Israel reproduced on a grander scale. It was certainly nothing like the worship of pagan temples. It was different in form, in content and in scope from all of these. It was practically related to day-to-day issues of a life lived in love, and eschatologically orientated at every turn. The New Testament communities were indeed worshipping 'neither in Jerusalem nor Gerizim', but worshipped the Father in Spirit and in Truth. In our concluding chapter we will reflect on what all of this might mean for us today.

Chapter 8

Worship in The Book of Revelation

Introduction
In the first chapter of this book we looked at a number of key biblical passages related to the theme of worship. Among them we gave some attention to Revelation 4–5, which we saw as giving us a view into the throne room of heaven, and which emphasised the importance of worship both for the heavenly host and the whole of the creation. We saw also how these chapters framed the entire book, with the letters to the seven churches preceding them and the extended recounting of the spiritual conflict that is the matrix for the Church's existence (at least in the time before the *eschaton*) following after them. Over all things, i.e. both the church and the world, the throne room in heaven reigns!

Our purpose in this chapter is to consider some aspects of the wider theology of worship in the book of Revelation, and to see how the teaching of this final and climactic book of the Bible relates to some of the themes we have seen emerging throughout our study.[1] The book is replete with references to worship, or allusions and imagery based on the Old Testament temple and its associated cultus. For the sake of brevity, the material has been ordered here under three headings: Trinitarian worship; worship and conflict; and the establishment of the true temple.

1. The Worship of Revelation is Trinitarian
The reality of the Trinitarian nature of God and the expression of worship in Trinitarian terms are clear in a number of places in the book. While there is no formal Trinitarian formula (cf. Matt. 28:19; 2 Thess. 2:13-14; 1 Cor. 12:4-6, etc.), the action of the book places the Father, the Son and the Spirit as One by implication.[2] In the very opening section of the book reference to a Trinitarian pattern emerges. God the Father gives Christ the revelation of the contents of the book to pass on to his servants (1:1), and when John writes to the seven churches who are to receive the revelation thus given, 'grace and

peace' come to them from 'him who was and who is and who is to come, and from the seven spirits who are before the throne, and from Jesus Christ' (1:4b-5). When the risen and glorified Christ speaks to the churches (see the repeated phrase 'The words of ...' in 2:1, 8, 12, 18, etc.) the churches are bidden to 'hear what the Spirit' is saying to them (e.g. 2:7, 11, 17, etc.).[3]

In the throne room of the heavenly temple itself – revealed for us in Revelation 4–5 – worship is offered to the 'Lord God Almighty' who is identified as the one seated on the throne (4:8 cf. 4:9, 10). The particular focus in Revelation 4 is on his nature as the Creator (4:11), and thus as the proper and exclusive object of worship. However, John needed to be in the Spirit to see any of this (4:2).[4] The 'Lamb' and the 'seven spirits of God'[5] (i.e. the Spirit himself) are seen in close association with the throne (5:6 cf. 7:17), and the Lamb himself is specifically mentioned as the object of worship (5:8b-10). Later, we see the 'great multitude' of the redeemed – so vast 'that no one could number' them – engaged in worship of God and the Lamb. Their worship is evoked by the fact that salvation comes from ('belongs to') them (7:10). Such worship by the human host of redeemed humanity also elicits enthusiastic worship from the heavenly host (7:11-12).

In this worship, the praise is a 'new song' i.e. a victory song,[6] because of the great work of redemption accomplished by the Lamb in the shedding of his own blood, thus establishing a new people who are 'king priests to our God [who] shall reign on the earth'. All of the angelic host (5:11-12) and ultimately the whole of the creation (5:13-15) falls down in worship of the Lamb and the One who is seated on the throne. The Lamb, as also the One seated on the throne, is worthy to receive 'blessing and honour and glory and dominion for ever and ever' (5:14). Indeed, the Lamb is in the 'midst' (or the 'centre' NIV; 'heart' NJB) of the throne itself (7:17).

The proclamation of God's victory over the kingdoms of this world and establishment of his reign causes worship to rise from the heavenly elders, who fall on their faces in adoration. In this case the praise they utter is because of God's just judgments, by which the wrathful nations have been overcome and by which the destroyers of the earth themselves have been destroyed (11:15-18). God's just judgements are praised in other places, also (e.g. 16:5-7; 18:20; 19:1-5), leading to praise of both God and the Lamb. 'God is worshipped because "He establishes justice in the earth," i.e. He judges all evil – in all its forms – and destroys it, thus purifying the creation and vindicating His own righteousness and love. This He does through the Lamb.'[7]

The defeat of evil is unspeakably important, both the future of the creation and for the vindication of God's holiness, and in many place in the Old Testament it forms the basis of rejoicing for God's people (e.g. Pss. 48:11; 58:10; 96:11-13; cf. Deut. 32:43; Isa. 26:21). The heavens are called to rejoice in the twin facts that the accuser has been defeated and that God's people are able to overcome him because of the blood of the Lamb (12:12). Later, worship is offered by the angelic beings because of the culmination of redemption: the marriage of the Bride and the Lamb (19:6-8), which of necessity has entailed the defeat of the enemies and the cataclysmic judgment of Babylon in particular. Even after the glorious victory of God over all the powers of evil, the matter of worship is not neglected. In two places human worship of angelic entities is entirely ruled out (19:10; 22:9), so that God alone is preserved as the One fitting object of worship in heaven or on the earth.

The whole message of the Book of Revelation magnifies the one true God, in all his Triune glory. The Lamb has redeemed a new humanity to act as king-priests in the new creation, to bring glory to his Father, and to work in concert with the Spirit, so that he and the Bride say, 'Come!'

2. Worship and Conflict

It is widely recognised that Revelation provides the church with a theology of history, however what is of great importance for our study is that this theology of history is built around the theme of worship. The action of the Son in shedding his blood to free us from our sins (1:5b) was so that we, the redeemed, would be made 'a kingdom, priests to his God and Father, to him be glory and dominion for ever and ever. Amen'. (1:6). The goal of redemption is worshipful service.[8]

In being thus constituted as a priestly kingdom, we are re-formed into the original purpose for which we were created. Both worship and dominion are placed in proper relationship to God, and to one another. Just as the Last Adam exercised (and exercises) his true dominion in and through his submission to God the Father, so it is for his people. The creation was formed to be headed up by a humanity living in joyful recognition of its dependence upon God, and in humble submission to his will. Dominion could only ever be exercised truly by a humanity that was submitted to the authority of God, manifesting that submission in authentic worship of him. The incarnate Son has come to both model and empower such worshipful submission for his people. However this redemptive action and its goal of a worshipping king-priesthood does not go uncontested.

Behind the scenes of history lie spiritual powers, unveiled in the book of Revelation for what they really are. The principle of their operation is imitative in that the seek to set up a counterfeit to the reality of God and his purposes. Thus,

> The red dragon – who is Satan – has the incarnation of his 'son' in the beast who is the counterpart of Christ, i.e. who is the Antichrist. He has a 'death' and a 'resurrection' (cf. 13:3), and the power of his death and resurrection is to make all men worship the beast. The second beast, who is the false prophet – the evil counterpart of the Holy Spirit – causes humanity to worship the image of the beast, and the beast is in collusion with the unholy woman, Babylon, who is the foul counterpart of the pure Bride – the church of Christ.[9]

The serpent/dragon is enraged that his power has been lost and causes a beast to rise out of the sea (of the restless nations, based on the information we are given in 17:15). This beast is worshipped for his supernatural power and miraculous resurrection (13:3-4), and vilifies the worship of God with blasphemous words (13:5, 6). The beast has power (for a season) over the saints of God (13:7), and this seems to encourage even more false worship of this one who seeks to usurp the place of God and the Lamb.

Ultimately, 'all who dwell on the earth' (with the exception of those whose names are written in the Lamb's book of life) are deceived into worshipping the beast (13:8). In this great conflict, to culminate in the last day, there is no middle ground. We have already commented that in the ordinary affairs of life there is no vacuum of 'non-worship'. Every human being is a worshipper of someone or something. In the end times this (now largely hidden) situation is magnified and brought out into the open. One is either a worshipper of God and the Lamb, or of the beast. One is either part of that humanity which forms 'a kingdom, priests to [Jesus'] God and Father' (1:6) or one is part of a fully apostate humanity thoroughly wedded to its illicit worship.

The blinding power of Satan, operating through his system of idolatrous shrines, receives stark comment in the theology of Revelation. This can be seen specifically, for example in Revelation 9:20, but principally throughout the book because Satan is seen to energise the whole worldly system that is opposed to God, together with its worship. The issue immediately in view in Revelation 9:20 is that those who worship idols refuse to repent in the face of the divine judgments that the Lord brings against them. That the idols represent demonic powers is taken for granted. However, this reinforces what we saw in the opening chapter of this book: idols fashion their worshippers in their image (cf. Pss. 115:8; 135:18). In particular, the spiritual powers behind the idols render the worshippers' hearts increasingly hardened and insensitive to the word of God, so that they become deaf, blind, and mute. Here, in Revelation 9:20, the insensitivity of heart is complete. Despite the plain destruction wrought by the divine judgments, those who observe such things do not have any change of heart. They have been completely formed into the demonic image that will not, and cannot, repent.

Given the theme of this book it is telling that the 'eternal gospel' to be proclaimed has the matter of worship at its heart. In Revelation 14:7 the sum of the eternal gospel is described 'And he said with a loud voice, "Fear God and give him glory, because the hour of his judgment has come, and worship him who made heaven and earth, the sea and the springs of water."' The language in the first part of this verse reminds us of Romans 1:21: 'For although they knew God, they did not honour [*glorify*] him as God or give thanks to him,' on which we have commented previously. Human sin is fundamentally a refusal to glorify God, a rejection of our created vocation to worship him. The 'good news' is that God has not completely rejected humanity in its abandonment of him, but that he has set out to redeem a new race through his Son to be his true worshippers. The possibility of repentance is thus part of the proclamation of the good news, and in this regard Paul's speech before the philosophers in Athens (on which we have commented in an earlier chapter) is entirely at one with the message of the 'eternal gospel' proclaimed here in summary form.

Where there is no repentance, however, the judgments of God press inexorably on, so that 'those who worship the beast and its image' are given to drink of the wine of God's wrath (14:10), an ironical exchange for the wine of sexual immorality peddled by the harlot (14:8), with whom the beast has been in league. Beast and Babylon alike are ultimately supported by the evil dragon, whose entire purpose is to eradicate the image of God from the earth and to overthrow God himself (as if such a thing were possible!). The worship of the beast and his image thus forms the pinnacle of demonic and human rebellion.

Who is this beast and what is his purpose? The long history of interpretation around this figure has consistently identified three biblical figures as referring to the same entity: the man of lawlessness (from 2 Thessalonians 4), the anti-Christ (from 1 John), and the beast (from Revelation 13). In 2 Thessalonians 2:1-12 Paul describes the activity of one there called 'the man of lawlessness', and this passage has many immediate points of comparison with the beast of Revelation. The 'man of lawlessness'[10] has such overweening pride that 'opposes and exalts himself against every so-called god or object of worship, so that he takes his seat in the temple of God, proclaiming himself to be God' (2 Thess. 2:4). He is the embodiment of evil, whose rise to power 'is by the activity of Satan with all power and false signs and wonders' (2 Thess. 4:9). As described in Revelation 13, the beast comes to power through the agency of the dragon (Satan), so that 'all who dwell on earth will worship it, everyone whose name has not been written before the foundation of the world in the book of life of the Lamb that was slain'. Morris is thus justified in commenting that 'the Man of Lawlessness is not simply a man with evil ideas. He is empowered by Satan to do Satan's work' and comes 'in a parody of the incarnation'.[11]

The beast's desire to be worshipped is not simply wrong, but evil in the extreme, for in so doing he seeks to unify the nations under his reign in an imitation of God's purpose to unify the rebellious nations under his. This accords with the situation seen elsewhere in the Bible and in ancient history. In a very real sense the divine kingship of Pharaoh embodied the unity of ancient Egypt. King Nebuchadnezzar set up images to be worshipped and thus impose unity on the nations under his rule (as is the clear implication of the repeated phrase 'all the peoples, nations, and languages' in Daniel 3:4; cf. 3:7).[12] At the time of John's exile on Patmos, Caesar worship was mandatory. It could also be argued that in more recent history the quasi-religious nature of the Nuremberg Nazi party rallies and the powerful personality cults surrounding such leaders as Hitler or Mao Tse Tung tap into the innate power of control available through unified worship. The attempts to impose a form of worship by force (e.g. the Spanish inquisition; the Act of Uniformity in England; the Crusades; Islamic Jihad; etc.) all share in the same character.

Of particular interest for our theme is that the 'man of lawlessness' demands absolute pre-eminence. It is not just God that he opposes, but he 'opposes and exalts himself against every so-called god or object of worship' (2 Thess. 2:4a). In Revelation 13, the beast likewise demands universal and exclusive worship. Thus it seems that, whereas in the current climate Satan is content to work through systems of idolatry in order to maintain power by blinding and ensnaring men and women, in the day of the unveiling of the 'man of lawlessness' Satan will cast all pretence aside and seek worship directly through the man completely conformed to his image.

There is doubtless a parody of the truth here, too. In the plan and purpose of God, the incarnate Son gives all glory to the Father. In the end, Christ Jesus gives all the kingdom to the Father, so that he, the Father, would be all in all (1 Cor. 15:24, 28). The Son is worshipped, and in so being, the Father is glorified. In the true pattern of self-giving love seen in the relationship between the Father and the Son, Paul says that 'Therefore God has highly exalted him and bestowed on him the name that is above every name, so that at the name of Jesus every knee should bow, in heaven and on earth and under the earth, and every tongue confess that Jesus Christ is Lord, to the glory of God the Father.' The 'therefore' is important, and in relation to our theme it is the fulcrum on which the difference between the Christ and the Anti-Christ hinges. The 'therefore' connects the exaltation of the Messiah with the humble obedience and atoning suffering of the Son on behalf of sinners. The exaltation of the Son is because of his love, and self-giving gracious action on behalf of others. He, the humble servant, is exalted. And in his state of exaltation, his humility is magnified in that all praise ascends through him to the Father. With the Anti-Christ, however, the action is pure egotism and haughty arrogance by which he seeks to gain mastery of the nations by deceit and to usurp completely the place of God. His is self-exaltation for his own glory, and by virtue of this fact his rule will always be destructive.

3. The Establishment of the True Temple[13]

We have drawn attention elsewhere to the connection between victory and temple building highlighted by Longman and Reid,[14] and in Revelation the situation in view is nothing less than the triumphant conclusion to all history. After the conflict comes the establishment of the final and eternal worship sanctuary. After the exodus came the establishment of the Tabernacle. After the wars of Saul and David, Solomon (whose name embodies *shalom*, 'peace') was commissioned to build the temple in Jerusalem. Here in the Book of Revelation, after the great cosmic conflicts of which these Old Testament events were the forerunners, the eternal temple is established.[15]

In this eternal worship-sanctuary the nations are brought under the reign and rule of God by his grace, and they are united in worship by love, borne out of redeeming holiness. The hostile and restless nations have been overcome by 'The Lord God, the Almighty' who has so acted in history that the anger of the nations has been turned to worship (15:4b). Here, we see the fulfilment of the prophetic vision of the Old Testament, seen not least in places such as Daniel 7:13-14: 'I saw in the night visions, and behold, with the clouds of heaven there came one like a son of man, and he came to the Ancient of Days and was presented before him. And to him was given dominion and glory and a kingdom, that all peoples, nations, and languages should serve him; his dominion is an everlasting dominion, which shall not pass away, and his kingdom one that shall not be destroyed.'

Temple imagery pervades the book. The conflation between the heavenly throne room, the presence of God and the temple is seen in many places. The term 'temple' (*naos* i.e. inner sanctuary) is itself used repeatedly (e.g. 7:15; 11:19; 14:15, 17; 15:5-8; 16:1, 17), while elsewhere objects or actions associated with the cultus are common. For example, an 'altar' – presumably the altar of incense – is mentioned repeatedly (e.g. 6:9; 8:3, 5; 19:13) seemingly without comment: its presence is assumed.[16] In 11:19 the 'ark of the covenant' is mentioned, but now not hidden from view behind the veil in the holy of holies, but in full view. The ark of the covenant was the divinely ordained repository of the Law, i.e. the Ten Commandments. These were God's own words, written by his own hand and cared for under the shelter of his own presence in the tabernacle and the temple. They form the basis of all moral action in the universe, and thus govern the moral shape of the new creation. In the end, the purified creation and all who dwell in it are conformed to every aspect of the holy will of God embodied in the Law,[17] and so it resides eternally in the heavenly temple.

Throughout the book, it is simply assumed that since God is present, the scene in heaven must be the temple, his dwelling place. The shorthand summary of the book's theme relates to being fitted to dwell in his presence, i.e. in his temple. Everything that does not comport with his holiness and which is not conformed to his moral glory is excluded, consigned to righteous and eternal judgement. The machinations of the evil powers seen in the book (such as the dragon, the beast, the false prophet, the harlot etc.) are all towards one end: to usurp the worship of God and conform the creation to their own image. The message of Revelation is plain. No matter what Satan seeks to do, or how deadly his intent, he is thwarted in his plans by the wisdom of God. Where Satan seeks to establish an eternal worship system based on his own pride, God overthrows all such activity and intent, to establish in eternity uncontested worship of the Father in Spirit and in Truth.

In earlier sections of this book we have seen that the tabernacle and the temple in Israel reflected the creation itself in their architecture and adornment. One of the implications of this observation is that the physical tabernacle or temple in Israel was a microcosm of the macrocosmic temple of creation. If we allow this assumption to stand, the whole of redemptive history pictured in Revelation has been with this point in view: to cleanse the macrocosmic temple of the defilement of evil and sin. Instead of an unholy temple of impure worship, the creation is brought to its proper end point, being constituted as the cosmic temple of God by both its initial creation and by his holy act of purifying redemption.

This cleansed creation-temple has its own priesthood. Just as the first creation had Adam as its (faithless) king-priest, so the new creation has the Last Adam – the Lamb – as the high priest over the house of God (to use the language of *Hebrews*). Those who by grace are united to him, form a kingdom of priests to lead the creation in its worship of the Triune God. The redeemed are therefore described as those who are 'before the throne of God, and serve him day and night in his temple; and he who sits on the throne will shelter them **from** his presence' (7:13). To those who overcome, the risen Jesus gives the promise: 'I will make him a pillar in the temple of my God. Never shall he go out of it, and I will write on him the name of my God, and the name of the city of my God, the new Jerusalem, which comes down from my God out of heaven, and my own new name' (3:12).[18]

Moreover, this new temple is thoroughly 'measured' (see 11:1ff.; cf. 21:15-17). This imagery goes back to the Old Testament, particularly as seen in Ezekiel's vision of the new temple in Ezekiel 40-48.[19] The clear implication of 11:2 (where the outer court is *not* measured and thus left to suffer judgement) is that the measuring provides security and protection for the *naos*, and those who dwell there. The action described in Revelation 21:15-17 has a similar purpose, in that 'the measuring of the city and its parts pictures the security of its inhabitants against the harm and contamination of unclean and deceptive people'.[20] In this way Revelation emphasises the utter purity of the new temple and the fact that the invasions and degradations brought about by sin and its associated idolatry are once and for all excluded from the new heavens and earth. It also indicates that while the church on earth (which is the new temple of Christ's spiritual body) may be caught up in the conflicts attending the rise and fall of nations, and while they may be persecuted by Satan and his cohorts to the point of death, the church is itself eternally safe. Death cannot harm its members, and the powers of evil will not ultimately triumph.

The fulfilment of the temple imagery is seen in Revelation 21–22, where in fact we are confronted with a conflation of images such as the Bride, the New Jerusalem, the Holy City, the Dwelling Place (21:1-4, 9-21) and the Garden (22:1-5).[21] There should be no surprise when we see this conflation of images. The original creation was the garden-sanctuary, the dwelling place of God with his children, the holy hill/city of his divine presence. The new creation will be all this at least, if not more. What is important is that this new city-temple 'has the glory of God' (21:11a), i.e. it reflects and shares in his moral radiance and everything within is holy. Ultimately, the temple is the Lord God Almighty and the Lamb (21:22f), which, whatever else it must mean, must imply 'direct and unmediated communion'[22] into which the nations bring their glory (21:26). This is the place of universally pure worship, and therefore of the universally accepted reign of God and the Lamb. The character of their holiness will forever form the joyful and life giving air of the new city.[23] In the light of this great and glorious outcome, and in view of the intensity of the battle along the way, it is no exaggeration to state that worship is indeed 'the primary matter of our universe.'[24]

Chapter 9

Conclusion

Introduction

It is always problematic to 'apply' the material of a book that is essentially a description and comment on a biblical theme. The material must be allowed to speak for itself, and the issues and implications for one reader or set of circumstances will not be exactly the same as those for the next. There is a real danger of becoming unhelpfully prescriptive in any comments. The human spirit is always prone to legalism, and it delights in laying down the law for another! Likewise there is the ever present danger of thinking that simply because one has understood certain things principially, the rest is easy! In all such cases we tend to focus on outward forms and to set up situations whereby we make judgments about others on the basis of our own practice.

It is also important to recognise that there are many areas of valid enquiry that we have not addressed in this book, on which the theme of worship has a bearing. These are what might be called the 'Worship and ...' issues. For example, we could discuss with some profit the relationship between worship and the sacraments of baptism and the Lord's Supper; worship and the place of preaching; the necessary association between worship and (or as) pastoral care; worship and the formation of/interaction with culture; or we could weigh into the current heated debate about worship and evangelism. In particular, I believe that there is a great deal yet to be done in considering issues related to the theme of worship and pastoral counselling, which is one of the most powerful routes into deliberations on matters to do with personal motivation, goals, ambitions, relational patterns and even addictions. Areas such as these could easily justify a full treatment in their own right.

With all these caveats included, however, it is appropriate to draw together some of the threads we have seen emerging from our discussion, and to seek the Lord's help in obeying that which is truly in accordance with his will. For the most part I have not added lines of evidence or support for the things that appear below, since I believe that they are self-evident from the material that has formed the first eight chapters of this book. There are many areas in which further reflection is needed, some of which may appear in another volume. The comments fall under four main headings: Idols and their influence; worship in the day-to-day; worship in the public assembly; and worship in the world to come.

1. Idols and Their Influence

The first and most obvious thing to say under this heading is that human beings have been created for worship. This means that every human being is a worshiper of someone or something, even if that person does not recognise it. There is indeed no vacuum of non-worship, and when the Lord is not the object of our worship something else will be. In overtly idolatrous societies the issue is more clear cut. In much of the western world the object of our worship is more subtle, but no less aberrant. The title of Paul Vitz's classic work, *Psychology as Religion: The Cult of Self Worship*, gives us a clue as to the nature of much worship in the western world. We worship and serve the creature (i.e. ourselves) rather than the Creator. When this is married to the pervasive idolatry of form and beauty that governs the advertising, fashion, glamour, and entertainment industries we see how powerful a force this can be for social and personal dislocation.

As the western world finds such self-worship to be morally bankrupt, however, we may yet see more clearly emerging forms of physical idolatry and paganism which will place us more firmly into the sort of social, cultural and religious setting of the first-century believers. If and when such developments occur, we will find ourselves more fully engaged with the overt battle for worship that forms much of the socio-religious environment of the biblical documents. However, we should not be deluded into thinking that simply because such overt expressions of idolatry are not yet numerous that idolatry does not exist. The drive for fame, power, wealth, position and prestige are just some of its manifestations, and these will lead men and women to sacrifice the lives of their children no less than the ancient gods of the Canaanites caused the kings of Israel to pass their offspring through the fire.

There is indeed no vacuum of non-worship, and there can be no doubt that idolatry has an effect on the relational and moral health of both individuals and society. This has been evident wherever we have looked in the Bible. There is a constant drive within human beings to worship: this is what they have been created for. They are worship-orientated creatures, who must find their direction in things that lie outside of themselves. Where they will not find their direction from God, issues of motivation, vocation, destiny and desire are answered in the idols who seem to provide such. Whether this be the idolatry of form in the media, the ambition of greed in business, the overt idolatry of false religion: in each and every case the direction of one's life is not rooted solely within one's own inner situation. Calvin says, 'The mind begets an idol: the hand gives it birth.'[1] Idols are not free standing, however. They are manifestations of human beings' unthankfulness to God, and are energised by demonic powers, so that they work as one with other enemies such as the world, the flesh, and the principalities and powers, so that the end point of their action will always be social, moral and ethical degradation.

In the New Testament idolatry is not just linked with physical representations, but with attitudes and actions. It 'understands idolatry as putting anything in the place that God alone should occupy as the proper focus of obedience and worship.'[2] In this connection it is also worth making some comments about greed, which is an expression of a heart that is not acting in true faith, and which is an attitude that is inherently idolatrous. Greed is faith misplaced in the treasure of this world – so much so that they are gathered at the expense of all other things. Relationships become captive to the gathering process, and people become objects to be used in the amassing of wealth.

In the prophets, denunciations against greed (often translated as 'dishonest gain') are often linked with the concept of unfaithfulness to God (as in Psalm 119:36 where the psalmist prays that his heart may be inclined to Yahweh's testimonies 'and not to dishonest gain') or as indication of Israel's transgression of her covenantal obligations (e.g. Jeremiah 22:17 in context). It indicates an attitude of distrust in God's provision, and an attempt (through false alliances, idolatry and deception) to increase one's own wealth at the expense of others. Covetousness (as *pleonexia* can also be translated) is the root of all manner of evil and is closely allied to an idolatrous heart.

Jesus' parable about the rich man who built more and bigger barns (Luke 12:13-21) is an extended illustration of the need to 'Beware and be on guard against every form of greed (*pleonexia*)'

(Luke 12:15 NASB), while in Colossians 3:5 greed is identified as being idolatry (*pleonexian ētis estin eidōlolatria*). In Ephesians 5:4 greed (as well as immorality or impurity) 'must not even be named among you' (i.e. the saints). Immediately following this statement, a 'covetous man' is equated with being an 'idolater' in 5:5: 'no covetous man, who is an idolater, (*pleonektēs ho estin eidōlolatrēs*) has an inheritance in the kingdom of God.' Lincoln quotes L. T. Johnson to good effect: 'All idolatry is a form of covetousness, for in refusing to acknowledge life and worth as a gift from the Creator, it seeks to seize them from the creation as booty.'[3] The attitude of conscious trust that is commended by Jesus in the Sermon on the Mount, or in the parable in Luke 12, is wholly different from the attitude of unbelief that gives rise to *pleonexia*. The knowledge of God, therefore, inescapably 'involves trust and reverence', as Calvin so eloquently argued (*Institutes* I.ii.2).[4]

What is clear from the discussion of this book is that *koinōnia* can only thrive where the power of idolatry is broken. Wherever it reasserts its power – in whatever form – self-serving and self-interest are the inevitable consequences. Conversely, where men and women 'turn to God from idols to serve the living and true God' (1 Thess. 1:9) the resultant fellowship of love is both empowered by the life of the Triune God and expressive of that life. To be sure, such turning from idols cannot happen without the gracious initiative of God, but he has shown himself to be the one who takes that initiative, whose grace we see fully in the crucified Son who is our Lord.

Little wonder, then, that John concludes his magnificent exposition of the propitiatory love of God and the union of love that he creates amongst believers (who are the Father's children) with the words, 'Little children, keep yourselves from idols' (1 John 5:21). We have been created not simply to render worship *to* the Triune God, but to do so *in* the Triune God. The fellowship of the Three-in-one is not so much a model for us to copy, but the realm in which our fellowship is created to exist. *Koinōnia* can only come through the Triune fullness of the worshiping community, and where this fulness is known the power of true worship has wider repercussions than we can tell.

2. Worship in the day-to-day
Given all that we have seen from the Scriptures, there can be no doubt that worship is conducted in the day-to-day events of life. The

deeds of love done in the service of the Lord are the authentic, bodily manifestation of our devotion to God the Father. It goes without saying that such deeds can only be done by the grace of God, but there can be no doubt that this action of well-doing is what we have been created for. 'We are his workmanship, created in Christ Jesus for good works, which God prepared beforehand, that we should walk in them' (Eph. 2:10). Repeatedly we see that deeds of love are the outcome of believing faith, so 'good works' that are pleasing to God are the goal of proclamation and conversion (e.g. Acts 9:36; 2 Cor. 9:8; Col. 1:10; 2 Thess. 2:7; 1 Tim. 6:18; 2 Tim. 3:17; Titus 2:14). These are not only our expression of worship *to* God, but they lead to the worship *of* God, as others see his love in action and glorify him on account of it (Matt. 5:21).

This emphasis needs to be magnified. The New Testament transformation of cultic vocabulary into relational categories is telling, defining the matter of new covenant worship along lines that have often been neglected. Too often, the emphasis has fallen on issues of form and function, on buildings and so-called sacred spaces, on liturgical actions and clerical roles or on other manifestations of a narrow perception of what worship is and how it is to be practised. While there is an important place for the worship of the public assembly of God's people, the wide sweep of events on which we have commented in this book bear testimony to the continual tendency for human beings to formalise and ritualise worship, avoiding the moral imperative of worship in the day-to-day.

When thinking more biblically, it is plain that worship 'becomes the category under which we order everything in our lives',[5] and that, consequently, the power of worship in the public assembly will be proportional to the authenticity of worship in the relationships of the congregation. Where worship in this sense is deficient, worship in the narrow sense of the public assembly will lack power. Conversely, the gathering for worship in the public assembly is not an end in itself. In and through the God-glorifying action of the public worship of God's people, worship in the day-to-day is strengthened. Through the mutual encouragement received in the public gathering, through the fresh in-filling of the Spirit that accompanies hearing the gospel with faith, and even through the admonishment of other believers, worship in the day-to-day is reinforced, and in so doing God is glorified in all aspects of life.

3. Worship in public assembly

While we need to recognise at the outset that 'there is no single passage in the New Testament that establishes a paradigm for corporate worship',[6] we must also recognise that this 'lack' is deeply providential. Had the Lord given a set pattern for the gatherings of the new covenant people of God we would be worshiping them, rather than him, to this day! The comments that follow, therefore, reflect the matters that must be given continual priority amongst Christian worshipers in the light of what we have seen biblically, but should not be taken as paradigmatic for any one occasion of worship.

Worship must be Trinitarian in order to be fully Christian. This means at least two things. Firstly, the forms of our public worship must give due weight to each of the members of the Triune God, while recognising that the Son himself has come to lead us to the Father. The liturgy and hymnody that we adopt must reflect the nature of God's Triune being in a way that is fully orbed and deliberate.

Secondly, we must bear in mind our earlier comments: worship is not just rendered *to* the Triune God but *in* the Triune God. This point means that Trinitarian worship must take into account the horizontal relationships amongst believers, as much as the vertical relationships between the congregation and God. As we have seen earlier, worship shapes individual and community character. In specific terms, it must be relational rather than institutional. For example – and here the trivial makes the point – we almost inevitably hear the person leading worship welcome people into the house of God. This is emphatically *not* the case! At best, the worship leader may welcome the house of God into the building in which they are meeting! Any language that suggests that the life of the people of God is known in its institutional and physical structures must be rejected. Through the events that take place in the public worship of God – such as the singing of God's praise; the reading and expounding of his Word; the prayers of intercession and adoration; the administration of the Lord's Supper; and all the other legitimate activities of public worship – the glorifying of God's name is at stake. His name is glorified most fully when the relationships within the congregation are congruent with those of the Triune God we worship.

One thing that follows from this is that the leading of worship in the public assembly must be seen as a facet of the pastoral care of the congregation. Its spiritual health is both measured by and also expressed in its worship. For this reason the whole idea of a 'worship leader' who is a non-elder of the congregation (or at least directly accountable to the eldership) must be held up to question. Through the public assembly of God's people for worship, his name is glorified and his people edified, for their blessing and joy. The task of leading worship, then, is far greater than simply leading praise. It is, given the fullest sense of the word 'worship', a leading into the relational unity and cruciform life that brings glory to God.

In many situations today we have an understanding of 'worship leading' that accentuates the affective side of human experience. Through mood, music, and lighting (for example), the affections of a congregation may be stirred, sometimes to seeming depth. This leads to a further diminution of meaning, so that it is not uncommon (at least amongst evangelical Christians) to hear comments like 'The worship was really moving this morning'. The problem is exacerbated by the new epistemology of popular culture, where the affections are the criteria for decision making: 'I feel, therefore I am' is enacted by 'This feels right for me, so ...'. In Christian circles this too readily becomes 'It feels good so it must be (of, from, in) God'.

Such statements should not be read to imply a belittling of the affective side of Christian experience. Rather, the opposite is the case: the affections are too important to be played (and preyed) upon in the public worship of God's people. Where they are moved they must be moved by the impact of the truth on the mind and conscience. Any attempt to bypass these is both wrong and dangerous.

In view of these comments, it is inescapable that the *content* of public worship is of immense importance. Writing in a different context, P. T. Forsyth said, 'The preacher is not there to astonish people with the unheard of, he is there to revive them in what they have long heard.'[7] What is so for preaching – which is in itself an act *of* worship which is foundational to any public assembly *for* worship – is also true for the context in which preaching takes place. Every element of the public worship of the people of God must communicate the true content of the faith, which finds its focus on the person and work of Jesus the Messiah. This emphasis excludes from true Christian worship any pluralistic and syncretistic trends, which we have seen tend to make their inroads into the people of God continually. Whether it be the worship of Baal in the Old Testament or the gnostic-like sects of the New, the drift has always been to blend the worship of God with other lines of devotion. The uniqueness of Jesus Christ and his claims will not allow this. True Christian worship is at one and the same time a rejection of all other means of access to God.

Thus, we must not allow in Christian worship any indication that access to God is mediated by any human agency. 'There is one God, and there is one mediator between God and men, the man Christ Jesus' (1 Tim. 2:5), a fact that excludes any form of human priest-craft. By priest-craft, I mean any attitude or action that indicates that one person has access to God in a special way that others to not, or knowledge of his will that others may not share, or the means to mediate blessing that others may not have. The people of the new covenant are themselves a kingdom of priests to God, who have direct access to the Father in the Son by the indwelling power of the Spirit.[8] No office of the church must be allowed to stand between the believer and his relationship with God, but rather every office of the church must encourage it.

There is one particular function of public worship that is exceedingly necessary in today's climate. We have seen that worship has a biblical history. That it has a theological and ecclesiastical history is no less true, but we have not examined the concept of worship through the lens of historical theology or church history in this book. The biblical narrative, itself, however, provides that which is sorely needed in these days: an overarching metanarrative in which men and women can find their meaning and destiny. We have traced the importance of worship through creation, fall, redemption and ultimate glorification. This biblical narrative serves not only to *describe* the movement of history, but also has an exegetical function. It is a powerful tool to *explain* the movements of history and the rise and fall of nations. While there are clearly other issues to be considered (e.g. the simple fact of the sovereignty of God expressed in the raising up of Cyrus as deliverer in Isaiah 44:28 or the commissioning of the Chaldeans for judgment in Habakkuk 1:6), there can be no doubt that the moral, ethical, spiritual and political future of the nations is closely tied with their worship. Moral decay does not happen in a vacuum. It is supported by the idolatry of the society at any given time, and expressive of its worship, even if such be completely unarticulated. In the public worship of the people of God the whole sweep of this biblical metanarrative must be brought to bear, so that the horizons of men and women are lifted and their own lives set in the context of

God's dealings with the nations. The worshiping community takes its place in the history of the redemption and judgment of the whole world. Worship that does not act as the vehicle for the expression of the great plan of salvation history becomes inevitably narcissistic.

4. Worship in the World to Come
We have been created for worship, not just in this world, but in the world to come. In my view, one of the most pressing needs of evangelicalism in the West is that of the recovery of the biblical priority given to eschatology. We have seen the eschatological dimensions of worship emerging repeatedly in our earlier material. The people of God worship the God in whose plan and purpose they have been caught up, and therefore their horizon is not simply the present, but the future. They are co-workers with God as his priest nation, who (in the use of spiritual weapons and means) are sharing in the divine purpose to bring about the *telos* which God himself has planned. While the new covenant communities thus live in the present evil age, they are aware that this age and its rulers are passing away, and that God's will *will* be done, on earth as it is in heaven.

In this new creation, all of the impurities of false worship will be done away, and the whole of the heavens and the earth will be led in praise to God by the great King-Priest, Jesus Christ. With him will be a multitude beyond human reckoning, in whose lives and relationships the image of the Son will be fully seen. Conformed to his image, they will be true worshipers of God, from whose hearts all idolatry will have been cleansed, and in whose minds and wills they find only love, empowering them to fulfil all the commandments of God with a willing spirit and perfect obedience. The glories of this age to come, though not understood at all by the spirit of this age, are communicated to believers through the ministry of God's own Spirit (1 Cor. 2:10), so that the people of God are filled with hope for the coming kingdom, and live by faith through the sufferings and trials of the current age in which the idols, and the demonic powers behind them, still make their impact.

Against this eschatological hope there is a 'downward pressure' continually in operation, which seeks to take that which is penultimate, and make it ultimate. For example, in *Hebrews*, the rest of which the writer speaks is the ultimate, eschatological rest of the people of God. To be sure, this is entered now by faith, but the very nature of hope looks for its consummation in the age to come. Against this eschatological reality, and in the face of the suffering that such eschatological hope brings in the present, the 'downward pressure' for the Hebrew believers came from the desire to know another form of 'rest' in the present. In their case, the 'rest' of returning to the old covenant worship of Judaism seemed to be on offer.

In our own day the downward pressure is no less real. For the converted Jew, it is to return to Judaism, rather than to face the suffering of holding to belief in Jesus as the Messiah. For the converted Muslim, to return to Islam, rather than to suffer the loss of home, family and even life for coming to know God as Father through Jesus his Son. In both examples, the pressure is in some senses parallel to that of *Hebrews*. But for the vast majority of evangelicals in the west, the downward pressure is simply to settle down and find in this life (through the abundance of one's possessions) a sort of 'paradise on earth' in which all my needs are met, all my goals fulfilled and all my dreams accomplished. In such a setting the gospel can become captive to a culture of narcissism, where the life, ministry, death, resurrection, glory and coming of the Son of God is all understood through the lens of what 'it means to me'.

The antidote to such 'downward pressure' is the continual eschatological emphasis of word and sacrament, of prayer and praise, and of *koinōnia* lived in the present in the light of the age to come. Where the eschatological vision is dimmed, the public worship of the people of God becomes lack-lustre and self-serving. Rather, we look forward to that day when the great multitude stand in the nearer presence of Father, filled to all the fullness of God the Spirit, through whom they are united with the Son. There they will look around and within, and find only worship. Despite all the attacks of the evil one, the drag of indwelling sin and the seductive power of the idols throughout their long history, their song will be one of praise drenched with wonder. In them the commandment will be completely fulfilled: they will have no other God but him. And in them the promise will be fully realised: he is their God and they are his people.

Bibliography

T. D. Alexander, *From Paradise to the Promised Land: An Introduction to the Pentateuch, Second Edition* (Second; Carlilse/ Grand Rapids: Paternoster/Baker Academic, 2002).

T. D. Alexander, *From Paradise to the Promised Land* (Carlisle: Paternoster, 1995).

T. D. Alexander, 'Messianic Ideology in the Book of Genesis,' *The Lord's Anointed: Interpretation of Old Testament Messianic Texts* (e. a. P. E. Satterthwaite; Carlisle: Paternoster, 1995) 27–32.

L. C. Allen, *Psalms 101–150* (Word Biblical Commentary; Waco, Texas: Word, 1987).

C. E. Arnold, *The Colossian Syncretism: The Interface Between Christianity and Folk Belief at Colossae* (Grand Rapids: Baker Books, 1996).

D. Atkinson, *The Message of Genesis 1–11* (The Bible Speaks Today; Leicester: IVP, 1990).

H. W. Attridge, *The Epistle to the Hebrews* (Hermeneia; Philadelphia: Fortress Press, 1987).

R. E. Averbeck, 'Môʿēʰd,' *NIDOTTE Vol. 2* (W. van Gemeren; Carlisle: Paternoster, 1996) 873–7.

R. E. Averbeck, 'Tabernacle,' *Dictionary of the Old Testament Pentateuch* (T. D. Alexander; Leicester: IVP, 2003) 807–26.

R. Averbeck, 'Miškân,' *NIDOTTE Vol 2* (W. A. VanGemeren; Carlisle: Paternoster, 1996) 1130–4.

J. Baldwin, *1 and 2 Samuel* (Tyndale Old Testament Commentaries; Leicester: IVP, 1988).

C. K. Barrett, *A Commentary on the Epistle to the Romans* (Black's New Testament Commentaries; London: Adam & Charles Black, 1962).

C. K. Barrett, *The Gospel According to John* (London: SPCK, 1960).

K. Barth, *The Epistle of to the Romans* (E. C. Hoskyns; Oxford: Oxford University Press, 1933).

R. J. Bauckham, *God Crucified: Monotheism and Christology in the New Testament* (Carlisle: Paternoster, 1998).

239

R. J. Bauckham, 'Jesus, Worship Of,' *Anchor Bible Dictionary Vol. 3* (D. N. Freedman; New York: Doubleday, 1992) 812–9.

R. Baukham, *Jude, 2 Peter* (Word Biblical Commentary; Milton Keynes: Word (UK), 1986).

G. Beale, *The Book of Revelation: A Commentary on the Greek Text* (The New International Greek Testament Commentary; Carlisle/ Grand Rapids: Paternoster/Eerdmans, 1999).

G. R. Beasley-Murray, *John* (Word Biblical Commentary; Waco: Word Books, 1987).

G. C. Bingham, *The Way and Wonder of Worship* (Blackwood: New Creation Publications, 1990).

E. M. Blaiklock, *Commentary on the Psalms Vol 2.* (London: Scripture Union, 1977).

H. Blocher, *In the Beginning: The Opening Chapters of Genesis* (David G. Preston; Leicester/Downers Grove: IVP, 1984).

H. Blocher, *In the Beginning* (Leicester: IVP, 1984).

D. I. Block, *Judges, Ruth* (The New American Commentary; Nashville: Broadman & Holman, 1999).

D. L. Bock, *Luke 9:51–24:53* (Baker Exegetical Commentary on the New Testament; Grand Rapids: Baker Books, 1996).

T. L. Brensinger, '*Nsh*,' *New International Dictionary of Old Testament Theology and Exegesis Vol. 3* (W. A. Van Gemeren; Carlisle: Paternoster, 1997) 111–3.

C. Brown, 'Sacrifice,' *The New International Dictionary of New Testament Theology Vol. 3* (C. Brown; Grand Rapids: Regency(Zondervan), 1986) 415–38.

W. P. Brown, *Seeing the Pslams: A Theology of Metaphor* (Louisville: Westminster John Knox Press, 2002).

F. F. Bruce, *The Book of the Acts* (The New International Commentary on the New Testament; Grand Rapids: Eerdmans, 1981).

F. F. Bruce, *The Epistle to the Hebrews* (New International Commentary on the New Testament; Grand Rapids: Eerdmans, 1964).

W. Brueggermann, *Theology of the Old Testament* (Minneapolis: Fortress Press, 1997).

J. Calvin, *Calvin's New Testament Commentaries 12: The Epistle of Paul the Hebrews and The First and Second Epistles of St. Peter* (D. W. & T. F. Torrance; 1963).

J. Calvin, *Genesis* (Calvin's Commentaries; Grand Rapids: Baker Books).

J. Calvin, *Hebrews and I & II Peter* (Calvin's New Testament Commentary; Grand Rapids: Eerdmans, 1963).

E. Carpenter, 'Exodus: Theology Of,' *NIDOTTE Vol. 4* (W. van Gemeren; Carlisle: Paternoster, 1996) 605–15.

E. Carpenter, 'Exodus, Theology Of,' *NIDOTTE Vol. 4* (W. Van Gemeren; Carlisle: Paternoster, 1997) 605–15.

D. A. Carson, *The Gospel According to John* (Leicester: IVP, 1991).

D. A. Carson, *Matthew* (Expositor's Bible Commentary; Grand Rapids: Zondervan, 1984).

D. Carson, 'Worship Under the Word,' *Worship by the Book* (D. Carson; Grand Rapids: Zondervan, 2002) 11–63.

B. Childs, *The Book of Exodus: A Critical, Theological Commentary* (The Old Testament Library; Louisville: The Westminster Press, 1974).

D. Chilton, *Paradise Restored* (Dominion Press, 1994).

A. Clarke, "Be Imitators of Me': Paul's Model of Leadership,' *Tyndale Bulletin* 49/2 (1998) 329–60.

R. E. Clements, *God and Temple* (Oxford: Basil Blackwell, 1965).

R. A. Cole, *Exodus* (Tyndale Old Testament Commentaries; Leicester: IVP, 1973).

P. Craigie, *Psalms 1–50* (Word Biblical Commentary; Waco: Word, 1986).

O. Cullman, *Early Christian Worship* (Studies in Biblical Theology: First Series; London: SCM, 1963).

J. Currid, *Ancient Egypt and the Old Testament* (Grand Rapids: Baker Books, 1997).

J. Currid, *Exodus Chapters 19–40* (Evangelical Press Study Commentary; Darlington: Evangelical Press, 2001).

E. Curtis, 'Idols, Idolatry,' *The Anchor Bible Dictionary Vol. 3* (D. Freedman; New York: Doubleday, 1992) 376–81.

R. Davidson, *Genesis 1–11* (The Cambridge Bible Commentary; Cambridge: Cambridge University Press, 1973).

D. R. Davis, 'Rebellion, Presence and Covenant: A Study in Exodus 32–34,' *Westminster Theological Journal* 44/1 (Spring 1982) 72–88.

M. Dawn, *Powers, Weakness and the Tabernacling of God: The 2000 Shaff Lectures, Pittsburgh Theological Seminary* (Grand Rapids: Eerdmans, 2001).

J. Day, 'Ashtoreth,' *ABD Vol. 1* (D. Freedman; New York: Doubleday, 1992) 492–4.

J. Day, 'Baal,' *Anchor Bible Dictionary Vol. 1* (D. Freedman; New York: Doubleday, 1992) 545–56.

R. de Vaux, *Ancient Israel Its Life and Institutions* (London: Darton, Longman & Todd, 1961).

J. Denney, *The Second Epistle to the Corinthians* (London: Hodder & Stoughton, 1916).

R. B. Dillard, 'The Chronicler's Solomon,' *Westminster Theological Journal* 43/2 (Spring 1981) 289–301.

J. F. Drinkard, 'Religious Practices Reflected in the Book of Hosea,' *Review and Expositor* 90 (Spring 1993) 205–18.

W. Dumbrell, *Covenant and Creation: An Old Testament Covenantal Theology* (Exeter: Paternoster Press, 1984).

W. Dumbrell, *The Faith of Israel: A Theological Survey of the Old Testament* (2nd ed.; Leicester: IVP, 2002).

W. Dumbrell, *The Faith of Israel* (Leicester: IVP/Apollos, 1989).

W. Dyrness, *Themes in Old Testament Theology* (Downers Grove/Carlisle: IVP/Paternoster, 1977).

J. H. Leith, *Creeds of the Churches: A Reader in Christian Doctrine from the Bible to the Present. Third Edn.* (Louisville: John Knox Press, 1982).

T. D. Alexander & S. Gathercole, *Heaven on Earth: The Temple in Biblical Theology* (Carlisle: Paternoster, 2004).

C. e. a. Jones, *The Study of Liturgy* (London: SPCK, 1978).

W. Eichrodt, *Theology of the Old Testament, Vol. 1* (London: SCM, 1961).

P. Ellingworth, *The Epistle to the Hebrews: A Commentary on the Greek Text* (The New International Greek Testament Commentary; Carlisle: Paternoster, 1993).

P. Enns, *Exodus* (The NIV Application Commentary; Grand Rapids: Zondervan, 2000).

S. B. Ferguson, *The Holy Spirit* (Contours of Christian Theology; Leicester: IVP, 1996).

J. Fitzmyer, *Romans: A New Translation with Introduction and Commentary* (The Anchor Bible; New York: Doubleday, 1992).

P. T. Forsyth, *Positive Preaching and the Modern Mind* (Reprinted from 107 edition; Blackwood: New Creation Publications Inc., 1993).

R. T. France, 'Pour,' *The New International Dictionary of New Testament Theology Vol. 2* (C. Brown; Grand Rapids: Regency(Zondervan), 1986) 853–5.

T. E. Fretheim, *Creation, Fall and Flood* (Minneapolis: Ausgburg Press, 1969).

T. Fretheim, "Because the Whole Earth is Mine': Theme and Narrative in Exodus,' *Interpretation* 50/3 (July 1996) 229–39.

R. E. Friedman, 'Tabernacle,' *Anchor Bible Dictionary Vol. VI* (D. Freedman; New York: Doubleday, 1992) 292–300.

P. Garber, 'Moriah,' *The International Standard Bible Encylopedia Vol. 3* (G. Bromiley; Grand Rapids: Eerdmans, 1986) 413.

L. Goppelt, *A Commentary on I Peter* (J. E. Alsup; Grand Rapids: Eerdmans, 1993).

R. P. Gordon, *Hebrews* (Readings: A New Biblical Commentary; Sheffield: Sheffield Academic Press, 2000).

W. Grudem, *1 Peter* (Tyndale New Testament Commentaries; Leicester/Grand Rapids: IVP/Eerdmans, 1988).

D. Guthrie, *New Testament Theology* (Leicester: IVP, 1981).

J. M. Hadley, 'Ashteroth,' *NIDOTTE Vol. 3* (W. A. van Gemeren; Carlisle: Patenoster, 1996) 562–3.

J. M. Hadley, 'Baal,' *NIDOTTE Vol. 4* (W. A. van Gemeren; Carlisle: Paternoster, 1996) 422–8.

S. Haffemann, 'Corinthians, Letters to The,' *Dictionary of Paul and His Letters* (G. Hawthorne; Leicester: IVP, 1993) 164–79.

D. Hagner, *Matthew 1–13* (Word Biblical Commentary; Dallas, Texas: Word, 1993).

V. C. Hamilton, *The Book of Genesis Chapters 1–11* (New International Commentary on the Old Testament; Grand Rapids: Eerdmans, 1990).

V. P. Hamilton, *The Book of Genesis 18–50* (The New International Commentary on the Old Testament; Grand Rapids: Eerdmans, 1995).

T. Hart, 'Atonement and Worship,' *Anvil* 11/3 (1994).

H. Heppe, *Reformed Dogmatics* (G. T. Thompson; London: Wakeman Great Reprints, 1950).

K. Hess, '*Latreuō,*' *The International Dictionary of New Testament Theology, Vol. 3* (C. Brown; Grand Rapids: Zondervan, 1976) 549–51.

R. S. Hess, *Joshua: An Introduction & Commentary* (Tyndale

Old Testament Commentaries; Leicester/Downers Grove: IVP, 1996).

J. H. Hilber, 'Theology of Worship in Exodus 24,' *Journal of Evangelical Theological Society* 39/2 (June 1996) 177–89.

J. K. Hoffmeier, 'Plagues of Egypt,' *NIDOTTE Vol. 4* (W. A. Van Gemeren; Carlisle: Paternoster, 1996) 1056–9.

P. R. House, *1, 2 Kings* (The New American Commentary; Nashville: Broadman & Holman, 1995).

P. E. Hughes, *A Commentary on the Epistle to the Hebrews* (Grand Rapids: Eerdmans, 1977).

P. E. Hughes, *A Commentary on the Epistle to the Hebrews* (Rend Rapids: William B. Eerdmans, 1977).

P. E. Hughes, *Paul's Second Epistle to the Corinthians* (The New International Commentary on the New Testament; Grand Rapids: Eerdmans, 1962).

L. W. Hurtado, *At the Origins of Christian Worship: The Context and Character of Earliest Christian Devotion* (Grand Rapids: Eerdmans, 1999).

Irenaeus, *Against Heresies* (The Ante Nicene Fathers; Edinburgh: T. & T. Clark, 1993).

M. E. Isaacs, *Sacred Space: An Approach to the Theology of the Epistle to the Hebrews* (JSNT Supplement; Sheffield: JSOT Press, 1992).

Isbell, 'Worship in the New Testament,' *Worship in the Presence of God* (Smith and Lachman; Greenville: Greenville Seminary Press, 1992).

J. G. Janzen, 'The Character of the Calf and Its Cult in Exodus 32,' *Catholic Biblical Quarterly* 52/4 (October 1990) 597–607.

J. B. Jordan, *Through New Eyes* (Brentwood, TN: Wolgemuth & Hyatt, 1988).

K. Jung, 'Ashtoreth,' *TISBE Vol. 1* (G. W. Bromiley; Grand Rapids: Eerdmans, 1979) 319–20.

E. Käsemann, *New Testament Questions of Today* (Philadelphia: Fortress Press, 1969).

S. J. Kistemaker, *Hebrews* (New Testament Commentary; Grand Rapids: Baker Books, 1984).

K. A. Kitchen, 'Pharoah,' *The International Standard Bible Encyclopedia Vol. 3* (G. W. Bromiley; Grand Rapids: Eerdmans, 1989) 821.

H. Klauck, 'Sacrifice and Sacrificial Offerings,' *The Anchor Bible*

Dictionary Vol. 5 (D. N. Freedman; New York: Doubleday, 1992) 870–91.

R. W. Klein, "Back to the Future': The Tabernacle in the Book of Exodus,' *Interpretation* 50/3 (July 1996) 264–76.

M. G. Kline, 'Oath and Ordeal Signs,' *Westminster Theological Journal* 27/2 (May 1965) 115–39.

M. Kline, *Images of the Spirit* (Grand Rapids: Baker, 1980).

M. Kline, 'Investiture with the Image of God,' *Westminster Theological Journal* 40/1 (Fall 1977) 39–62.

G. N. Knoppers, 'Rethinking the Relationship Between Deuteronomy and the Deuteronomistic History: The Case of Kings,' *Catholic Biblical Quarterly* 63 (2001) 393–415.

A. König, *The Eclipse of Christ in Eschatology: Towards a Christ-Centred Approach* (Blackood: New Creation Publications, 1999).

H.-J. Kraus, *Worship in Ancient Israel: A Cultic History of the Old Testament* (Geoffrey Buswell; Oxford: Basil Blackwell, 1966).

W. L. Lane, *Hebrews 1–8* (Word Biblical Commentary; Dallas: Word Books, 1991).

W. L. Lane, *Hebrews 9–13* (Word Biblical Commentary; Dallas: Word Books, 1991).

W. L. Lane, 'Hebrews,' *Dictionary of Later New Testament & Its Development* (R. Martin and P. Davids; Leicester: IVP, 1997).

W. LaSor, 'Artemis,' *TISBE Vol. 1* (G. W. Bromiley; Grand Rapids: Eerdmans, 1979) 306–8.

W. Liefeld, *1 & 2 Timothy/Titus* (The NIV Application Commentary; Grand Rapids: Zondervan, 1999).

A. T. Lincoln, *Ephesians* (Word Biblical Commentary; Dallas: Word, 1990).

B. Lindars, *The Gospel of John* (New Century Bible Commentary; Grand Rapids: Eerdmans, 1972).

G. Lohfink, *Does God Need the Church? Toward a Theology of the People of God* (Collegeville: Michael Glazier/Liturgical Press, 1999).

R. N. Longenecker, *New Wine Into Fresh Wineskins: Contextualizing the Early Christian Confessions* (Peabody: Hendrikson Publishers, 1999).

T. Longman III, *Immanuel in Our Place: Seeing Christ in Israel's Worship* (The Gospel According to the Old Testament; Phillipsburg: Prebyterian & Reformed Publishing, 2001).

T. Longman III, T., & Reid, D., *God is a Warrior* (Studies in Old Testament Biblical Theology, Grand Rapids: Zondervan, 1995).

M. Luther, *Lectures on Genesis 1–5* (Luther's Works; Concordia Publishing House, 1958).

D. Macleod, D., *Behold Your God* (Fearn: Christian Focus Publications, 1995).

I. H. Marshall, *The Acts of the Aposltes* (Tyndale New Testament Commenataries; Grand Rapids: Eerdmans, 1980).

I. H. Marshall, 'Church and Temple in the New Testament,' *Tyndale Bulletin* 40/2 (November 1989) 203–22.

I. H. Marshall, *The Pastoral Epistles* (The International Critical Commentary; Edingburgh: T. & T. Clarke, 1999).

I. H. Marshall, 'Worshipping Biblically,' *Scottish Bulletin of Evangelical Theology* 20/2 (Autumn 2002) 146–61.

R. P. Martin, 'Worship in the Early Church,' *Worship in the Early Church* (Grand Rapids: Eerdmans, 1974).

K. A. Mathews, *Genesis 1:1–11:26* (New American Commentary; Nashville: Broadman & Holman, 1996).

U. W. Mauser, *Christ in the Wilderness* (Studies in Biblical Theology; London: SCM, 1963).

A. D. Mayes, *Deuteronomy* (The New Century Bible Commentary; Grand Rapids: Eerdmans, 1979).

J. L. Mays, *The Lord Reigns: A Theological Handbook to the Psalms* (Louisville: Westminster John Knox Press, 1994).

J. McCann, 'Exodus 32:1–14,' *Interpretation* 44 (July 1990) 277–81.

G. McConville, 'King and Messiah in Deuteronomy,' *King and Messiah in Israel and the Ancient Near East: Proceedings of the Oxford Old Tesament Seminar JSTOT 270* (J. Day; Sheffield: Sheffield Academic Press, 1998).

J. G. McConville, *Deuteronomy* (Apollos Old Testament Commentary; Leicester/Downers Grove: Apollos/IVP, 2002).

J. G. McConville, 'Exodus,' *NIDOTTE Vol. 4* (W. A. van Gemeran; Carlisle: Paternoster, 1997) 601–5.

J. McKeown, 'Blessings and Curses,' *Dictionary of the Old Testament Pentateuch* (T. D. &. B. Alexander, D. W.; Leicester: IVP, 2003) 83–7.

S. McKnight, 'Cain,' *Dictionary of the Old Testament Pentateuch* (T. D. &. B. Alexander, D. W.; Leicester: IVP, 2003).

S. McKnight, 'Collection for the Saints,' *Dictionary of Paul and His Letters* (G. F. Hawthorne; Leicester: IVP, 1993) 143–7.

S. McKnight, 'Seth,' *Dictionary of the Old Testament Pentateuch* (T. D. &. B. Alexander, D. W.; Leicester: IVP, 2003).

P. D. Miller, *The Religion of Ancient Israel* (Library of Ancient Israel; London/Louisville: SPCK/Westminster John Knox Press, 2000).

P. Miller, *Deuteronomy* (Interpreters' Bible Commentary; Louisville: John Knox Press, 1990).

R. W. Moberly, 'Christ as the Key to the Scripture: Genesis 22 Reconsidered,' *He Swore and Oath: Biblical Themes from Genesis 12–50* (R. Hess, G. Wenham and P. Satterhwaite; Carlisle/Grand Rapids: Paternoster/Baker, 1994) 143–73.

D. J. Moo, *The Epistle to the Romans* (The New International Commentary on the New Testament; Grand Rapids: William B. Eerdmans, 1996).

D. J. Moo, *Romans* (The NIV Application Commentary; Grand Rapids: Zondervan, 2000).

L. Morris, *The Atonement: Its Meaning and Significance* (Leicester: IVP, 1983).

L. Morris, *The Epistle to the Romans* (Grand Rapids: Eerdmans, 1988).

L. Morris, 'The Saints and the Synagogue,' *Worship, Theology and Ministry in the Early Church: Essays in Honor of Ralph P. Martin* (Micael J. Wilkins and Terence Paige; Sheffield: JSOT Press, 1992) 39–52.

H. Morrison, 'The Function of the "Spirit of Yahweh/God' in some early narratives of the Hebrew Bible, University of Glasgow,1993.

A. Motyer, *Look to the Rock* (Leicester: IVP, 1996).

S. Motyer, 'The People of God in Hebrews,' Unpublished conference presentation Tyndale Fellowship Conference, Nantwich, July, 2000).

W. Mounce, *Pastoral Epistles* (Word Biblical Commentary; Nashville: Thomas Nelson Publishers, 2000).

J. Murray, *The Epistle to the Romans* (The New International Commentary on the New Testament; Grand Rapids: Eerdmans, 1968).

N. Needham, *The Age of the Early Church Fathers* (2000 Years of Christ's Power; London: Grace Publications, 1997).

J. Niehaus, 'The Central Sanctuary: Where and When?' *Tyndale Bulletin* 43/1 (May 1992) 3–30.

P. O'Brien, 'Benediction, Blessing, Doxology, Thanksgiving,' *Dictionary of Paul and His Letters* (G.F. Hawthorne, R. P. Martin and D. G. Reid; Leicester/Downers Grove: IVP, 1993) 68–71.

P. O'Brien, *Colossians, Philemon* (Word Biblical Commentary; Waco: Word Books, 1982).

O'Mathúna D. P., 'Divination, Magic,' *Dictionary of the Old Testament Penateuch* (T. D. Alexander; Downers Grove: IVP, 2003) 193–7.

W. Osborne, 'Babel,' *Dictionary of the Old Testament Pentateuch* (T. D. &. B. Alexander, D. W.; Leicester: IVP, 2003) 73–75.

J. N. Oswalt, 'The Golden Calves and the Egyptian Concept of Deity," *Evangelical Quarterly* 45 (1973) 13–20.

D. Peterson, *Engaging with God: A Biblical Theology of Worship* (Leicester: Apollos, 1992).

D. Peterson, *Engaging with God: A Biblical Theology of Worship* (Leicester: IVP, 1992).

A. Resner, *Preacher and Cross: Person and Message in Theology and Rhetoric* (Grand Rapids: Eerdmans, 1999).

A. P. Ross, *Creation and Blessing: A Guide to the Study and Exposition of Genesis* (Grand Rapids: Baker Books, 1996).

E. Sauer, *The King of the Earth* (Carlisle: Paternoster, 1967).

P. Schaff, *The Creeds of Christendom, 3 Vols.* (New York, 1919).

A. Schlatter, *Romans: The Righteousness of God* (1995; S. S. Schatzmann; Peabody, Mas.: Hendrikson, 1995).

R. Schnackenburg, *The Epistle to the Ephesians* (Edinburgh: T & T Clark, 1991).

T. R. Schreiner, *Romans* (Baker Exegetical Commentary on the New Testament; Grand Rapids: Baker Books, 1998).

H. Schwönweiss and C. Brown, '*Proskyneo*,*' (1976) 875–9 *The International Dictionary of New Testament Theology, Vol. 2* (Colin Brown; Grand Rapids: Zondervan.)

D. Sheriffs, *The Friendship of the Lord: An Old Testament Spirituality* (Carlisle: Paternoster, 1996).

T. Smail, *The Giving Gift: The Holy Spirit in Person* (Leicester: IVP, 1989).

B. Strawn, 'Pharaoh,' *Dictionary of the Old Testament Pentateuch* (T. D. &. B. Alexander, D. W.; Downers Grove: IVP, 2003) 631–6.

S. Stuart, 'A New Testament Perspective on Worship,' *The Evangelical Quarterly* 68/3 (July 1996) 209–21.

A. Thistleton, *The First Epistle to the Corinthians: A Commentary on the Greek Text* (The New International Greek Testament Commentary; Grand Rapids/Carlisle: Eerdmans/ Paternoster, 2000).

D.Thomas, *Proclaiming the Incomprehensible God: Calvin's Teaching on Job* (Christian Focus, 2004).

L. E. Toombs, 'When Religions Collide: The Yahweh/Baal Confrontation,' *When Religions Collide and Other Essays. Essays in Biblical Literature and Archaeology in Honor of Willard Hamrick* (L. Toombs; Lewiston: Edwin Mellen, 1995) 13–46.

J. B. Torrance, 'The Place of Jesus Christ in Worship,' *Theological Foundations for Ministry* (R. Anderson; Edinburgh: T. & T. Clark, 1979) 348–69.

J. B. Torrance, *Worship, Communion and the Triune God of Grace* (Carlisle: Paternoster, 1996).

T. F. Torrance, *The Mediation of Christ* (Edinburgh: T. & T. Clark, 1992).

L. A. Turner, 'Genesis, Book Of,' *Dictionary of the Old Testament Pentateuch* (T. D. &. B. Alexander, D. W.; Leicester: IVP, 2003).

C. van Dam, 'Golden Calf,' *Dictionary of the Old Testament Pentateuch* (T. &. B. D. W. Alexander; Downers Grove: IVP, 2003) 368–71.

W. A. VanGemeren, *Psalms* (Expositor's Bible Commentary; Grand Rapids: Zondervan, 1991).

J. von Allmen, *Worship: Its Theology and Practice* (New York: Oxford University Press, 1965).

G. von Rad, *Genesis* (Old Testament Library; London: SCM, 1972).

A. W. Wainwright, *The Trinity in the New Testament* (SPCK Large Paperbacks; London: SPCK, 1962).

L. Walmark, 'Hebrews, Theology Of,' *EDBT* (A. Elwell; Grand Rapids: Baker Books, 1996).

B. Waltke, *Genesis: A Commentary* (Grand Rapids: Zondervan, 2001).

J. H. Walton, *Genesis* (The NIV Application Commentary; Grand Rapids: Zondervan, 2001).

A. Weiser, *The Psalms A Commentary* (Old Testament Library; London: SCM, 1962).

G. J. Wenham, 'The Religion of the Patriarchs,' *Essays in the Patriarchal Narratives* (A. &. W. Millard, D.; Leicester: IVP, 1980) 157–88.

G. Wenham, *Genesis 1–15* (Word Biblical Commentary; Waco, Texas: Word Books, 1987).

G. Wenham, 'Sanctuary and Symbolism in the Garden of Eden Story,' Proceedings of the World Congress of Jewish Studies, *9* (1986).

B. F. Westcott, *The Epistle to the Hebrews* (London: Macmillan & Co., 1914).

C. Westermann, *Genesis* (D. Green; Edinburgh: T & T Clark, 1988).

R. A. Whitacre, *John* (The IVP New Testament Commentary Series; Leicester/Downers Grove: IVP, 1999).

H. G. Williamson, 'Samaritans,' *Dictionary of Jesus and the Gospels* (M. Green, Marshall; Leicester: IVP, 1992) 724–8.

P. R. Williamson, 'Abraham,' *Dictionary of the Old Testament Pentateuch* (T. D. &. B. Alexander, D. W.; Downers Grove: IVP, 2003) 8–17.

B. Witherington III, *Conflict and Community in Corinth* (Carlisle/ Grand Rapids: Paternoster/Eerdmans, 1995).

B. Witherington III, *John's Wisdom: A Commentary on the Fourth Gospel* (Cambridge: The Lutterworth Press, 1995).

B. Witherington III, *Revelation* (The New Cambridge Bible Commentary; Cambridge: Cambridge University Press, 2003).

J. W. Wright, 'Genealogies,' *Dictionary of the Old Testament Pentateuch* (T. D. &. B. Alexander, D. W.; Leicester: IVP, 2003).

J. L. Wu, 'Liturgical Elements,' *DLNTD* (Martin & Davids; Leicester: IVP, 1997).

Notes

Chapter 1: The Battle for Worship

[1]This latter point is significant for the method we have adopted. Our method in this book is to examine the matter of worship from the viewpoint of biblical theology rather than from the standpoint of systematic or practical theology. The passages to be considered in this chapter indicate some significant markers in the landscape that forms the biblical theology of worship, and they touch on issues that will be developed in later chapters. A recurring them, however, will be the pressing reality of the battle for worship and its consequences. A quick glance at the indexes or tables of contents of books dealing with the matter of worship from the viewpoints of practical or systematic theology will indicate that this theme is under-represented in other treatments. By providing a biblical theology approach to the issues, it is hoped that this will feed into further necessary reflection in the realms of systematic or practical theology.

[2]Or perhaps because of it. See Mauser, U. W. (1963), *Christ in the Wilderness,* Studies in Biblical Theology, SCM, p. 100.

[3]Ibid.

[4]de Vaux, R. (1961), *Ancient Israel Its Life and Institutions,* Darton, Longman & Todd, p. 64.

[5]'Anointed one' is the translation of the Hebrew *mashiaḥ*; 'Messiah' is its transliteration.

[6]Note the close connection between the king's throne and Yahweh in such places as 1 Chronicles 28:5: 'And of all my sons (for the LORD has given me many sons), He has chosen my son Solomon to sit on the throne of the kingdom of the LORD over Israel,' and 29:23: 'Then Solomon sat on the throne of the LORD as king instead of David his father; and he prospered and all Israel obeyed him.' The king had no authority of himself, but only as he was the chosen and anointed one of Yahweh. For this reason David refused to raise his hand against Saul (e.g. 1 Sam. 24:6, 11; 26:9-12, 23), and for this reason also the king was meant to be a hearer and doer of the word of Yahweh, obeying the Torah and heeding the voice of the prophets.

[7]In the case of Solomon there is no specific mention of his reception of the Spirit, but it is certainly implied in his gift of wisdom

(1 Kings 4:29; cf. Isa. 11:2). There is probably a difference implied here between the earlier charismatic kingship of Saul and David, and the dynastic kingship model that emerged after David's reign. It may not be that the lack of reference to a special Spirit anointing is indicative of a kingship of lesser authority, but that the anointing on the king at the head of the dynasty (in this case, David) stands as representative of the whole. For discussion of this point I am indebted to my Old Testament teaching colleague, Hector Morrison.

[8]A theme prominent in Matthew (e.g. 1:1; cf. 3:17; 16:16; 17:5; 26:23; 28:18), but implicit throughout the synoptic Gospels.

[9]Tremper Longman III and Daniel Reid have drawn attention to the role of Yahweh as Divine Warrior. Among other fine observations, the point is well made that 'God was not at Israel's beck and call in warfare. He would not provide the victory for them in any and every situation. They had to obey the covenant, otherwise they were liable to God's judgement. At such times God turned against Israel as an enemy. This reversal of holy war came about particularly when the king trusted his weapons more than the Lord (Isa. 30:15-16; Amos 2:13-16)' (Longman III, T., & Reid, D. [1995], *God is a Warrior*, Studies in Old Testament Biblical Theology, Zondervan, p. 60). The identification of the king's false trust in the weapons of mere men, or in alliances with other nations is doubtless fair comment. However, at this point the writers miss the larger connection between the judgement of Israel – where Yahweh effectively constitutes himself as Israel's enemy – and the corruption of worship, for which the kings in particular were held responsible.

[10]This statement summarizes the theme of the letter to the Hebrews, about which we will say more in a later chapter.

[11]Weiser, A. (1962), *The Psalms A Commentary,* Old Testament Library, SCM, p. 695.

[12]Allen, L. C. (1987), *Psalms 101–150,* Word Biblical Commentary, p. 87. Mays comments on the importance of Psalm 2 for its links with the kingship of Jesus the Messiah, suggesting that 'One way to identify and describe the uniqueness of the kingship about which Psalm 2 speaks is to say that it has a prophetic origin, a prophetic history and a prophetic destiny' (Mays, J. L. [1994], *The Lord Reigns: A Theological Handbook to the Psalms,* Westminster John Knox Press, p. 113).

[13]In Psalm 105:15 (= I Chronicles 16:22), the prophets generally are described as Yahweh's "anointed ones".

[14]Hector Morrison has drawn attention to the connection between anointing and covenantal commitment. Drawing on the work of Kutsch and Mettinger, whose studies into the use of anointing oil in the ancient Near East indicate that it had a contractual or covenant fixing role, Morrison comments, 'The anointing by the people ... implies a contract between king and people (2 Sam. 5:3), while the anointing by Yahweh signals a contractual relationship between Yahweh and the king in which Yahweh pledges himself to the king and becomes obligated to him as protector while the king in turn is consecrated to Yahweh and becomes his vassal' (Morrison, H., [Unpublished MTh Dissertation, Glasgow University, 1991], p. 172.

[15]The wording is itself significant. This is a conflation of Psalm 2 and Isaiah 42, and as such brings together the themes of the Kingship and the Suffering Servant. The nature of Jesus' kingship is thus declared from the very outset of his ministry.

[16]This is a consistent line of New Testament teaching, which can be traced all the way back to the promise of Genesis 3:15, that one would come from woman who would crush the Serpent's head. See, for example, John 12:31; 16:11; Acts 10:38; Colossians 2:13-15; Hebrews 2:14-15; 1 John 3:8b; Revelation 20:10.

[17]Ferguson, S. B. (1996), *The Holy Spirit,* Contours of Christian Theology, IVP, pp. 46f. Tom Smail draws attention to a similar idea. He suggests that the baptism 'was not simply a dramatic manifestation of what had been his from the start; it involved his being given by the Father, in a real and dynamic transaction, that which was appropriate to the stage in his life and mission that he had now reached and that would not have been appropriate before.... His relation to his Father is indeed eternal; yet it is also pneumatic, that is, it is lived out in the ever active power and creative freshness of the Spirit. It can, therefore, be expressed in all sorts of different ways at different stages of the development of his human life and his messianic mission' (Smail, T. [1989], *The Giving Gift: The Holy Spirit in Person*, IVP, pp. 96-97.

[18]Allen, L. C. (1987), p. 99.

[19]This text is disputed, and does not appear in all the ancient manuscripts. The fact that it should appear at all, however, bears testimony (at least in the early church's exposition of the events in Gethsemane) to the depths of suffering inherent in this deep trial.

[20]In this aspect the Spirit is seen reprising his role of the leader and guide of the king in Israel, and also as the one who is present with his

people even in the wilderness (Isa. 63:9-10). The question that both the king and Israel needed to face was, 'Do we trust God, or do we not?' The refusal to trust him, i.e. to act in unbelief, was the root of all their sin. In particular it was the root of their idolatry, since such false worship (connected as it often was with fertility) expressed their unbelief in Yahweh's essential goodness and his faithfulness to his promises.

[21]This question of trust is the other side of the issue of obedience. Paul tells us that 'anything that does not proceed from faith is sin' (Rom. 14:23), while the writer to the Hebrews, in his discussion of Israel's refusal to enter God's rest in chapters 3 and 4, clearly aligns disobedience with unbelief. To trust God's word is to obey him; to obey him is to trust his word and act accordingly.

[22]While Luke's account does not repeat the phrase, it does stand at the head of his account as the rubric under which the temptations are clustered.

[23]See for example, the mountain in the region of Moriah, where the dramatic events of Abraham's sacrifice of Isaac take place in Genesis 22; the references to Horeb/Sinai as the mountain of God where he meets with his people in the events of the exodus (e.g. Exod. 3:1, 12; 15:17; 19:12ff.; 24:12ff.), where the Lord spoke to Moses 'face to face in the midst of the fire' (Deut. 5:4); God's 'holy mountain', Zion (e.g. Pss. 48:1ff.; 99:9) where he caused his glory and name to dwell in the Temple; the mountain of the Lord that would be the blessing of the nations (e.g. Isa. 2:1ff.; 11:9; 25:6ff; 65:25); the revelation of Jesus' kingdom teaching that takes place in the sermon on the mount (Matt. 5:1f.); and the mountain to which John is taken in the Spirit so that he can see the bride, the wife of the lamb (Rev. 21:10).

[24]Psalm 2:7f.: 'He said to me "You are my son, today I have begotten you. Ask of me and I will surely give the nations as your inheritance, the ends of the earth as your possession." '

[25]Hagner, D. (1993), *Matthew 1–13*, Word Biblical Commentary, p. 68.

[26]The link between Satan and idolatry (seen in such places as Deuteronomy 32:17; Psalm 106:37; 1 Corinthians 10:14-22; Galatians 4:8; Revelation 9:20 etc.) is one to which we will return later.

[27]Carson, D. A. (1984), *Matthew*, Expositor's Bible Commentary, Zondervan, p. 114.

[28]See, for example, Allen, L. C. (1987), p. 109.

[29]Blaiklock, E. M. (1977), *Commentary on the Psalms, Vol 2.*, Scripture Union, p. 84. Weiser points to significant features of the Psalm that indicate an earlier origin, and thus concludes that 'a pre-exilic origin for the liturgy is not excluded, even though the lack of particular references makes the exact dating of the psalm impossible' (Weiser, A. [1962], p. 715).

[30]The Hallel Psalms were extremely significant in the liturgical life of Israel. There are three main collections, The Egyptian Hallel (113-118); the Great Hallel (120–136); and the concluding Hallel psalms (146–150). 'The Hallel Psalms had a significant part in the praise (*hallel*) of the Lord. The Egyptian Hallel and the Great Hallel ... were sung during the annual feasts (Lev. 23; Num. 10:10). The Egyptian Hallel psalms received a special place in the Passover liturgy, as 113–114 were recited or sung before and 115-118 after the festival meal (cf. Matt. 26:30; Mark 14:26) (VanGemeren, W. A. (1991), *Psalms,* Expositor's Bible Commentary, Zondervan, p. 713. Allen (following Gunkel and Weiser) gives a fair reconstruction of the way in which this psalm may have been used in the public worship of God's Old Testament people, perhaps involving a priest's encouragement and an antiphonal response (1987, p. 108f.).

[31]VanGemeren, W. A. (1991), p. 720.

[32]Allen, L. C. (1987), p. 111.

[33]William Brown comments on Psalm 115's declaration of 'God's efficacious presence in contrast to the lifeless idols', particularly in the ascription of the full range of senses to Yahweh (in contrast to the idols who have none). 'Speech, sight, hearing, smell, touch, even locomotion ("walk") are covered in this taxonomy of agency. Rather than delimiting the deity, the bodily senses highlight God's unbounded freedom.... Divine freedom, moreover, is shared by those who cast their allegiance on God ... much in contrast to the idol worshipers, whose own senses are numbed to the point of death' (Brown, W. P. [2002], *Seeing the Psalms: A Theology of Metaphor*, Westminster John Knox Press, p. 127.

[34]Moo, D. J. (2000), *Romans*, The NIV Application Commentary, Zondervan, p. 59. Author's italics. Paul is, of course, drawing upon Old Testament theology here. For example, in Isaiah the proclamation of good news is to be seen in the context of the experience of chastisement and judgment under the hand of God.

[35]Morris, L. (1983), *The Atonement: Its Meaning and Significance*, IVP, p. 169, Author's italics.

[36]Barrett, C. K. (1962), *A Commentary on the Epistle to the Romans*, Black's New Testament Commentaries, Adam & Charles Black, p. 36.

[37]Schreiner, T. R. (1998), *Romans*, Baker Exegetical Commentary on the New Testament, Baker Books, p. 88. Schreiner goes on to make the powerful and biblically correct statement that 'Since refusal to honor and glorify God is described in terms of ἀδικιά [unrighteousness], we have a clue here that both the saving and judging righteousness of God are rooted in a desire to see his name glorified. His wrath is inflicted upon the world because he is not prized, esteemed, and glorified.'

[38]Schlatter notes how Paul's analysis exposes the self seeking nature of human religion. 'Whatever they are seeking for themselves by means of their religious acts, namely, to secure and increase their happiness, to atone for their guilt, and to gain for themselves the assistance of the deity, all this is put aside. The individual is godless if he fabricates religion in his own interest, for the sake of his own happiness' (Schlatter, A. [1995], *Romans: The Righteousness of God*, Hendrikson, p. 40.

[39]Moo, D. J. (1996), *The Epistle to the Romans*, The New International Commentary on the New Testament, William B. Eerdmans, p. 111.

[40]Bingham, G. C. (1990), *The Way and Wonder of Worship*, New Creation Publications, p. 43.

[41]Barth, K. (1933), *The Epistle of to the Romans*, Oxford University Press, p. 51.

[42]'Revelation' is simply the English translation of the Greek *apocalypsis*, which is the first word of the book in the Greek text: *apocalypsis Iēsou Christou* i.e. [the] revelation of Jesus Christ. *apocalyptō* (the verb) and its cognates means to reveal, disclose, uncover. It is not a process of discovery from the human side of things, but of unveiling from the divine side.

[43]Witherington III, B. (2003), *Revelation*, The New Cambridge Bible Commentary, Cambridge University Press, p. 40.

[44]Beale points to a number of indicators that the theme of God's sovereign action dominates the book. He draws attention to the intensity of occurrences of the word *thronos* (throne) in chapters 4

and 5; to its use throughout the rest of the book (e.g. that all the judgments unleashed on earth begin from the throne in heaven as in Rev. 6:1-8; 8:3-6; etc.); to the central position occupied by the throne in heaven; and to the fact that 'all earth's inhabitants are appraised on the basis of their attitude to God's claim to rule over them from his heavenly throne (cf. 6:16-17; 20:11-12)' (Beale, G. [1999], *The Book of Revelation: A Commentary on the Greek Text*, The New International Greek Testament Commentary, Eerdmans, p. 320.

[45]For full discussion of these points, see Longman III, T., & Reid, D. (1995), pp. 83–88.

[46]Ibid, p. 45.

[47]Ibid, pp. 121–24.

[48]In particular Bingham, G. C. (1990), *The Way and Wonder of Worship,* New Creation Publications; Bingham, G. C. (1989), *The Clash of the Kingdoms*, New Creation Publications Inc.; and Bingham, G. C. (1981), *Dear and Darling Idols: Lords and Gods Piffling and Appalling*, New Creation Publications Inc.

[49]Much of this has been in the context of personal discussion or preaching engagements, not least at the author's recent induction service!

[50]Cranfield, C. E. B. (1958, October), 'Divine and Human Action: The Biblical Concept of Worship,' *Interpretation, 12* (4), p. 387.

Chapter 2. Worship in the Biblical Prologue: Genesis 1–11
[1]We should also bear in mind references to the council of God, in which the role of the angels is also portrayed: e.g. Jeremiah 23:18; 22; Job. 15:8.

[2]An alternative translation runs 'the fullness of the whole earth is his glory'.

[3]The Hebrew word means 'burning ones' and they are thus associated with the holiness of God, which is pictured as a consuming fire.

[4]There are over 65 references to *cherubim* in the Bible. There are no Hebrew words of the same root, so the meaning is debateable. Characteristically, however, they are associated with the presence of God. Far from the benign childishness implied in our English version of the word (cherubic), they are seen as powerful and active servants of God.

[5]There are some parallels between the description of the living creatures in Revelation 4:6-9, and the *seraphim,* but they are not identical.

[6]Blocher, H. (1984), *In the Beginning*, IVP, p. 71. So also Walter Brueggemann (1997, *Theology of the Old Testament*, Fortress Press, p. 157), who argues that the lively response of the creation in obedient fruitfulness is its praise to the Creator.

[7]A polemical strain runs throughout the opening books of the Old Testament, not least in the opening chapters of Genesis. Many of the elements described in these chapters are delineated in sharp contrast to the belief system and worship practices of the surrounding nations in the ancient Near East. For example, Lohfink comments, 'The sun and the moon, which in the entire East were a god and a godess of the foremost significance, are deprived of their divinity; God simply hangs them in the heavens as "lights", mere utensils (1:14-18). That is demythologization so radical that we can scarcely appreciate it nowadays' (Lohfink, G. [1999], *Does God Need the Church? Toward a Theology of the People of God*, Liturgical Press, p.8.

[8]This thought is reflected, for example in Luther's *Small Catechism*. In relation to the first article of the Apostles' Creed, 'I believe in God the Father Almighty, maker of heaven and earth,' the *Catechism* says, 'I believe that God has created me and all that exists; that he has given me and still preserves to me body and soul, eyes, ears, and all my limbs, my reason and all my senses; and also clothing and shoes, food and drink; house and home; wife and child; land, cattle and all my property; that he provides me daily with all the necessities of life, protects me from all danger and preserves and guards me against all evil; and all this out of his pure paternal goodness and mercy, without any merit or unworthiness of mine, for all which I am in duty bound to thank, praise, serve and obey him.'

[9]Irenaeus, *Against Heresies*, The Ante Nicene Fathers, Book IV, Ch. xiv, para. 1, T. & T. Clark.

[10]Wenham, G. (1987), *Genesis 1–15*, Word Biblical Commentary, Word Books., p. 53.

[11]My italics.

[12]Hart, T. (1994), 'Atonement and Worship,' *Anvil, 11*(3), 203.

[13]We notice in passing that both extremes have been seen in human history. Not only is idolatry tied to the representation of physical forms (as in Romans 1:18-32), but angelic and other beings have also been the objects of human worship (see, for example, the practice implied in Colossians 2:18 and the abundance of New Age books on this and related topics today). For further detailed discussion on the background

to the Colossian heresy and its implications, see Arnold, C. E. (1996), *The Colossian Syncretism: The Interface between Christianity and Folk Belief at Colossae*, Baker Books. Arnold argues that the worship of angels alluded to in Colossians 2:18 'refers essentially to a magical invocation of angels, especially for apotropaic purposes' [i.e. intended to ward off evil] (p. 10). It is, of course, the supreme irony that Satan, an angelic creature, should seek to have the Son of God worship him in the temptation narratives. Hebrews 1:6 provides an appropriate comment: 'when he brings the firstborn into the world, he says, "Let all God's angels worship him."'

[14]Hart, T. (1994). Atonement and Worship. *Anvil, 11*(3), 203.

[15]See, for example, Alexander, T. D. (1995). *From Paradise to the Promised Land*, Paternoster, p. 21; Jordan, J. B. (1988), *Through New Eyes*, Wolgemuth & Hyatt, p. 136; Wenham, G. (1987), *Genesis 1–15*, Word Biblical Commentary, Word Books, p. 65; Wenham, G. (1986), 'Sanctuary and Symbolism in the Garden of Eden Story [Proceedings of the World Congress of Jewish Studies],'. in *9*, pp. 19-25; Chilton, D. (1994), *Paradise Restored*, Dominion Press, p. 44; Sauer, E. (1967), *The King of the Earth*, Paternoster, pp. 90ff.

[16]See also Ezekiel 28:13-14 and the repeated theme of the 'mountain of the Lord', 'the holy mountain' and 'Mt. Zion', often associated with Edenic imagery, and the identification of this mountain with the Temple, both geographically and theologically.

[17]Chilton, D. (1994), *Paradise Restored*, Dominion Press, p. 44.

[18]Wenham, G. (1987), p. 67.

[19]It is also possible to see this as a direct rebuke to Satan. The 'you' could be taken as specific. The commandment was as applicable to him as to any other created being. Jesus may be saying to him, '*you* should worship God alone', as much as 'I will worship God alone'.

[20]Colin Brown, '*Proskuneō,*' *The International Dictionary of New Testament Theology*, Vol. 2., Zondervan, p. 875.

[21]Hess suggests that the meaning of *latreuō* covers 'the service of God by the whole people [i.e. not just the priests, for which the word *leitourgeō* is normally used] and by the individual, both outwardly in the cultus and inwardly in the heart' (C. Brown, [1976], *Latreuō, The International Dictionary of New Testament Theology*, Vol. 3, Zondervan, p. 550.

[22]Walton, J. H. (2001), *Genesis*, The NIV Application Commentary, Zondervan, p. 203.

[23]Fretheim, T. E. (1969), *Creation, Fall and Flood*, Ausgburg Press, p. 69.

[24]Fretheim, T. E. (1969), p. 80.

[25]The provenance of the term is disputed. Does it come from *nechosheth*, 'brass', or *nachash*, 'serpent'? It does not much matter. The point at issue is that it has become an object of worship, either as The Serpent image or The Brass image (emphasizing its powers of deliverance).

[26]There is, of course, a deep irony in the use of this Psalm by the devil in the New Testament temptation narratives. In Matthew 4:6 the devil is shown to test Jesus in relation to his trust in God, quoting from Psalm 91:11,12. The same Psalm, however, shows that by the very act of trusting God 'the young lion and the serpent' will be trampled down!

[27]The allusion is almost universally acknowledged (e.g. Cranfield, Moo, Morris, Fitzmyer, Schreiner *et.al.*) What is debated is whether the allusion carries a temporal or eschatological weight. Is it speaking of the cosmic victory of the Kingdom of God over the Devil, or the more immediate manifestation of this in the defeat of the false teachers who are opposing the gospel? Whatever the case, the identification with Genesis 3:15 means that the one who works evil in the world now, or the one who will be finally judged and cast into the lake of fire then, in Paul's theology is the same as the one who deceived the first couple in Eden with his cunning. Certainly Paul's language chimes with the wider New Testament perspective in which the apostolic/ believers' authority is to tread serpents under foot and thus gain victory over the devil (e.g. Luke 10:19 in its context).

[28]The ones to whom the epithet *satan* are ascribed in the Old Testament are varied. The word means an 'adversary', and can thus be used both of people (e.g. 1 Samuel 29:4; 2 Samuel 19:22) and spiritual/supernatural beings (e.g. Zechariah 3:1-3). Its context is always important. In Numbers 22:22f, for example, the Angel of Yahweh is designated as a *satan* against Balaam. Wherever it appears it has a legal background, which is also widely attested to in non-canonical writings of the period of Second Temple Judaism. For details of the latter, see Beale, G. (1999), *The Book of Revelation: A Commentary on the Greek Text*, The New International Greek Testament Commentary, Eerdmans, pp. 661ff.

[29]His descriptive titles portray his character and action. He is variously called the Tempter (Matt. 4:5; 1 Thess. 3:5), Beelzebub

(Matt. 12:24), the Enemy (Matt. 13:39), the Evil One (Matt. 13:19, 38; 1 John 2:13,14; 3:12, and particularly 5:18), the Father of Lies and a Murderer (John 8:44), Belial (2 Cor. 6:15), the Adversary (1 Peter 5:8), the Deceiver (Rev. 12:9) and the (Great) Dragon (Rev. 12:3).

[30]cf. David Atkinson's comments in the context of his discussion of Genesis 3:1-5: 'Some habit, some possession, some secret sin, some bitter resentment – in the context of our whole life, it seems so small, and yet it is at that one point that our trust in God is tested. If we will not let God be God at this one, small, trivial, yet so crucial a point, then we really do not trust him where it matters at all' (Atkinson, D. [1990], *The Message of Genesis 1–11*, The Bible Speaks Today, IVP, p. 84).

[31]This statement assumes that the provision of animal skin coverings implies instructions about sacrifice and atonement. God's gracious provision was not just in furnishing Adam and Eve with coverings against the elements, but with the means of offering acceptable worship. While one cannot argue absolutely for this point from the exegesis of Genesis 3:21 alone, it does match with a long history of exegesis along these lines, and certainly accords with the content and meaning of the subsequent description of Abel's worship, and provides part of the contrast between his (acceptable) and Cain's (unacceptable) worship. Likewise, Noah's acceptable worship is predicated on sacrificial offerings that must have had a provenance in the earlier history of the race.

[32]Old Testament scholars are not united on the exact meaning of the words (at least in their original intention). For some of the difficulties of vocabulary and grammar, see, Wenham, G. (1987). *Genesis 1–15*, pp. 79ff.; von Rad, G. (1972), *Genesis*, SCM, pp. 92ff.. Despite this divergence, there are a number of reasons for taking this as a Messianic reference. The subsequent emphasis on the 'seed' (*zera'*) in the Pentateuch; its central place in the Abrahamic covenant, especially as interpreted by Paul in Galatians; other New Testament allusions such as Romans 16:20; Hebrews 2:14; Revelation 12; and the fact that from the early history of the church this verse has been spoken of as the 'protoevangelium'; these all indicate that the verse is of Messianic significance. For further discussion, see Alexander, T. D. (1995), 'Messianic Ideology in the Book of Genesis,' in P. E. Satterthwaite, *The Lord's Anointed: Interpretation of Old Testament Messianic Texts*, Paternoster, pp. 27-32.

[33]Cain's name (*qayin*) is based on the Hebrew 'acquire, possess, get' and forms a word play with the latter part of the verse: 'I have gotten (*qânîtî*) a man with the help of the LORD' (ESV). Other translations handle the text in similar ways e.g.: 'With the help of the LORD I have brought forth a man' (NIV); 'I have gotten a manchild with the help of the LORD' (NASB); 'I have gotten a man from the LORD' (KJV). The word play may indicate something of Cain's character, with his name acting as 'a foreshadowing of his primary proclivities' (Waltke, B. [2001], *Genesis: A Commentary*, Zondervan, p. 96. The translations above indicate a preference for interpreting Eve's comment as an expression of gratitude, which is not the only option (it could be taken as a boast, see the discussion in Walton, J. H. [2001]. *Genesis*, The NIV Application Commentary, Zondervan, pp. 261-62; Wenham, G. [1987], *Genesis 1–15*, pp. 101-02), and there may be 'an ambiguity about her expression which may suggest that she covertly compared her achievement with Yahweh's greater works and hoped that he would be with her son' (Wenham, G., p. 102).

[34]See this theme in the later prophets also: e.g. Malachi 1:6-14

[35]Calvin, commenting on Genesis 4:4, says: 'for he does not simply state that the worship which Abel had paid was pleasing to God, but he begins with the person of the offerer; by which he signifies that God will regard no works with favour except those the doer of which is already previously accepted and approved by him' (Calvin, J. *Genesis*, Calvin's Commentaries, Baker Books, p. 194). McKnight's comment is apt: 'the narrative suggests that the rite itself and the intent of the worshiper are to be distinguished, with the latter carrying the load of what God considers acceptable' (McKnight, S., 'Cain,' in *Dictionary of the Old Testament Pentateuch*, IVP, p. 108.

[36]Hughes, P. E. (1977), *A Commentary on the Epistle to the Hebrews*, Eerdmans, p. 454.

[37]Luther, M., *Lectures on Genesis 1–5,* Luther's Works. Concordia Publishing House, p. 259..

[38]Luther sees Cain as being typical of many first-born sons in the Bible: 'Relying on their right [of primogeniture], they despised and lorded it over their brothers. But God is the God of the humble and resists the proud (1 Peter 5:5). Because they are proud, the firstborn sons are deprived of their right.... Thus Abel – whom Adam, Eve and Cain despised as a worthless person – is given a position before God as Lord of heaven and earth' (Luther, M., *Lectures on Genesis 1–5*, p. 245).

[39]Blocher, H. (1984), *In the Beginning: The opening chapters of Genesis*, IVP, p. 198.

[40]Psalm 51 clearly identifies acceptable sacrifice with the humble and penitential faith of the offerer. David knew that there was no provision to cover the sin he had committed, yet he looked to God to be merciful to him for he knew that 'the sacrifices of God are a broken spirit: A broken and contrite heart, O God, you will not despise' (Ps. 51:17). This is the worship that Cain refused to offer. In the history of Israel his failure was to be repeated on a national scale.

[41]There are numerous parallels between the incident of Cain's sin and that of the sin of Eve (and then Adam) in the garden. '(1) sin is graphically described (Gen. 3:5-7; 4:6-7); (2) the sinner undergoes divine interrogation (Gen. 3:3-13; 4:9-12; (3) the ultimate divine question is one of personal location ("Where are you?") and social location ("Where is your brother?"; Gen. 3:9; 4:9); (4) the sinner is cursed (Gen. 3:14, 17; 4:11-12); and (5) the clothing of Adam and Eve and marking of Cain are similar, as is their banishment to the east (Gen. 3:21, 24; 4:15-16)' (McKnight, S., 'Cain,' in *Dictionary of the Old Testament Pentateuch*, IVP, p. 107. The parallels serve both to indicate the continuity of Cain's sin with that of his parents, and to indicate that God's attitude to each is consistent.

[42]Wenham quotes Procksch, who calls it 'The most obscure verse in Genesis' (*Genesis 1–15*, p. 104. For similar comments on the difficulty of the verse, see, for example, Mathews, K. A. (1996). *Genesis 1:1–11:26.*, New American Commentary, Broadman & Holman, p. 269; and Hamilton, V. C. (1990), *The Book of Genesis Chapters 1–11*, New International Commentary on the Old Testament, Eerdmans, p. 225.

[43]Mathews, K. A. (1996), p. 269.

[44]McKnight, S., 'Seth,' in *Dictionary of the Old Testament Pentateuch*, IVP, p. 739.

[45]See the discussion in Sheriffs, D. (1996). *The Friendship of the Lord: An Old Testament Spirituality*, Paternoster, chapter 2, 'Walking with God: Three Genesis Prototypes.' Sheriffs makes the appropriate link with Hebrews 11:5 and 12:1f. in the New Testament, and suggests that 'What comes through in the descriptions of Hebrews and in Gen. 5:24 is the continuity of relationship with God. Death does not break it – neither the death pronounced in the Eden story (Gen. 2:17 and 3:19), nor the termination of life in old age' (p. 33).

[46]Motyer, A. (1996), *Look to the Rock*, IVP, pp. 44–45, provides further discussion on this repeated emphasis.

[47]There is, of course, a converse idea seen in the concept of walking with the wicked: e.g. Psalm 1:1; Proverbs 4:14; Ephesians 2:2.

[48]The original divisions in the Genesis narrative are marked out by the recurring *tôledôt* formula. This is translated by the NIV as 'account', but derives from the Hebrew word to beget, bear, or bring forth. It is seen in Genesis 2:4; 5:1; 6:9; 10:1; 11:10, 27; 25:12, 19; 36:1, 9; 37:2, and acts as a sort of chapter marker for the unfolding narrative. 'The overall function of *tôledôt* formulas ... is to juxtapose narrative and genealogical blocks, a feature that has a significant impact on the theology of the book as a whole' (Turner, L. A., 'Genesis, Book of,' in *Dictionary of the Old Testament Pentateuch*, IVP, p. 350. The genealogies associated with the *tôledôt* divisions serve to underscore the development of themes in the narrative such as the place of the 'seed', the unfolding of God's purpose etc. 'The genealogical structure of the *tôledôt* formula gives Genesis its distinct nature as the story of a particular family amidst all the families of the earth. Even as the narrative develops linearly, the genealogical structure brings the readers' attention back to this particular family, the family of Jacob/ Israel.... They reveal that Genesis is unique among the books of the Pentateuch in its nature as the story of God's calling of a particular family amidst God's good creation, now gone bad' (Wright, J. W., 'Genealogies,' in *Dictionary of the Old Testament Pentateuch*, IVP, p. 348.

[49]So Blocher, 'The earth is now so filled with violence (Gn. 6:11f.) that God must deploy the most gigantic ablution to wash it free of its stain. He himself uses the verb 'blot out' (Gn. 6:7; 7:4, 23). The universality of the scourge corresponds to the universality of the corruption' (Blocher, H. [1984], *In the Beginning: The opening chapters of Genesis*, IVP, pp. 205-06.

[50]Motyer, A. (1996), *Look to the Rock*, p. 43.

[51]Motyer, A. (1996). *Look to the Rock*, p. 43.

[52]Walton, J. H. (2001). *Genesis*, p. 311. He continues: 'This is in accord with the normal usage of these terms throughout the Old Testament, where they do not generally indicate someone's absolute righteousness or blamelessness relative to God's standards but indicate one's status on the human scale'. He offers Genesis 18:23-28; 2 Samuel 22:24-26 and Ezekiel 33:12-18 as examples. The quotation in the text

preserves his italics.

[53]See Dumbrell, W. (1984), *Covenant and Creation: An Old Testament Covenantal Theology*, Paternoster, p. 13: 'The term "righteousness" in the Old Testament generally refers to conduct logically arising from the prior establishment of a relationship. Such conduct would be appropriate to and consistent with the relationship established.'

[54]Waltke, B. (2001). *Genesis: A Commentary*, p. 142.

[55]Wenham suggests that the verse could be paraphrased, 'The Lord smelled the Noahic sacrifice' (*Genesis 1–15*, p. 189), while Hamilton suggests the translation 'Yahweh smelled the rest-inducing aroma' (*The Book of Genesis Chapters 1–11*, p. 308). There are many lines in this account that emerge as significant themes in the later history of Israel. The division between clean and unclean animals, the nature of the offering (as a whole burnt offering), and the mention of the soothing aroma are all ideas which recur in the theology of the later sacrifices of atonement in the temple. While Old Testament scholars debate the sources and chronology which underlie the Genesis account, the ancient readers of Genesis (who were Israelites, we must remember) would have been left in no doubt that this worship was propitiatory. It was an effective act of atonement no less than those sacrifices offered in faith in the temple.

[56]Although writing with a different point in view Walther Eichrodt's comment is nonetheless apposite: 'the whole tenor of ancient Israel's belief in Yahweh is irreconcilable with the idea that God is fed by the sacrifice, bound up as this idea is with God's dependence on man. The central concept of the covenant asserts no less than that Yahweh already existed and had proved his power, before ever Israel sacrificed to him' (Eichrodt, W. [1961], *Theology of the Old Testament*, SCM, p. 143). In the immediate context of the Noahic sacrifice, Waltke comments on the contrast between the Genesis Flood narrative and the gods in the Gilgamesh epic in which 'the Mesopotamian gods gather "like flies" around the sacrifice' (*Genesis: A Commentary*, p. 142).

[57]Osborne, W., 'Babel,' in *Dictionary of the Old Testament Pentateuch*, IVP, p. 75.

[58]Wenham, G. (1987). *Genesis 1–15*, p. 239.

[59]Wenham, G. (1987). *Genesis 1–15*, p. 241.

[60]Clements, R. E. (1965), *God and Temple,* Basil Blackwell, p. 3;

cf. R. Davidson, 'The ziggurats were the cathedrals of the ancient near east, expressions of man's piety. They symbolised the connection between heaven and earth, the gods and men.' In the building of this tower, Davidson suggests, 'Man unites in the anthem, "Glory to man in the highest", and the outcome is division and confusion' (Davidson, R. [1973], *Genesis 1–11*, The Cambridge Bible Commentary, Cambridge University Press, p. 105.

[61]Walton, J. H. (2001), pp. 373-78.

[62]Walton, J. H. (2001), p. 376. Walton goes on to comment on the irony embedded in the Babel story: 'The builders construct the ziggurat so that deity can come down into their midst – and indeed Yahweh does come down (v. 5), but he is displeased. He views this as a first step with inevitable results – human beings have crossed a significant threshold from which there will be no turning back' (p. 378).

[63]Dumbrell, W. (1984), *Covenant and Creation: An Old Testament Covenantal Theology*, Paternoster, p. 60.

[64]Hence Wenham's comment: 'for all its vaunted height, so far short of heaven did this so called skyscraper fall that God could hardly see it: he had to come down to look at it!' (*Genesis 1–15*, p. 345).

Chapter 3. The Patriarchs and the Exodus: Contrast and Conflict

[1]Blocher comments, 'With Abram ... the tenth from Noah, as Noah was the tenth from Adam, begins the decisive implementation of the plan of God. The sights are set on its goal; on that descendant of Abraham by whom all the nations of the earth will have their share in blessing. The sights are set on Jesus Christ and on those who in him constitute the true descendants of the father of those who believe, that humanity that is gathered together by grace' (Blocher, H. [1984)], *In the Beginning: The opening chapters of Genesis,* IVP, p. 211).

[2]See the discussion of McKeown, J. (2003), 'Blessings and Curses,' in *Dictionary of the Old Testament Pentateuch* [2003], IVP, pp. 86-87).

[3]Interestingly enough, Joshua 24:14 indicates that many of the Israelites still worshiped these gods, all these centuries later! Joshua's exhoration is that they would put away these gods from their midst. Passages such as Genesis 35:2-4, where Jacob and his extended household rid themselves of the various foreign gods they had amongst them (though by hiding them rather than destroying them!), indicate

the antiquity of the practice. These idols had come from the household of Laban, who had remained beyond the River. The evident purity of Abraham's worship from his call onwards, provides a counterpoint and contrast to the worship of his descendants. By implication, it also provides a pattern for them to follow.

[4]The word 'hearing' is not specifically mentioned but his obedience is clear: 'according to what the Lord has spoken to him'. There is a close connection throughout the Old Testament between 'hearing' and 'obeying'.

[5]Hess comments, 'When God took Abram from this land he also removed him from ties with his ancestral deities. Laban, having remained *beyond the River* in Haran, had continued with these ties. God's work with Israel began by enabling Abram to worship God alone' (Hess, R. S. [1996], *Joshua: An Introduction & Commentary*, IVP, p. 302). Walton likewise indicates the connections: 'The issues of land and family ... have significance here [in Gen. 12:1-3] with regard to the role of deity. In the ancient world many deities were associated with land or with people groups (nations, tribes, clans, families).... Thus, when Abram is asked to put his land and his family behind him, the request entails walking away from any territorial or patron gods' (Walton, J. H. [2001], *Genesis*, The NIV Application Commentary, Zondervan, p. 392).

[6]The nature of the patriarchs' religious experience has been debated, and such debates have often been linked to discussions about the underlying sources of the Genesis narrative based on the names of God used in different sections. Other aspects of the debate have focussed on the comparison between their religious expression and that of other Ancient Near East religions. In addition, the issue of the nature of patriarchal religion is complicated by various interpretations of Exodus 6:3 (especially when compared with Exodus 3:13-15), where it appears that a new name of God is being revealed to Moses, a name unknown to Abraham. G. J. Wenham, in his 'The Religion of the Patriarchs' (in A. and W. Millard, D., *Essays in the Patriarchal Narratives* [1980], IVP, pp. 157–88), gives a good overview of the debates and interrelated questions and themes, while a glance at the bibliographies of the various commentaries on the passage will reveal how much critical activity has surrounded this passage. None of this, however, should obscure the central thought. Canonically, Abraham is held up as a model of true worship, i.e. obedient service, to the one,

true God. P. R. Williamson, in his article 'Abraham', is justified in commenting: 'While debate on the precise significance of Exodus 6:3 will continue, there can be no question as to the identity of Abraham's God as far as the final editor of Genesis is concerned: Abraham was a follower of Yahweh, and thus his religion, however primitive, was a form of Yahwism' (*Dictionary of the Old Testament Pentateuch* [2003], IVP, p. 13).

[7]Miller observes that 'The absence of any god but Yahweh from a central place in the course of Israel's religion is matched by the absence of Yahweh from any place in the pantheons or in the cultus of any other people of the ancient Near East. While it is possible that signs of such worship may yet turn up, the fact is rather remarkable, for there are many indications of the sharing of deities among the various groups of the Near East' (Miller, P. D. [2000], *The Religion of Ancient Israel*, Library of Ancient Israel, SPCK/Westminster John Knox Press, p. 3). While arguing from silence is never conclusive, the seeming absence of Yahweh from the rest of the nations' worship underlines the veracity of the patriarchal accounts, and the subsequent development of the unique nature of Israel's religion.

[8]Peterson, D. (1992), *Engaging with God: A Biblical Theology of Worship*, Apollos, p. 25.

[9]Peterson, D. (1992), p. 25.

[10]Currid, J. (1997), *Ancient Egypt and the Old Testament*, Baker Books, chapter 2.

[11]Currid, J. (1997), pp. 47–48.

[12]Brensinger, T. L. (1997), *Nsh*, in W. A. Van Gemeren, *New International Dictionary of Old Testament Theology and Exegesis*, Vol. 3, Paternoster, p. 112.

[13]Conversely, the thread of those who are shown to be disobedient hearers is also strong. The rebellion of Adam, who not only disobeyed God's command but also ran from the voice of God in the garden, is echoed throughout the Old Testament with the effect that God's statement, 'I have called, but you have not answered/listened/heeded,' becomes something of a refrain in his account of Israel's disobedience (e.g. Prov. 1:24; Is. 65:12; 66:4; Jer. 7:13). This thought stands behind Jesus' parable in Matthew 22:2-7, where judgment falls on those who have not heeded the voice of the servant of the King inviting them to the wedding feast: 'But they paid no attention and went off, one to his farm, another to his business, while the rest seized his servants, treated

them shamefully, and killed them. The king was angry, and he sent his troops and destroyed those murderers and burned their city.'

[14]Commentators are not united on this. For example, Walton argues for a different location, other than Jerusalem; one not preserved in any way in subsequent Old Testament history, while Waltke suggests that this 'probably refers to Jerusalem'. Westermann sidesteps the issue; Hamilton argues for a more definite connection with Jerusalem on the basis of the implicit identification of the site with 'the mountain of the LORD' in verse 14, a line also taken by A. P. Ross and Moberly, though with more commitment. Garber is representative of the middle ground which argues that 2 Chronicles 3:1 deliberately 'intends to associate the temple mount with the theophanies of both 2 S. 24 and Gen. 22:14'. Whatever the case, the importance of the site in the traditions of both Judaism and Islam is built on the identification. This matter was also one of the differences, of course, between the Samaritans (who claimed that Mt. Gerizim was the mountain on which the incident took place) and the Jews, who worshipped in Jerusalem. Jesus' words to the Samaritan woman in John 4:22 may be taken to affirm the Jews' position, but in any case, with the advent of Jesus' new temple (John 2:19-21) they render any such location-based worship obsolete.

[15]Dyrness, W. (1977), *Themes in Old Testament Theology*, IVP, p. 154.

[16]See also the comments by Tremper Longman, who outlines not only the ubiquity of the '*ōlâh* sacrifices, but links this prevalence with the purpose of atonement. (Longman III, T. [2001], *Immanuel in Our Place: Seeing Christ in Israel's Worship*, Presbyterian and Reformed, p. 84.

[17]A 'foreshadowing of the three-day journey of Israel into the wilderness to sacrifice to God (see Exod. 3:18; 5:3; 8:27)', a possibility raised by Ross, A. P. (1996), *Creation and Blessing: A Guide to the Study and Exposition of Genesis*, Baker, p. 398.

[18]*Calvin's New Testament Commentaries: Vol. 12. The Epistle of Paul the Hebrews and The First and Second Epistles of St. Peter* (Torrance edition, 1963), p. 173.

[19]'It is interesting that the word used to describe what Abraham was about to do to Isaac is *slaughter* (*šahat*) ... used of the slaughter of animals for both secular and sacred purposes ... [and] used to describe the slaughter or sacrifice of children to false gods in pagan

cults (see Isa. 57:5; Ezek. 16:21; 23:39). Its use in Gen. 22:10, then, makes Abraham's sacrifice of Isaac assume an even more dreadful aspect' (Hamilton, V. P. (1995), *The Book of Genesis 18–50*, The New International Commentary on the Old Testament, Eerdmans, p. 111.

[20]Ross, A. P. (1996), *Creation and Blessing*, p. 402..

[21]For a fascinating discussion of the relationship between the ritual of circumcision and its spiritual meaning, the events of Genesis 22 and their significance for the Old Testament understanding of consecration and sacrifice, and the links of all these things with the life and death of Jesus Christ, see Kline, M. G., 'Oath and Ordeal Signs,' *Westminster Theological Journal,* 27.2, May, 1965), 115-39. The following gives a flavour: 'With this demand laid upon Abraham to perfect the circumcision of his son, he was confronted with the dilemma of circumcision-consecration. The son of Adam who would consecrate himself to God in the obedience of covenant service can do so only by passing through the judgment curse which circumcision symbolizes. Isaac must be cut off in death at the altar of God. In the circumcision of the foreskin on the eighth day he had passed under the judgment knife of God apart from God's altar in a merely symbolic, token act of conditional malediction. But this cutting off of the whole body of Isaac's flesh to be consumed in the fire of the altar of God was a falling under the actual judgment curse. This was an infliction in reality of that curse which was but symbolized by the ordinary circumcision made with hands (p. 121).

[22]We have already commented on the fact that Abraham's departure from his own land was also a sign of his separation from the idolatrous worship associated with the nations from which he had been called. It is significant, therefore, that the problem of idolatry made its way back into Abraham's grandchildren through the links with Laban, who had stayed in Haran (Gen. 27:43; 29:1ff.).

[23]Adrio König rightly reminds us of the nature and meaning of biblical promises. 'The promises of the Bible are not predictions which serve as predictions for future history, so that the future can be described in advance and calculated in detail. If this were so, a promise would become impotent immediately upon its fulfillment and thereafter be of no more than historical interest.... Rather, they retained their character as promises and repeatedly drew the eyes of faith toward the future' (König, A. [1999], *The Eclipse of Christ in Eschatology:*

Towards a Christ-Centred Approach, New Creation Publications, p. 20). In an accompanying footnote he expands the point: 'It is generally agreed by Old Testament scholars ... that certain promises are repeated throughout Old Testament history and often provisionally fulfilled, but that the promises are never replaced by these fulfillments. Often a promise retains its force and opens even wider vistas so that "repeated" or "more extensive" fulfillments of a promise are spoken of.'

[24]Enns, P. (2000), *Exodus*, The NIV Application Commentary, Zondervan, p. 200.

[25]Enns, P. (2000), *Exodus*, p. 205.

[26]Currid, J. (1997), *Ancient Egypt and the Old Testament*, Baker Books, p. 115.

[27]Currid, J. (1997), p. 115.

[28]Currid, J. (1997), p. 118.

[29]'The idea of order was critically important to the Egyptian conception of eternal happiness. When a person died, the heart was weighed against the feather of truth and righteousness – actually the feather of *maat* – to determine one's fitness for heavenly bliss ... Even in death there had to be harmony, stability, and order' (Currid, J. [1997], p. 118).

[30]Kitchen, K. A., 'Pharaoh,' in *The International Standard Bible Encyclopedia*, Vol. 3 , Eerdmans, p. 821.

[31]Pharaoh was regarded as both 'the incarnation of Horus' and 'the son of Re, the sun god'. He was 'the god of the Egyptian state, and was responsible to maintain cosmic order, or *maat* on earth' (Hoffmeier, 'Plagues of Egypt,' in W. A. Van Gemeren (1996), *NIDOTTE Vol. 4*, Paternoster, p. 1057.

[32]Currid, J. (1997), p. 119.

[33]Strawn, B. (2003), 'Pharaoh,' in *Dictionary of the Old Testament Pentateuch*, IVP, p. 635.

[34]It is somewhat surprising to see that T. Longman III and D. Reid, *God is a Warrior* (Studies in Old Testament Biblical Theology; Zondervan, 1995) do not pick up on this point in their treatment. They mention the fact that the Warrior released his people from Egypt (p. 31) and that this indicates that Israel know him to be the Warrior God from their early history, but do not press the matter back to the events of the exodus itself, nor provide any comment on the three key passages outlined above.

[35]Later in Israel the theme is revisited in the prophets as they look for a new exodus from Babylon (e.g. Jer. 16:14-15) and it forms much of the background to the imagery of Isaiah chapters 40-55. Of all the allusions that appear, 'chapter 43 furnishes the best example. The link is most clearly made in a reference to the fate of the pharaoh's chariots (vv. 16-17). Thereafter, there is guidance and provision in the desert, for the people who are characterized as Yahweh's chosen (vv. 19-21). The logic of the Exodus story it mimicked too, for the deliverance should lead to worship but it does not (vv. 22-24)' (McConville, J. G. [1997], 'Exodus,' in W. A. van Gemeren, *NIDOTTE*, Vol. 4, Paternoster, p. 604.

[36]There is, of course, deep irony in Pharaoh's statement in Exodus 5:2: 'Who is the LORD, that I should obey his voice and let Israel go? I do not know the LORD, and moreover, I will not let Israel go.' The theme of knowing God echoes like a refrain throughout the story of the exodus (e.g. Exod. 6:7; 7:5; 14:4; 16:6), where it is shown to be a double-edged concept. Those who are his covenant people come to know him as the God who brings deliverance and salvation; those who refuse to hear his voice know him as the God who brings judgment.

[37]The matter comes to a head in Exodus 5:18, where Pharaoh's command is reduced to 'Go now and work' (*abad*), the same word used in Exodus 4:23, 'Let my son go that he may serve (*abad*) me.' In other places it is made plain that the people of Israel did not generally recognise what was at stake. The cry of the people in Exodus 14:12, ('Is this not what we said to you in Egypt, "Leave us alone that we may serve the Egyptians"? For it would have been better for us to serve the Egyptians than to die in the wilderness'), is expressive of their deep ignorance of the contrast between serving Pharaoh and serving Yahweh. This is the first numerous 'murmuring' passages that run like a thread throughout the books of Exodus and Numbers, though the nascent grumbling evident in this passage is given more detailed attention in the longer murmuring passages that follow (e.g. in Exod. 15; 16; 17; Num. 14; 16-17). We should bear in mind that 'the murmuring motif is not designed to express a disgruntled complaint. Quite the contrary, it describes open rebellion' (Coates, quoted in Currid, J. [1997], p. 145). Currid himself then goes on to point out that 'The groaning began already in Egypt (Exod. 5:21). In fact, whenever the Hebrews complained, they mentioned Egypt.' They

even take descriptions of the land promised to them as their resting place and apply these to Egypt (e.g. Num. 16:13-14). Throughout, Israel is portrayed as an ungrateful people, whose hearts and minds are continually straying from Yahweh as their deliverer. This theme is taken up elsewhere in the Scriptures with some force (e.g. Deut. 9:6-24; 31:25-30; Judg. 2:19; Pss. 78:8; 81:10-13; Jer. 5:21-25; cf. Acts 7:51-53; Heb. 3:10 especially when seen in the context of the larger discussion of sin and unbelief in Hebrews 3-4), and emphasises the need for a new covenant, in which the hearts and not just the flesh of the community is circumcised (Deut. 10:16; cf. 30:6).

[38]The links between creation and exodus are clearly interwoven in Psalm 136, which was unquestionably used as an antiphonal response psalm in the setting of public worship. It begins with creation, moves through the events of the exodus, and returns to praise of God as the faithful creator and sustainer of all things, as the 'God of heaven' whose 'lovingkindness is everlasting'. The existence of the psalm in the psalter demonstrates that the theological connections between the events of creation and the exodus were accepted as normative: there is no need to explain these connections; they were understood as central to the worship of the God who is the Creator and Redeemer. Interestingly enough, the worship scene given to us in the throne room of heaven in the book of the Revelation follows the same pattern. Revelation 4 focuses on the worship of God as Creator and Revelation 5 on the worship of God as Redeemer.

[39]Carpenter, E. (1997), 'Theology of Exodus,' in W. Van Gemeren, *NIDOTTE, Vol. 4*, Paternoster, p. 607.

[40]van Dam, C., 'Golden Calf,' in *Dictionary of the Old Testament Pentateuch*, IVP, p. 368. Cole points out that the Hebrew word *'egel* may be used of animals up to three years old, so we should not think in the more limited way in which the word 'calf' is used in English (Cole, R. A. (1973), *Exodus*, IVP, p. 214.

[41]I am assuming the integrity and unity of the golden calf incident, and thus look to the most likely influences given the most natural *Sitz im Leben* of the perpetrators. The view taken by some critical scholars that this incident is a *de novo* creation of the Deuteronomic editor of 1 Kings 12:25-33 (in order to bolster rejection of Jeroboam's calf cult) seems unnecessarily cynical and is well refuted by Childs ([1974], *The Book of Exodus: A Critical, Theological Commentary*, The Old Testament Library, The Westminster Press, Chapter XXI) and

Davis ('Rebellion, Presence and Covenant: A Study in Exodus 32-34,' *Westminster Theological Journal, 44*[1], 1982, Spring, pp 72–88), though for different reasons. For background to the some aspects of the bull cults in Egypt, see Oswalt, J. N. (1973), 'The Golden Calves and the Egyptian Concept of Deity,' *Evangelical Quarterly, 45,* 13-20.

[42]Janzen, J. G. (1990, October), 'The Character of the Calf and its Cult in Exodus 32,' *Catholic Biblical Quarterly, 52*(4), 598.

[43]Childs, B. (1974), p. 564.

[44]McCann, J. (1990, July), 'Exodus 32:1–14,' *Interpretation, 44,* 277. His italics.

[45]Childs, B. (1974), p. 564.

[46]Childs, B. (1974), p. 507. John Hilber draws attention to the four central themes for worship embedded in the account of Exodus 24: 'response to the covenant relationship, which is characterised by God's presence, defined by his word, and mediated through sacrifice.' On the basis of this observation he makes a useful link with the New Testament: 'Exodus 24 served as the pattern for covenant inauguration when Jesus instituted the Lord's table. So the theology of Exodus 24 offers pertinent instruction for the worship of the Christian community.' (Hilber, J. H. 'Theology of Worship in Exodus 24,' *Journal of Evangelical Theological Society*, 39.2; June 1996, 188f.).

[47]Detailed attention to these elements would draw in too much extraneous material. However, it is worth noting the thoroughness with which the matter of idolatry is addressed and the very robust nature of Moses' response to it. The destruction of the calf, for example, could not have been more complete, since Moses knew that to allow the preservation of even a fraction of it would have been a snare for the people from then on.

[48]Childs, B. (1974), p. 579.

[49]'It is especially with respect to the intercession motif that one could say that Moses is so crucial that Israel's destiny hangs on his girdle. This does not suggest some "merits of Moses" idea but does try to take account of him as covenant mediator and as evidently the only Israelite still in covenant fellowship with God and unstained by the smear of apostasy. Yet it must be noted that even Moses has perimeters that limit him ... and, though he ever remains the bold and adventurous supplicant, he nevertheless remains a supplicant. Here we see but a forerunner of the One Mediator' (Davis, D. R. [1982], p. 86).

[50]See the use of this image in places such as Deuteronomy 32:11-12; Isaiah 63:9, and Jesus' use of the not wholly dissimilar image of the hen and her chicks in Matthew 23:37.

[51]Fretheim suggests that the Exodus 19:3-6 is the lens through which the entire book of Exodus (and beyond) is to be viewed. His discussion is particularly stimulating for the connections he draws between God's purpose in the exodus and his plan and purpose for the creation. The statement that 'the whole earth is mine' is connected closely with the phrases regarding Israel's unique identity (as a kingdom of priests etc.). While there is no doubt an elective element (i.e. God is sovereign over the whole earth, and as sovereign king he chooses a people for himself), Fretheim also argues that the emphasis is on the mission of God. 'The use of such language in other texts (e.g. 8:22; 9:14, 16, 29) suggests a more comprehensive sense, best captured by this translation: *Because* (*kî*) all the earth is mine, so you, you shall be to me a kingdom of priests and a holy nation. This links with the missional purpose of God, which is first articulated in Genesis 12:3b' (Fretheim, T., 'Because the Whole Earth is Mine': Theme and Narrative in Exodus,' *Interpretation*, 50.3, July 1996, 237).

[52]Dumbrell, W. (1984). *Covenant and Creation: An Old Testament Covenantal Theology.* (p. 87). Exeter: Paternoster, p. 87.

[53]'It is ... best to refer to I Kg. 18:28 and also to certain texts from Ugarit ... as illustrating at least the custom of self-laceration as part of the ritual by which the death of the fertility god Baal was mourned. Israel's status as sons of Yahweh means that her participation in rites proper to the worship of any other god must be considered apostasy' (Mayes, A. D. [1979], *Deuteronomy*, The New Century Bible Commentary, Eerdmans, p. 239).

[54]Childs, B. (1974), p. 367.

[55]McCann, J., 'Exodus 32:1–14,' *Interpretation*, 44, July 1990, 279.

Chapter 4. Worship in the New Land

[1]The land here is shown to be the servant of the Creator, accomplishing his will in accordance with his covenantal conditions (in this case acting to carry out the condition of the covenant curses). This is one indication of an important truth in the Bible: the earth (and/or the material world) is not evil. It may be affected by the fall of its vice-regent head, but it is still 'good' in terms of its fundamental relationship to God, who still rules over it. It thus serves the purposes of God, and

continues to be the means by which men and women may experience joy and blessing (as in the Noahic covenant), or conversely it may be used by God to bring chastisement and/or judgment (as in the effects of the curses in Deuteronomy 28).

[2]Hadley, J. M., 'Baal,' in W. A. van Gemeren, *NIDOTTE*, Vol. 4, Paternoster, p. 427.

[3]Block, D. I. (1999). *Judges, Ruth*, The New American Commentary, Broadman & Holman, p. 124.

[4]Block, D. I. (1999). *Judges, Ruth*, p. 124.

[5]Hadley, J. M., 'Ashteroth,' in W. A. van Gemeren, *NIDOTTE*, Vol. 3, Paternoster, p. 563.

[6]Block, D. I. (1999). *Judges, Ruth*, p. 125. Jung and Sayce indicate that the Astarte probably derives from the ancient Babylonian Ishtar, who was recognised under a variety of names in Egypt, Assyria, and Canaan. In Babylon Ishtar was 'a personification of the productive principle in nature, and more especially the mother and creatress of mankind' (Jung. K., 'Ashtoreth,' in G. W. Bromiley, *TISBE*, Vol. 1, Eerdmans, p. 320. There may also be a connection with the Greek goddess Artemis (the Roman Diana), though lines of direct linkage are difficult to trace. For more details, see LaSor, W., 'Artemis,' in G. W. Bromiley, *TISBE*, Vol. 1, pp. 306-08. Since goddess worship was widespread throughout the ancient world we should not be surprised at the similarities between the diverse systems and deities. It is also generally recognised that the vocalisation of the name 'is a deliberate scribal distortion ... reflect[ing] the vowels of the Hebrew word *bōðet* "shame", a term employed in place of the divine name Baal in such references as Hosea 9:10 and Jer. 11:13 as well as in some personal names' (Day, J., 'Ashtoreth,' in D. Freedman, *Anchor Bible Dictionary*, Vol. 1, Doubleday, p. 491.

[7]See 'Aspects of Canaanite Religion' in Kraus, H.-J. (1966), *Worship in Ancient Israel: A Cultic History of the Old Testament*, Basil Blackwell, pp. 36-43. For a different interpretation of the relationship between Baal, Mot and seasonal patterns, see Day, J., 'Baal,' in D. Freedman, *Anchor Bible Dictionary*, Vol. 1, pp. 545-46. There is also a helpful discussion of the main features of Baalism in Toombs, L. E. (1995), 'When Religions Collide: The Yahweh/Baal Confrontation,' in L. Toombs, *When Religions Collide and Other Essays. Essays in Biblical Literature and Archaeology in Honor of Willard Hamrick*, Edwin Mellen (pp. 13-46), and much useful

background material in Drinkard, J. F. (1993, Spring), 'Religious Practices Reflected in the Book of Hosea,' *Review and Expositor, 90,* pp. 205-18.

[8]In the worldview of Baalism, sex and sexual activity 'were the dynamos which generated power to keep the vital natural cycles going. The sexual act was not something to be done in darkness or secrecy. As an essential part of the structure of reality, it was sacred, and therefore, it belonged in the temple. Prostitutes, male and female, were part of the personnel of a Canaanite temple. Their services allowed worshipers to identify themselves with the gods whose vigorous sexual activity helped create and maintain the world order' (Toombs, L. E. (1995), p. 33.

[9]Although Israel had been forbidden from worshiping other gods in the high places by Moses (Deut. 7:5; 12:2-3; cf. Exod. 34:13), and although they were expressly warned not to worship Yahweh there (presumably because of the danger of syncretism, see Deut. 12:11-14), it is clear that the high places persisted throughout the period of the divided monarchy. Indeed Solomon himself is said to worship at the high places until the Temple is built (1 Kings 3:3) and the construction of high places as illegitimate locations of worship was part of the great sin of Jeroboam (1 Kings 12:31). One of the benchmarks for the radicalness of the reforming kings was whether they managed to remove the high places (e.g. 1 Kings 15:9-13; 2 Kings 12:3; 15:4 etc; cf. Hezekiah in 2 Kings 18:1ff.)

[10]McConville, J. G. (2002), *Deuteronomy,* Apollos Old Testament Commentary, IVP, p. 205.

[11]These comments are based on the nature of 'magic' in the formal sense, which 'attempts to use supernatural powers to influence people, events or other supernatural beings.... Magic and divination are human efforts to understand, control or manipulate the divine realm by methods believed to practically guarantee the desired results' (O'Mathuna, D. P., 'Divination, Magic,' in *Dictionary of the Old Testament Pentateuch,* IVP, p. 193).

[12]Block, D. I. (1999), *Judges, Ruth,* p. 129.

[13]Dumbrell, W. (1989), *The Faith of Israel,* IVP, pp. 79-80. Elsewhere, Dumbrell comments on the nature of the judges and the extent of their role in contrast to dynastic kingship: 'They [the judges] are raised up by Yahweh, they are men of the Spirit (cf. Judg. 6:34; 11:29; 15:14; etc.) and they are said in each case to exercise authority

over all Israel. But they are, we might note, surrogates only for Yahweh himself who is *the* Judge of Israel (cf. Judg. 11:27). That the term Judge can be (and is probably primarily) applied in this way should make us reluctant to interpret it in a merely narrow juridical sense, and here we should note that the Hebrew verb 'to judge' (Heb. *shâpat*) in early Semitic conveyed a basic meaning of 'rule' or 'administer'. The role of the Judge would thus have been an extremely wide one, and being episodic, non-transferable, and non-predictable, is antithetical to dynastic kingship' (Dumbrell, W. [1984], *Covenant and Creation: An Old Testament Covenantal Theology*, Paternoster, p. 130).

[14]Dumbrell, W. (1989). *The Faith of Israel*, p. 80. So also, Block: 'These are apostate Israelites, acknowledging no king, neither divine nor human. But there is no need for a king in the estimation of the narrator. Wickedness is democratized; everyone does what is right in his own eyes, and the results are disastrous' (*Judges, Ruth*, p. 583).

[15]Dumbrell, W. (2002). *The Faith of Israel: A Theological Survey of the Old Testament*, IVP, 2nd ed., p. 83.

[16]Baldwin, J. (1988), *1 and 2 Samuel*, IVP, p. 116.

[17]There is an implicit contrast here with so much of Israel's earlier (and later!) history. Moses had warned the people that they should not 'forget the LORD their God' when they entered the land and when they dwelt securely in their houses with an abundance of good things. Indeed they should see these very blessings as a reason for 'remembering' God and giving thanks to him (Deut. 8:11-20). These good things were to be seen as testimonies to God's goodness, not the people's innate might or power. Later, Israel's suffering under the covenant curses is said to be caused by such unthankfulness: 'Because you did not serve the LORD your God with joyfulness and gladness of heart, because of the abundance of all things, therefore you shall serve your enemies whom the LORD will send against you, in hunger and thirst, in nakedness, and lacking everything' (Deut. 28:47-48; cf. the theme as it is taken up in Nehemiah's prayer of national repentance, e.g. Neh. 9:35). It is no surprise, then, to see that Paul locates the root of sinful rebellion in humanity's refusal to honour God or give thanks to him (Rom. 1:21). David thus embodies the appropriate response to God's goodness, at least in spirit, even if his action is not permitted at this stage.

[18]For discussion of this point, see the relevant commentaries. Dumbrell is probably right in stating that if there is a rebuke here it is

only a mild one. Rather the issue relates to the timing and the initiator of the construction. 'That Yahweh must initiate the move might have been discernible from the fact that David had to await the divine pleasure before the ark could be brought to Jerusalem, as well as from the fact that Jerusalem itself had been put into David's hands by Yahweh. Thus the marking off of the site and the movement of the ark had both of them been divine decisions. The timing of the building and the person of the builder must also be' (*Covenant and Creation: An Old Testament Covenantal Theology*, p. 148).

[19]The issue of forced labour under Solomon is a difficult one. Elsewhere the narrative makes it plain that Solomon did not enslave any of the Israelites (1 Kings 9:20-22), and from the reference in 5:13-18 it seems clear that the conscripts had favourable conditions granted to them: one month on site and two months at home. However, the later division of the kingdom under Rehoboam and Jeroboam hinges in no small part on the matter of the harsh yoke Solomon had placed on the people (1 Kings 12:1-15), where Rehoboam's foolish and arrogant disregard for the counsel of the elders leads to the division of the northern and southern tribes. The pronounced emphasis on quasi-slavery in this passage is seen in the repeated use of the term 'yoke' (1 Kings 12:4, 10, 11, 14). This was a word freighted with meaning for Israel (e.g. Lev. 26:13; Deut. 28:48; cf. Isa. 9:4; 10:27; 14:25; 47:6; 58:6; Jer. 2:20; Ezek. 34:27), and connoted slavery under Pharaoh as well as the servitude under oppressive powers such as Babylon or Assyria. In Deuteronomy 28:48 the yoke of the oppressor is described as part of the harvest of covenant curses to be reaped for Israel's continued idolatry. We will see later that the biblical assessment of Solomon's reign is not universally positive. The matter of forced labour is one indication that the model of kingship found in the surrounding nations began making its impact on Solomon from the early days of his reign.

[20]Knoppers, G. N. (2001), 'Rethinking the relationship between Deuteronomy and the Deuteronomistic History: The Case of Kings,' *Catholic Biblical Quarterly, 63,* 398.

[21]McConville, G. (1998), 'King and Messiah in Deuteronomy,' in J. Day, *King and Messiah in Israel and the Ancient Near East: Proceedings of the Oxford Old Tesament Seminar JSTOT 270,* Sheffield Academic Press, p. 276.

[22]McConville, J. G. (2002), *Deuteronomy*, p. 44.

[23]Miller, P. (1990), *Deuteronomy*, Interpreters' Bible Commentary, John Knox Press., p. 16.

[24]McConville ([1998], 'King and Messiah in Deuteronomy,' pp. 276f.) points to a difference in emphasis between the role of the king as portrayed in Deuteronomy and the picture presented in the 'Zion theology' of the Psalms, as seen for example in Psalm 2. In the former, the emphasis is on the solidarity of the king with Israel, his 'brothers', and with the subjection of the king to God with a consequent and significant delimitation of his powers and privileges. The latter points to a situation in which the king specifically is designated the 'son of God' and emphasises the power and glory of his reign. It is significant, however, that both in Deuteronomy and the Psalms the king is appointed by God and still subject to him. He is still installed and anointed by God, who is the one who glorifies him before the nations. The exaltation of the king in Zion, and his rulership over the nations, is in fact the obverse of his subjection to God. The former is not possible without the latter, as the history of kingship in Israel so dramatically demonstrated. When the king did not serve God and his people, particularly by leading them in covenantal faithfulness (seen especially in the matter of idolatry), both king and nation suffered the ignominy of exile, being placed under (rather than over) the surrounding nations.

[25]House, P. R. (1995). *1, 2 Kings*, The New American Commentary, Broadman & Holman, p. 165.

[26]House, P. R. (1995). *1, 2 Kings*, p. 184.

[27]The account of Jehu's purge of the leadership of the nation and the slaughter of the priests and prophets of Baal is detailed and bloody (2 Kings 9:14–10:35). Despite the fact that it removed institutionalised Baalism from the land it was driven by an excessive ruthlessness, so that Hosea is instructed by the Lord to call his firstborn son Jezreel, 'for in just a little while I will punish the house of Jehu for the blood of Jezreel, and I will put an end to the kingdom of the house of Israel' (Hosea 1:4). Excessive brutality in war is likewise shown to be a cause for judgment upon Assyria (e.g. Isa. 10:5-7); Syria (Amos 1:3) and Babylon (Hab. 1:6ff.; cf. 2:8ff.), notwithstanding the fact that each is said to have been raised up by God for the purpose of judgment. Underlying the actions of such nations is their own pride and arrogance by which they do not acknowledge God. In their actions they in fact give praise to their gods, and thus render themselves ripe for divine

punishment. In no case does God leave the guilty unpunished. The Old Testament prophets saw questions of theodicy worked out in the long view they took of history and God's dealings with the nations over time.

[28]See the prophetic commentary on this event, and its relation to the principle enunciated in the preceding footnote, in Isaiah 10.

[29]Readers are directed to the various Bible Dictionaries and Encypclopaedias where the construction materials of the tabernacle, its dimensions, its contents, and its location in the midst of the camp are all very well described. There is little point in reproducing here the diagrams and detailed descriptions found in such places. Likewise, such resources usually comment on the theological significance of the various implements and the numerous forms of sacrifice offered.

[30]See Averbeck, R., 'Miškân,' in W. A. VanGemeren, *NIDOTTE*, Vol 2, Paternoster, pp. 1130-31, for further examples.

[31]Thus, Klein comments: 'The reality and freedom of God's presence, so memorably expressed by *miškân* ("tabernacle") and by the technical verb of the priestly tradition *šakan*, are echoed in the prologue to John's Gospel: "And the Word became flesh and pitched his tent in our midst".' (Klein, R. W. [1996, July], '"Back to the Future": The Tabernacle in the Book of Exodus,' *Interpretation, 50* (3), p. 275). The issues of God's power, indwelling glory and the place of human weakness are explored in a stimulating discussion in 'The Tabernacling of God and Human Weakness', Chapter 2 of Dawn, M. (2001), *Powers, Weakness and the Tabernacling of God: The 2000 Shaff Lectures*, Pittsburgh Theological Seminary, Eerdmans.

[32]The event of the golden calf aptly illustrates what sort of worship the people themselves would devise!

[33]Currid comments on Exodus 25:9: 'It is often assumed ... that God merely provided for Moses, in a sense, exact blueprints for what is to be built. But, in reality, it was much more than that – the word 'pattern' almost exclusively refers to an imitation of something that already exists in reality. The tabernacle, then, is modelled on something else. It is a replica of a celestial archetype – that is, the heavenly sanctuary. (For further textual support for this idea see Micah 1:2-3 and, especially, Hebrews 9:23-24) (Currid, J. [2001], *Exodus Chapters 19–40*, Evangelical Press, p. 150. See also Meredith Kline's comments in his *Images of the Spirit*, (1980), Baker, pp. 35-47). The 'existing reality' may be assumed to be something akin to the revelation

that John received on the isle of Patmos, and recorded for us in the Book of Revelation. The whole of this majestic book is saturated with depictions of the vibrant nature of heaven as the great cosmic worship centre, in which the throne of God and the Lamb dominate the vista, both in heaven and on the earth.

[34]Though see Averbeck, R. E., 'Môʿēd,' in W. van Gemeren, *NIDOTTE*, Vol. 2, Paternoster, pp. 875-86, for a discussion on the relationship between the tent of meeting specifically designated as the meeting place of Moses and Yahweh (as in Exodus 33:7-11) and the tabernacle as the tent of meeting for the assembly as a whole.

[35]Kline is right in identifying this as one of a number of lines of similarity between the original creation (the macro-temple of God), and the structure of the tabernacle (as a microcosm of the macrocosmic temple/dwelling place of God seen in the creation narratives). 'The Spirit who structured the cosmic temple in the beginning by divine wisdom was also the primary builder of the tabernacle, present and acting through Bezalel and Oholiab, whom he filled and endowed with the wisdom of craftsmanship' (Kline, M., 'Investiture with the Image of God,' *Westminster Theological Journal*, 40 (1), 1977, Fall, p. 42).

[36]It appears that Solomon's temple effectively doubled the size of the tabernacle, while maintaining the same floor plan to scale.

[37]Dillard, R. B., 'The Chronicler's Solomon,' *Westminster Theological Journal*, 43 (2), 1981, Spring, pp. 296-99.

[38]For an indication of the presupposed nexus between tabernacle and temple in Israel, it is instructive to note the wording of the command of the reformer-king Hezekiah in 2 Chronicles 28:4-8: 'He brought in the priests and the Levites and assembled them in the square on the east and said to them, "Hear me, Levites! Now consecrate yourselves, and consecrate the house of the LORD, the God of your fathers, and carry out the filth from the Holy Place. For our fathers have been unfaithful and have done what was evil in the sight of the LORD our God. They have forsaken him and have turned away their faces from the habitation of the LORD and turned their backs. They also shut the doors of the vestibule and put out the lamps and have not burned incense or offered burnt offerings in the Holy Place to the God of Israel. Therefore the wrath of the LORD came on Judah and Jerusalem, and he has made them an object of horror, of astonishment, and of hissing, as you see with your own eyes."' The phrase translated as

the 'habitation of the Lord' in verse 6 is literally, 'the tabernacle/tent (*miškân*) of Yahweh.' There are a number of possibilities. This may be an unconscious allusion on Hezekiah's part, reflecting the essential unity of the two structures in the thinking of Israel. Conversely, it could be a deliberate allusion, used by Hezekiah to indicate to an apostate priesthood and nation the historical and theological pedigree of the temple, and thus using the identification with the ancient tabernacle as a means of goading them into action. The same sort of identification is seen in the parallelism of Psalm 74:7, speaking of the destruction of the temple: 'They set your sanctuary on fire; they profaned the dwelling place (*miškân*) of your name, bringing it down to the ground.' In either case the weight of the instruction lies in the moral authority inherent in the tabernacle/temple continuity. A third option is that the actual tabernacle itself was set up within the temple, an idea favoured by Friedman (see Friedman, R. E., 'Tabernacle,' in D. Freedman, *Anchor Bible Dictionary*, Vol. VI, pp. 293-94). This seems unlikely, since one would expect specific mention of such a significant occurrence in the accounts of Solomon's furnishing of the temple. All we read of is the ark of the covenant being brought in, rather than of the erection of the tabernacle itself. The centrality of the ark is of undoubted importance to both tabernacle and temple theology, and it is fitting that the glory of the Lord descended upon Solomon's temple at the time of the installation of the ark. This glory-filling corresponded to that of the original tabernacle, thus underlining the temple as the new, divinely ordained and ratified centre for worship, and thus as the replacement for (rather than repository of) the original tabernacle.

[39]The Temple in Biblical Theology (T. Desmond Alexander & Simon Gathercole eds.) Paternoster, Carlisle 2004; Greg Beale, The Temple and the Church's Mission: A biblical theology of the dwelling place of God, New Studies in Biblical Theology Series 17 Apollos, Downers Grove, 2004

[40]Alexander, T. D. (2002), *From Paradise to the Promised Land: An Introduction to the Pentateuch*, Second Edition, Paternoster, p. 192.

[41]This statement houses a huge biblical theme. It could be argued that the whole of the biblical narrative can be understood in terms of the theme of God's presence. Creationally, human beings have been structured to know that presence above all else, such knowledge being

the key to true human hope and happiness. The Fall, of course, excludes humanity from the immediate presence of God, and the whole of salvation history indicates the way in which God works to restore the blessing of his presence to a renewed humanity. In the end the eschatological vision of the Scriptures has the manifest presence of God amongst his people as the goal of all things (see Revelation 21-22). While the presence is necessary to human blessing, it is also the reason for divine judgment on sin. Sin cannot appear in his presence, a fundamental assumption that lies behind the principle of substitutionary atonement throughout the Scriptures, so that the presence of the holy God also brings down wrath upon evil. In the end, even the lake of fire burns in the presence of God and the Lamb (Rev. 14:10), so that the horror of eternal judgment is in part explained by his presence as much as by his absence.

[42]See, for example, the preponderance of first person personal pronouns at key points in the narrative such as Exodus 6:6-9; 7:1-6, etc.

[43]Neither should we miss the integral relation that exists between the concepts of 'presence' and 'shepherd' imagery. The shepherd imagery of the Old Testament is extensive and makes a much neglected contribution to many New Testament themes and categories.

[44]Carpenter, E., 'Exodus: Theology of,' in W. van Gemeren, *NIDOTTE*, Vol. 4, Paternoster, p. 611.

[45]Kline, M., 'Investiture with the Image of God,' *Westminster Theological Journal, 40* (1), 1977, Fall, pp. 43-44.

[46]A phrase for which I am indebted to my friend and teacher Geoffrey Bingham.

[47]See part IV of Niehaus, J., 'The Central Sanctuary: Where and When?' *Tyndale Bulletin, 43* (1), 1992, May, pp. 3-30.

[48]McConville, J. G. (2002), *Deuteronomy*, p. 220.

[49]Averbeck, R. E., 'Tabernacle,' in T. D. Alexander, *Dictionary of the Old Testament Pentateuch*, IVP, p. 824.

[50]House, P. R. (1995), *1, 2 Kings*, p. 144.

[51] So also, Hosea 11:1ff..

[52] The Old Testament prophecies of restoration and the associated full knowledge of the Father could only ever be fulfilled finally and completely in the redemption secured by the Son. The events of the Old Testament are 'ensamples', to use the KJV translation of 1 Corinthians 10:11's *typos*, better expressing the word's weight than mere 'example'. Just as there is a new exodus brought about in Christ,

there is also a new restoration.

[53] In John 1:12 we are told, 'But as many as received him [Christ], to them he gave the right to become children of God, even to those who believe in his name.' John habitually uses the words child/children (*teknon*) as the equivalent of son/sons (*huios*) in terms of status and responsibility (e.g. 1 John 2 and 3), though rarely he uses both terms together (e.g. Rev. 12:5). In John, *huios* is used almost exclusively of *the* Son, through whom men and women come to know the Father. John thus distinguishes between the ontological and eternal Son, and those who come to son status by belief in Jesus as the Messiah. Paul distinguishes between *the* Son and the *sons* not by using the word 'child' (though he is not averse to it: see, for example, Romans 8:16-21), but by the more formal use of the language of adoption. In either case, however, the emphasis is on the gracious action of God in bringing men and women into a new status.

[54]There is an echo here of the way in which God's eyes are said to be on the land (e.g. Deut. 11:12), which is also preserved in the narrative of 1 Kings 9:3. Behind these may be Edenic allusions to the way in which God provided all that was needed for the garden of Genesis 2, which he had created as his special provision for his royal children, and into which they had been placed (Gen. 2:7, 15). We have commented on the Edenic imagery in the tabernacle and temple elsewhere, but we should not miss this added line of connection with the land. Just as the land would vomit the inhabitants out should they pollute it with idolatry, so also the temple (as the visible representation of Eden, and the place which granted people access to the divine presence) would be taken from them should they repeat the sin of Adam's Edenic rebellion. In a very real sense Adam in the garden was the first 'to worship the creature rather than the creator' (to take Paul's words from Romans 1:25), as he turned from God to give heed to the voice of the serpent. If Israel were to continue in such sinful worship, they, too would be expelled from land and temple, which each in their own way declared God's gracious provision of restored access to him.

Chapter 5. Jesus and the Transformation of Worship

[1]von Allmen speaks of 'the Christological basis of the Church's worship' (von Allmen, J. [1965], *Worship: Its Theology and Practice*, Oxford University Press, p. 25).

[2]It is not germane to our theme to discuss the relationship between this account of the temple cleansing (standing at the outset of Jesus' ministry) and the synoptics' accounts of the cleansing (which take place following Jesus' entry to Jerusalem at the close of his public ministry: Matthew 12:12ff.; Mark 11:15-17; Luke 19:45f.). The differences between John's account and the synoptics' are noticable, and even within the synoptic accounts there are some minor variations and distinctions in emphasis. Bock summarises the main options and their proponents succinctly and gives his own view that the 'differences between the Synoptics and John make it slightly more likely that there were two temple cleansings', though acknowledging that no proposed reconstruction is completely problem free (Bock, D. L., [1996], *Luke 9:51–24:53*, Baker Exegetical Commentary on the New Testament, Baker, pp. 1576-77). The important thematic and theological developments embedded in John's account are in no way affected by these debates, and these are the focus of the discussion that follows.

[3]For example, in Deuteronomy 28:47 God provides abundance in the land/resting place he had given them – and lack of thankfulness for this abundance is one of the reasons for his justified acts of judgment; in 1 Chronicles 29:16 the point is made that the abundant provisions for the temple came from God's own abundance to the people, so that they are only giving to him what is already his own; in Isaiah 66:11 the people of Judah are invited to drink deeply of the abundance of God in the vision of a restored Jerusalem, from which (using the image of the nursing mother) there is bountiful provision of life-nurturing, comforting milk; etc.

[4]The 'now' and 'not yet' aspect of the new covenant is important for our discussion as we go forward into the following chapters. We have seen previously that a new covenant was needed, and that under the provisions of the old covenant Israel's propensity to idolatry was not only not curbed, but made all the more culpable. It was clear that a new situation needed to be brought into being, where the all-embracing circumcision of the heart of which Moses spoke was radically effected. The gifts of the new covenant are indeed abundant: new birth, faith, repentance, forgiveness of sins, justification, reconciliation, adoption, sanctification, ongoing Spirit fullness and promised glory, to name some of the most significant. In possession of all these, the new covenant meant that true worship of God from

the heart could be established. However, it would not be secured in all its fullness this side of the eschatological *telos* (goal) to which God is currently bringing all things. The glory is the *promised* glory; the fullness of the Spirit is contested and (depending on the sort of 'gospel' we hear) not guaranteed; justification is real and actual now, but still known only by faith; and so on. The success of the new covenant in cleansing human hearts from idolatry should not be judged while we are still living in the penultimate age! We know only too well how much we are engaged in a spiritual battle against the powers of darkness, and how the plans and purposes of the evil one are still active in seducing the world (and providing deep and intense temptations to God's own people) in the matter of idolatry, with all its associated ethical and moral consequences. The ultimate age is where the real and eternal fruits of the new covenant will be revealed, but we have already begun to taste of them in the present.

[5]'Perichoresis' is a term used to describe the relation between the persons in the Godhead, which preserves their unique identity yet stresses their mutuality. The term refers to 'mutual indwelling or, better, mutual interpenetration' so that each person has '"being in each other without any coalscence" (John of Damascus)' (Smith, S., 'Perichoresis,' in W. A. Elwell, *Evangelical Dictionary of Theology*, Baker, p. 843. Because of their perichoresis, 'everything in the Trinity is triadic. Each Person acts in union with the others, even when we consider actions belonging to one or attributed to one: creation by the Father, the incarnation of the Son, the coming of the Spirit' (Boff, L. [1988], *Trinity and Society*, Burns and Oates, p. 6. Donald Macleod comments that the word houses three related concepts: the fellowship (*koinōnia*) of the persons of the Trinity, their mutual indwelling of each in the others, and the circulation of divine power amongst all three (Macleod, D. [1995], *Behold Your God*, Christian Focus Publications, pp. 203-04). Since believers have been united to Christ, and dwell in the Father through union with him by the power of the Spirit, they have been inducted into this perichoretic life of mutuality. This forges the pattern for their relationships in the present, and will be the full substance of their relational life in eternity.

[6]We give more attention to this in chapter 7, where we comment on various instances of what David Peterson calls 'transformed cultic language' to illustrate the metamorphosed nature of New Testament worship. See, for example, Peterson's use of the phrase in his chapter

on the Pauline theology of worship in his *Engaging with God: A Biblical Theology of Worship*, (1992), IVP, p. 203.

[7]A number of commentators pick up the change of tense evident in John's use of Psalm 69:9. John changes the past tense original to a future: 'Zeal ... *will* consume me.' This may be a pointer to the long term orientation of Jesus' action, a pointer given more weight when we see that the phrase is used in conjunction with the 'remembering' of the disciples (John 2:17a). When did they remember? It is clear that they did not understand the meaning of the action at the time, so it is likely that the 'remembering' took place after the resurrection (as in v. 22). They then understood themselves and the whole church of God to be the temple of the new covenant, and so the 'zeal' that they saw in operation was in fact directed to a larger and more glorious goal than the temporary cleansing of a physical structure. They 'remembered' the fact that zeal would consume him (on the cross) for the purpose of establishing this new temple of which they were a part.

[8]Marshall, I. H., 'Church and Temple in the New Testament,' *Tyndale Bulletin, 40* (2), 1989, November, p. 222.

[9]Williamson points to the comments of Josephus in his *Antiquities* which 'may be regarded as symptomatic, though told from a Jewish standpoint. For instance, between A.D. 6 and 7, some Samaritans scattered bones in the Jerusalem Temple during Passover ... while in A.D. 52 Samaritans massacred a group of Galilean pilgrims at *Engannîm*' (Williamson, H. G., 'Samaritans,' in *Dictionary of Jesus and the Gospels*, IVP, p. 727. For further helpful detail on the history of the Samaritans and their beliefs, see the 'Historical Horizon' section related to this passage in Witherington III, B. (1995), *John's Wisdom: A Commentary on the Fourth Gospel*, Cambridge: The Lutterworth Press, pp. 117-23. Fascinatingly, Witherington indicates that there was still (at the time of his writing in 1995) a small group extant, offering sacrifices on Mt. Gerizim according to their ancient practices.

[10]'It appears that by Jesus' day, Samaria as a land was regarded by many of the religiously observant Judean and Galilean Jews as unclean, and contact with these people, especially their women, or sharing a meal or a common cup with them was widely held to render a Jew unclean' (Witherington III, B. [1995], pp. 117-18).

[11] Hence the added power in the parable of the good *Samaritan* (Luke 10:30-36).

[12] In passing, it is worth noting the fact that Jesus draws a distinction between marriage and cohabitation in verse 18: 'you have had five husbands, and the one you now have is not your husband.' This distinction has implications for the way in which many folk in our own day virtually equate the two states, and it certainly takes away any authority for young Christian couples to live together before marriage, as has become increasingly popular. Often the excuse used is that they are 'married in the eyes of God'. Clearly Jesus thinks that this could not be the case! A couple may be cohabiting while unmarried, or they may be married and thus lawfully cohabiting, but Jesus' words cannot be taken to mean anything else than cohabitation without the public exchange of vows is not marriage.

[13]Though see the comments by Williamson, who argues that the Samaritans 'did not see themselves as the remnant of the old northern kingdom of Israel, but as a separate group alongside them' ('Samaritans,' *Dictionary of Jesus and the Gospels*, p. 725).

[14]While the Samaritans had the Pentateuch as their holy book, it may well have been that their worship had been deeply influenced by other factors. Certainly the origin of northern worship in the division of the kingdom was syncretistic, and it is likely that further layers of extraneous belief and practice would have made their impact on worship over the subsequent centuries.

[15]Though they did not have a full copy of the Jewish scriptures (or at least they did not acknowledge them as being valid), they did share in a messianic expectation, probably based on Moses' words in Deuteronomy 18:18-22, though we have seen that the theme of a promised deliverer runs like a thread through the Pentateuch.

[16]Carson, D. A. (1991), *The Gospel According to John*, IVP, p. 223.

[17]Bingham, G. C. (1990), *The Way and Wonder of Worship*, New Creation Publications, p. 9.

[18]Walton's comment on these verses is helpful: 'Because the garden in Genesis was planted in a well-watered place (Eden), it took Eden as its name. But technically speaking, the garden should be understood as adjoining Eden because the water flows *from* Eden and waters the garden (see Gen. 2:10). In the same way, therefore, that a garden of a palace adjoins the palace, Eden is the source of waters and the residence of God, and the garden adjoins God's residence. The picture presented is of a mighty spring that gushes out from Eden and is channeled through the garden for irrigation purposes' (Walton, J. H.

[2001], *Genesis*, The NIV Application Commentary, Zondervan, p. 168).

[19]Having preached on this and related themes many times, I am firmly of the opinion that many of our best evangelical congregations are wedded to the ancient heresy of Docetism (from the Greek *dokeō*, 'to seem'), in which the Son takes on human flesh like a man may put on a coat, only to discard it when it is no longer needed. The incarnate Son abides as a man in heaven still, and by so doing he continues to faithfully fulfil his office as high priest for the people of God.

[20]There are some very helpful treatments of this subject available, which take the reader to much more depth than is possible here. See, for example Hurtado, L. W. (1999), *At the Origins of Christian Worship: The Context and Character of Earliest Christian Devotion*, Eerdmans (to which we refer more fully in the next chapter); Wainwright, A. W. (1962), *The Trinity in the New Testament*, SPCK, especially chapter 6; Bauckham, R. J., 'Worship of Jesus,' in D. N. Freedman, *Anchor Bible Dictionary,* Vol. 3, pp. 812-819; Bauckham, R. J. (1998), *God Crucified: Monotheism and Christology in the New Testament*, Paternoster.

[21]At various points in the Old Testament, this declaration of the divine name echoes out, often at very critical times of Israel's history. For example, the wording appears in the accounts of the giving of the Decalogue, where it acts as a sort of commentary on the first and second commandments in both Exodus (Exod. 20:3-6) and Deuteronomy (Deut. 5:7-10). In Moses' intercessory prayer of Numbers 14:11-19, Moses takes the explanation of the Name on his own lips and by it beseeches that God would have mercy on the rebellious nation who have refused to enter the resting place of the land (see Numbers 14:18-23 in particular). In effect, he asks God to live up to his Name! It echoes through Daniel's confession during the time of the captivity (Dan. 9:4) and its strains are heard in Nehemiah's prayer of repentance after the return from exile (Neh. 9:23). It finds a place in a number of the Psalms (e.g. 86:5, 15; 100:4; 103:8; 130:4-7; 145:1), and is the basis for calls to repentance in the prophets (e.g. Joel 2:13; Mic. 7:18). The last part of the utterance, which refers to the visiting of the iniquity of one generation on another, needs to be taken in its wider context. The words which Moses hears at the time of the revelation of the glory in Exodus 34 take up words given earlier in the context of the Decalogue. There we read that the visitation is

'on the third and fourth generation *of those who hate me*' (Exod. 20:5; cf. Deut. 5:9). Later in Israel's history God had to rebuke his people for the fatalistic attitude that they had attributed to the principle of such divine visitation. In Ezekiel 18 there is an extended discussion of the matter, where the prophet clearly spells out the correct understanding of the principle: the soul that sins it will die. This means that if a son has an idolatrous father, he cannot blame his father for his own idolatry. He, himself, is responsible. If he turns and repents, then it will go well with him. In Israel, the proverb 'the fathers have eaten sour grapes, and the children's teeth are set on edge' (Ezek. 18:2), was being quoted as a twisted form of the principle. As a sort of fatalistic slogan, it was used to excuse the people's idolatry and its associated moral and ethical transgressions on the basis of these being someone else's fault. Rather, if a son should repent from idolatry and *thus cease to hate God*, it would go well with him. God visits the generations of those who continue in rebellion against him, and in this way he does not leave the guilty unpunished. He causes the sins of the fathers' rebellion (e.g. the moral and physical pollution of the land) to rest on a generation *that continues to rebel*, but this is not a fixed and unalterable state. Repentance changes the whole picture.

[22]See, for example, Jesus' words in Luke 19:41-44; 23:27-31; cf. 21:20-24.

[23]There are a number of connections between Isaiah 6 and Isaiah 52:13–53:12 (perhaps the greatest of all the Servant Song passages in relationship to Christ) and also a substantial series of allusions to this passage in John 12. For a full discussion of these, see Carson, D. A. (1991), *The Gospel According to John*, IVP, pp. 448-50.

[24]Whitacre, R. A. (1999), *John*, The IVP New Testament Commentary Series, IVP, p. 322.

[25] This accords with Peter's statement that the prophets of old were moved by the Spirit of Christ within them to speak of the things concerning him, especially in relation to his suffering and death (1 Peter 1:10-12).

[26]This naturally raises a theological problem that has been addressed since the early days of Christian theological reflection: how can worship and prayer be offered to the *man* Jesus? Is this not some form of idolatry? The answer, of course, lies in the unique person of the Son, who is both God the Son and the Son of Man. His person has no

paradigm. Heppe thus states, 'the honour of worship does not belong to Christ's humanity as such, but because the divine Logos has taken it up into his personality, which is by nature *adorabilis*.' He then quotes Wolleb, Keckermann, Zanchius and Voetius on the point (Heppe, H. [1950], *Reformed Dogmatics*, Wakeman Great Reprints, p. 438. See also the comments by Turretin in his *Institutes* 14:XVIII where he quotes both Athanasius and Augustine.

[27]See, for example, Jones, C. (1978), *The Study of Liturgy*, SPCK; Schaff, P. (1919), *The Creeds of Chrisendom*, 3 vols.; Leith, J.H. (1982), *Creeds of the Churches: a Reader in Christian Doctrined from the Bible to the Present*, third edition, John Knox Press.

Chapter 6. Worship in Hebrews.

[1]I have adopted the convention of italicising the name of the book, to make a clear distinction between the book *Hebrews* and its recipients – who were 'Hebrews', of some sort at least!

[2]The academic interest in *Hebrews* is fed by a number of sources, e.g. its relationship to first century Hellenistic Judaism; its relationship or otherwise to the theology of the Qumran community; its use of the Old Testament; the origins of its Christology; etc. None of these, however, need be addressed in this chapter.

[3]Marcion (d. AD 160) was a leading gnostic heretic of the second century, who produced his own radically emended New Testament. In his *Antitheses* he set out 'the contradictions of the Old and New Testaments (as he interpreted them) in order to prove that the God of Judaism was not the heavenly Father of Jesus Christ'. In his own version of the New Testament 'he threw out everything that had a Jewish element, accepting only Luke's gospel and most of Paul's letters', though even these he did not leave untouched (Needham, N. [1997], *The Age of the Early Church Fathers*, 2000 Years of Christ's Power, Grace Publications, p. 96.

[4]Peterson, D. (1992), *Engaging with God: A biblical theology of worship.* (p. 228). Leicester: IVP.

[5]Were they 'readers' or 'hearers'? The book's self designation as a 'word of exhortation' (13:22) is taken by commentators to refer to a sermon/exposition/homily of some sort. It certainly lacks many of the normal features of a New Testament epistle. The epistles, in any case, would have been read aloud in the assembly of the people of God, but this piece of work has its own character, and is replete with rhetorical

and sermonic devices. For this reason some commentators refer to the recipients of the letter as 'addressees', rather than 'readers'.

[6]Lane, W. L. (1991), *Hebrews 1–8*, Word Biblical Commentary, Word Books.

[7]See, for example, Hughes, P. E. (1977), *A Commentary on the Epistle to the Hebrews*, Eerdmans, pp. 15ff. for some alternatives.

[8]Lane, W. L. (1991), *Hebrews 1–8*, p. cxxxviii. Note also the comment by Attridge: 'The creative heart of the doctrinal reflection of Hebrews is clearly its christology, which is treated so explicitly and carefully. Other elements of the faith of Hebrews are in large measure the background of the christologically based paranaesis. They never become in and of themselves the subject of exposition' (Attridge, H. W. [1987], *The Epistle to the Hebrews*, Hermeneia, Fortress Press, p. 27.

[9]I take the position that the present tense references associated with the cultus (in 5:1-4; 7:21, 23, 27f.; 8:3, 4f.; 13; 9:6f., 9, 13, 25; 10:1-3, 8, 11; 13:10-11) indicate that the temple in Jerusalem is still standing. Even if this is not the case (as Lane and others argue), the point remains. The old worship cultus, associated with Moses, Sinai and the piacular sacrifices, has been completely overtaken by the eternal reality to which it pointed.

[10]Isaacs comments: 'In many ways Jesus' work may be compared with that of his biblical predecessors, namely Moses and the high priest, but in each case it is sonship which is used to highlight the contrast between his status and theirs. Like them his task is to cross the boundary which divides the human from the divine, the sacred from the profane. Yet whereas their achievement is flawed and partial, Jesus has definitively crossed over into the realm of the sacred in entering heaven, the superior Mt. Sinai and the true holy of holies' (Isaacs, M. E. [1992], *Sacred Space: An Approach to the Theology of the Epistle to the Hebrews*, JSOT Press, p. 178.

[11]Walmark, L. (1996), 'Hebrews, Theology of,' in A. Elwell, *Evangelical Dictionary of Biblical Theology*, Baker Books, p. 335.

[12]Westcott, B. F. (1914), *The Epistle to the Hebrews*, Macmillan & Co., p. 7. So also Lane, 'The eternal, essential quality of Jesus' sonship qualified him to be the one through whom God uttered his final word,' (Lane, [1991], *Hebrews 1–8*, Word Biblical Commentary, p. 11).

[13]Lane, W. L. (1991), pp. 12ff.

[14]Hughes thus echoes the earliest Christian theological reflection on these verses when he comments, 'Of the two expressions "the radiance of his glory" and "the very stamp of his nature", the former, which implies the consubstantiality of the Son with the Father, is balanced by the latter, which implies the distinction of the person of the Son from that of the Father, and both designate the function of the Incarnate Son, who as the Light and the Truth ... is the Revealer of God to mankind' (Hughes, P. E. [1977], *A Commentary on the Epistle to the Hebrews*, Eerdmans, p. 44.

[15]Guthrie, D. (1981), *New Testament Theology*, p. 320.

[16]Hurtado, L. W. (1999), *At the Origins of Christian Worship: The Context and Character of Earliest Christian Devotion*, Eerdmans, p. 97. On the same page Hurtado indicates how the impact of the revelation of Jesus Christ, responded to in worship, informs the development of theology: 'This unusual "mutation" in monotheistic practice in turn contributed heavily to the subsequent complicated effort to develop a new doctrine of God, which occupied Christians for the next several centuries.' Theology arises out of worship, not *vice versa*!

[17]Lane comments on the unusual word order of the verse, indicating that it 'is calculated to arouse attention; it conveys an element of surprise as well as emphasis.... On seven other occasions the writer will introduce the proper name and in each instance it is given a position of great emphasis by its position at the end of the sentence (3:1; 6:20; 7:22; 10:19; 12:2, 24; 13:20). There is nothing corresponding to this in any other New Testament writer' (Lane, W. L. (1991), *Hebrews 1-8*, pp. 48f.

[18]Bruce, F. F. (1964), *The Epistle to the Hebrews*, New International Commentary on the New Testament, Eerdmans, p. 37.

[19]Isaacs, M. E. (1992), *Sacred Space: An Approach to the Theology of the Epistle to the Hebrews*, JSOT Press, p. 174.

[20] With some insight, Lane also suggests that the verse constitutes an allusion to 1 Samuel 2:25 ('If one man sins against another, God will mediate for him; but if a man sins against the Lord, who can intercede for him?'), which he suggests forms a transition into chapter three (Lane, W. L. [1991], *Hebrews 1–8*, p. 65).

[21]Torrance, J. B. (19), 'The Place of Jesus Christ in Worship,' in R. Anderson, *Theological Foundations for Ministry* T. & T. Clark, p. 351.

[22] While J. B. Torrance in particular turns to *Hebrews* to substantiate his ideas, it is curious that the language of union with Christ ('in Christ', 'with Christ' etc.), so prevalent in the rest of the New Testamwnt letters and in Paul in particular, is wholly absent from Hebrews. Torrance also misses the fact that even here, outside of *Hebrews*, the language of union with Christ is almost exclusively related to his work on the Cross – and believers who have become spiritually united with him by grace through faith in this atoning death expressed in baptism – rather than being related to his incarnation.

[23] See, for example, Torrance, J. B. (1996), *Worship, Communion and the Triune God of Grace*, Paternoster, Chapter 3.

[24] Torrance, T. (1992), *The Mediation of Christ*, T. & T. Clark, pp. 62, 68.

[25] Hughes, P. E. (1977), *A Commentary on the Epistle to the Hebrews*, Eerdmans, p. 120.

[26] Attridge, H. W. (1987), *The Epistle to the Hebrews*, Hermeneia, Fortress Press, p. 90.

[27] Calvin, J. (1963), *Hebrews and I & II Peter*, Calvin's New Testament Commentary, Eerdmans, p. 27.

[28] This may be why it does not figure significantly in some treatments of New Testament worship. For example, neither Cullman, O. (1963), *Early Christian Worship*, Studies in Biblical Theology: First Series, SCM, nor Martin, R. P. (1974), *Worship in the Early Church*, Eerdmans, make much reference to *Hebrews* in their works, a pattern continued to some extent in Hurtado, L. W. (1999), *At the Origins of Christian Worship: The Context and Character of Earliest Christian Devotion*, Eerdmans. David Peterson (1992), *Engaging with God: A Biblical Theology of Worship*, Apollos) is something of an exception, devoting a whole chapter to it.

[29] There may be a possible reference to the Lord's supper in 13:10, but even then, 'it must be noted, however, that there is no support for the view that the "altar" is a description of the Lord's table, for nowhere else is such an identification made in the New Testament. The point of the statement is not to present an interpretation of the ordinance, but to demonstrate the superiority of Christianity over the Jewish cultus' (Guthrie, D. [1981], *New Testament Theology*, IVP, p. 781.

[30] Attridge, H. W. (1987), *The Epistle to the Hebrews*, Hermeneia, Fortress Press, p. 290.

[31]Hughes, P. E. (1977), *A Commentary on the Epistle to the Hebrews*, Eerdmans, p. 418.

[32]There is, of course, a deep sense of continuity with the Old Testament in all this. The two greatest commandments govern all the Law and the Prophets, so that wherever formalism threatened to replace wholehearted love of God and service of one's neighbour, the prophetic oracles were withering (e.g. Isa. 1:10-17; cf. Jer. 22:3, 15-17; Micah 6:8; Zeph. 2:3; Zech. 7:9-10). God has always looked for the congruence of his people's hearts with his own.

[33]Hughes, P. E. (1977), *A Commentary on the Epistle to the Hebrews*, Eerdmans, p. 415. So also the comment by Kistemaker: 'The author's exhortation to "spur one another on to love" precedes his remarks about church attendance. When the believer attends the worship service, he expresses his love for Jesus. He realises that Jesus, the head of the church, is present at the service and desires his presence' (Kistemaker, S. J. [1984], *Hebrews*, Baker, p. 291).

[34]Bruce, F. F. (1964), *The Epistle to the Hebrews*, New International Commentary on the New Testament, Eerdmans, p. 384.

[35]Ellingworth, P. (1993), *The Epistle to the Hebrews: A Commentary on the Greek Text*, The New International Greek Testament Commentary, Paternoster, p. 692.

[36]Kistemaker, S. J. (1984), *Hebrews*, Baker, p. 401. So also this comment by Lane: 'Christians under the new covenant are to enter into an experience of maturity in which all of life becomes an expression of worship. Authentic worship is a grateful response to covenantal blessings already experienced and to the certainty of the reception of an unshakeable kingdom (v 28). It is deepened by the frank awareness of the awesome character of God's holiness, which was disclosed in the fiery epiphany of Sinai (v 29)' (Lane, W. L. [1991], *Hebrews 9-13, * Word Biblical Commentary, Word, p. 491).

[37]Hughes, P. E. (1977), *A Commentary on the Epistle to the Hebrews*, Eerdmans, pp. 583f.

[38]Craigie, P. (1986), *Psalms 1–50*, Word Biblical Commentary, Word, p. 367.

[39]Attridge, H. W. (1987), *The Epistle to the Hebrews*, Hermeneia, Fortress, p. 401. So also Calvin, who comments on 13:16: 'It is no common honour that God regards what we do for men as sacrifices offered to Himself, and that He so values our works which are worth nothing that He calls them holy. Therefore where there is no love

among us, we not only deprive men of their right, but God Himself who has solemnly dedicated to Himself what He commanded to be done to men' (Calvin, J. [1963], *Hebrews and I & II Peter,* Calvin's New Testament Commentary, Eerdmans, p. 212).

[40]Lane, W. L. (1991), *Hebrews 9–13*, Word Biblical Commentary, p. 573. Lane sees the topic of worship as pervading the final section of Hebrews, with the whole of 13:1-21 being an elaboration of 12:28. He suggests that the entire section of the book (identified by him as running from 12:14–13:25 under the heading 'Orientation for life as Christians in a hostile world') is 'a skilfully constructed admonition to worship God acceptably…. Authentic worship is an expansive concept that makes sacred all of life. It presupposes the willing adoption of a lifestyle pleasing to God. Worship, accordingly, cannot be restricted to formal or informal expressions of praise and prayer, but infuses every aspect of public and private life with the character of consecrated service to God. The writer focuses the attention of the assembled Christians upon shared life within the confessing community because he perceives worship comprehensively' (p. 572).

[41]We have already made passing reference to this verse, but here note the comment of Calvin: 'This is a fine analogy *(anagoge)* from the old rite of the Law to the present state of the Church. There was a solemn kind of sacrifice, which is mentioned in Lev. 16, of which no part was given back to the priests and Levites. He says, using a neat allusion, that this has now been fulfilled in Christ, since He was sacrificed on the condition that those who serve at the tabernacle should not feed on Him. By the ministers of the tabernacle he understands all those who performed the ceremonies. He therefore means that we must renounce the tabernacle in order to have a share in Christ. Just as the word altar includes a sacrifice and a victim, so the tabernacle includes all the outward types which were joined to it' (Calvin, J. [1963], *Hebrews and I & II Peter*, Calvin's New Testament Commentary, Eerdmans, pp. 209ff.). In my view the emphasis Calvin brings to the verse is appropriate: the weight of meaning lies in the contrast between the former and latter manners of worship. I do not take this 'altar' as being a reference to a new, Christian cultus since all other evidence – not least in the verses that follow – indicates that the writer has in view the informal, spiritual worship of believers, rather than formal acts of worship in a public assembly.

[42]Motyer, S. (2000, July), 'The People of God in Hebrews,' Unpublished conference presentation, Tyndale Fellowship Conference, Nantwich, p. 13.

[43]Wu, J. L. (1997), 'Liturgical Elements,' in *Dictionary of Later New Testament & Its Development,* IVP, p. 661.

[44]Longenecker, R. N. (1999), *New Wine into Fresh Wineskins: Contexualizing the Early Christian Confessions*, Hendrikson, Chapter 1. In brief, the criteria (not all of which need be present in any given case) are: the presence of *parallelismus memborum*, even though the material is not poetry; the presence of *hapax legomena*; a preference for participles over finite verbs; an affirmation regarding the work or person of Jesus Christ; use of the noun *homologia* or the verb *homologeo*; the use of *hoti recitativum*; verbs for preaching, teaching or witnessing to introduce confessional material; and a participial construction or relative clause introducing the material in question. Longenecker has similar criteria for identifying hymnic fragments, and single statement affirmations.

[45]Attridge, H. W. (1987), *The Epistle to the Hebrews*, Hermeneia.,Fortress, p. 26.

[46]Lane, W. L. (1997), 'Hebrews,' in *Dictionary of Later New Testament & Its Development*, IVP, p. 451.

[47]Attridge, H. W. (1987), *The Epistle to the Hebrews*, p. 24.

[48]Motyer, S. (2000, July), 'The People of God in Hebrews,' Unpublished conference presentation, Tyndale Fellowship Conference, Nantwich, p. 13.

[49]Hurtado, L. W. (1999), *At the Origins of Christian Worship: The Context and Character of Earliest Christian Devotion,* Eerdmans, p. 4.

[50]Guthrie, D. (1981), *New Testament Theology*, IVP, p. 778.

[51]Isaacs, M. E. (1992), *Sacred Space: An Approach to the Theology of the Epistle to the Hebrews*, JSOT Press, pp. 21f..

[52]Gordon, R. P. (2000), *Hebrews*, Readings: A New Biblical Commentary, Sheffield Academic Press, pp. 21f.

[53]'Yet the heavenly Jerusalem, like God's "rest" and the holy of holies entered by Jesus, is more than simply the counterpart of its earthly type, the earthly Jerusalem. The holy city, like all the rest of Israel's sacred ground, is but a foretaste of the real thing – which is heaven itself. This holy mountain, the heavenly Zion, has been scaled by someone closer to God than Moses; Jesus the Son of God' (Isaacs,

M. E. [1992], *Sacred Space: An Approach to the Theology of the Epistle to the Hebrews*, JSOT Press, p. 126).

[54]Isaacs, M. E. (1992), *Sacred Space: An Approach to the Theology of the Epistle to the Hebrews*, p. 67.

Chapter 7. Worship in The Letters of Peter and Paul.

[1]Klauck, H. (1992), 'Sacrifice and Sacrificial Offerings,' in *The Anchor Bible Dictionary,* Vol. 5, Doubleday, p. 891.

[2]This is the reason we have not given consideration to Jude, James or the letters of John. I have taken instances of cultic terminology as the route into the underlying theology of worship of the writers. In these other letters such terminology is not evident. However, I believe that a careful reading of these letters will confirm the general pattern that emerges in this chapter.

[3]Schlatter, A. (1995), *Romans: The Righteousness of God*, Hendrikson, p. 228.

[4]Morris, L. (1988), *The Epistle to the Romans*, Eerdmans, p. 434.

[5]Murray, J. (1968), *The Epistle to the Romans*, Vol. 2, The New International Commentary on the New Testament, Eerdmans, p. 114.

[6]Barrett, C. K. (1962), *A Commentary on the Epistle to the Romans*, Black's New Testament Commentaries, Adam & Charles Black, p. 232.

[7]'The Christian finds out the will of God not to contemplate it but to do it... And even the renewed mind needs a good deal of instruction: hence the detailed advice and exhortation in the following paragraphs' (Barrett, C. K. [1962], *A Commentary on the Epistle to the Romans*, p. 233).

[8]Schreiner, T. R. (1998), *Romans*, Baker Exegetical Commentary on the New Testament, Baker, p. 766.

[9]Peterson, D. (1992), *Engaging with God: A Biblical Theology of Worship*, Apollos, p. 181.

[10]Käsemann, commenting on Romans 12:1, emphasises the radical nature of Pauline theology at this point: 'where the worship of Christians takes the form of their bodily obedience, there is in principle an abandonment of the cultic sacred place which is characteristically a place of divine worship for the ancient world.... Sacred times and places are superseded by the eschatological public activity of those who at all times and at all places stand "before the face of Christ" and from this position before God make the every-day round of so-

called secular life into the arena of the unlimited and unceasing glorification of the divine will ... the total Christian community with all its members is the bearer of this worship and ... not only sacred functions but also cultically privileged persons lose their right to exist ... so far from there being any room left for cultic thinking, the use of cultic terminology becomes itself the means of making clear, through a paradox, the extent of the upheaval' (Käsemann, E. [1969], *New Testament Questions of Today*, Fortress, pp. 191–92).

[11]For a succinct summary of the issues and the likely dates of Paul's various visits to Jerusalem, see Hughes, P. E. (1962), *Paul's Second Epistle to the Corinthians*, The New International Commentary on the New Testament, Eerdmans, pp. 283-86. See also McKnight, S. (1993), 'Collection for the Saints,' in *Dictionary of Paul and his Letters*, IVP, pp.143–47).

[12]Denney, J. (1916), *The Second Epistle to the Corinthians*, Hodder & Stoughton, p. 285.

[13]Our 1 Corinthians is probably Paul's second main letter to them, while our 2 Corinthians is probably the fourth of Paul's letters to them. It is clear that, in both, Paul picks up issues that the Corinthians had raised with him, and also that he addresses issues of which he has heard by way of first-hand report.

[14]Witherington III, B. (1995), *Conflict and Community in Corinth*, Eerdmans, p. 95.

[15]Haffemann, S. (1993), 'Corinthians, Letters to the,' in *Dictionary of Paul and His Letters*, IVP, p. 165.

[16]For details, see Schreiner, T. R. (1998), *Romans*, Baker Exegetical Commentary on the New Testament, Baker, p. 797; and Fitzmyer, J. (1992), *Romans: A New Translation with Introduction and Commentary*, The Anchor Bible, Doubleday, p. 736.

[17]On the basis of the archaeology Witherington suggests a maxium of 50 for the very largest houses in Corinth (Witherington III, B. [1995], *Conflict and Community in Corinth*, Eerdmans, p. 30.

[18]Witherington's estimate seems reasonable: 'In 11:8 Paul seems to envision the whole Christian community in Corinth coming together in one house to celebrate the Lord's Supper in the context of a meal. In even notable Roman villas the dining room, where people reclined on couches for meals, normally only accommodated nine to twelve people ... and even making allowances for dining in the atrium, kitchen and elsewhere in the house, a dining party in a home would at most

allow for a crowd of around fifty or perhaps sixty people. Unless this meal was held in a pavilion or tent, which was in fact done in Roman antiquity, frequently on the grounds of a temple, we may conjecture that there were about sixty people in Corinth' (*Conflict and Community in Corinth*, p.114).

[19]For a very helpful discussion of the background, see on 'Status Inconsistency' and on 'Debates About the Socioeconomic Status of Paul and his Converts' in Thistleton, A. (2000), *The First Epistle to the Corinthians: A Commentary on the Greek Text*, The New International Greek Testament Commentary, Eerdmans, pp. 12-17, 23-29.

[20]Marshall, I. H. (1980), *The Acts of the Aposltes*, IVP, p. 83. Grand Rapids: Eerdmans; also Bruce, F. F. (1981), *The Book of the Acts*, The New International Commentary on the New Testament, Eerdmans, p. 79.

[21]Bauckham, R. (1986), *Jude, 2 Peter*, Word Biblical Commentary, p. 85.

[22]The nature of the 'remembering' is significant. The Greek word *anamnésis* is best taken in the light of the Old Testament background provided by the theology of 'remembering' the deeds of God in accordance with his covenantal promises and his deliverance, particularly in the matter of the Passover. Israel was to 'remember' God and his deeds (e.g. Exod. 13:8; Deut. 5:15; 8:2; 16:12), and their disobedience could be characterised as forgetting him, or not remembering what he had done (e.g. Judg. 8:34; Pss. 78:11; 106:21; Jer. 2:32). Such remembering was always with a view to increased trust in God in the present, and continuing obedience. In the context of the Lord's Supper the Corinthians were to remember the sacrificial action of God in Christ, whereby he had established the promised new covenant in his blood (see Exod. 24:8; cf. Jer. 31:31-34). They were to see the Lord's Supper as the present gift of the Lord to spur them on in loving obedience that shares in the nature of his self-giving sacrifice by the concrete expression of *koinōnia* in the new covenant community.

[23]Thistleton, A. (2000), *The First Epistle to the Corinthians: A Commentary on the Greek Text*, p.899.

[24]In principle, the judgment that falls on Ananias and Sapphira in Acts 5 and that which is described here in 1 Corinthians 11 is the same. In each situation the transgression is against the love of the

fellowship, which was the great hallmark of their new covenant status as God's beloved people.

[25]For more details, see 'Roman Corinth: Religion' in Witherington III, B. (1995), *Conflict and Community in Corinth*, pp. 12–19). See also the extensive treatment given to the socio-political and religious context of Roman Corinth by Thistleton in his 'Roman Corinth in the Time of Paul' (*The First Epistle to the Corinthians: A Commentary on the Greek Text*, pp.1–17).

[26]'Several temples in Corinth had dining rooms where feasts were held on many occasions, including birthdays. Temples were the restaurants of antiquity. There is archaeological evidence at the Asklepion in Corinth of a dining room with couches along four walls and a table and brazier in the center' (Witherington III, B. [1995], *Conflict and Community in Corinth*, p.188).

[27]Outside of this section of 1 Corinthians the term only appears in two other places in the New Testament (Rev. 2:14, 20), where it is cited as one of the reasons for the risen and glorified Lord's judgement against the churches of Pergamos and Thyatira respectively. This does not mean it was not an issue elsewhere, for Paul has to address the issue of eating meat (presumably because of its idolatrous associations) in Rome also (Rom. 14:21).

[28]According to Louw and Nida, *eidōlothuton* is a 'semantically complex word meaning literally "that which has been sacrificed to idols." There is no specific element meaning "meat", but the stem meaning "sacrifice" implies "meat". Part of the sacrifice was normally burned on the altar, part was eaten during a ritual meal in a temple, and part was sold in the public market. According to Jewish tradition this meat was unclean and therefore forbidden … [it] is normally translated by a phrase, for example, "meat which had been offered to idols" or "meat of an animal which had been sacrificed to idols" or "meat of animals killed in honor of false gods".'

[29]Witherington III, B. (1995), *Conflict and Community in Corinth*, p.190.

[30]Witherington III, B. (1995), *Conflict and Community in Corinth*, p.226.

[31]I am assuming Pauline authorship of Ephesians, though the comments below are not materially affected by taking a contrary view. The doctrine of Ephesians is, at the very least, Pauline.

[32]The idea of walking with God draws on rich Old Testament imagery, but includes concepts such as being in fellowship with God, being accepted by him, and at peace with him. Overall,

however, it relates to the matter of obedience to him. One may be a member of covenant Israel, but not be walking with him in this sense. For more, see the chapter on 'Walking with God' in Sheriffs, D. (1996), *The Friendship of the Lord: An Old Testament Spirituality*, Paternoster.

[33]Lincoln, A. T. (1990), *Ephesians*, Word Biblical Commentary, p. 141.

[34]'The objective situation of hostility because of the law's exclusiveness engendered personal and social antagonisms. The laws which forbade eating or intermarrying with Gentiles often led Jews to have contempt for Gentiles which could regard Gentiles as less than human. In response, Gentiles would often regard Jews with great suspicion, considering them inhospitable and hateful to non-Jews, and indulge in anti-Jewish prejudice.... This lively mutual animosity was one of the uglier elements in the Greco-Roman world' (Lincoln, A. T. [1990], *Ephesians*, p.142.

[35]Lincoln, A. T. (1990), *Ephesians*, pp.161-62.

[36]This point is well made by Rudolph Schnackenburg (1991), *The Epistle to the Ephesians*, T & T Clark, p. 115.

[37]Schnackenburg, R. (1991), *The Epistle to the Ephesians*, p.116.

[38]In the LXX *prosphora* and *thysia* are habitually used to translate *zebah* and *minhâh* respectively. The former is a 'generic word for sacrifice' while the latter 'means a gift or present ... tribute ... and an offering made to God of any kind, whether of grain or animals' ('Sacrifice,' in C. Brown [1986], *The New International Dictionary of New Testament Theology*, Vol. 3, Zondervan, pp. 422, 421). It would seem that by using such wide terms, Paul is speaking of an all-encompassing action of worship.

[39]This helpful term comes from Resner. 'Paul's call to "imitate me" is not a plea for a pragmatics of persuasion. Nor does it suggest that either Paul's right living or his readers' right imitation of Paul makes efficacious the gospel message. Rather, his imitation call is ethical in the Pauline sense of the call to the cruciform life (I Thess. 1-2). The life so lived becomes a lived parable of the gospel message, an existential witness of the death and resurrection of Christ continuing to work its judging and redeeming power in the world' (Resner, A. [1999], *Preacher and Cross: Person and Message in Theology and Rhetoric*, Eerdmans, p. 152).

[40]Clarke, A. (1998), '"Be Imitators of Me": Paul's Model of Leadership,' Tyn*dale Bulletin*, 49(2), 360.

[41]Lincoln, A. T. (1990), *Ephesians*, p.3 10.

[42]France, R. T. (1986), 'Pour,' in *The New International Dictionary of New Testament Theology*, Vol. 2, Zondervan, pp. 854-55. Colin Brown suggests that 'the use of the word *thysia* and the fact that Paul was in prison expecting the possibility of execution' means 'Paul was thinking of his death, not as a propitiatory sacrifice but as a freewill offering for the sake of the church' (*The New International Dictionary of New Testament Theology*, Vol. 3, p.432.

[43]For a survey of some of the options available in identifying Paul's opponents in Philippi, see Bateman IV, H. (1998, January), 'Were the Opponents at Philippi Necessarily Jewish?,' *Bibliotheca Sacra*,155, (617), 39–61. Bateman comes to the conclusion, *inter alia*, that 'Although traditional historical reconstructions about the opposers in Philippi suggest that the Judaizers were ethnic Jews, it would be a mistake to rule out a priori the possibility that those who opposed the Christians at Philippi were Gentile Judaizers who claimed to be Christians' (p. 60). Whatever the case, it is clear from the context that they were insisting on circumcision and other Jewish practices as a mark of spiritual maturity and as a badge of salvation.

[44]For more detail on this point, see deSilva, D. (1994, Spring), 'No Confidence in the Flesh: The Meaning and Function of Phil. 3:2–21,' *Trinity Journal*, 15(1), 35.

[45]Hawthorne, G. F. (1983), *Philippians*, Word Biblical Commentary, p. 127.

[46]O'Brien, P. (1982), *Colossians, Philemon*, Word Biblical Commentary, p. 211.

[47]Peterson, D. (1992), *Engaging with God: A Biblical Theology of Worship*, Apollos, p. 221.

[48]'Paul mentions the subject of thanksgiving in his letters more often, line for line, than any other Hellenistic author, pagan or Christian. The *eucharistō* word group turns up forty-six times in the Pauline corpus and appears in many important contexts in every letter except Galatians and Titus' (O'Brien, P. [1993], 'Benediction, Blessing, Doxology, Thanksgiving,' in *Dictionary of Paul and his Letters*, IVP, p. 69.

[49]Liefeld, W. (1999), *1 & 2 Timothy/Titus*, The NIV Application Commentary, Zondervan, p. 19.

[50]For example, Mounce is more favourably disposed to Pauline authorship (through an amanuensis), while Marshall is of the opinion that direct Pauline authorship must be subject to serious doubt. For

discussion, see the extensive discussion given over to the matter in the Introductions of their commentaries (Marshall, I. H. [1999], *The Pastoral Epistles*, The International Critical Commentary, T. & T. Clark; Mounce, W. (2000), *Pastoral Epistles*, Word Biblical Commentary.

[51]The issues of authorship and date are closely interrelated. Pauline authorship would demand a period of ministry on Paul's part following his release from house arrest in Rome, which is where we see him at the end of the Book of the Acts. If this were the case, the letters would have been written in the years following his release but before the death of Nero in AD 68 (under whose persecution he was almost certainly martyred). If one opts for non-Pauline authorship, the date becomes more flexible, but even here we are probably not looking at something beyond AD 70. Marshall, for instance, suggests that while 'It is true that we know so little about the "tunnel period" from c. AD 70 to AD 100 that it could be argued the PE might fit in anywhere in this period without serious difficulty. On the whole, however, the PE reflect an undeveloped ecclesiology that more naturally belongs to the earlier part of this period' (Marshall, I. H. [1999], *The Pastoral Epistles*, p.57).

[52]See Howard Marshall's helpful discussion of the connection between worship in the day-to-day and worship in the public assembly, particularly in the way in which he adapts terms from speech analysis (the 'illocutionary' and 'perlocutionary' functions of an utterance) to illustrate the nexus between broad and narrow understandings of worship (Marshall, I. H. [2002], Worshipping Biblically. *Scottish Bulletin of Evangelical Theology*, 20 (2), 146-61.

[53]Cranfield, C. E. B. (1958, October), 'Divine and Human Action: The Biblical Concept of Worship,' *Interpretation*, 12 (4), 395.

[54]'That Christians are the "people of God" because they are people of the new covenant is emphasized by Paul in order to distinguish them as the eschatological fulfillment of Israel. Hebrews does the same thing in order to make the readers certain of that which is eschatological/ultimate and is given to them to counter the inner doubt caused by not seeing. But I Peter emphasizes identity as "God's people" in order to characterize the addressees' place in society and their historical mission' (Goppelt, L. [1993], *A Commentary on I Peter*, Eerdmans, p. 151).

[55]Grudem, W. (1988), *1 Peter*, IVP, p. 98.

[56]See, for example, Leon Morris' discussion of this relationship in 'The Saints and the Synagogue,' in Michael J. Wilkins & Terence Paige (1992), *Worship, Theology and Ministry in the Early Church: Essays in Honor of Ralph P. Martin*, JSOT Press, pp. 39-52. Marshall also draws attention to both similarities and differences (Marshall, I. H. [1989], 'Church and Temple in the New Testament,' *Tyndale Bulletin*, 40 (2), pp. 203-22.

Chapter 8. Worship in The Book of Revelation

[1]Our purpose is to engage with the theme of worship *per se*, rather than to buy into debates related to eschatological chronology or engage in interpretation based on one prophetic schema or another. While the view of the author is essentially amillennial and broadly in line with Hendriken's understanding of the structure of the book of seven sections in parallel (Hendriksen, W. [1954], *More Than Conquerors: An Interpretation of the Book of Revelation*, Baker), the theological reflection contained in this chapter is free standing enough to be embraced by others whose persuasions are different. Apocalyptic imagery and symbolism is so extensive and so powerful that it is impossible to exhaust the meaning of any single image or collection of allusions without nailing the literature down to an imposed rigidity that it was never designed to bear.

[2]For an extensive discussion of the doctrine of God contained in the book, see Swete, H. B. (1907), *The Apocalypse of St. John: The Greek Text with Introduction, Notes and Indices*, London: Macmillan and Co., pp. clviii-clxv. Other helpful material is to be found in Wainwright, A. W. (1962), *The Trinity in the New Testament*, SPCK; and Peterson, D. (1992), *Engaging with God: A Biblical Theology of Worship*, Apollos, especially chapter 9. For a useful overview of the theme of worship in the Book of Revelation, see Bingham, G. C. (1990), *The Way and Wonder of Worship*, New Creation Publications, chapters 2 and 3.

[4]The necessity of the Spirit's present and enabling power is a repeated theme in the book (e.g. Rev. 1:10; 17:13; 21:10), and is as much needed to see the things of heaven as the things of hell. Unaided human reason would never be able to grasp either the mysteries of grace nor those of iniquity. In relation to the latter, Caird comments: 'John uses the most offensive language he can to delineate his spiritual

enemies (Balaamite, Jezebel, fornication, monster, whore), because he is aware that they present themselves to the world in a much more attractive light. No man chooses evil because he recognises it to be evil, but always because, for the moment at least, is appears to be good. The essence of evil is deception and counterfeit' (Caird, G. B. [1984], *The Revelation of St. John the Divine*, Black's New Testament Commentaries, A & C Black, p. 294).

[5]Ladd is correct to identify the seven-fold references to the Spirit (1:4; 3:1; 4:5; 5:6) as signifying the Spirit in all his fullness. He then comments, 'The source of the idea appears to be Zech. 4, where the prophet described a candle-stick with seven lamps which are the eyes of the Lord ranging over the whole earth. The meaning of the vision was "Not by might, not by power, but by my Spirit, says the Lord of hosts" (Zech. 4:8)' (Ladd, G. E. [1972], *A Commentary on the Revelation of John*, Eerdmans, p. 25). Caird indicates something of the significance of such references for the theme of worship and conflict, commenting that John's use of 'the seven spirits, lamps or stars was a direct challenge to the imperial myth of the divine ruler, and, since defiance of emperor-worship was one of the main themes of his vision, it is reasonable to suppose that the challenge was intended' (Caird, G. B., *The Revelation of St. John the Divine*, p. 15).

[6]Longman III, T., & Reid, D. (1995), *God is a Warrior*, Studies in Old Testament Biblical Theology, Zondervan, p. 45.

[7]Bingham, G. C. (1990), *The Way and Wonder of Worship*, New Creation Publications, p. 30.

[8]We have seen that this was the pattern for ancient Israel. The exodus was with a view to service. 'Let my son go that he may serve me' (Exod. 4:22-23) at one and the same time indicates the dignity of Israel (adopted son of God) and the destiny of his people (to worship and serve him). In Exodus 19:3-7 we read that 'The LORD called to him out of the mountain, saying, "Thus you shall say to the house of Jacob, and tell the people of Israel: You yourselves have seen what I did to the Egyptians, and how I bore you on eagles' wings and brought you to myself. Now therefore, if you will indeed obey my voice and keep my covenant, you shall be my treasured possession among all peoples, for all the earth is mine; and you shall be to me a kingdom of priests and a holy nation. These are the words that you shall speak to the people of Israel." So Moses came and called the elders of the people and set before them all these words that the LORD had

commanded him.' We have already commented on this passage in a previous chapter, but note one crucial difference with the language of Revelation 1:6 and parallel passages. In Revelation any hint of conditionality is removed. Where we saw that Israel did not obey his voice and keep his commandments (and so they effectively forfeited their status as his king-priest nation), the redeemed of the new covenant in Revelation are shown in a different light. In them, the circumcised heart promised in the Old Testament has been granted.

[9]Bingham, G. C. (1993), *The Revelation of St. John the Divine*, New Creation Publications Inc., p. 303.

[10]'Man of lawlessness' (*anthrōpos tēs anomias*) is the best translation, but the more common phrase 'man of sin' (as in the KJV) has had such a long, popular usage that it will no doubt continue to be used! In the end, as John tells us, 'sin is lawlessness' (1 John 3:4).

[11]Morris, L. (1959), *The First and Second Epistle to the Thessalonians*, The New International Commentary on the New Testament, Eerdmans, p. 231.

[12]Motyer's comment is helpful: 'Chapter 3 [of Daniel] tells of one king's attempt to dictate the world's theology and worship, as though it were for him to determine the nature of God' (Motyer, A. [2001], *The Story of the Old Testament*, Baker Books, p. 149. It is telling that the phrase 'all peoples, nations, and languages' appears later in the account, but only with reference to what God has done in defeating human pride and vindicating himself as the only One worthy of worship (e.g. Dan. 3:29-30; 4:1-3; cf. 5:19; 6:25; 7:14).

[13]For more detailed attention to this theme, see Beale, G. K. (2004), *The Temple and the Church's Mission: A biblical theology of the dwelling place of God*, New Studies in Biblical Theology, Apollos, especially chapter 10; and Dumbrell, W. (1985), *The End of the Beginning: Revelation 21–22 and the Old Testament*, Lancer Books, especially chapter 2.

[14]For their comments on the Old Testament and ancient Near Eastern background, and the pattern in Revelation, see Longman III, T., & Reid, D. (1995), *God is a Warrior*, Studies in Old Testament Biblical Theology, Zondervan, pp. 84-88 and 190-92 respectively. Although he does not develop the matter extensively (as he refers to this 'on the way' to making another point), Vern Poythress has assembled an impressive table of references to support the sequence of deliverance, house building and worship; see Table 2 in Poythress, V. S., 'Ezra 3,

Union with Christ and Exclusive Psalmody,' *Westminster Theological Journal, 37*(1), 1974, Fall, p. 78.

[15]In keeping with the nature of apocalyptic language and symbolism, there is some fluidity in the way in which the temple is described. If we allow that the visions of the heavenly realm are visions of the heavenly temple-throne room of the Great King, then the temple is where God dwells, in heaven. Other indications (for example the 'measuring' of the temple in Revelation 11) seem to apply the image to the saints of God on the earth. In the end, the new creation is the temple-city of God, and ultimately God and the Lamb are the temple. In speaking of the establishment of the eternal temple, then, we should not limit the thought to one aspect or another, as all are related.

[16]Which altar is signified? The Greek word *thusiastērion* 'does not of itself determine whether it alludes to the altar of sacrifice or the altar of incense, which is described in Exodus 30:1-10. The description given in Revelation seems to fit the altar of incense better than the great altar of sacrifice which stood near the door of the tabernacle. The altar in Revelation is connected with the prayers of the martyrs (Rev. 6:9), its fire is used to light the incense of the golden censer (8:3, 5), and its location is "before God", which would accord much more closely with the place of the altar of incense that stood on the border between the Holy Place and the Holy of Holies, the inner shrine of the tabernacle' (Tenney, M. C. [1957], *Interpreting Revelation*, Eerdmans, p. 172).

[17]By way of contrast, see the list of those excluded from the new creation (e.g. in Revelation 21:8) and compare with the substance of the commandments.

[18]Swete's comment is helpful: 'As the pillar cannot be moved out of its place while the house stands, so a lapse from goodness will be impossible for the character which has been fixed by the final victory' (Swete, H. B. [1907], *The Apocalypse of St. John: The Greek Text with Introduction, Notes and Indices*, Macmillan and Co., p. 57).

[19]Other Old Testament connections may be seen in Zechariah 2:1-2 and Jeremiah 31:38-40.

[20]Beale, G. K. (2004), *The Temple and the Church's Mission: A biblical theology of the dwelling place of God*, New Studies in Biblical Theology. Downers Grove: Apollos, p. 315.

[21]For an extended treatment of these themes, see Dumbrell, W.

(1985), *The End of the Beginning: Revelation 21–22 and the Old Testament*, Lancer Books.

[22]Ladd, G. E. (1972), *A Commentary on the Revelation of John*, Eerdmans, p. 285.

[23]In commenting on Revelation 21:22, Caird points out that the physical tabernacle or temple essentially offered the world the demarcation between the holy and the unholy, the pure and the unclean. This it did not just by its presence, but by the rules associated with the cultus itself. 'The temple was therefore the symbol of God's claim on the secular world, and of his abhorrence of the unclean. But no such symbol is needed any longer.... The sphere of the holy has expanded to include all that is capable of being offered to God, and all that is unfit for God has been for ever excluded.The presence of God, no longer confined to the sanctuary apart, pervades the whole of the life and being of the city, which accordingly needs no created light' (Caird, G. B. [1984], *The Revelation of St. John the Divine,* Black's New Testament Commentaries, A & C Black, p. 279).

[24]Bingham, G. C. (1993), *The Revelation of St. John the Divine*, New Creation Publications Inc., p. 263.

Chapter 9.

[1]*Institutes* I.xi.8

[2]Curtis, E. (1992), 'Idols, Idolatry,' in D. Freedman, *The Anchor Bible Dictionary*, Vol. 3, Doubleday, p. 381.

[3]Lincoln, A. T. (1990), *Ephesians*,Word Biblical Commentary, Word, p. 324.

[4]Calvin's argument is creational. We are made for such creaturely acknowledgement, which in turn acts as the motive force for true service. 'Until men recognise that they owe everything to God, that they are nourished by his fatherly care, that he is the Author of their every good, that they should seek nothing beyond him – they will never yield to him willing service' (*Institutes* I.ii.1). He states this more positively a little later: 'Indeed, no one gives himself freely and willingly to God's service unless, having tasted his fatherly love, he is drawn to love and worship him in return' (I.v.3). It goes without saying that such trust can only be engendered in the heart of fallen human beings by the work of God in Christ the Mediator (I.ii.1). Calvin's pastoral application of such trust is astute (I.ii.2). My attention has recently been drawn to Dr. Derek Thomas' book, *Proclaiming the*

Incomprehensible God: Calvin's Teaching on Job. Thomas' masterful survey of Calvin's Joban sermons clearly enunciates the fundamental place that trust plays in the Reformer's understanding of the Christian faith, and in our relation to God and his providential dealings with us. This should not be confused with a resigned Stoicism. For Calvin, the very incomprehensibility of God's own nature and his dealings with us becomes a powerful factor in sanctifying mind and spirit, as we submit to his providences and honour him in the process. 'For Calvin the very heart of godliness is submission to a God who cannot ultimately be fathomed' (Christian Focus, 2004, pp. 374-75).

[5]Carson, D. A. (2002), 'Worship Under the Word,' in D. A. Carson, *Worship by the Book*, Zondervan, p. 46.

[6]Carson, D. A. (2002), 'Worship Under the Word,' p. 55.

[7]Forsyth, P. T. (1907, rpt 1993), *Positive Preaching and the Modern Mind*, New Creation Publications Inc., p. 62.

[8]In the gathering for public worship we should therefore ensure that our attitudes, actions and liturgical statements adequately reflect the nature of life in the new covenant. For example, in many evangelical settings shared congregational confession of the faith through the Creeds, liturgical responses and prayers has been virtually abandoned. In its place we often have a pseudo-priesthood of minister or worship leader who 'performs', while others look on. The Reformers understood the nature and power of the priesthood of all believers, and ensured that in their liturgies they included corporate prayers, confessions and creeds so that worshipers could take on their own lips the great truths of the faith and express their corporate response to God in an ordered way.

CONTRIBUTORS

Rev. Terry L. Johnson • Dr. Robert S. Godfrey

Dr. Joseph A. Pipa, Jr. • Dr. Morton H. Smith

Rev. Brian Schwertley • Rev. Benjamin Shaw

Rev. Cliff Blair

The Worship of God

Reformed Concepts of Biblical Worship

The Worship of God

Essays from the Greenville Spring Theology Conference

"There can be no more important *issue* than that of worship. There can be no more important *question* than that of how God is to be worshipped."

In the 21st century, as has been the case throughout history, different interpretations of worship continue to divide churches and denominations. Worship expresses our theology and if we are to worship in truth we must submit to scriptural revelation.

'The Worship of God' offers an invaluable companion to those seeking to enhance their understanding of the purpose, history and different forms of worship. Dealing with subject areas from the regulative principle of worship to the distinctives of reformed liturgy, from Heart worship to the place of Psalms and contemporary worship music, this book gives us unique insights on an issue that demands our attention.

'Convinced of the importance of worship for the health of the Church, we offer this book to the public. The purpose of this book is to address a number of the major issues that create tensions in our practice of worship. Our intent, however, is not simply to critique those who differ from us, but also to offer a blueprint for a more biblical, God-honoring worship. Thus we deal with the purpose of worship, the rule for worship, and the practice of worship.'

Joseph A. Pipa, Jr.

Contributors include:
Robert S. Godfrey, Westminster Seminary, Escondido, California.
Terry L. Johnson, Independent Presbyterian Church, Savannah, Georgia.
Joseph A. Pipa, Jr., Greenville Presbyterian Theological Seminary, Greenville, North Carolina.

ISBN 1-84550-055-5

NEW TESTAMENT
**BACKGROUND
COMMENTARY**

A NEW DICTIONARY OF WORDS,
PHRASES AND SITUATIONS
IN BIBLE ORDER

W. HAROLD MARE

New Testament
Background Commentary

A new dictionary of words, phrases and situations in Bible order

W. Harold Mare

The New Testament is a fascinating collection of documents that illuminate the life and ministry of Jesus of Nazareth. It contains an amazing number of details in its texts that can easily be lost on the modern mind. This means that the full impact can pass by the reader, yet sometimes that snippet of information has major consequences for the meaning of the passage.

Commentaries are of some use as they cannot always pause long enough to develop the detail as they explain the main teaching of the passage. Bible dictionaries are helpful, but they are more interested in expressing the meaning of words rather than the significance of situations.

Harold Mare has helped the modern reader by combing the best elements of both in his New Testament Background Commentary. It is both a commentary and a dictionary of words, phrases and situations that shed light on the point the writer is trying to make. He accomplishes this by placing the explanations in *Bible order* so that it is easy to access the background comments of this book as you read through the Bible passage.

It is an invaluable companion to any reading of the New Testament. It is such a helpful tool you will wonder how you managed without one before.

W. Harold Mare(1918-2004) was a founding trustee of Covenant Seminary, St Louis, Missouri in 1963 and served as Professor of New Testament until his retirement in 1984. After his retirement, Dr. Mare continued to teach as an emeritus professor at Covenant Seminary until his death in 2004 while doing archaeological excavations in Jordan.

ISBN 1-85792-955-1

'The wit of an evangelical Chesterton, prophetic insight of Francis Schaeffer and the accessibility of John Stott.'
Melvin Tinker

THE WAGES OF
SP I N

CRITICAL WRITINGS ON HISTORIC & CONTEMPORARY EVANGELICALISM

CARL R. TRUEMAN

The Wages of Spin

Critical Essays on Historic and Contemporary Evangelicalism

Carl Trueman

DO YOU HAVE AN OPINION?

There is an increasing tendency in Evangelical circles to regard disagreement in our allegedly post-modern world as inherently oppressive. Too many people sit on the fence and ignore, or are unaware of, the fact that Christianity is an historical religion. As Laurence Peter once said *"History repeats itself because nobody listens."*

The point of having a debate is not to have a debate and then agree to differ (sitting around in a mutually affirming love-fest) - the point of debate, as the Apostle Paul clearly demonstrates time and again in the book of Acts, is to establish which position is best.

With this collection of essays, Carl Trueman will provoke you into thinking for yourself - and to have an opinion on THINGS THAT MATTER!

'I cannot think of a young evangelical writer and theologian whose works I more eagerly read than Carl Trueman.'
Mark Dever, Capitol Hill Baptist Church, Washington, D.C

'...affirms the historic evangelical faith with great force, clarity and excellent judgement.'
Paul Helm, Emeritus Professor, University of London

'The wit of an evangelical Chesterton, prophetic insight of Francis Schaeffer and the accessibility of John Stott.'
Melvin Tinker, Author and Vicar of St John, Newland, Hull.

Carl R. Trueman is Professor of Church History and Historical Theology at Westminster Theological Seminary, Philadelphia.

ISBN 1-85792-994-2